A DEADLY LEGACY

A DEADLY LEGACY

GERMAN JEWS AND THE GREAT WAR

Tim Grady

YALE UNIVERSITY PRESS
NEW HAVEN AND LONDON

For Victoria

For information about this and other Yale University Press publications, please contact:
US Office: sales.press@yale.edu   yalebooks.com
Europe Office: sales@yaleup.co.uk   yalebooks.co.uk

Set in Adobe Garamond Pro by IDSUK (DataConnection) Ltd
Printed in Great Britain by TJ International Ltd, Padstow, Cornwall

Library of Congress Control Number: 2017942330

ISBN 978-0-300-19204-9

A catalogue record for this book is available from the British Library.

10 9 8 7 6 5 4 3 2 1

CONTENTS

ABBREVIATIONS

BArch Berlin	Bundesarchiv, Berlin
BArch MA	Bundesarchiv-Militärarchiv, Freiburg
CAHJP	Central Archive for the History of the Jewish People, Jerusalem
CJA	Centrum Judaicum Archiv, Berlin
CV	Central Association of German Citizens of the Jewish Faith (Centralverein deutscher Staatsbürger jüdischen Glaubens)
GStA PK	Geheimes Staatsarchiv Preußischer Kulturbesitz, Berlin
HstAS	Hauptstaatsarchiv Stuttgart
IfS	Institut für Stadtgeschichte, Frankfurt am Main
JFB	Jewish Women's League (Jüdischer Frauenbund)
JMB	Jüdisches Museum Berlin
KfdO	Committee for the East (Komitee für den Osten)
KRA	War Raw Materials Section (Kriegsrohstoffabteilung)
LAB	Landesarchiv Berlin
LBINY	Leo Baeck Institute Archive, New York
PA–AA	Auswärtiges Amt–Politisches Archiv, Berlin
RjF	Reich Association of Jewish Frontline Soldiers (Reichsbund jüdischer Frontsoldaten)
SPD	Social Democratic Party of Germany (Sozialdemokratische Partei Deutschlands)
StAHH	Staatsarchiv Hamburg
USPD	Independent Social Democratic Party of Germany (Unabhängige Sozialdemokratische Partei Deutschlands)

VJOD   Association of Jewish Organisations in Germany for the
                Protection of the Rights of the Jews in the East
                (Vereinigung jüdischer Organisationen Deutschlands zur
                Wahrung der Rechte der juden des Ostens)
ZVfD   Zionist Organisation for Germany (Zionistische
                Vereinigung für Deutschland)

ILLUSTRATIONS

ACKNOWLEDGEMENTS

When I first started to think about this book, the brutal events of the First World War seemed to lie firmly in the distant past. The extremes of chauvinistic nationalism, racism and state-sanctioned violence appeared to be slowly declining, as liberalism, tolerance and international collaboration slowly – though always partially – became more firmly rooted. The year 2016 certainly shook some of this optimism. It can only be hoped that the centenary of the First World War will go some way to reminding us of the importance of dialogue and understanding both within and across national borders. Writing a book of this length requires these values in abundance. I am, therefore, deeply indebted to the archivists and librarians in Britain, Germany, Israel and the United States who have kindly helped me in researching this book. Their advice on source collections, long-forgotten materials and even the best local restaurants has been invaluable.

Above all, though, it has been the kindness of friends, family and colleagues that has made writing this book possible. In this respect, I must give my words of deepest thanks to Matthew Stibbe and Hannah Ewence, who took time out of their own busy lives to read every page of the draft manuscript. Their careful and thoughtful advice not only highlighted crucial omissions but also pushed me to think in different ways about the topic. Caroline Sharples, Gavin Schaffer, Neil Gregor, Mathias Seiter, Alana Vincent, Tony Kushner, Klaus Gietinger, Anja Löbert and Rory Castle all helped me immensely along the way with their own views on particular aspects of this vast history. I would also like to thank Heather McCallum and Rachael Lonsdale for their great care in bringing this project all the way from proposal to finished book.

At Chester, I am grateful to all my colleagues in history and archaeology who over the years have made the department such a warm and friendly place in which to work. Much of this, it must be said, has been down to the sound guidance of the dean of humanities, Rob Warner, but also to the diligence and good humour of Keith McLay during his time as head of department. Finally, I would like to thank Orla, Frieda and Victoria. The book is dedicated to Victoria, who not only supported me all the way through but also read multiple drafts of the manuscript.

INTRODUCTION

In August 1914, the popular *Berliner Illustrierte Zeitung*, which published some of the most enduring images of Germany's struggle during the First World War, printed a striking photograph of a cavalry battalion proudly making its way down Berlin's central thoroughfare, Unter den Linden (see Plate 1). All eyes in the photograph are on the central uniformed figure, mounted on a powerful military horse. Reaching down to the two civilians running alongside – both dressed, somewhat incongruously, in formal clothes – the soldier bids his final farewells before making his way to the front. Such scenes played themselves out in German towns and cities up and down the country upon the outbreak of war.

What the newspaper failed to mention was the fact that all three protagonists in the image were German Jews. Willy Liemann, a young Berlin student, was the soldier purposefully heading into battle, while the two individuals on the street below were Fritz Schlesinger, a Berlin engineer, and his young wife, Emma.[1]

Liemann and the Schlesingers occupy a fairly typical place in the history of the First World War: they are visible as Germans but invisible as Jews. During the conflict, almost 100,000 German Jews served in military uniform, as soldiers, sailors, airmen and administrators. But these individuals have largely disappeared into the massed ranks of the wider military machine. Jewish men and women, who staffed hospitals, ran soup kitchens or laboured away in factories, are also hard to find. The same is true of German Jews as business owners, captured prisoners or interned civilians overseas. The very ordinariness of many Jewish lives helped to submerge their wartime experiences within the wider landscape of the First World War.

In contrast, finding examples of a distinctly Jewish wartime experience, where Jews suddenly became visible, is far easier. This is most obviously the case with the history of anti-Semitism. The First World War had no shortage of anti-Semitic incidents, accusations of war profiteering at home or of war shirking at the front being the most pervasive. But it is the infamous Jewish census of 1916, when the War Ministry inexcusably decided to count the number of Jewish soldiers in the armed forces, that has most often come to define the history of German Jews during the conflict.[2] There can be no doubting that moments of anti-Semitic attack threw German Jews into the public gaze.

Yet such examples can easily mislead. For much of the time, the way German Jews experienced the conflict was not exceptional; it was simply ordinary.[3] Taking the idea of Jewish 'normality' as its starting point, the first aim of this book is to write Jews back into the wider history of Germany's First World War. This means viewing Jews as active participants in the German military, long before they became its victims. There is an understandable inclination to approach the history of Jewish life in Germany from the perspective of its 'vanishing point', whether this is 1933, 1938 or even 1941.[4] However, writing this long history backwards makes it much trickier to recover the joys, pains, sorrows and losses that Jews, like other Germans, experienced during the First World War. In uncovering these histories, the book gives equal weight to the various frontlines as well as to life on the home front. The different spaces within which Jews and other Germans lived the First World War were never isolated. Developments at home or at the fighting front always had a significant effect on the other sphere.[5]

Whether people were stuck in a waterlogged trench in France, a submarine in the North Sea or a factory in the Ruhr, their lives were immeasurably tied together. For the most part, therefore, German Jews were not 'fighting different wars', but were instead neck-deep in the same bloody conflict as all other Germans.[6] They fought alongside other Germans in battle, died with them in the same muddy fields or drowned together in the same freezing cold seas. At home, members of Jewish communities suffered economic hardship, starved during catastrophic food shortages and had to struggle by in unheated buildings, but then so did almost all other Germans. There was, then, no distinct Jewish path through the First World War; the conflict was lived in multiple ways by both Jews and other Germans alike.[7]

The fact that Jews experienced the conflict not separately as part of a distinctive subculture, but as part of wider society would be unworthy of further comment if this were a history of popular entertainment or the urban environment.[8] But the historical stakes at play in the First World War were clearly much higher.[9] At its core, the war was a clash between nations, empires and peoples; it was an attempt by one power to subjugate another. The means of achieving this goal was realised through industrialised warfare. Machine guns, artillery, tanks, submarines and gas were all employed to kill the enemy. From home, whole economies and cultures came to be directed towards securing victory. Mutilation, smashed bodies and mass death, therefore, were inherent elements of the First World War. The conflict created untold loss, pain and suffering. It left somewhere in the region of 10 million dead, 20 million wounded, 9.5 million displaced and many more lives permanently changed.

This was not only a conflict on a massively destructive scale, but it was also one in which Jews were full participants. The book's second main argument stresses this very fact. It maintains that German Jews have to be seen as 'co-constitutive' in shaping what quickly turned into a bloody and brutal conflict, sharing the same hopes and values as many other Germans.[10] If Jews are to be rightly recognised as active participants in the conflict, then this means moving beyond the rather straightforward registers of Jewish loyalty, patriotism and heroism. Participation statistics, Iron Crosses, heroic battle stories and silent war memorials, which dominate existing histories, capture only one small part of the conflict.[11] Indeed, to focus on these celebratory elements alone is to silence the grim horrors of the actual war. Jews appeared in the conflict not just as heroes and victims, but also as trained killers, cultural propagandists and war enthusiasts.[12]

With the huge scale of death, destruction and suffering, there can be little in the way of positives to rescue from Germany's history of the First World War. But then Germany is far from unique in having a rather uncomfortable history of the conflict. All the belligerent powers have their own problematic episodes: the British with their policies in Ireland; the French with their response to the large-scale army mutinies of 1917. And Germany is no exception. During the course of the conflict, the German army invaded Belgium, occupied much of Eastern Europe, employed chemical weapons, utilised forced labour and launched a campaign of unrestricted submarine warfare.

However, seven aspects of the German war effort, which are discussed in detail in the book's main chapters, warrant particular attention. The first concerns the depths of war enthusiasm during the early months of the war when Jews and other Germans often let their patriotic spirit run wild. Second is the issue of total war. From very early on, the lives of all those at home were directed towards the war effort: schools were closed, valuable food supplies were rationed and the economy was gradually subjugated to the needs of the military. Third is a culture of destruction. Amongst almost all sections of society there was a general acceptance of violence and the destruction of the enemy's culture; these were seen as a legitimate means to wage war.[13] The fourth theme concerns Germany's war aims, in particular the willingness of some Jews and other Germans to push the case for annexations and territorial expansion.[14]

The way that Germans approached the war started to create dangerous social problems during the conflict. This can be seen in the final three defining characteristics of the German war effort. The fifth aspect focuses on the denigration of internal and external minorities during the war, which left not only Jews but also other supposedly outsider groups viciously exposed. Sixth is the divisions both at home and amongst the frontline troops; these came more and more to the fore, the longer the war went on. The seventh and final point is the infamous 'stab in the back' myth, which suggested that the German army had been defeated not in battle but by the machinations of the home front.

It may be tempting to assume that it was predominantly the political right that defined these seven markers of the German war effort. This would also have the advantage of placing Germany's Jewish population, who were generally seen as being fairly liberal-minded, outside the war's more extreme narratives.[15] However, in the case of the First World War, these presumptions are false on two counts. For one thing, German Jews spanned the political spectrum; they were certainly never just in the liberal political camp. Their numbers may have been small, but Jews could be left-wing radicals, passionate conservatives or even in some cases right-wing agitators.[16] For another, extreme ideas during the conflict were not confined solely to the political right. Germans from a range of different social and political backgrounds supported territorial expansion or the use of more extreme weapons, for example. Differences when they occurred – at least until the war's final months – were rarely about the ethics of Germany's war effort, but were rather about the most appropriate method of achieving a German victory.[17]

What needs to be recognised, therefore, is that Jews and other Germans jointly helped to define the way in which the German war effort was conducted. And this in itself was not without consequence: more than four years of violence, death and destruction could not suddenly be erased with the cessation of hostilities. This was most obviously the case for the bereaved, the war-wounded and those whose lives had been irreparably altered by the conflict. But even where people managed to reconstruct families, communities and businesses, the war often still cast a dark shadow over interwar state, politics and society.[18] Returning to the bright summer of 1914, as most Germans acknowledged, was an impossible dream.

The book's third main argument, therefore, is that traces of the wartime culture that Jews and other Germans had helped to define left dangerous legacies for the postwar world. In particular, the seven features of the German war effort – war enthusiasm, total war, a culture of destruction, annexations, the 'other', divisions and the 'stab in the back' myth – defined both the social and the political atmosphere of the postwar Weimar Republic. The instability and chaos that resulted from these legacies was eventually exploited by the National Socialists as they made their own bid for power. The rise of Nazism, therefore, cannot be explained solely by long-term continuities in German history stretching back to German unification or the peculiarities of nineteenth-century colonialism.[19] Instead, it was the specifics of Germany's First World War – a conflict that Jews and other Germans had jointly shaped – that provided the foundations for Hitler's eventual path to power.[20]

There was of course never a straight line from the conflict, and the way in which it was fought, through to the formation of these postwar legacies. Standing as an immovable barrier between the periods of war and peace were the triumvirate of defeat, revolution and the Treaty of Versailles. The collective turmoil of these three events, which provoked fears of Bolshevism and national decline, determined how the seven features of the German war effort transposed into postwar Germany.[21] Amidst the chaos of postwar Germany, some elements of the wartime culture struggled to make the journey from war to peace at all. The legacy of war enthusiasm, for example, remained rather dormant in the early 1920s, presumably because in the wake of defeat, few people wanted to be reminded of their earlier excitement for the conflict. Conversely, the 'stab in the back' myth, which had first emerged in the final year of the war, came to be even more fiercely contested once the war had reached its depressing conclusion.

However, the most radical shift in Germany's wartime culture occurred with the actual protagonists involved. Following the conflict's messy conclusion, a series of small, radical right-wing groups, often filled with individuals too young to have fought at the front, started to claim the war's legacies for themselves.[22] Where German Jews had once helped to shape Germany's approach to the conflict, after the war they were gradually pushed to the side-lines, as the political right looked to the conflict as a means to legitimise its own existence. These shifts, however, took place extremely slowly. There was certainly nothing preordained or inevitable about them. In the early postwar years, some German Jews maintained an active interest in the war's multiple legacies, whether this was the question of Germany's position in the east or the rapid spread of political violence after the revolution. It was only as anti-Semitism hardened during the late 1920s that the position of Jews in these narratives became much more fragile.

As the National Socialists rose to become a genuine force during the Great Depression, they gave new life to the legacies of the 1914–18 conflict. The self-styled party of the war, which had emerged amidst the upheaval of defeat and revolution, had always placed great weight on the experience of the First World War, on militaristic values and on reversing the Versailles 'Diktat'.[23] But it was only after their electoral breakthrough in September 1930 that Hitler's party was in a position to fundamentally reshape the war's legacies. Thereafter, though, it quickly made its influence felt. The movement valor-ised the war and the war dead by making alterations to Germany's existing memory culture; it sought to recreate the apparent unity of August 1914 through the idea of a *Volksgemeinschaft* ('people's community') as a means to heal social divisions; and it defended itself against a second 'stab in the back' by persecuting those accused of ushering in Germany's defeat in 1918: Jews and communists.[24] This was all preparation for a future total war, albeit one of unparalleled dimensions. Eastern Europe remained an object of Hitler's territorial desires, but unlike in the First World War, this was only a starting point and not the end of an expansionist dream.[25]

During the First World War, nobody – neither Jews nor other Germans – could have imagined that the experience of war would provide the dangerous legacies that would feed into a second – far more deadly – clash. But this is precisely what happened.[26] Germany's path through the First World War not only destabilised German politics and society; it also opened people's minds to the power of violence and destruction. Other groups on Germany's polit-ical right also toyed with these legacies, but it took the National Socialist movement to apply them to a Second World War. But in this new conflict, German Jews were no longer joint protagonists; instead, they became the victims, murdered along with 6 million other European Jews in the National Socialists' war of genocidal destruction.

I

PRECEDENTS

In mid-July 1914, just as Europe was teetering on the brink of a world war, General von Kleist, a withered veteran of the nineteenth-century Wars of Unification, found the time to pen an article for the conservative *Kreuz-Zeitung*. The subject was not military strategy or the latest weaponry – seemingly important issues at this time – but rather the question of whether Jews should be allowed to become military officers. Kleist was firmly of the view that Jews should not be commissioned, offering a string of reasons to this effect. 'The army is racially pure' was one; 'Germany is a comprehensively Christian state' was another.[1] For all the polemics of his article, Kleist was actually preaching to the converted. Germany's conservative circles had long been of the opinion that it would be inappropriate for Jews to hold command over Christian soldiers. The Prussian officer corps, whose members generally held Jews in low esteem, also saw little reason to alter the status quo.

By the time of Kleist's article, it had actually been almost thirty years since the last Jew had been awarded a reserve commission in the Prussian Army, although the situation was slightly more favourable in Bavaria where a handful of Jewish officers had been installed.[2] In the intervening period, a whole string of Jews from well-to-do backgrounds, who under other circumstances would have reached officer rank, had been denied promotion. What stopped them being commissioned into the army were the racial underpinnings of military selection. The German military establishment held a fixed idea of the physical attributes that made a good fighter. Notions of bravery, fearlessness and aggression all featured prominently. In common with other societies of this time, the dominant belief was that some 'races' displayed these traits while others did not. As far as the German military was concerned, the Jews fell into the latter category and were thus deemed to possess questionable fighting qualities. The label of cowardice, which had long been attached to Jewish men, proved difficult to shake off. As a result, it was easy for military doctors to write the Jewish body off as weak, feeble and inferior.[3]

This deep-seated aversion to Jewish officers did not stop Jews from applying. Albert von Goldschmidt-Rothschild, part of the wealthy Frankfurt banking family, had sought a position as a reserve officer in 1904. The then chancellor, Bernhard von Bülow, stepped in to make the young man's case, but to no avail. As Goldschmidt-Rothschild's disappointment demonstrated, not even wealth and influence could buy a German Jew entry into the officer corps.[4] Angry and frustrated at this treatment, Jewish groups had long campaigned for a change in the military promotions process. But all this led to was more talk. Since 1904, the issue of Jews as army officers was discussed on an almost annual basis in the Reichstag, but always without any resolution. In far more conciliatory tones than Kleist had been able to muster, the War Ministry repeatedly maintained the line that promotion to the officer corps was free of any form of discrimination. This may have been so, but it did not answer the question of the shocking deficit in Jewish officers.[5]

Yet a mere two weeks after Kleist had made his defence of the military's discriminatory practices, the situation changed completely. In August 1914, after entering a war on the side of its Central European ally, Austria-Hungary, Germany found itself rapidly embroiled in a global conflict. With the army fighting on all fronts, the War Ministry could no longer afford to be picky; it needed all the men it could lay its hands on, including those who happened to be Jewish. To the excitement of the Jewish press, which followed these developments with glee, German Jews started to be promoted, with the names of the first few Jewish reserve officers listed in newspapers for posterity.[6] There was no doubting that Germany had undergone a rapid transformation during the summer of 1914. The path to war, it seemed, had finally brought the German people together, erasing previous internal divisions and uniting Jews and other Germans behind a single national cause. This may have proved to be a short-lived illusion, but in the summer of 1914 it was one in which many people willingly placed their faith.

Distant Murders and Distant Wars

The tumultuous events of that summer started with what on the face of it should have been a simple car journey; but never has one brief drive had such devastating consequences for world peace. On 28 June, Archduke Franz Ferdinand, the man in line to be the next emperor of Austria-Hungary, was on a state visit to the Bosnian capital, Sarajevo. Having already narrowly escaped one assassination attempt earlier in the morning, Franz Ferdinand and his wife, Sophie, risked the car again later that same day. This proved to be a fatal mistake. As the motorcade wound its way slowly through the centre of the city, a young Bosnian Serb nationalist, Gavrilo Princip, seized his chance; he strode up to the open-topped car, pulled out a revolver, then fired at the arch-duke and duchess from point-blank range. Austria-Hungary's leading elite, which had already been struggling to keep their patchwork empire together, reacted to the assassinations with shock and anger, but also with considerable determination. The answer, as far as they saw it, was to launch some form of military action against Serbia. Not that anyone realised it at the time, but the path to a world war had been laid.[7]

Public shock at the events in Sarajevo was on full display in the main Austrian towns and cities. Newspapers ran long features eulogising the royal pair, black flags fluttered from people's homes, while public buildings flew the state colours at half-mast.[8] Jewish communities throughout the empire also played their own part in these public rituals. Special services of mourning for the archduke were held in synagogues and many communities also composed their own telegrams of condolence. 'In loyal devotion to throne and father-land', wrote the Viennese Jewish community, 'Austrian Jewry is united as one in deep, heartfelt prayers.'[9] In Germany, in marked contrast, there was far less fuss. The assassination of the archduke and duchess was undoubtedly a signif-icant event, but it was still not enough to warrant special synagogue services, prayers or telegrams. Even the German-Jewish press barely mentioned the Sarajevo murders in their general news pages. Presumably the assassination of a foreign monarch in a distant city was deemed to be of little interest to Germany's Jewish communities.

Certainly, very few Germans were prepared to let the two murders inter-rupt their daily routines. After all, the archduke and duchess had had the misfortune to be killed in early summer, which for well-off Germans just happened to be when they hoped to be enjoying their annual holidays. As with most aspects of Imperial Germany, Kaiser Wilhelm II set the standard in this respect. Each year, he took an extended cruise to Scandinavia aboard his royal yacht, *Hohenzollern*. The summer of 1914 proved to be no exception. Clearly the kaiser had no intention of letting the small matter of an impending war alter his plans. As chance would have it, Arthur Stern, a Berlin-based medical doctor, had also been holidaying in Scandinavia that summer. Scanning out to sea with his binoculars, Stern managed to catch a glimpse of the kaiser entertaining on the deck of the *Hohenzollern*, seemingly without a care in the world.[10] Like Stern, other German Jews were also determined to relax and recuperate over the summer. Theodor Kirchberger, for example, enjoyed a break in the small seaside resort of Wustrow on the Baltic, while 14-year-old Charlotte Stein-Pick spent an idyllic few weeks with her family in the Alpine hills near Oberammergau.[11]

The vast majority of German Jews, though, spent the summer of 1914 neither in Scandinavia nor relaxing in Germany's domestic holiday resorts. Nonetheless, there was still plenty to occupy their minds. The excitement in Berlin came in the form of a new Jewish hospital built in the northern district of Gesundbrunnen to replace a much smaller facility in the city centre. The new building promised patients 'brighter, larger rooms, more air and gardens'.[12] At the time of its dedication in late June, nobody had an inkling that only a matter of weeks later, this gleaming new hospital would start to fill with wounded soldiers. During June and July, Jewish communities in Germany's provincial towns were also in the midst of a building spree. In the port town of Wilhelmshaven, for example, local dignitaries gathered at the end of June to lay the foundation stone for the town's very first synagogue. Symbolising the communities' tight connection to Germany, an urn containing national coins and newspapers was also sealed in the synagogue's foundations.[13]

These new buildings hinted at the growing confidence of Jewish communities. Full emancipation had arrived with German unification in 1871. After decades of restrictions in their daily lives, German Jews had finally been able to look to the future with some optimism. Gradually the number of Jews in previously restricted professions, such as the judiciary, academia and politics, started to rise. German Jews may have enjoyed far greater freedoms, but anti-Jewish sentiment remained very much alive. Encouraged by the historian Heinrich von Treitschke and the court preacher, Adolf Stoecker, political anti-Semitism increased during the 1880s. Fears of economic and political liberalism were transposed onto Jewish communities, who for the German right came to represent all the ills of the new German Empire.[14]

Despite this simmering anti-Jewish sentiment, German Jews chose to focus on the positives: their position in society was strengthening and over time, they hoped, old hatreds would gradually die out. As far as they were concerned, the days of keeping a low profile and avoiding any signs of extravagance were long gone. This was most obviously the case in Berlin, which was home to almost

150,000 Jews out of a total Jewish population in Germany of between 550,000 and 600,000. The glimmering gold cupola of the city's New Synagogue had provided a statement of emancipatory intent when it was built in 1866. Almost half a century later, this same sense of belonging and rootedness had started to spread out to the regions, where there was also a growing stability to Jewish life. Before the outbreak of war, then, German Jews constituted a proud, and for the most part, prosperous section of German society.

Yet beyond this image of stability, considerable divisions amongst Germany's Jewish population also existed. The problem was simply that there had never been just one single Jewish community in Germany, but rather an 'overlapping multitude' of different 'German-speaking Jewries'.[15] Religious differences between liberal and Orthodox Jews provided one source of internal Jewish division. During the first half of the nineteenth century, a liberal Jewish movement, which sought to turn Jews into modern 'Germans', had gradually usurped the existing Orthodox communities. And in doing so it had replaced an older set of liturgical traditions with organ music and German-language prayers. However, while the Orthodox communities may have lost some of their previous dominance, they never died out. What remained in most urban areas, therefore, were divided Jewish communities, where liberal and Orthodox synagogues operated side by side.

But the biggest and most bitter divides were ideological. Acculturated Jews fought an acrimonious battle for influence with the much newer Zionist movement, which sought to construct a Jewish future in a new national home. Representing the former was Germany's largest Jewish organisation, the Central Association of German Citizens of the Jewish Faith (Centralverein deutscher Staatsbürger jüdischen Glaubens, the CV). Founded in 1893 to defend against anti-Semitism, the CV grew rapidly: by the start of the war its membership was about 38,000. Its policies, which revolved predominantly around the issue of German citizenship, fitted the belief structures of the association's mainly liberal, middle-class supporters.[16]

The CV's ideological rival, the Zionist Organisation for Germany (Zionistische Vereinigung für Deutschland, the ZVfD), had been founded four years after the CV in 1897. In contrast to its older sister, the ZVfD failed to flourish. It never managed to energise much of the German-Jewish population, counting some 6,000 paid-up members before the war, which represented not even a quarter of those joining the CV. Unsurprisingly, the ZVfD's policies concentrated primarily on Jewish nationalist issues.[17] During the July crisis, for example, the main talking point in Zionist circles was not the threat of war, but rather the tenth anniversary of Theodor Herzl's death. Alongside a series of memorial services, one publisher offered a special edition of Herzl's speeches and a series of postcards featuring portraits of the great man.[18]

Further complicating this picture of divergent Jewish communities was Germany's swelling Eastern European Jewish population. From the 1880s onwards, the intensification of pogroms, persecution and economic hardship in Russia had encouraged thousands of Jews to flee westwards. Most of the Eastern European Jews who entered Germany were transmigrants, hoping to build a better life in the United States. Shipping agents fought for their custom in Eastern Europe. Samuel Chotzinoff recalled how the family home 'was alive with these agents', each offering the cheapest price for a journey from Vitebsk to New York. Eventually, Chotzinoff and his family embarked on their precarious journey westwards. After a fleeting stay in Germany, they boarded a ship in Stettin to take them to their new life in America. However, like many desperate migrants, the Chotzinoffs were duped. Their ship took them not across the Atlantic, but rather to London's Tilbury Docks.[19] While this had clearly never been their goal, the Chotzinoffs at least made it further than some of their fellow travellers. Many of the transmigrants ended up stuck in Berlin or in other major German cities as plans changed or finances dwindled.

In Germany's urban environment, Jewish transmigrants were joined by other Eastern European Jews, many of whom had entered Germany illegally. Alexander Granach, a young Galician Jew, had crept over the border from Austria-Hungary into Prussian Silesia; once across, he and his companion bought train tickets for Berlin, where they hoped to chance their luck. By the turn of the century, somewhere in the region of 70,000 Eastern European Jews lived in Germany.[20] Unlike the existing Jewish population, which was predominantly middle class, these newer – mainly Yiddish-speaking – arrivals often lived on or below the poverty line. Exaggerated fears of disease and epidemics also made them a ready target for anti-Semites as well as for new state restrictions. On several occasions, Jews were even deported from Prussia en masse and returned to Russian territory. On the eve of war, therefore, the Eastern European Jews remained on the margins of both German and German-Jewish life. Their outsider status meant that they had little power to influence Germany's gradual creep towards war in July 1914. They could only look on fearfully as their current home – Germany – made preparations to fight the country whose citizenship they often continued to hold: Russia.[21]

Just as large numbers of Eastern European Jews entered Germany, so members of the existing German-Jewish population also left the country to pursue interests overseas. Britain and the United States, in particular, had small but significant communities of German Jews. The likes of Ludwig Mond, the successful chemist, or the banker and financier Ernest Cassel, had all flourished after exchanging Germany for Britain. Some Jews, such as the economist and historian Moritz Bonn, had left Germany for a much shorter sojourn overseas.[22] Married to an Englishwoman and with a reputation as something of a cosmopolitan, Bonn had readily accepted a visiting fellowship at the University of California in Berkeley, seeing it as an opportunity to discover more about American university life. Bonn left for the United States at a rather inauspicious time, sailing from Bremen on 26 July 1914 and arriving in New York in early August. In making this long transatlantic journey, Bonn did little more than to exchange one set of divisions for another; he escaped the rifts that ran through German-Jewish and German society more generally, but had to watch from afar as Europe descended into war.[23]

War in Sight

During the first half of July, most German Jews were blissfully unaware of the deadly conflict rushing over the horizon. What occupied people's minds were the rhythms of daily life – work, family and community – or in Moritz Bonn's case, finalising his preparations for travelling to California. However, this was not a case of people wilfully closing their eyes and ears to international developments. The public was certainly aware of the potential for armed conflict. What it did not know, however, was just how close this possibility actually was, for the watchword during July was secrecy. At the start of the month, the kaiser, the chancellor, key ministers as well as representatives of the Austro-Hungarian Empire met in Berlin to discuss their response to the Sarajevo murders. It was out of these secret diplomatic meetings that the Germans offered the Austrians the infamous 'blank cheque' that assured their ally of support should they decide to take a military line with Serbia.[24]

Despite the general fog of ignorance that hung over the German public, a small number of German Jews were close enough to the ruling elite to know that something dangerous was afoot. As head of a state with limited democratic structures, the kaiser had always attracted a motley group of industrialists, press barons and politicians, who all desperately sought influence at the very highest level. Among this entourage were several Jews, whom Chaim Weizmann, later the first president of Israel, dubbed rather disparagingly the *Kaiserjuden*.[25] The Hamburg banker, Max Warburg, whose personal drive had helped to catapult the family's banking house M.M. Warburg into the international elite, had been late to join this privileged circle. He had first met with the kaiser in 1903 to discuss finance reforms; thereafter they saw one another at least once a year.

Even with his limited contact to power, Warburg could sense the approaching storm clouds. In late June 1914, Warburg attended a sumptuous banquet for the kaiser at the residence of the Prussian envoy, Hans Alfred von Bülow. As befitted a royal guest, the event was deeply ostentatious. The house had been filled with different plants and flowers especially for the occasion. The grand dining table itself was covered with exotic orchids and horned pansies, which barely left space for the guests to make use of Bülow's best dinner service. As the evening drew to a close, the kaiser spent a lot of time chatting and socialising with fellow guests. At one stage, he took Warburg to one side and, seemingly unprompted, decided to outline the state of international affairs. Playing with the idea of a pre-emptive strike against the Entente, he pondered whether 'it might not be better to strike now rather than to wait'.[26]

Warburg's friend and Hamburg colleague, Albert Ballin, was even more in the know. Ballin, born in the 1850s into a far from privileged Hamburg Jewish family, had risen dramatically from these fairly humble beginnings. After starting out in his father's emigration business, Ballin joined the HAPAG shipping line in 1886, becoming its director-general in 1899. What eventually brought this self-made Jewish businessman and the kaiser together was a shared love of ships, the sea and German naval power. During the annual Kiel Week, Ballin liked to wine and dine the kaiser aboard one of the HAPAG's great liners. A dozen or so other visits occurred regularly throughout the year. To call the pair friends would be to miss the mark, for the kaiser's personality was such that he could quickly swing into a deep rage over the most trivial of matters. Yet there could be no denying that they both found some form of comfort in each other's company.[27]

Ballin was first briefed on the developing international crisis in mid-July. Gottlieb von Jagow, the German foreign secretary, interrupted the shipping magnate's spa break in Bad Kissingen to outline the dangers of a proposed Anglo-Russian naval treaty. Having already ruined Ballin's holiday, Jagow had no reservations about adding to the bad news. In a private meeting between the two, Jagow asked Ballin to prepare the HAPAG fleet for the possibility of war; similar instructions also went to the head of the rival Norddeutscher Lloyd shipping line.[28] Soon after these discussions, Ballin departed for London on a fact-finding mission to discover the extent of the Anglo-Russian agreements and the current state of British attitudes towards Germany. The shipping magnate had form in such matters, though not necessarily success, having received the British secretary of state for war, Lord Haldane, in 1912. Following up on a suggestion from Ballin, Haldane had travelled to Berlin in the hope of finding ways to improve the already strained Anglo-German relationship. Neither side, though, proved particularly willing to give ground, making an already bad situation even worse.[29]

If the 1912 mission proved to be a failure, then the 1914 equivalent was nothing short of a disaster. Ballin enjoyed high-powered meetings with Haldane, with Edward Grey, the British foreign secretary, and with Winston Churchill, the first lord of the Admiralty. With access to some of the leading members of the British government, it should have been possible to gain a good sense of British views. However, something clearly went awry. Over dinner with Churchill, Ballin had asked directly whether the British would intervene in a continental war, even one in which Germany took French colonies as an indemnity. Churchill had responded obliquely that Britain would 'judge events as they arose'.[30] For some reason, this response proved enough to reassure Ballin, who departed for home firm in the belief that the British would not get involved in a continental war. This must surely have been a case of misplaced optimism on Ballin's behalf, as Churchill had reportedly begged the HAPAG director to do everything to avoid war. 'My dear friend, don't let us go at war!' were Churchill's parting words.[31]

It was only during the final week of July that the general public started to get an idea of just how precarious the international situation had become. On 23 July, in a move that was widely reported in the German press, the Austrians issued a strict ultimatum to the Serbian government. The terms, when they arrived, were far harsher than Belgrade could possibly have expected. The Austrians demanded a Serbian crackdown on all pro-nationalist, anti-Austrian activity, but also suggested that Austrian forces should partake in the suppression of these groups, which posed an obvious threat to Serbian sovereignty. The young German-Jewish satirist, Walter Trier, captured the Serbians' surprise at the Austrian 'note' in a brilliantly sardonic cartoon (see Plate 2). Showing a merciless disregard for Serbian sensitivities, Trier sketched the Serbian king, Petar Karađorđević, sitting relaxed awaiting the arrival of the 'Viennese note', which he imagines will be a mellow flute recital. But when the Austrian arrives, he is playing a very different tune. A large trumpet blasts the poor Serb king loudly into the air.

For the Serbs, there was very little to lift the mood music. Given only forty-eight hours in which to respond, people across Europe waited anxiously for the Serbs to make their next move. Yet while German newspapers wound themselves into a frenzy, the Jewish press remained largely silent. The lead article in the Zionist *Jüdische Rundschau*, for example, dealt not with events in Belgrade, but with 'The Realisation of Zionism': an ongoing debate over how best to bring about a Jewish homeland. More appropriately perhaps, the weekly *Allgemeine Zeitung des Judentums* ran with a story on the fast day of Tisha B'Av, which marks a series of tragedies in Jewish history.[32] Admittedly the focus of Germany's Jewish newspapers had always been more on community and religious matters than on actual news events. Nonetheless, their general silence bespoke a general failure to grasp the seriousness of European affairs.

The German-Jewish press may have been slow to recognise the enormity of the situation; other Jews, however, sensed the danger much more quickly. During the final week of peace, people across Germany started to give public expression to the possibility of war. But in doing so, they also revealed just how divided the country actually was. Although the citizens of Bavaria, Prussia and Württemberg, along with those from another twenty-three states, had been fused into a single German nation in 1871, deep regional divisions remained in terms of dialect, custom and culture.[33] Even Jewish communities retained a regional divide. Local communities, which existed in most towns, had to fight for their members' attention with national movements, such as the CV and the ZVfD, as well as with large regional organisations like the Federation of East Prussian Synagogue Communities (Verband der Synagogengemeinden Ostpreußens), which also attracted people's loyalties.

However, the most problematic fractures in German society ran along political lines. On paper at least, the German Empire was a parliamentary monarchy, but in reality older groups of conservative elites maintained a tight grip on power. Elections were unequal and parliament itself lacked complete independence from the emperor. The Social Democratic Party of Germany (Sozialdemokratische Partei Deutschlands, the SPD), which claimed to speak for Germany's growing proletariat, therefore found itself in a paradoxical situation: it was the largest parliamentary party, but it still lacked the power to invoke meaningful change.

The threat of war provided the perfect setting for the playing out of these various divisions. During July, a minority of Germans spoke out in support of war, prioritising above all the defence of Austria in the face of Russian aggression; others, meanwhile, sought peace and did their utmost to avert military confrontation. Some German Jews, such as the longstanding editor of the liberal *Vossische Zeitung*, Georg Bernhard, tentatively dipped their toes into the pro-war waters. Bernhard, a lifelong newspaper man, certainly recognised the potential dangers of a continental war. He repeatedly used his newspaper to express the hope that a peaceful solution to the crisis could be found. But at the same time, he refused to rule out the necessity of war. 'Germany wants peace', he stressed, 'but we are not afraid to pick up the gauntlet, if we are forced to.' As far as Bernhard was concerned, it was not Austria that was pushing Europe over the brink, but Serbia and Russia. What had Serbia done in response to the Sarajevo murders, he asked. 'It has done nothing, absolutely nothing.'[34]

But for all the fury of the war enthusiasts, the vast majority of Jews and other Germans sought peace, or at the very worst a small, local conflict. These voices of moderation found their most visible representation in a series of peace demonstrations that swept the country during the final days of July. In the capital, where the protests had begun, several thousand protesters marched through the city centre singing working-class songs and calling for peace.[35] Just as Bernhard had sympathised with the pro-war movement, so German Jews also appeared at the anti-war protests. In Berlin, Oskar Cohn, committed socialist and an SPD parliamentarian, took centre stage at a protest demonstration held in a Friedrichshain brewery. Cohn, after many years as a lawyer and two in the Reichstag, was already an accomplished speaker. When he stood in front of his audience on this midsummer's evening, back upright and shaggy moustache glistening, Cohn took aim at both the monarchy and the Austrian ultimatum. Yet to the astonishment of the conservative *Die Post*, Cohn also blamed the move towards war on the machinations of Austrian agriculture. 'No, you didn't mishear this; it was definitely said', mocked the newspaper.[36]

While Cohn was doing his best to win a local Berlin audience for peace, two other prominent Jews attempted to do something similar, only on an international level. Hugo Haase, a mild-mannered Jewish lawyer from East Prussia, who also happened to be the SPD's co-chairman, joined Karl Kautsky, the leading Marxist theoretician, in Brussels. The pair were in the Belgian capital to represent Germany at what became a frantic meeting of the International Socialist Bureau. Haase gave an energetic performance. He defended the SPD's record, citing the 'thousands of workers' protesting against war on Germany's streets. Despite these impassioned words and two days of furious talking, little progress was made. By the time Kautsky and Haase had packed their bags and made for home, Europe was on the brink of war.[37]

Negative Integration

Haase arrived back in Germany to be thrown straight into a rather dispiriting meeting of the SPD parliamentary group. On Friday 31 July, the party's leading lights gathered in the SPD's Berlin headquarters, a six-storey block in working-class Kreuzberg, to discuss recent developments. The central question for the group to decide was whether or not to support the allocation of war credits, which were crucial for the government's war budget. Haase remained typically defiant on the matter and opened the meeting by declaring that 'without doubt we have to vote against the war credits'. But he faced strong opposition from some within his own party. Eduard David and Friedrich Stampfer, who like Haase were Jewish SPD members, held the view that the time for outright opposition had passed. Stampfer, although not part of the SPD's parliamentary group, was most outspoken in his support for war credits.[38] To Haase's chagrin, Stampfer went as far as drafting an article in support of war. 'We do not want our women and children to become the victims of Cossack bestialities', he declared dramatically, before adding that the party would do its 'duty'. Haase was outraged and demanded the article be withdrawn, but by then the damage had already been done.[39]

At first glance, these disputes within the SPD appeared to be merely a continuation of the fractures that had for so long riddled German society. However, events on the world stage very quickly changed the contours of these discussions. On the very day that the SPD's leading members were ensconced in Berlin going through the finer details of war credits, news of the Russian general mobilisation order spread through the capital. According to the press, the Russians were now preparing to mobilise their entire army and their naval fleet. The next day, 1 August, Germany responded by declaring the full mobilisation of its armies; the wheels of war were now in motion and could not be stopped. The SPD's party organ could do little more than express its horror at the speed of events. 'May this mass murder end as quickly as possible', it urged, 'so that all efforts can be directed once again towards creating a peaceful social culture.'[40]

The outbreak of war helped to assuage some of the deep-seated divisions in German society. The anti-war movement and peace protests, for example, fizzled out very quickly. With soldiers marching off to the front, the moment to stop a deadly conflict had already passed. Despite this easing of public tensions, Germany's political elite still realised that they needed to take decisive action if they were going to unite a divided population behind the war.

The kaiser provided just the tonic when on 1 August he spoke to the German people with power, passion and belief – qualities that were not normally associated with him. Taking to the balcony of the royal palace in Berlin, he declared a 'civic truce' or *Burgfrieden*. 'I no longer recognise any parties or any confessions; today we are all German brothers and only German brothers', he pronounced rather optimistically to the thousands gathered in the square below.[41]

Wilhelm II's words had the desired effect as his opponents started to fall into line. On 3 August, the SPD's parliamentary committee finally agreed to back the provision of war credits. An internal vote saw seventy-eight party members vote in favour with only fourteen against. The next day, Hugo Haase stood before parliament to read out a pre-prepared statement of support. Against his better judgment, Haase confirmed that the SPD would back the war, declaring that 'in this hour of danger, we are not deserting the fatherland'. At the end of the parliamentary session, the entire house rose to its feet and the vaults of the chamber filled with 'several minutes of thunderous clapping and applause'.[42] In a matter of days, the SPD had embarked on a remarkable journey, turning itself from an anti-war party into one publicly supporting the conflict.

The entire notion of a 'civic truce', so brilliantly encapsulated in the kaiser's speech, had a similarly transformative effect on Germany's Jewish communities. What most appealed to German Jews was the promise of national unity, of a country free of divisions, where Jews and other Germans could live as equals in the same nation. However, this long-held desire for complete equality should never really have been held, as, technically, all Germans, regardless of their religious beliefs, enjoyed the same rights. Under a law of 1869, which was subsequently incorporated into the Imperial German constitution of 1871, religious freedom and equality were guaranteed. Yet, as members of Jewish communities knew all too well, legal guarantees in the past had not always equated to full equality. Jews who wanted to work in the civil service, in universities or in the military could often start a career, only to discover that the higher echelons remained unofficially closed to them. At the turn of the century one Jewish politician gave voice to this situation when he complained that it took on average eighteen years for the state to employ Jewish lawyers, but only eight years to appoint Christians to posts.[43]

For many Jews wishing to escape such prejudices, the only option over the years had been to convert to Christianity. Baptism suddenly opened the door to professions, including the officer corps, where access had previously been barred. The experience of Fritz Litten is a case in point. Born into a Königsberg Jewish family, Litten had defied his parents to convert to Christianity in the 1890s, a decision that allowed entry to the officer corps and then later to the higher ranks of academia.[44] The success of Litten and others no doubt went some way in encouraging German Jews to follow the baptismal path, not necessarily for spiritual reasons, but as a means to become 'more German'. Between 1880 and 1919, 16,479 people had converted to the Protestant Church alone.[45] Categorising these converts is difficult, particularly as many people retained a deep connection to their Jewish identities long after they had been baptised.[46]

The significance of the kaiser's 'civic truce' for German Jews, therefore, was that it appeared to offer a means to end longstanding discriminatory practices without the need to convert. But as such, it must be seen as a form of negative integration. The 'civic truce' encouraged German Jews to back the war, not as Germans, but under the promise that they too could finally become part of a united German nation. However, in August 1914, with Germany entering a major war, the small matter of this linguistic sleight of hand did not concern that many people.

Instead, the kaiser's words immediately took on an almost symbolic role for Jewish communities. A number of the main Jewish newspapers republished his words in full, while others publicly lauded the idea of a 'civic truce'. The CV declared enthusiastically that the kaiser's declaration of unity 'should be a watchword for us Jews' and even the Zionists embraced the patriotic spirit, repeating the line that there was now 'no difference between [Jews] and other Germans'.[47] Such was the power of the 'civic truce' that the CV's chairman Maximilian Horwitz even penned his own celebratory poem, pasting it onto the front cover of the association's monthly newsletter. The verse itself may not have warranted such a prominent position, but the sentiment was certainly heartfelt. 'Yes, we stand together! Every difference has disappeared from where it once existed. Whether high or low, whether Christian or Jew, now we are one people in one nation', ran the start of the final stanza.[48]

With the 'civic truce' in place, those Jews who had previously harboured doubts about their place in Germany found a new sense of belonging. The journalist Ludwig Strauss, who was later to marry Martin Buber's only daughter Eva, provides a good example. An ardent Zionist, Strauss's relationship to Germany had been ambivalent at best, but with the outbreak of war and talk of inner unity, he suddenly felt an overwhelming sense of attachment to the nation. 'I believe that after this war, in which I am firmly convinced we will be victorious, it will be great and joyous to be a German citizen', he wrote.[49] Here, Strauss also highlighted the basis of many Jews' sudden support for the war, which stemmed not only from the current conflict, but also from the idea that the war would bring about a more united and more equal Germany.

In late August, the German-Jewish impressionist painter Max Liebermann attempted to commit the new spirit in Germany to paper. His lithograph, produced for the newly launched artists' journal *Kriegszeit*, depicts the kaiser's 'civic truce' address to the crowds gathered in front of the royal palace in Berlin (see Plate 3). Barely distinguishable as individuals, the outbreak of war has turned this dark mass of people into one unified group. At the bottom of the page, Liebermann repeats the kaiser's words: 'I no longer recognise any parties, I know only Germans.' Inevitably Liebermann's print could only ever capture one aspect of the war's outbreak. There was certainly no mention of the divisions, anxieties and fears that had fractured both German-Jewish and German society. But then the start of hostilities was all about the promise of a new and better future; it was not the time to dwell on the divisions of the past.

Patriotic Unity

The last major conflict in Central Europe had been the German Wars of Unification, which in 1871 had led to the creation of the German Empire under Bismarck's strong leadership. Theobald von Bethmann Hollweg, the latest chancellor to attempt to fill Bismarck's shoes, lacked his predecessor's aura, though he did have his own 'enigmatic' charms.[50] In the pre-war years, Bethmann Hollweg had managed to pick his way through Germany's political divisions by pursuing a 'politics of the diagonal'; he offered certain entice-ments to the left and the right to win their support. With the outbreak of hostilities, Bethmann Hollweg suddenly had to call upon all his years of polit-ical experience to explain why Germany suddenly found itself at war. The answer that Bethmann Hollweg offered involved placing all of the blame onto the Russians. Speaking to a special session of the Reichstag, Bethmann Hollweg explained that it had been Germany's wish 'to continue to live in peaceful industry'. But despite its best efforts to keep the peace, 'Russia has thrown a firebrand into the house'. As cheers filled the chamber, Bethmann Hollweg stated simply: 'we have been dragged into a forced war with Russia and France'.[51]

If the declaration of the 'civic truce' had been about negative integration, then Bethmann Hollweg's focus on national defence offered more positive reasons for Jews and other Germans to back the conflict. The language of 'defence' invoked the idea that a foreign power had taken Europe to war. Germany may have joined in, but according to Bethmann Hollweg, Germans were innocent participants in a conflict that was not of their making. Instead, sole responsibility for this turn of events rested with Russia. The Tsarist regime's decision to mobilise its forces, partially on 29 July, and then fully on 31 July, added considerable weight to this interpretation of events. This was certainly all the evidence that Ludwig Haas needed. Writing in the left-liberal *Berliner Tageblatt*, the Jewish parliamentarian had no hesitation in explaining to his readers that 'Russia is responsible for the greatest crime in world history'.[52]

Like Haas, Albert Ballin – fresh from his London peace mission – also subscribed to the view that the descent into war had not been of Germany's making. The shipping magnate joined a committee of politicians, industrialists and bankers who made it their job to convince the rest of the world, but in particular the United States, of Germany's complete innocence. What emerged from their deliberations was a rather drab little pamphlet that offered a detailed exposition as to the origins of the world war. The one theme that repeatedly emerged from Ballin's outline was the fact that Germany had never wanted war. 'Never would a German government dare to contemplate a war for the sake of dynastic interest, or for the sake of glory', the pamphlet confidently stated. 'This would be against the entire bent of our character.' If Germany had not sought war, then the only explanation for the conflict was that the country had been 'threatened by war'. And this was thus a fight in defence of the fatherland.[53]

The vast majority of German Jews saw the start of hostilities through the same patriotic lens as Haas and Ballin. Most had been born and raised in Germany, and as such had no qualms in supporting their country in its hour of need. 'We German Jews are indelibly connected . . . with heart and soul, with life and limb, with blood and possessions to our German fatherland', explained the monthly *Liberales Judentum*.[54] It was this sense of duty that led so many German Jews to throw themselves wholeheartedly behind the war effort. For most Jews, there was never any question as to whether or not they would stand behind Germany: it was simply a given. 'We are acting as demanded by our duty and conscience', explained Eugen Fuchs, a lawyer and co-founder of the CV.[55]

If the thought of fighting a defensive war presented German Jews with one reason to back the war, then the fact that the enemy was Russia provided further grounds for optimism. Tsarist Russia had long been held in low esteem by Germany's Jewish communities. Memories of the Russian anti-Jewish pogroms of the late nineteenth and early twentieth centuries were still fresh among many Jews. The 1903 Kishinev pogrom, in particular, which had seen almost fifty Jews killed and hundreds injured, remained a byword for Russian barbarism. The outbreak of war with Russia, then, offered an opportunity to avenge this violence. As the Zionists' main newspaper, the *Jüdische Rundschau*, declared, the Russians 'will be taught a lesson'. 'Revenge for Kishinev', it cried.[56] However, while revenge may be sweet, it tends to be only short-lived. For many people, therefore, ensuring that Russia's Jews were saved from a life of servitude was equally important. 'We are fighting', stated one German-Jewish publication, 'to protect our holy fatherland, to rescue European culture and to liberate our brothers in the east.'[57]

Despite all the bravura of August 1914, it is hard not to escape the impression that many people simply did not know what they were really letting themselves in for. Put simply, Jews and other Germans had very little knowledge of the dangerous potential of modern warfare. After all, the last major continental clash had been the Franco-Prussian War, almost fifty years earlier.[58] With little direct experience of the horrors of war, Germans and other Europeans marched naïvely over the brink and into battle. The German-Jewish industrialist, thinker and sometime politician Walther Rathenau was, like many Germans, rather blasé about the onset of war. He may have been privately sceptical about war, but in public he concealed these views and instead let his deep patriotism shine through. Invoking Carl von Clausewitz's famous dictum that war is the continuation of politics by other means, Rathenau found it easy to justify armed struggle. In an article for the *Berliner Tageblatt*, he suggested that if Russia made demands against Austria-Hungary, then this in turn would create 'a politically intolerable world situation'. Under these circumstances, Germany would have the 'right and duty' to 'fight on Austria's side for a worthy goal', he insisted.[59]

Rathenau's valiant attempt to justify war covered the same ground as that of many other German intellectuals. The prominent historian Friedrich Meinecke, for example, backed the war on the basis that it was a defence of German culture against the threat of Slavism from the east.[60] What the tensions of the July crisis had done was to give a disparate group of people something to rally around. Jewish communities, which had themselves been riddled with divisions, found as much reason to back the war as all other Germans. Yet divisions within society had not permanently vanished; they had just been covered over with a strong blast of patriotic optimism. Behind the scenes, it was clear that uncertainty still reigned supreme. In private, even Rathenau viewed the onset of war very differently to his public pronouncements. 'The world has gone mad!' he complained to a close friend.[61] It was all very well to hide the madness of war under the veil of wartime unity, but as Jews and other Germans would quickly discover, national harmony could unravel just as quickly as it had appeared.

2

WAR ENTHUSIASM

'Mobilisation': the front-page headline of the liberal *Vossische Zeitung* was unambiguous. On 1 August, after a month of heated negotiations, Germany joined sides with its ally Austria-Hungary and declared war on Russia. The First World War had now begun in earnest. The editor of the *Vossische Zeitung*, the German-Jewish journalist Georg Bernhard, immediately threw his full weight behind the conflict. Nothing but positive news filled the first wartime editions: Russia was solely responsible for the war's outbreak; Germany was ready to achieve a 'total victory' and the German people were apparently thrilled that the war had finally started. On the streets of Berlin, suggested the newspaper, 'many thousands of men and women' stood together to sing 'patriotic songs'. Their jubilation was so great that 'nobody could think of sleep'; all they wanted to do was to celebrate the start of hostilities.[1]

Had the *Vossische Zeitung* cast its net a bit wider, it would have captured a very different image of Germany. Not everyone was banging the drum for war. City dwellers worried about food shortages (some even began to hoard supplies), farmers fretted at the thought of losing labourers for the harvest, and in Germany's border regions the very real threat of invasion caused more panic than patriotic exuberance. German Jews also had to deal with their own concerns in August 1914. At a time of national crisis, some sections of Jewish communities feared being pushed to the margins amidst a wave of patriotic fervour. Yet, despite the wide variety of responses to the conflict, which ranged from anxiety to determined support, it did not take long for one single narrative of the war's outbreak to emerge. This narrative stressed enthusiasm and excitement over scepticism and panic, and national unity over petty divisions.

In short, the German people were united, enthusiastic and more than willing to march onto the battlefield in defence of their country.

Such was the strength and simplicity of the message that the 'spirit of 1914', as it was dubbed, became the watchword for Germany's supposed wartime unity. The 'spirit of 1914' may have offered at best a one-dimensional, highly selective account of the public's response to war, but it proved to be one that the people found easy to embrace. German Jews, whose response to the July crisis had spanned a gamut of emotions, managed to project an image of unified war enthusiasm once the conflict was in full swing. Any hesitancy or scepticism that individuals may have held was rapidly subsumed by a message of support and patriotic gusto. In this sense, then, German Jews played a central role in helping to construct the 'spirit of 1914'. They were not meekly sitting on the sidelines in August 1914 waiting for the conflict to be over, but were also pushing Germany forwards into battle.

The 'Spirit of 1914'

In an attempt to capture some of the momentum of the 'spirit of 1914', the kaiser declared 5 August to be a day of patriotic prayer. Under the glare of the summer sun, Germany's synagogues joined the Catholic and Protestant churches in throwing open their doors to crowds of curious people. In Berlin, as elsewhere, the synagogues of the Orthodox and liberal communities were filled to breaking point. Such was the demand that one liberal community was forced to hold a second service immediately after its first, just to ensure that nobody missed out. Once inside, patriotic prayers and tub-thumping speeches added to the feverish atmosphere. Rabbi Leo Baeck, who officiated at the service in the Fasanenstrasse Synagogue, told the congregation that the war would 'decide the future culture and ethos of Europe'.[2] Across Berlin, in the majestic New Synagogue, passions rose even higher. German victory prayers and a spontaneous rendition of the *'Deutschlandlied'* – *'Deutschland, Deutschland über alles'* – echoed through the building.[3] No doubt, many people sat through these services with tears in their eyes, worrying about the future; but amidst the fervour of August 1914, such fears vanished from view.[4]

By declaring their unconditional support for the conflict, the main Jewish associations helped to lay the groundwork for the 'spirit of 1914'. Germany's largest Jewish organisation, the heavily acculturated CV, led the way with a powerful call to arms. 'In this fateful hour, the fatherland calls its sons to join up', the organisation urged. 'It goes without saying that every German Jew is ready to sacrifice property and blood as duty demands.'[5] For added publicity, the CV repeated this call in the *Frankfurter Zeitung*, a mainstream liberal newspaper. If the organisation was going to support the war, it was important that other Germans be made aware of this fact too. The Zionists, along with almost all of the smaller Jewish associations, followed suit. 'We call on you', the main Zionist organisation urged, 'to give yourself . . . to serve the fatherland.'[6]

It would be easy to dismiss the Jewish organisations' carefully staged gatherings and weighty statements as nothing more than public posturing. However, the fact that many individual Jews also actively participated in this early war enthusiasm must indicate a genuine and widely held commitment to the conflict. The most visible evidence of this patriotic sentiment came from the large numbers of Jewish men who volunteered for military action. During August alone, an estimated 250,000 Germans of all ages flocked down to their local recruitment depots, hoping to be selected for the front. How many of this number were Jewish is hard to say. In Württemberg, where some statistics exist, it is clear that Jewish volunteers were over-represented.[7] In an attempt to replicate this information for the remainder of the country, Jewish communities conducted their own statistical surveys. However, the scale of the task was such that these surveys also failed to reveal accurate numbers.[8]

In a sense, there was never any real need for Jews or for any other Germans to sign up voluntarily for the war as Germany's system of conscription would have rounded them up in the end. Of course, it was not always a streak of patriotism that encouraged these early volunteers; pay, a desire to fulfil masculine ideals or even a love of adventure was also motivation enough. Nonetheless, a wish to defend the country appeared to be a significant factor for many Jews. Otto Braun, for example, who had only just turned seventeen, defied his parents and joined the military. For this adolescent schoolboy, testing his masculinity in the military clearly overrode his parents' fears. I was 'mightily proud and happy', he wrote.[9] Elsewhere, Hubert Plaut, a 25-year-old Jewish mathematics student, was also desperate to join up. He 'was quite looking forward to the adventure', he later recalled, so he 'tried at once to enlist'. Plaut ran down to his local recruiting depot in Hamburg and joined a huge crowd 'pressing forward' at the gates. But as in many cities, the army was completely overwhelmed with recruits and simply turned away many young men, like Plaut, who had been desperate to serve at the front.[10]

Other volunteers, though, were more successful. Stories abounded of German Jews, overseas when the conflict started, who rushed back to sign up.

Isaac Hurwitz, who had spent the previous nine years in Argentina, wanted to return to serve his 'second fatherland'. 'I have to be a part of it', he pleaded.[11] With slightly less distance to travel, Otto Stern managed to evade the French authorities to travel back from Paris to Aschaffenburg. Grateful to have made it home, Stern pledged to help defend 'German soil . . . from our enemies with our own blood'.[12] Jewish newspapers quickly seized on any stories of German Jews, like Hurwitz and Stern, who had gone beyond the call of duty to fight in the war. They proudly declared Germany's youngest volunteer to be a 14-year-old Jewish boy from Königsberg and also managed to unearth two of the army's oldest recruits: a 63-year-old from Aachen and a 64-year-old from Würzburg. The pair were Jewish veterans of the Franco-Prussian War keen to have one last shot at their old enemy.[13]

The general excitement of the war's first week took many forms. Alongside the war volunteers or the curious crowds on the streets, there was also a cultural dimension to the 'spirit of 1914'. Artists, journalists and playwrights lined up to capture this moment of national unity. Walter Trier, for example, repeatedly reached for his sketchbook during these first weeks. Trier had plenty of reason to celebrate the apparent coming together of the German people. Born into a middle-class Jewish family in Prague, he was something of a double outsider in Imperial Germany. But now circumstances appeared to have changed for the better. Perhaps the most well-known of Trier's wartime cartoons is based on a map of Europe (see Plate 4). Each of the warring parties is depicted in satirical fashion – the British by a kilted Scotsman; the Irish by a bulldog ready to bite its master across the Irish Sea; and the Serbs by a dirty pig. At the centre of these goings-on are the Germans, who face a jumbled mess of bodies in the west, representing the French, and an oversized, moustachioed head in the east, standing for the Russians. Amidst the chaos around them, the neat, well-groomed German soldiers in contrast represent one unified national body.

Like Trier, Anton and Dorat Herrnfeld, two Hungarian-born Jews, also found much to celebrate in the 'spirit of 1914'. As directors of Berlin's Herrnfeld theatre company, the pair were able to bring their excitement to the stage. Wasting little time, the pair immediately sat down to draft a special, celebratory play: *He Will Return* (*Er kommt wieder*). Set in a village on the Austria–Germany border, the play revolves around the departure of a young Jewish soldier, Jacob, for the front. But the plot really just serves as a vehicle for displaying a string of heavily patriotic lines, extolling German values while decrying those of the Russians. In one scene, Jacob's father, Moses, asks 'is there anything more beautiful than to be able to defend the kaiser and

Reich?' before going on to explain how this 'sense of duty' had previously led him to fight in the 1866 Austro-Prussian War.[14]

However, for all its patriotic spirit, the Herrnfelds' play also hinted at some of the deeper fears affecting German Jews at this time. In the pre-war years, the Herrnfeld brothers had been self-confident in their use of a wide range of local dialects on stage. Their theatre on Berlin's Kommandantenstrasse, just to the south of the centre, had routinely produced popular plays in which Eastern European Jewish characters took to the stage and regaled the audience with a mixture of German, Hebrew and Yiddish words. However, none of these previously strong traits survived the outbreak of hostilities. *He Will Return* was an entirely straight play, in which the main characters all spoke in standard German, free of dialect. Moses, meanwhile, may be Jewish, but he is an acculturated, highly patriotic Jew; the more complex Eastern European Jewish characters of old were nowhere to be seen.[15]

This marked shift in the Herrnfelds' work stemmed from the 'spirit of 1914' itself; the idea may have symbolised unity, but it also spread considerable disunity. It exalted Germans, but left anyone deemed to be a non-citizen, including Eastern European Jews, dangerously marginalised, particularly as the country erupted into spy fever. Local and national newspapers dedicated many column inches to unmasking French and Russian spies, who, if the stories were to be believed, had already managed to infiltrate every corner of the country. Many of the stories were completely far-fetched. The SPD's Friedrich Stampfer recalled witnessing a crowd turn on a 'Russian spy' in the centre of Berlin. However, on closer inspection their 'spy' turned out to be a Bavarian army officer; he managed to escape, slightly shaken by the experience.[16]

Of the hundreds of 'spies' arrested each day, very few, if any, were actually involved in espionage. But this was not the point. The intensity of this spy fever created an atmosphere of deep suspicion. If a Bavarian officer could be attacked in the German capital for being a spy, then Germany's Eastern European Jews stood even less of a chance. Indeed, many of the column inches that newspapers dedicated to unmasking spies happened to mention foreign Jews. In Würzburg, a Jewish businessman was accused of harbouring spies; the police investigated claims that a Jew in Stettin had sold German military uniforms to the Russians; and in the East Prussian town of Insterburg a 70-year-old Jew had apparently filled his cellar with bombs, ready for an attack on Germany.[17]

The *Israelitisches Gemeindeblatt* in Cologne complained that the press never reported the arrest of a Greek Catholic spy, a 'Protestant' spy or a

'Calvinist' spy; 'Jewish spies' were all they were interested in.[18] However, the response of the larger German-Jewish groups to these incidents was remarkably low key. The CV, the main Jewish defence organisation, did little more than to write to the government expressing its concerns. 'In future, details about [spies] belonging to Judaism should cease in all reports', it politely requested.[19] The German-Jewish communities conveniently overlooked the fact that they were supposedly going to war to help Eastern European Jews, like those now under attack at home. The excitement and enthusiasm of August 1914, it seems, outweighed such inconvenient technicalities. During the first weeks of the conflict, Jews and other Germans expended most of their energy in publicly demonstrating their support for the conflict. This was supposed to be a moment of national unity. Rather than rock the boat, German Jews steered themselves towards calmer waters and joined in with the public excitement for war.

Mobilising the Home Front

With the Russians mobilising in the east and the Entente starting to do the same in the west, Jews and other Germans also needed to mobilise the home front for war. The general impression that reigned during August was of an excited public willingly preparing for the fight that lay ahead. German Jews again contributed to this aspect of the 'spirit of 1914', whether this came through volunteering in hospitals or making community buildings available for military purposes. However, public impressions could also be deceptive. At its core, mobilisation was about change. It required Jews and other Germans to alter daily routines, adapt their lives and make sacrifices in order to prepare the country for war. As people very quickly discovered, none of this was at all easy.

The speed of change took many families by surprise. In Königsberg, Gerda Luft's father had only recently made the momentous decision to retire. He sold his import/export business and was all ready to dedicate his twilight years to a quiet life of study. The outbreak of hostilities, however, changed his retirement plans in an instant; price rises and inflation wiped out his savings, forcing him to take a lesser job in a bank. 'It was painful', his daughter later recalled, to see her father on the way to work every morning 'slowly walking with his stick, stopping, gasping for breath.'[20] During the first weeks of war, similar stories of personal upheaval could be found in every corner of the country. Looking back at the mobilisation process, a Jewish care charity in

Frankfurt recorded how many more people had been pushed into poverty as a result. 'Mobilisation deprived many families of their breadwinner, their tenant or boarder', it noted. 'Businesses faltered, owners of insufficiently sound businesses fell into financial difficulty, employees lost their jobs or were put onto half-wages.'[21]

It was not just families that were suddenly forced into a period of rapid transition; all types of public institutions had to adapt to the demands of war. Some schools, for example, had to give up physical space to the war, as the military's rapid growth led it to requisition buildings or sometimes whole institutions.[22] The government was particularly keen to exploit the potential of schoolchildren as both workers and future fighters. Young people aged sixteen or over were to undertake war work, while schools were asked to set aside time for military training.[23] Young Zionists, organised in the Blau-Weiss youth movement, leapt at this chance to take part in war games. Even if these only meant chasing a pretend enemy through the woods of Berlin, they still offered a fantastic opportunity for young German Jews to demonstrate their masculinity. Rallying its members to action, the leadership of the Blau-Weiss told them that this was now the moment 'for us self-assured young Jews to rebut the insults' suffered during peacetime. Male military strength was to provide a strong rejoinder to anti-Semitic accusations of Jewish frailty.[24]

As far as most Germans were concerned, military mobilisation – and thus war games in schools – was strictly an all-male affair. Women and girls had a far more important role ascribed to them: they were to take care of the family, the home and the wounded. Sticking to this familiar line, one Jewish author called on women to 'energetically intervene wherever help is needed'. Ideally, she explained, they should sign up for medical roles to 'care for the wounded and the sick'.[25] Käthe Frankenthal, who had only recently completed her medical studies, followed this call and volunteered for the front. The authorities confirmed that while they did indeed need doctors, what they actually had in mind were male doctors. Military doctors, it turned out, also enjoyed the rank of officer. It would have 'endangered military discipline', Frankenthal was told, if men had to report to her. As the German army put gender hierarchies over medical needs, Frankenthal offered her services to the Austrians, who immediately installed her as a military doctor.[26]

When Germany society encouraged women to take up medical positions, what it had in mind were auxiliary positions, at best the nursing profession. However, even here, the image of the female nurse bravely tending the wounded at the front proved something of an ideal. In reality, very few women had either the time or the finances to undergo training in nursing; only about 25,000 women had served by the war's end.[27] Initially, most of the Jewish women who ended up serving in medical roles were already professional nurses, rather than volunteers. This was the case with Stuttgart's Jewish hospital. At the start of the conflict, a contingent of nine nurses, led by Dr Gustav Feldmann, made themselves available for military duties. They were immediately sent to a military hospital in Breisach, which lay on one of the main Rhine crossing points used by troops heading towards the fighting in Lorraine.[28]

Clearly aware of this insurmountable obstacle, Germany's main women's groups sought to find alternative ways of mobilising their female membership for the war. The Jewish Women's League (Jüdischer Frauenbund, the JFB), led since its formation in 1904 by the formidable Bertha Pappenheim, joined with its Christian and Social Democratic sister organisations to form a wartime action committee, the National Women's Service (Nationaler Frauendienst).[29] Under these auspices, the JFB and other local Jewish groups worked vigorously to ready their members. Within a matter of weeks of the outbreak of war, for example, a Jewish women's group in Berlin established soup kitchens for the poorest families, a clothes bank and a large needlework centre. So many women wanted to help in the tailoring facility that the group ran out of sewing machines and had to limit recruitment to women who could work from home.[30]

The JFB's motivation for its rapid mobilisation was not entirely altruistic. It was acutely aware that the war offered a means to advance its twin goals of improving female and Jewish rights. However, in August 1914 it was not these long-term hopes that were on public display but rather the organisation's patriotism. Not wanting to miss out, Jewish communities throughout Germany rushed to demonstrate their own patriotic spirit by mobilising behind the war. In Berlin, the Jewish community offered the Red Cross exclusive use of the Jewish workers' colony (Arbeiter-Kolonie) in Weissensee. The organisation's red-brick building stretched over four floors and could house ninety residents in comfortable surroundings; as the workers' colony suggested, it was the ideal setting for a military hospital.[31] However, despite agreeing to expel the home's existing residents, the two sides failed to reach an agreement. The Geneva-based institution made it clear that it would only take on the building if the workers' colony left it fully equipped, covered the staffing and provided all meals. Even 'with the best will in the world', the workers' colony explained, there was no way that it could afford these extra costs.[32]

Acrimony over the workers' colony building only served to deepen Jewish disquiet with the Red Cross. Rumours of selective recruitment practices, which had allegedly led to the exclusion of Jewish doctors and nurses, were also doing the rounds at this time. In an attempt to quash such claims, the Red Cross issued a statement of apology, which the CV immediately accepted.[33] With mobilisation under way on all fronts, this was not the time to start debating the place of Jews in the national imagination. Instead, quite the opposite was true: Jews and other Germans were to be united together as one. Arnold Zweig, the great German-Jewish author, expressed this sentiment even more clearly: 'In my inherently Jewish way, I will make Germany's cause, my cause', he wrote. However, for good measure, he added that 'I am not going to stop being a Jew'.[34] In this new Germany his Jewish and German identities were, for the first time, fully in sync.

Yet for German Jews, national unity came at the price of religious solidarity. Fighting for Germany meant by implication fighting, and quite possibly killing, French, Russian and British Jews. While this was undoubtedly an unsavoury prospect, the majority of German Jews accepted their separation from Jewish communities in the Entente as a necessary part of their spiritual mobilisation for war. After all, the conflict also pitted German Catholics and Protestants against fellow believers in the east and west. For the literary scholar Ludwig Geiger, the fact that Jews were now at war with other Jews was proof of the normality of German-Jewish life. They could no longer be considered a minority group, more international than national, but rather were loyal German citizens. 'The German Jew, just as much as the French Jew, has not for a second paid any attention to the fact that he is first and foremost a Jew', wrote Geiger; 'instead, he sees himself as purely a member of his own country.'[35]

As an ideological stance, Ludwig Geiger's promotion of national identities over Jewish fraternalism turned out to be fairly modest. Other German Jews went much further and attempted a more fundamental break from Germany's wartime enemies. The Alliance Israélite Universelle – a French organisation that was dedicated to protecting Jewish rights – should have been harmless enough. Yet at the start of the war, one of the organisation's members from Mainz decided to quit with immediate effect. 'I resigned', he explained, 'because as a German, I cannot belong to a society under French leadership.'[36] His response was in keeping with a wave of popular patriotism, which targeted anything associated with the three Entente powers. Businesses Germanised their names, obliterating any trace of English or French; theatres stopped performing the plays of Sheridan or Tolstoy; and newspapers made a point of avoiding foreign words.[37] Max Liebermann was one of many intellectuals to return British and French academic awards and prizes.[38]

By all accounts, German Zionists, as members of a transnational movement, should have found it much harder to renounce their ties to the outside world. After all, the conflict appeared to be the very antithesis of their long-term goal of Jewish unity. Yet, aside from a few notable individuals such as the young Gershom Scholem, most German Zionists easily managed to circum-navigate the moral dilemma of fighting other Jews. Justifying their stance, though, required some effective verbal gymnastics. Arthur Hantke, chairman of Germany's main Zionist organisation, acknowledged that fighting other Jews might 'smother any remnants of a community feeling'. Yet a far more likely outcome, argued Hantke, was that the war would 'reignite an already lapsed sense of nationhood by making the ultimate consequences of a diaspora plain to see'.[39]

German Zionists' decision to back Germany's war effort highlighted the extent to which Jewish communities as a whole mobilised during the late summer of 1914. Previously more on the margins of Jewish life, their sudden burst of patriotism surprised many observers. As one liberal rabbi sardonically commented, 'even the Zionists have discovered their natural German heart'.[40] The appeal of the 'spirit of 1914' for many Jews, whether liberal or Zionist in outlook, was the idea of a deepening bond between Germans of all social, religious and economic backgrounds. This was certainly how Martin Buber viewed the opening weeks of the conflict. 'Never has the concept of the *Volk* been such a reality to me than during these last weeks', he remarked excitedly in a letter to a fellow Zionist, Hans Kohn.[41] Amidst the clamour to mobilise, the occasional flickers of anti-Semitism proved easy to downplay. These moments of discrimination may have laid down an ominous marker for the future, but in August 1914 they did little to derail Jewish support.

Germans to the Front

Throughout August, the men who had appeared to volunteer so willingly started to depart for the front. Hugo Rosenthal and his four brothers all left their home in the western district of Lippe in quick succession. Just a few weeks earlier, the family had gathered together to celebrate Rosenthal's older brother's wedding. Now all that his mother wanted to do was to sit 'crying at her window seat'. The image remained deeply etched in his mind.[42] On the streets, emotions also ran high. Towns across Germany witnessed the choreo-graphed spectacle of uniformed soldiers marching to local railway stations, ready to be whisked off to the front. Often crowds of curious onlookers jostled to get a glimpse of the soldiers marching by, perhaps unsure when or if they would see a loved one again. These were not scenes of excitement, but rather of fear and trepidation for the future.

During the first weeks of the war, most of the new recruits ended up in the west. Indeed, at one point, troop trains, crammed full with fresh-faced soldiers, trundled across the Rhine at Cologne at ten-minute intervals.[43] From here, the 1st, 2nd and 3rd Armies moved on towards Belgium, which according to the so-called 'Schlieffen Plan', was a mere stepping stone on the way to Paris.[44] Gottfried Sender, an energetic young Jewish educator, was part of the early advance through the lowlands. 'The journey is long and hot. But we're longing for action', he explained to those at home.[45] Further south, the German-Jewish Social Democratic politician Ludwig Frank, who had not so long ago turned forty, was despatched to Lorraine. The job of Frank and his colleagues was to hold the line against the French, while Sender and the main armies swept through Belgium. In the east, where the Russians were not expected to offer much initial threat, the aim was simply to defend the lines until France was defeated. Harry Marcuse, who like Sender was a member of Berlin's Jewish community, was one of the first to arrive in the east, albeit in a medical, rather than a combat, capacity.[46]

For the German General Staff, the initial military operations passed off fairly smoothly. However, it did not take long for the German advance to run into difficulties. One major problem, which Sender experienced, was the sheer physicality of the westward march. 'After only a few days, my feet were torn to shreds', he complained. 'I doubt that there's a single infantryman who would not rather take a bullet than have to suffer this torment in the heat and dust', he added for good measure.[47] If the strains of the march were not enough, the advancing soldiers also had to take on the Belgian army, which was making a valiant attempt to defend the country's neutrality. The tenacity of the Belgian soldiers appeared to catch the advancing Germans off guard. 'As we came further into the country, so they became more treacherous and hostile', explained one German-Jewish soldier somewhat indignantly.[48]

The German attack on France, with troops advancing through Belgium and also through Alsace-Lorraine, came at a high cost. From the Belgian army alone, there were some 30,000 casualties, and from the German roughly 2,000. Ludwig Frank, who had so cheerfully departed Germany in August, was killed on 3 September, becoming the first parliamentarian to die in the conflict. During a major frontal offensive, Frank's regiment came under heavy fire from the French lines; a bullet or piece of shrapnel shot across, striking Frank in the left temple. He died immediately, although such was the intensity of the battle that his body could only be recovered the following day. The loss of Frank, who had been seen as something of a rising star, hit both German Jews and his political party hard. The SPD's newspaper in Mannheim, Frank's political stronghold, appeared with a black border and three simple words: 'Ludwig Frank Falls'. Elsewhere, the main Jewish organisations mourned the loss of 'one of the greatest Jews' with a series of lengthy speeches and heartfelt obituaries.[49]

What quickly became clear during the first weeks of fighting was that large numbers of civilians were also going to be casualties of the war. This was particularly evident in Belgium, where the invading army brutally executed people accused of sabotage and drove many thousands of civilians from their homes. In the university town of Louvain, which before the war was renowned for its 'old houses with handsome façades', German troops wilfully set fire to several of the city's most beautiful buildings.[50] The historic centre, the church of St Peter and the university library, containing some 300,000 books, were reduced to a charred pile of smouldering ashes.[51] Felix Theilhaber, a Jewish doctor from Berlin, registered the destruction when his battalion entered what remained of Louvain, but found actual sympathy harder to come by. 'These collapsing ruins didn't make much of an impression on us ... We'd already seen enough destroyed houses' in Belgium, he remarked.[52] Wartime destruction, it seems, had already become an accepted part of the war experience.

Even though they had never been invited to march through the country, the Germans were very quick to blame any military excesses on the Belgians themselves. The main accusation was of Belgian underhand tactics, with civilians acting as saboteurs in place of regular troops. Oskar Brieger, a Jewish infantryman from Posen, certainly struggled to hide his anger after surviving a Belgian ambush. As his battalion entered a quiet village centre, he and his comrades were greeted by 'tremendous fire; the entire civilian population, including the women, shot continually at us'. Brieger managed to drag himself to the safety of a nearby barn, only to see 'a Belgian soldier shooting our wounded'. Already fired up from the ambush, he seized an opportunity to rescue his comrades. 'As the wretch went to reload his gun', Brieger explained, 'I dug my bayonet into his heart.'[53] The adrenalin was clearly still pumping as Brieger penned his account. But this in itself was part of the problem. The more jittery the invading soldiers became, the more willing they were to sense danger around every corner. Often they took their revenge on the local population before it had even shown any resistance.[54]

Despite their slow progress, the German army eventually started to make some headway. After an eleven-day battle, the heavily fortified city of Liège finally fell on 16 August. The German forces were now on a roll. They captured Brussels, defeated the British at Mons and then moved across the border into France, seemingly on an unstoppable path to Paris. Writing in early September from the front, Karl Blank, a young Jewish student from Hanover, felt confident enough to declare that the war in the west would soon be won. '[We] have enjoyed victory after victory', he commented. Hopefully 'the French will [soon] have had enough of all the blows'.[55]

Sadly for Blank, the popular idea that the war would be over by Christmas (a cliché so beloved of historians) was never likely to become reality. Germany may have sent the majority of its troops into battle in the west, but the conflict was never destined to be a mere rerun of the Franco-Prussian War. From the very start, this was a global conflict with multiple protagonists. In Africa, for example, the British and French managed to place Germany's African forces very quickly onto the back foot. German Togoland fell within the first month of the conflict; the Cameroons were all but lost the following year; and Germany's control of South-West Africa ended in July 1915. German Jews played only a limited role in the African campaigns. Richard Kandt, a well-known colonial administrator of Jewish descent, was on leave in Germany in 1914 and was unable to return. Nonetheless, German Jews still had some presence on the continent. In total, seventeen Jews fought in Paul von Lettow-Vorbeck's army, which put up resistance in German East Africa until the very end of the conflict.[56]

Brutal as they were, these colonial campaigns were still only a sideshow to the clashes on the European mainland. According to the 'Schlieffen Plan', the German army was supposed to have defeated the French in a matter of weeks, before turning its firepower on the Russian army in the east. The Russians, though, had their own plans, which turned out to be very different to the role the Germans had assigned to them. Harry Marcuse, who was by now sporting a 'magnificent full beard', reported heavy skirmishes with the Russians, 'several hours of [enemy] artillery fire each day' and a continual stream of wounded.[57] What Marcuse witnessed was the Russian assault on East Prussia, which left over 1,000 civilians dead and some 100,000 buildings destroyed.[58] Johanna Klunower from the lakeside town of Lötzen lost her home and possessions in these clashes. The stress of all this took a toll on her health, leaving her suffering from both heart and kidney problems. Destitute and in ill health, Klunower decided to contact her late husband's synagogue community for help.[59] Unfortunately it is not clear whether her pleas were answered, but what they do highlight is the precarious situation for both Jews and other Germans in the eastern borderlands.

In East Prussia, it took the German military until the end of August to regain the initiative. The famous battle of Tannenberg saw the Germans gradually overpower their Russian adversaries over a five-day period, forcing them back across the East Prussian border. Victor Klemperer, the German-Jewish literary scholar, noted in his diary simply: 'magical successes!'[60] The German victory was not quite as overwhelming as Klemperer suggested; nonetheless the Russian advance had been halted and by early September East Prussia was liberated. Perhaps the longer-term significance of Tannenberg was that it helped to turn the generals Paul von Hindenburg and Erich Ludendorff into national heroes. Although the duo had only been drafted in as commanders shortly before Tannenberg, Hindenburg, in particular, had no qualms about taking full credit for the army's triumph. A congratulatory telegram from the kaiser in which he hailed Tannenberg as a victory 'unique in history' was plastered across the front of many newspapers.[61]

Jewish journalists also helped to sow the seeds of what was to become a veritable Hindenburg myth. In glowing terms, the *Allgemeine Zeitung des Judentums* reported 'General Hindenburg's wonderful feat of arms' which had resulted in a 'great victory in East Prussia'.[62] The Viennese journalist Paul Goldmann went a stage further and published a rather obsequious article about the great general that read more like a celebrity interview than a serious discussion of Germany's military strategy. Hindenburg looked younger than his sixty-seven years, the article revealed. He received fan mail almost daily and has been sent more fingerless gloves than he knew what to do with. 'I would have to have 40 hands if I wanted to wear all the ones I've been given. For heaven's sake, don't send me any more fingerless gloves', joked Hindenburg.[63]

Goldmann's portrayal of this jovial character helped to cement the image of Hindenburg as both a military leader and a relaxed commander of men. Instead of regaling journalists with chirpy anecdotes, Hindenburg should really have been more concerned about Germany's failure to achieve a decisive breakthrough on either front. Yet such concerns could wait. In autumn 1914, the German military leadership still had many reasons to be confident. They had enjoyed a euphoric victory at Tannenberg, the Russians had been expelled from East Prussia, Belgium was occupied, and German troops were encamped in France.

The soldiers in the field faced much greater risks than the members of the General Staff. By the end of 1914, out of the 7 million soldiers from both sides involved in the opening skirmishes, a million had lost their lives.[64] Yet even for the troops on the frontline, Germany's apparent military gains helped to mask some of the harsher realities of war. Many soldiers shared a mixture of pride and genuine relief that the German army, of which they were a part, had achieved so much in such a short space of time. 'We hear that the German cavalry is within a few kilometres of Paris', one Jewish soldier remarked excitedly.[65] As rumours of the German army's successes spread through the ranks, people began to dream of a rapid end to hostilities. 'Beaming with joy, we just heard the wonderful news of our victories in east and west', remarked Richard Friedmann. Rather optimistically, he concluded that 'the dawn of peace has now begun to shine through'.[66] In early autumn 1914, any talk of victory was clearly somewhat premature. But the advances and moderate victories of the first month gave Jewish soldiers, like Friedmann, plenty to cheer. For now at least, the future seemed bright.

Sensing Victory

Aside from Russia's incursion into East Prussia, all of the fighting throughout the war took place outside Germany. The German public, therefore, did not have to witness directly the moment when a soldier was struck by a bullet or was thrown to one side by an exploding shell. Those at home were also less aware of the military reverses, of the intensity of French and Belgian resistance or of the endless waves of men that the Russians could throw into action. Removed from the horrors of battle, the home front found it even easier than the fighting troops to place a positive slant on developments. In early September, before the failure of the battle of the Marne, German war enthusiasm reached a new peak, as Germans of all social and religious backgrounds soaked up the euphoria of the army's first successes.

The public may have been removed from the full horrors of battle, but they were not completely ignorant of events. Newspapers passed on some information, though always with a highly patriotic gloss. Far more useful as mediators of frontline news were soldiers' letters, which tended to be widely circulated between groups of friends and relatives. In Würzburg, the members of one German-Jewish student fraternity even gathered every morning over coffee to read the 'eagerly awaited' letters.[67] Although much of this correspondence was fairly banal, it was still possible to get a sense of daily life for the Jewish soldiers at the front. Harry Marcuse, for example, wrote keenly about long evenings spent with comrades in the mess. Once the drink started flowing, he joked, the conversation was not always 'suitable for ladies' ears'.[68] Marcuse seemed to enjoy the novelty of this fairly crude male bonding, which was very different to his middle-class home life.

However, as is to be expected in war, not all of the news from the front was good. In other letters, Marcuse broached the subject of war damage, destroyed buildings and smashed-up bodies. But for those at home, none of this could have come as a surprise. The horrors of war were hard to escape. People often witnessed the return of the most severely wounded and the first casualty lists were also readily accessible.[69] Many of the Jewish newspapers shared this information, publishing the names of their own war dead, partly for information and partly to remind people of the extent of Jewish participation.[70]

Yet the belief that Germany was on course for a rapid victory stopped people from focusing for too long on these lengthening casualty lists. Across the country, news of the army's heroic exploits in the east and west was greeted with great celebration. On learning of Germany's successes in Lorraine, even Theodor Wolff, the Jewish editor of the *Berliner Tageblatt*, put his earlier scepticism to one side and let the flags be raised above the newspaper's offices.[71] The mood was also buoyant in the offices of the *Frankfurter Zeitung*. Visiting the newspaper in late August, the Danish politician Hans Peter Hanssen bumped into Adolf Warschauer and August Stein, two German-Jewish writers, who exuded confidence. 'They all thought that the war would soon be over', he sceptically reported.[72]

On a communal level, the main German-Jewish organisations also helped to fuel the general public's insatiable enthusiasm for the conflict. Synagogue sermons often talked not of the sorrow of war but of its elemental power. Their focus was not on the destruction of Belgium but on the soldiers who had carried 'the German flag from victory to victory'.[73] Many Jewish community newspapers also allowed themselves to get carried away by the army's early successes. The Kartell-Convent, umbrella organisation for Germany's numerous Jewish student fraternities, launched a special war edition of its newspaper. Other publications regaled readers with heroic tales of Jews in past conflicts, such as the Franco-Prussian War, while almost all Jewish newspapers started to publish patriotic letters from Jewish soldiers fighting at the front.[74]

German Jews' public enthusiasm for the conflict was certainly not unique; the Catholic and Protestant churches also gave their enthusiastic support for the war, seeing in it a moment of spiritual renewal.[75] What was different, however, were the levels of emotional currency that Jews invested in the conflict. This was no ordinary war; it was also a fight for a more secure Jewish future. Both Zionists and liberals began to compare the Central Powers' current fight with the ancient struggles of the Maccabees. In the same way that the Maccabean forces had crushed the ancient Greeks to re-establish Jewish rights in biblical Jerusalem, German Jews were now fighting to free 'Russia and the world from unprecedented tyranny', argued the Zionist *Jüdische Rundschau*.[76] In short, Jews were engaged in a new 'holy war', not against Greek but against Russian oppression.[77] Should any German Jews have harboured doubts about the direction the war was taking, then the knowledge that they were engaged in a religious war, similar to the heroic struggles of past Jewish history, was supposed to allay their fears.

Such conviction in the righteousness of Germany's military struggle also helped to define the way Jews perceived the enemy. It seems it was not enough simply to defeat the opposition forces on the battlefield; people demanded that the French, British and Russians be completely crushed. Max Liebermann's early wartime lithographs for the *Kriegszeit* journal encapsulated this rather vengeful attitude. One particularly striking image depicts a cavalry officer galloping at full pelt into battle (see Plate 5). With his sword swinging high above his head, the officer is clearly not looking to take prisoners but is instead ready to crush any opposition encountered. The line at the bottom of the page – 'Now we will thrash them' – stems from one of the kaiser's speeches. The message was clear: there was to be no empathy with Germany's opponents; they were to be destroyed by the superiority of German military might.

The work of Jewish writers and artists, such as Max Liebermann, did much to colour the atmosphere of the early war period. Their literary offerings in newspapers, pamphlets and even street posters fed this extreme chauvinism. One of the most notorious examples of this war culture came from Ernst Lissauer, a moderately successful Jewish poet and passionate Prussian. Lissauer was slightly overweight, round in the face and no longer in the full flowering of youth. Nonetheless, as a convinced German patriot, he was eager to fight in the war. When he was rejected from the army – somewhat inevitably – on health grounds, Lissauer, like many writers and artists, sought to serve his country in the cultural sphere instead. As Lissauer himself put it, this was 'military service of an intellectual kind'.[78]

Lissauer put pen to paper as soon as the war began, managing to produce a steady stream of rather mediocre poems. His 'Motto 1914' ('Spruch 1914'), for example, attempted to articulate Germany's new sense of unity:

> A people
> Seventy million as a single force
> Those with the guns
> On land, air and sea
> The Iron Cross
> The Red Cross
> To the east and north and west
> We stand close together
> A block.[79]

However, with the country awash with patriotic ditties of varying qualities, writers needed to produce something special if they wanted to stand out. Lissauer managed to achieve his greatest moment of personal fame in September 1914, when he published his 'Hymn of Hate against England' ('Haßgesang gegen England'). What forced this poem to the forefront of the public's imagination was not its literary style, but rather its basic message. After dismissing Russia and France as countries to be neither loved nor hated, the final lines end in a sustained and spiteful attack on Britain:

> We have one and only one hate
> We love as one, we hate as one
> We have one foe and one alone:
> England![80]

Published amidst the excitement of autumn 1914, the 'Hymn of Hate' took Germany by storm. Stefan Zweig aptly described it as exploding 'like a bomb in a munitions depot'. Newspapers published the poem in full, soldiers sung it at the front and schoolchildren learnt the words off by heart.[81] The kaiser even awarded Lissauer the Order of the Red Eagle in recognition of this great patriotic achievement.[82] The general public may have lapped the poem up, but for some Germans Lissauer's message of hate went too far. The *Frankfurter Zeitung* and Theodor Wolff's *Berliner Tageblatt* criticised it for damaging future relations with Germany's neighbours, while one SPD politician complained that the song was corrupting the minds of young people.[83]

These liberal voices undoubtedly made a valid point. After the German army's early victories against the French, Belgians and Russians, an uncontrollable wave of euphoria swept through the nation. Artists, writers and poets stressed German superiority, whilst at the same time vilifying its enemies, often in the cruellest of fashions. And in this sense, Lissauer, with his 'Hymn of Hate', was one of the worst offenders. The notorious anti-Semitic publicist, Houston Stewart Chamberlain, suggested that a fierce hatred of the enemy was a Jewish, rather than a German trait.[84] This was obviously nonsense as Germans of all religious backgrounds lined up to denigrate the enemy. The zoologist Ernst Haeckel, for example, launched a ferocious attack on Britain in his essay 'England's Blood Guilt for the War'. Neither Lissauer's poem nor Liebermann's sketches, then, were a peculiarly Jewish form of war culture. Instead, what they demonstrate is that Jews, just as much as other Germans, helped to develop an atmosphere of hyper-patriotism during autumn 1914. Against this backdrop, the war turned into a bitter and spiteful clash between all those involved.

War Aims

Amidst the upheaval and excitement of the first weeks of war, the question of what Germany was actually fighting for was never properly answered. Bethmann Hollweg and the kaiser had skilfully managed to brand the conflict as a defensive war. With the nation apparently under attack from all sides, it proved easy for Germans from across the political spectrum to accept the logic of the conflict. After all, if people failed to pick up their guns, then the Russians would stream in from the east and the French and British from the west. But if the First World War was being fought to defend Germany's borders, what was to be its end point? Did France, Britain and Russia need to be completely defeated or was it enough simply to subdue the enemy? On these issues, German Jews were divided, in common with the wider population.

In public at least, the SPD flew the flag for a moderate peace. When the party had agreed to back a defensive military campaign, they did so on the basis that it would be a limited conflict avoiding any untoward 'aggression or conquest'. Hugo Haase, the party's German-Jewish joint chairman, made this argument explicit in his Reichstag speech that had committed the SPD to war. Once Germany's enemies had been repelled, stressed Haase, the war was to 'be brought to an end by a peace treaty that makes friendship with our neighbours possible'.[85] Plenty of other German Jews were sympathetic to these rather moderate aims. Theodor Wolff avoided laying out an explicit plan, but his articles and notes made it clear that he was firmly opposed to any form of annexations.[86] Eugen Fuchs, a prominent spokesman of the CV, followed a similar line. 'We have not been striving for world power', he stressed. 'We merely wanted a moderate place in the sun.'[87]

However, Fuchs's final demand also revealed one of the difficulties facing the advocates of a moderate peace. The further the German army advanced, the greater people's expectations for the future became. In the minds of many, there had to be some reward for the human and financial sacrifices that Germany had already made. It seemed inconceivable that the German army would simply march back home, returning Europe to the previous status quo. The reward could be a mere 'place in the sun', as Fuchs suggested, or something much grander. Some members of the SPD even ended up coming down in favour of territorial gains. Max Cohen-Reuß and Eduard David, two Jewish politicians on the party's right, argued that there should be 'no territorial annexation'. But they then demanded in the next breath that the Belgian and French Congo regions become the basis of a new German colonial empire spreading across equatorial Africa.[88]

Cohen-Reuß and David's support of an expansive war-aims policy was at the more moderate end of the annexationist spectrum. Far more ambitious in scope was the *Mitteleuropa* or 'Central Europe' idea, most commonly associated with the politician Friedrich Naumann, but actually first pushed into the political arena by Walther Rathenau, the German-Jewish industrialist. Rathenau, whose father had founded the AEG electrical conglomerate in 1887, chaired the company's board of directors, but also found time to dabble in literature, philosophy and politics. It was in this latter context that he penned two memoranda for Bethmann Hollweg outlining his ideas for a new *Mitteleuropa*. In Rathenau's view, a European customs union dominated by Germany was preferable to direct annexations. Under this plan, German industry would flourish to rival the British Empire, all without the need for direct control of more European territory.[89] The *Mitteleuropa* plan gained the tacit support of leading figures in the world of German banking, shipping and light industry.[90]

Far-reaching as it was, the *Mitteleuropa* plan failed to light a spark with Germany's more conservative thinkers. Heavy industrialists and right-wing politicians called for even grander war aims, more befitting Germany's current position of military strength. Rather than just economic dominance, they desired wide-ranging territorial annexations too. Heinrich Claß, chairman of the radical Pan-German League (Alldeutscher Verband), went furthest in his public demands. The northern two-thirds of Africa must become German colonies, France and Belgium be entirely crushed, and all annexed territories be ethnically reconfigured, with Germans replacing the existing populations. The government, which was trying to keep the debate over war aims in check, hit Claß with a publishing ban for his efforts.[91]

On the face of it, there looked to be a wide spectrum of competing war aims, with German Jews mainly drawn to the moderate camp, while the annexationists were dominated by the political right. However, the dividing lines between these factions were actually more blurred than the groups themselves cared to admit.[92] Deep down, all sides believed that the war had to end with Germany in a more dominant position, ideally usurping Britain to become the leading European power. Although they placed less weight on annexations, the supporters of a liberal war-aims policy, who included many Jews, remained open to the idea of some form of territorial expansion. Rathenau admitted that 'significant changes to the map' of Europe were possible, while the shipping magnate Albert Ballin suggested that Germany needed to consider the 'annexation of valuable overseas territories'.[93] There was also agreement on the desirability of war indemnities; it was just the actual figure that differed. Rathenau favoured imposing an indemnity of 40 billion gold francs on France; Claß also thought a figure running into the billions should suffice.[94]

It was all very well for Rathenau and Ballin to dream of overseas expansion or for Bethmann Hollweg to demand annexations in east and west, but with Russia, Britain and France still resolutely fighting, these musings were nothing more than wishful thinking. While waiting for the inevitable defeat of the Entente powers, Germany's military and political leaders had to content themselves with Belgium, which became something of a test case for the differing war-aims policies. All sides in the debate agreed that Belgium could not simply be returned to its pre-invasion state. Not only was the country of strategic importance, but the fear of Belgian saboteurs also continued to haunt German minds. Thus, in the short term at least, Belgium was to remain occupied.[95]

Germany may not have annexed Belgium entirely, as many were demanding, but this was still far removed from the idea of a more benign customs union. Yet Rathenau and other Jewish members of the supposedly liberal war-aims camp seemed unperturbed by such realities. Rathenau made it clear that he regarded Belgian requisitions as essential.[96] Georg Solmssen, the Jewish-born director of the Disconto-Gesellschaft banking group, went further. He demanded that Belgium be 'politically and economically chained to the Empire through military occupation and a customs and currency union'.[97] As would be proved time and again, it was only degrees of graduation that separated the different war-aims policies. Over the question of whether Germany needed to strengthen its standing in the world, there was near unanimity amongst Jews and other Germans.

The German army had military reasons for marching through Belgium. It could also make a convincing argument for the economic exploitation of Belgian industry. The British, though, who had entered the war in defence of Belgian neutrality, rightly viewed events very differently. British propaganda efforts emphasised civilian casualties, the destruction of Louvain and the harsh occupation of this small, innocent state. The words 'brave little Belgium' were on everybody's lips. For British propagandists, the Belgian question represented a clash of cultural values, between European humanitarianism and German savagery. British Jews happily joined in these attacks. According to the cultural Zionist Israel Zangwill, not only had the entire conflict been 'made in Germany', but Germany's wartime behaviour had also been 'barbarous'.[98] Building on these themes, Britain's chief rabbi, Joseph Hertz, described a cultured nation as one that 'vindicates the eternal values of life – conscience, honour, liberty'. 'Judged by this test', he concluded, 'two of the littlest of peoples, Judaea in ancient times and Belgium to-day, and not their mighty and ruthless oppressors, are among the chief defenders of culture, champions of the sacred heritage of man.'[99]

The criticisms of Zangwill and Hertz particularly riled Germany's Jewish communities. They could see no reason to brand Germans as perpetrators in the face of Russia's recent history of barbarism and Belgium's reported use of saboteurs.[100] If Belgian women were amusing themselves by 'poking the eyes out of wounded German soldiers', as Martin Buber complained, then it was surely the Belgians rather than the Germans who were responsible for inhuman savagery.[101] German Jews, like Buber, proved particularly belligerent in their defence of Germany's actions and certainly seemed to have little time for the protests of Britain's chief rabbi or the complaints of other British or French Jews. Arnold Zweig produced one of the most sensational rebuttals of British propaganda with his short story, 'The Beast' ('Die Bestie'). In this fictional account, a Belgian farmer slits the throats of three innocent German soldiers before butchering their remains for pigswill. In this light, the farmer's arrest and execution the following day are more than justified.[102]

Europe's intellectuals now took aim at each other in a vicious and increasingly bitter war of words. Julius Bab, German-Jewish dramatist, theatre critic and Berlin socialite, took to recording many of these exchanges in a popular poetry anthology dedicated to the war. But it was through his own poetry and verse that he did the most to stir up tensions with his non-German contemporaries. In his poem 'Germany' ('Deutschland'), from the first month of the war, Bab portrayed himself as being at one with Germany's defensive struggle: 'I stand and fall with Germany which is me.'[103] Amidst the chauvinism of the war's first months, previous friendships counted for very little, as Bab himself proved. In autumn 1914, he launched a scathing attack on Belgium's foremost poet, Emile Verhaeren, whom Bab had previously held dear. Bab's writing in 'The Belgian' ('Die Belgier') and 'To Verhaeren' ('An Verhaeren') depicted the poet as an overwrought Belgian nationalist who had naïvely propagated the idea of German brutality. This was 'a vicious poison that had infected an entire people', lamented Bab.[104]

What most angered German-Jewish intellectuals was the suggestion from Verhaeren and others that the German war effort had destroyed the very idea of humanity.[105] It was inconceivable to think that the rest of Europe was somehow more cultured than the people who had given the world Goethe and Schiller. The young Jewish designer Louis Oppenheim, already well known for his work as a graphic artist for some of Berlin's leading firms, committed this argument to paper. He produced a poster depicting Germany's cultural achievements as being much higher than those of its enemies (see Plate 6). The Germans apparently spent more on schooling, paid out higher social insurance, published more books and had given the world fourteen Nobel Prize-winners compared to Britain's five and France's three. To illustrate these differences, a caricatured image represents each category of achievement. Thus, the minuscule face of a German worker, representing the low number of illiterates in Germany, compares favourably to the bulging face of a rosy-cheeked Frenchman, in whose country illiteracy apparently reigns supreme. The title at the top of the poster – 'Are we the barbarians?' – made it clear that Germany's culture, even in the midst of war, was superior to that of the French and British.

However, it was left to the German-Jewish playwright Ludwig Fulda to make the most incendiary intervention. In early October, at a point when hopes of a swift victory still continued to flicker, Fulda drafted a petition addressed to the 'cultural world'. Its basic aim was to refute all criticism of Germany's wartime conduct levelled from abroad. Thus, Germany was not 'guilty of causing this war': its invasion of Belgium had been fully justified; and the German army, so the petition argued, had not violated 'the life and property of a single Belgian citizen'. The protest ended with a rather empty plea:

'we shall fight this war to the very end as a cultured people to whom the legacy of Goethe, Beethoven and Kant are as sacred as hearth and home'. Ninety-three leading scholars, writers and scientists signed the petition. Besides Fulda, several German-Jewish intellectuals, including Liebermann and Fritz Haber, put their names to the protest. In excusing the military's excesses in this way, the signatories effectively placed Germans above international cultural values and exchange. And in doing so, they damaged further the very ideas they were looking to protect: Germany's claim to be a cultural nation.[106]

Fulda's petition to the 'cultural world' was naïve in the extreme. As the intellectuals who signed the petition would surely have known, it was impossible to make a judgment on Germany's wartime conduct without recourse to evidence. A few academics, in particular Albert Einstein, were more astute and wanted nothing to do with this increasingly bitter war of words. More sober voices could also be found in society at large, where some Jews looked on with anguish at wartime developments. Yet amidst the excitement of August and September 1914, these views carried less weight than those advocating an increase in German power or the exploitation of Belgian industry. What counted more than anything was the impression of patriotic unity, to demonstrate that Germans of all backgrounds were behind the war. Most German Jews performed this task to perfection. They gave the conflict their full backing, decried the Entente's tactics and celebrated Germany's early victories. In late autumn 1914, this seemed a sensible stance to take. Although the German army had not advanced as far as it might have hoped, it still seemed to be in control in both east and west. Victory was surely within the grasp of Jews and other Germans.

3

TOTAL WAR

There was little evidence of the usual New Year's exuberance as Germany entered 1915. Theodor Wolff spent a thoroughly glum evening with the Austrian-born Jewish director Max Reinhardt, who at that time headed up Berlin's Deutsches Theater. Discussion soon turned to absent friends, in this case to one of Reinhardt's colleagues, Karl von Gersdorff, who had celebrated with the pair the previous year. 'Now he lies covered in earth in France with so many others.' Not surprising, therefore, that Wolff noted in his diary simply: 'absolutely no New Year's Eve atmosphere whatsoever'.[1] The streets of Berlin were just as morose. Aside from visitors to the cathedral and the other churches, there was little going on; even the restaurants on the Friedrichstrasse reported only a few visitors.[2] The contrast with the crowds of early August could not have been starker. If the military campaigns had gone to plan, then the German people should have been toasting victory at the end of 1914. Instead, they were preparing themselves for another year of fighting.

Jews and other Germans had good reason to be glum. Despite an optimistic spin on events in the press, it became increasingly obvious that the military's tactics had not gone entirely to plan. One major setback had occurred earlier in the autumn, when the French had forced the Germans back on the Marne. This dramatic reverse had seen the kaiser's new favourite, Erich von Falkenhayn, replace Helmut von Moltke as chief of the General Staff. But more significantly, the battle of the Marne also ushered in trench warfare in the west. On the Eastern Front, some movement remained, although the overall picture was also one of increasing bloodshed for very little success. By the year's end, then, it was clear that Germany was now embroiled in a two-front war – the very scenario that the 'Schlieffen Plan' had been designed to avoid.[3]

To lift the growing gloom, significant changes had to be made to the way in which the country approached the war. In short, greater sacrifices needed to be made at home to support those at the front. Many German Jews not only embraced these demands, but were also at the forefront of these changes, helping to push the country further down the path to total war. The hallmarks of this kind of warfare were the formation of a war economy, a closer alignment between the home front and the frontline, the utilisation of new military technologies and finally changes to the army's structure. When placed together, these major adjustments ensured that the home front came to be increasingly subordinated to the needs of the various frontlines.[4] The creeping militarisation of German society ran counter to the professed ideals of a supposedly liberalising state. Yet very few Germans, whether Jewish, Catholic or Protestant, did anything to resist the conflict's intrusion into the rhythms of daily life.

Hunger

The first signs of a creeping militarisation at home occurred in people's bellies. The German navy's failure to do much more than sit in port made it very difficult to import vital food supplies. Admittedly, there had been the odd naval skirmish, which had mainly served to confirm Germany's shortcomings. The battle of the Heligoland Bight in late August, for example, saw the British sink three German light cruisers – *Cöln*, *Mainz* and *Ariadne*. The son-in-law of Emil Sulzbach, whose family ran the influential German-Jewish bank Gebrüder Sulzbach, went down on the *Ariadne*, becoming one of Germany's earliest naval casualties.[5] Such one-sided battles encouraged the Germans to leave the High Seas Fleet in port, rather than risk another bruising encounter. However, this gave the British an enormous strategic advantage. It meant that Britain's military strategists could execute their pre-war plan to blockade German shipping. In effect, this saw British ships intercepting any cargo, including food, heading towards the Central Powers. The blockade started slowly but proved increasingly effective as the Entente ratcheted up its control measures during 1915.[6]

The effective closure of Germany's main ports had a dramatic impact on international trade. The ships of Albert Ballin's HAPAG line, which had once proudly plied the globe, now lay mothballed either at home or in ports overseas. For a company whose entire business model rested on the transportation of goods and people, this was devastating, so much so that Ballin launched a campaign for government compensation to cover the worst of his financial losses.[7] However, a more immediate and potentially far more devastating impact of the naval blockade concerned the availability of food. Before the war, Germany had imported up to 30 per cent of its basic food supplies from other countries. But with the major ports now sealed, this was clearly no longer a viable option. If the German population was not to starve, then Germany would either have to fight an extremely short war or to find alternative ways of managing food supplies.[8]

However, it became immediately clear that the German military was not in a position to provide a solution to the problem of food supply. Preparing military tactics and organising armies had clearly taken priority over the more mundane issues of the population's basic needs. Fortunately for the military's planners, Ballin, who had previously drafted a paper on the very topic of food supplies, viewed matters with greater foresight. In early August the Interior Ministry, after suddenly grasping the urgency of the situation, packed off a representative to speak with Ballin in Hamburg. The journey proved worthwhile, for out of the meeting came the idea to establish a private organisation to supply food to the public.

The Reichseinkauf, as it was initially called, started life in Hamburg under the direct control of HAPAG. The organisation sent its officials to neutral countries with the express purpose of buying essential provisions for Germany's civilian population. By January, the organisation had grown to such an extent that it needed to move to larger premises in Berlin. It now came under direct state control and took on a new name: the Zentraleinkaufsgesellschaft. After the move to Berlin, HAPAG continued to play an important role in the concern, sending company representatives to procure food from longstanding contacts overseas.[9] Besides Ballin, other German-Jewish businessmen did their best to keep food supplies moving. Carl Melchior, another Hamburg man, was responsible for what the Zentraleinkaufsgesellschaft called 'the most successful example of its activity'.[10] After being wounded and discharged from the army, Melchior, a lively, upright figure with a ravenous intellect, led a delegation to Romania early in 1915. He returned with a contract for 2.25 million tons of grain to be delivered to the Central Powers, which went some way to stemming the worst shortages.[11]

Despite the best efforts of Ballin, Melchior and others, food, or to be more precise the lack of it, became a persistent problem for Germany's civilian population. After only a few months of fighting, shoppers in Berlin's bakeries found the shelves empty, and in early 1915 the government introduced the first ration cards for bread in the capital.[12] Meanwhile, the prominent German-Jewish social reformer Alice Salomon calculated that the availability of protein had already dropped by some 33 per cent.[13] Food shortages inevitably led to price rises for basic foodstuffs, even though the government attempted to fix price ceilings for the main staples. The effect of inflation and shortages, though, was extremely mixed. For the working classes, a meal of *Schmalzbrot* (bread and lard) with potatoes quickly became something of a luxury. Yet while one section of society was scavenging for food scraps, Germany's wealthier citizens remained resolutely unaffected by the situation. Theodor Wolff, for example, who regularly made a note of his eating habits in his diary, commented on the 'very extensive' menu at Dressel's, one of Berlin's finest restaurants: 'caviar, scrambled egg with truffles, sole, ice cream'.[14]

Responsibility for Germany's food supply problems ultimately lay with the (all-male) government which after all had been elected to protect and care for its citizens. Yet the job of resolving these shortages fell almost entirely into the hands of the country's female population. Put simply, the expectation was that women needed to do their patriotic duty and make the food that was available go much further. Henriette Fürth, SPD member and prominent feminist activist, gave concrete expression to this sentiment in her own 'war-cookbook': 'Just as the men in the army are defending the wellbeing of the fatherland, so we women want to contribute to a victorious outcome to this harsh war by prudent austerity and with a sense of duty for the population as a whole.'[15]

Although Fürth produced her book for a general rather than a Jewish audience – even though she herself was a proud German Jew – her general line of argument found favour with the main Jewish organisations. Orthodox communities, after all, had long held the belief that women were the ones best placed to ensure the family followed ritual food laws. But liberal Jews too accepted the important role that women played within the household. For example, Siddy Wronsky, a social reformer like Fürth, explained to Berlin's main Jewish community that it was a housewife's responsibility 'to furnish their tables with nutritious and varied meals in spite of all the constraints'.[16]

Speaking in patriotic tones about the need to make sacrifices at the dining table was relatively easy. Actually persuading people to change their eating habits proved much trickier. The government's attempts to conserve meat supplies, for example, fell flat. During 1915, it introduced a series of meat-free days, when meat products could not be sold. But as Theodor Wolff laconically observed, all the public did was to 'lay siege to the butchers' the day before.[17]

Lilli Manes and Minna Schwarz, who organised a Jewish soup kitchen in the Charlottenburg district of Berlin, experienced similar degrees of public reticence. They implemented part of the government's food policy, which was to eat potatoes in their skins rather than peeled, but found the whole experiment a disaster. People simply refused to eat unpeeled potatoes so just ate more bread instead. One of the kitchen's workers took matters into her own hands. She peeled the potatoes for eight people herself when dishing out their food, 'just to avoid them giving the food back again'.[18]

Trying to get people to eat a potato cooked in an unconventional fashion was one of the more minor food-related problems that Jewish communities had to tackle. With less produce being imported, the supplies of kosher food also came under pressure. Even though the number of Jews keeping kosher outside the Orthodox communities was low, restrictions on the availability of kosher goods still caused considerable difficulties. Many liberal Jews, for example, followed a non-kosher diet most of the time, but returned to Jewish dietary laws on special occasions such as religious festivals, mainly as a means of maintaining their ethnic identity.[19] One method of circumnavigating shortages in the supply line was to utilise alternative ingredients. The Jewish community in Berlin conceded to the use of rye and potato flour in Passover matzos, assuring its members that these changes were acceptable under religious law and 'only impaired the taste a little'.[20] Replacing fresh ingredients with preserved versions also became popular, but again more out of necessity than as a matter of taste. A firm in Frankfurt, for example, did a good trade in ritually certified tinned meat which it claimed would last for up to ten years if kept in the right conditions.[21]

Because of the importance of food not just for public health but also for people's morale, the authorities were quick to play down any shortcomings in the system. If German propagandists were to be believed, the Zentraleinkaufsgesellschaft had nullified the effects of the Entente's naval blockade of Germany. Indeed, it was almost preposterous to think that the German people were short of anything. A postcard one Jewish soldier sent home from the front used humour to encapsulate this very message (see Plate 7). Under the heading 'English starvation!', the postcard depicts a group of healthy-looking soldiers posing beside two large animal carcasses. If the rather rotund man with the butcher's knives was anything to go by, the German army was evidently not short of provisions. On receiving the postcard, however, the soldier's family probably had fewer reasons to laugh. Food shortages, price rises and the daily grind of queuing in front of shops had all become part of life on the home front. In a war that was becoming total, geographic distance from the battlefields counted for little.

A War Economy

The German state proved to be as ill-prepared in its economic planning as it had been in securing vital food supplies. When Germany first entered the war, its economy was not at all geared up for the pressures that lay ahead. Three months down the line and many businesses still appeared to be stuck in a peacetime mode of thinking. Advertisements spread across the back pages of the main Jewish newspapers must have seemed rather incongruous to a public in the midst of a world war. 'Pianos and grand pianos' could be bought from Ed. Nold & Sohn of Frankfurt, while the Schuh-Haus Louis Spier tried to tempt readers with its high-heeled ladies' brogues.[22] Even at this early stage in the conflict, it was obvious that the German army had a more pressing need for guns, shells and winter boots than the general population had for pianos or luxury shoes. It was clear to observers that Germany's economic mobilisation still had a long way to go. If Germany was going to win the war, the economy would have to be rebalanced away from the peacetime domestic market to the needs of the military instead.

The Entente's naval blockade added a degree of urgency to Germany's economic mobilisation. Without shipments from overseas, existing stocks of copper, wool, rubber, jute and tin would not even last for twelve months.[23] Fortunately for the German war effort, another German Jew – this time Walther Rathenau – was prepared to do for the economy what Ballin had done for food supplies. Himself an industrialist, Rathenau was all too aware of Germany's reliance on imported raw materials. But he feared – rightly as it turned out – that the military was rather lackadaisical about such serious shortcomings. These concerns led him to push for a series of meetings with high-ranking officials in the War Ministry, including Erich von Falkenhayn, then its head. In his discussions with Falkenhayn, which took the better part of one morning, Rathenau forcefully laid out the supply problems facing Germany and his solutions for solving them.[24]

Rathenau must have made a convincing case, for the meeting ended with Falkenhayn agreeing to the establishment of the War Raw Materials Section (Kriegsrohstoffabteilung, the KRA). This new organisation had the express aim of acquiring and then distributing essential raw materials to the industries that most urgently required them. This was supposed to ensure that factories could maintain full production for however long the war continued. As if the implementation of a new economic model was not enough of an achievement, Falkenhayn also immediately named Rathenau as the new organisation's head. Appointing a German Jew to a powerful position within the conservative War Ministry provided a further sign of doors slowly opening for Germany's Jewish minority. Although Rathenau never shied away from taking full credit for this important development, much of the recognition should also be given to the engineer Wichard von Moellendorff, whose thoughts on Germany's war economy had shaped Rathenau's own thinking.[25]

However, it was Rathenau rather than Moellendorff who became the figurehead of the KRA. It was also Rathenau who toiled away to set the organisation up, working long hours with only a little music for relaxation.[26] For Rathenau, running the KRA offered some compensation for his failure to be accepted into the army as a volunteer at the start of the war. Presumably the War Ministry had been of the opinion that the frontline was not the best place for a wealthy middle-aged industrialist with a penchant for philosophical musings. The KRA, as a department of the War Ministry, certainly afforded Rathenau some of the trapping of military power. He was given an office in the War Ministry in Berlin, which, as he later remarked, enjoyed a marvellous view over the ministry's private garden.[27]

Rathenau approached his work in the KRA as if he were commanding an offensive on the battlefield. 'This is a military campaign, only for materials', he remarked to one acquaintance.[28] He recruited from the business and financial community what was in effect his own General Staff, and then laid down a strategy for those working under him to follow. Under Rathenau's leadership, the KRA set out to acquire all raw materials deemed essential for use in the war industries. Following Rathenau's repeated demands, this also included the procurement of materials captured from occupied Belgium. Once in the hands of the KRA, these resources were then to be distributed to firms that produced weapons, munitions and vital goods for the war effort.

This was undoubtedly a massive undertaking. Even though the KRA had limited its work to the war industries, this still left it with a huge range of materials to oversee. Manufacturing gunpowder required cotton and saltpetre, while shells and bullets needed copper, much of which Germany had to import from Scandinavia. To cope with the complexity of distributing such a large range of resources, War Raw Materials Corporations (Kriegsrohstoffgesellschaften) were created, with each one given responsibility for a specific category of raw material. The first of these, set up in early

September, took up the control and distribution of metals; others focusing on smaller areas, such as cotton and leather, followed. Within a short space of time, Rathenau sat at the head of a colossal organisation that controlled vast swathes of the economy. At the time of its formation, the KRA occupied a handful of rooms in the War Ministry. One month later the number had risen to ten, and by 1917 at least 1,800 people worked for the KRA in a sea of different offices.[29]

Nobody could fail to notice the rapid growth of the KRA, an organisation that had come from nowhere to tower over German economic life. This, as well as its radical working methods, very quickly led it to become a target of popular anger. A backlog in the supply of materials, the growth of state power along socialist lines and accusations of profiteering were amongst the most serious of the claims thrown in the KRA's direction. Rathenau's dual role as chair of the board of directors of the AEG and head of the KRA made refuting these attacks much harder than it need have been. A conflict of interest existed, which became even more visible when the AEG signed a series of lucrative contracts with the War Ministry. Barbed wire, military aircraft as well as parts for the navy's ships all started to pass out of the AEG's factory gates.[30] Wilhelm von Meinel, a 'big name' in the Bavarian civil service, was not alone when he complained that the AEG enjoyed an advantage over other companies when trying to secure increasingly scarce raw materials.[31]

The sense that Germany's new war economy privileged the few at the expense of the majority quickly gained ground. More worrying was the fact that some of the criticism of both Rathenau and the war economy was tinged with anti-Semitism. This was certainly the case in Frankfurt. After the military had agreed contracts for the supply of horse saddles, the director of one local firm angrily rejected the decision. He listed the six companies awarded contracts, complaining that these 'Jewish firms', as he labelled them, had 'no previous experience of military work'.[32] In reply, the army pointed out that the complainant had conveniently failed to mention non-Jewish companies awarded contracts and stressed that decisions were made without 'confessional consideration'.[33] The presence in the KRA alongside Rathenau of other German Jews provided further grist to the anti-Semites' mill. Eugen Wallerstein, for example, was a leading light in the shoe and leather corporation, while Moritz Goldstein briefly took on a pivotal role in the chemical corporation.[34] This fact alone was too much for some Germans. As the war progressed, right-wing groups made it their mission to prove that the KRA was fully in Jewish hands, publishing statistics to this effect.[35]

In April 1915 – only eight months after founding the KRA – Rathenau handed in his resignation. His decision is often attributed to rising anti-Semitism, but is more likely to have stemmed from the heavy demands of a role that he combined with other business activities. Long hours coupled with intense public scrutiny had already led him to suggest 'leaving the running [of the KRA] to others' in February 1915, so his decision to step down two months later came as no surprise.[36] Despite the lack of public gratitude, at the time of his departure Rathenau had much to be proud of. He had helped to shift an economy suffering from acute supply problems into one robust enough to deal with the rigours of a protracted war. As the economist Kurt Wiedenfeld proudly observed, the creation of the KRA meant that 'we can fight the war for so long as we deem it militarily and politically expedient to do so'.[37] Saving Germany from economic disaster, though, came at a hefty price. Thanks to Rathenau's efforts, the economy was placed on a war footing, with all other activity subordinated to the needs of the military. The foundations for a total war were now starting to take shape.

This turn towards a war economy had a mixed effect on German businesses. As many industrialists discovered, moving from domestic to wartime production took time. For example, the Mertons, a prominent German-Jewish family from Frankfurt, struggled to keep the Metallgesellschaft, their giant metal-trading firm, afloat. Not only did they lose their trading partners abroad, but domestically the firm also had to fit into the KRA's new arrangements. The firm's first wartime report stated despairingly that the war had created 'shocks to economic life that have never previously been observed'.[38] Yet for other businesses, the conflict also brought with it a wealth of new opportunities. Expanding into the German-occupied territories in the east and west offered one particularly opportunistic way for firms to offset the war's financial impact. As in so many other areas of the conflict, Rathenau had led calls for the exploitation of Germany's vanquished foes, seeing in Belgium a means to acquire essential raw materials for the war effort and by implication for German business too.[39]

In the eastern war zone, one of Rathenau's business contemporaries, Eduard Arnhold, attempted to perform a similar feat of economic exploitation. Arnhold, the fourth of eight children born to a wealthy Jewish family, had built up a massive coalmining empire in Silesia. Like Rathenau, at the outbreak of hostilities Arnhold threw himself behind the German war effort with considerable gusto. His wife Johanna helped to establish a military hospital in Berlin, while Arnhold advised the government on maintaining coal supplies in the country's eastern provinces.[40] As the German army pushed further into the east, Arnhold's companies managed to take effective control of the coalmines in southern Poland. He then used these mines to fulfil contracts with the German military for the supply of coal.[41]

It was all very well for the War Ministry to agree large contracts with Arnhold for coal or to procure great quantities of raw materials through the KRA, but ultimately all these resources came at a considerable financial cost. They all had to be paid for. And it is in this respect that German planners struggled. In contrast to the French and British banks, Germany's financial institutions found it difficult to raise much-needed foreign capital. The size and strength of the London money market over its Berlin equivalent allowed the British to account for about one-quarter of their wartime debt through overseas borrowing, while the Germans had only the domestic market to turn to.[42] At the start of the war, the Hamburg banker Max Warburg had attempted to acquire loans from the American bank director Jacob Schiff, whose German-Jewish heritage might have been expected to make him sympathetic to Germany's plight. But Warburg's efforts were in vain as Schiff chose to respect the neutrality of the United States.[43]

Reluctant to hit public morale by raising taxes, the government was forced to seek other ways to cover the unprecedented costs of a world war. It was particularly drawn to the idea of issuing war bonds (*Kriegsanleihe*), which were in effect a more complex method of domestic borrowing. At regular intervals during the war, the government issued a public sale of war bonds. Initially the scheme proved an unqualified success. The first three calls raked in some 24 billion Marks, with each subscription campaign recording an increase over the previous one.[44] The promised 5 per cent return over a ten-year period presumably helped to focus people's minds. But this was not the only reason for the success of the war bonds. The scheme functioned through its ability to tap into the public's competitive instincts. Donating to the war effort allowed people to flaunt their patriotism by giving more than their neighbour. Ever the patriot, Eduard Arnhold himself pressed this emotional button in an attempt to encourage fellow business leaders to buy bonds. Citing the decision of the BASF and Bayer chemical conglomerates to subscribe to 4 million Marks' worth of bonds, he suggested to Franz Oppenheim of Agfa that his firm should do something similar.[45]

The chances that anyone could have missed the release of war bonds were slim. Speeches, flyers and posters encouraging Germans to dig deep into their pockets accompanied each sale. Even the CV joined in on the act and distributed its own leaflets urging the group's members to donate to the war effort.[46] In this respect, the introduction of war bonds provided a particularly visible indication of the transformation of Germany's economy during the first months of the war. The country's military and political leaders did not just require their citizens to fight on the battlefield; they also needed them to make financial sacrifices at home. When these shifts were placed alongside Rathenau's formation of the KRA to control war materials and Ballin's work to import foodstuffs from abroad, it was clear that Jews and other Germans were now living in a war economy, whether they liked it or not.

Communities on the Move

The war itself unleashed a tremendous wave of migration – much of it forced – which continued well into the postwar period. From both east and west, people fled across the German border to escape the approaching armies. Determined to help the newly displaced, German Jews in Frankfurt, as elsewhere, threw themselves into relief work. Jakob Liebmann, a prominent Jewish lawyer in the city, headed up an organisation dedicated to helping one specific group: the 'German and Austrian refugees from Belgium'.[47] At the same time as Liebmann was busy with his German refugees, the German-Jewish industrialists Wilhelm Merton and Leo Gans sat on a committee dedicated to helping 'expelled Germans from enemy territory'.[48] It was not just in Frankfurt where Jews took a significant role in the care of refugees; a similar process happened in most German cities. The Jewish community in Cologne, for example, offered practical aid to a group of people who had fled the fighting in Belgium. It closed its reading room and allowed some of the refugees to live for a short while in amongst the books.[49] The pattern that emerged here was of German Jews rushing to the aid of other Germans who had been displaced by the war.

When it came to helping non-German refugee groups, the role played by Jewish communities remained slightly more opaque. Jewish communities already contained a large number of foreign Jews, who had often lived in Germany for years but never acquired full citizenship. With the outbreak of hostilities, their position in the country was once again thrown into doubt. Some younger Eastern European Jews saw in the war an opportunity to become naturalised. This was the case with the brothers Joseph and Leo Chaimoff, who both signed up for the army and were rewarded with German citizenship soon after.[50] Older Jews, though, were not in a position to strike such a deal. An S. Krankinowsky, for example, had lived and worked in Breslau and Berlin for thirty-seven years; his eldest son had even joined the German army in August 1914. However, as Krankinowsky still retained Russian citizenship, he fell under immediate suspicion. He was ordered to report to the police every three days, a considerable hindrance for a travelling tobacco salesman.[51]

Yet of far greater concern for the established Jewish communities were groups of Russian Jews who had been holidaying in Germany in July 1914. Most had planned a short break in the country, perhaps to visit one of the many spa resorts for rest and recuperation. When war started, these visitors discovered that not only was their holiday in tatters, but that they were now also stranded in enemy territory. The Zionists, who evinced more sympathy for this group than the liberal associations, rightly described the situation as 'a double disaster': the displaced were ostracised both as Jews and as Russians.[52] This was certainly the case in Frankfurt, where the local authorities turned angrily against those Eastern European Jews who were using the city's public baths. The main complaint was that this Jewish minority, 'infested with scabies [and] with ripped, stinking underwear', were driving German customers away. The last thing that guests wanted, insisted the authorities, was to have to 'bathe with such people in a comparatively small pool', particularly as there was always the risk of coming into 'contact with their – likely naked – bodies'.[53] Frankfurt's established Jewish community kept well clear of this dispute, happy to maintain distance between itself and the new arrivals.

The situation was similar in other Jewish communities, where a deep-seated embarrassment towards Eastern European Jews encouraged more ambivalence than actual sympathy. Put simply, many German Jews had no wish to be associated with their supposedly less cultured co-religionists.[54] This was certainly the case in Leipzig. The city's Jewish community made it clear that it wanted nothing to do with a large group of practically destitute Russian Jews who had ended up stranded there. With their requests for help falling on deaf ears, the Russian Jews were forced to turn instead to the Jewish community in Chemnitz for financial help and for the provision of kosher food.[55] Even concrete relief plans were met with some disdain. When the Aid Association of German Jews (Hilfsverein der deutschen Juden) devised a plan to help the thousands of stranded Russian Jews, some of Germany's established Jewish communities were horrified. 'Hundreds of overpatriotic Jews protested against it', recalled Bernhard Kahn, secretary-general of the Aid Association.

Doing their best to ignore this hostility, Kahn and other members of the association set out to put their rescue plan into motion. What they hoped to do was quickly to return as many people as they possibly could – both Jews and non-Jews – to Russia. Pleased to see the situation taken out of its own hands, the German government gave the Aid Association its full backing. Yet the process of repatriation was still far from straightforward. With the Russia–Germany borderlands a war zone, the displaced could not simply be pushed across the border. Instead, a convoluted route to Russia through neutral Sweden had to be agreed. Eventually seventeen trains packed full of Russian citizens left Berlin; a further four trains from Frankfurt followed.[56]

For an improvised rescue, the movement of Jews from Germany back to Eastern Europe progressed relatively smoothly. Indeed, as far as some German Jews were concerned, the whole operation was far too successful. One Jewish orphanage complained that it had been left almost empty of children as a result. At the start of the war, Pinkus Klibansky's boys' home cared for a large number of Polish children ranging in age from ten to eighteen, all of whom had been raised, according to the owner, with 'German national spirit and German patriotism'. However, as a result of return migration at the start of the war, most of the boys headed home to Poland leaving Klibansky facing, in his own words, 'economic ruin'.[57]

Other Germans were also far from pleased to hear that so many civilians had returned eastwards. There was a concern that with their departure Germany was losing a much-needed supply of labour. This reason alone had already led to restrictions being placed on thousands of Eastern European seasonal workers whom the authorities had forced to remain in Germany.[58] In the Stettin administrative district, the deputy commanding general, Hermann von Vietinghoff, had his own set of strategic reasons for questioning the repatriations. Vietinghoff accused the Aid Association of having committed a traitorous act. Once home, he argued, these people would be set loose to fight against the Germans.[59] With so many critical voices making themselves heard, the German authorities gradually started to take a much harder line. Spurred partly by Britain's decision to intern its own enemy aliens, the German authorities changed tack in autumn 1914 and began to round up British, French and Russian citizens. The policy was no longer to send them home, but to ensure that they remained.[60]

This move to a policy of civilian internment caught many foreigners living in Germany off guard. Among those unpleasantly surprised by this development was Israel Cohen, a British journalist and member of the World Zionist Congress, who had lived in Germany for several years, first in Cologne and then in Berlin.

Cohen received a knock on his door early one Friday morning. The policeman standing on his doorstep gave Cohen a few minutes to gather together some possessions before taking him into custody. Cohen was eventually taken to Ruhleben, the old racecourse in the west of Berlin, which was to see some 5,500 internees pass through its doors during the course of the war. Ruhleben had all the trappings of a military camp; the internees were kept under guard and provided with only basic accommodation in the former racecourse stables. Yet, as the camp was only 9 kilometres from the very centre of Berlin, those interned there were never entirely cut off from the outside world. Diplomats from neutral states visited frequently and a soup kitchen in Berlin delivered kosher food each day.

This seemingly benign arrangement inadvertently sparked one of the worst incidents of anti-Semitism in Ruhleben's short history. In order to make it easier to distribute kosher supplies, the camp's acting commandant decided to send all the Jewish internees to a separate barracks. This may have simplified mealtimes, but at the same time it gave the distinct impression that Jewish internees were being singled out. Conditions in the new barracks were much worse than elsewhere in the camp; overcrowding, straw mattresses and a lack of heating greeted the new residents. The irony in all this, as Cohen pointed out, was that most of the Jews interned in Ruhleben 'had expressed no prefer-ence for ritual fare' in the first place. This enforced segregation only came to an end in spring 1915, when James Gerard, the American ambassador, visited the camp and demanded improvements.[61]

In the wake of Gerard's visit, the Prussian War Ministry gradually started to make some much-needed investment into Ruhleben's infrastructure. With the aim of easing some of the worst overcrowding, it agreed to the construc-tion of nine new wooden barracks. The internees, cut off from friends, family and civilian life, now settled in for the long haul. For those like Cohen, who had lived comfortably in Germany for years, the sudden change in their circumstances was particularly distressing: from freedom in what had appeared to be a stable society to a life behind barbed wire in a matter of months. Their fate, dramatic as it was, merely reflected Germany's shift towards 'total war'. The diversity and breadth of the pre-war Jewish communities were gradually sacrificed to German wartime unity.

'Toxic' Weapons

The conflict's steady intrusion into daily life excited some German Jews, but for others it only brought a growing sense of dread. Albert Einstein was not alone in wishing to escape from the 'mad, degenerate species' surrounding him. 'If only there were somewhere, an island for the benevolent and the prudent', he fantasised.[62] Rising anxieties at home added a degree of urgency to the military situation. People were willing to make sacrifices on the basis that the army would make rapid progress against the Entente and thus bring the war to a successful conclusion. Unfortunately for the German public, defeat at the Marne and the start of trench warfare made this scenario less and less likely. If the German public were going to continue to consent to the war, then the military needed to find a way to break the deadlock. This thought helped to focus minds. During the first winter of the war, politicians, the army leadership and scientists all engaged in a frantic search for a means to wrestle the military and diplomatic advantage away from the Entente.

As a way of securing victory, there was something reassuringly straightforward in the idea of simply increasing the availability of manpower. Carl von Clausewitz, the great Prussian military strategist, might have stressed that tactics, leadership and clear political aims rather than merely numerical superiority decided battles, but even Clausewitz had had to admit that numbers were 'the most common element in victory'.[63] Presumably conscious of this dictum, Moltke and his predecessors in the General Staff had lobbied unsuccessfully before 1914 to increase the size of the army by 300,000 men.[64] When Falkenhayn replaced Moltke after the debacle of the Marne, he was forced to acknowledge that the Central Powers could never match the Entente in terms of manpower. Therefore, he increasingly placed the emphasis on defending the German lines in the east, while at the same time chipping away at the Entente's morale in the west with a more offensive strategy.[65]

The numbers game was also played in the diplomatic arena. When the war first started, numerous countries, on both the European and the world stage, stood looking on from the sidelines. For the Entente and the Central Powers, the aim was simple. They needed to win over as many of these neutral countries as possible, in the belief that each one could bring some strategic and numerical advantage. Germany notched the first victory in this high-stakes game of diplomatic poker when it managed to coax Turkey to join the Central Powers in November 1914. Eugen Mittwoch, the German-Jewish Orientalist, did his best to play up the significance of this development. He explained to the German public that Turkey's declaration of a 'holy war' (jihad) offered a major advantage as it targeted Christians in the Entente, not those in the Central Powers.[66] But like so many apparent breakthroughs during the war, Turkey's entry did nothing to bring victory a step closer. With an army large in numbers but lacking the latest weaponry, initially Turkey's main contribution was merely to extend the war's geographical parameters.

The ears of German Zionists, though, pricked up at the news of Turkey's decision to enter the conflict on Germany's side. Turkey on its own would not have warranted that much excitement. But Turkey, as a part of the large Ottoman Empire, which included Palestine, was a very different matter. In rather understated language, the Zionist *Jüdische Rundschau* observed that this new 'fight for the future of the Orient will also be of importance for us'.[67] However, if the Zionists were to make any gains from Germany's new alliance with Turkey, they also needed to convince Germany's military and political leadership that Palestine was important for them too. As Palestine was of limited strategic importance, this was never going to be the easiest of tasks.

German Zionists' solution to this conundrum was to ensure that their interests in Palestine tied in very closely with Germany's own expansionist war aims. During the early years of the war, the German Zionist movement went into propaganda overdrive with a constant stream of letters, talks and pamphlets that outlined a rosy future for both Jews and Germans in the Middle East.[68] One of the most provocative statements in this regard came from Kurt Blumenfeld, who would later serve as president of the German Zionist movement. Presumably in an attempt to curry favour with German imperialists, Blumenfeld published his thoughts in the journal *Das größere Deutschland*, which had already gained something of a reputation for its pro-expansionist stance. Blumenfeld maintained that there was a unique cultural and linguistic bond between Germans and Jews. Increasing Jewish settlement in Palestine, he argued, would have the knock-on effect of securing German economic dominance in the whole region. In effect, the Jews would act as 'the economic intermediary between the Oriental world and Germandom'.[69]

Blumenfeld's exuberant support for German expansionism could easily be dismissed as an embarrassing necessity that had to be swallowed for the good of Zionism. Yet this would be to overlook the extent to which many German Zionists were also passionate supporters of Germany's war effort. For obvious reasons, the German Zionist movement expended much of its energies on Palestine and Turkish diplomacy. But Blumenfeld and his colleagues also willingly backed Germany's diplomatic negotiations when there was no direct correlation to their own ideological aims. Italy, which had remained belligerently neutral in August 1914, is a case in point. Although of little value to their own interests, the Zionists Hermann Struck and Adolf Friedemann did their best to win over Italian Jews to Germany's cause. They even arranged a propaganda trip to Italy to drum up Jewish support.[70] However, all of this ended in frustration: the Italians joined the side of Britain, France and Russia in May 1915. Rathenau dismissed these *Leichenfledderer* ('vultures') as a military irrelevance, but Italy's decision was an undoubted diplomatic setback for Germany.[71]

However, with the United States following a policy of wartime neutrality, there were far more important prizes still to be won. Both sides in the conflict recognised very quickly the decisive role that this burgeoning world power could play and were determined to win the American people over to their own particular cause. With the US's Jewish population numbering well over 1.5 million, the German government identified a potential propaganda opening that it hoped German Jews could exploit. The Kantian philosopher Hermann Cohen volunteered to undertake a propaganda trip across the Atlantic to the United States, but this came to nothing.[72] Being in his mid-seventies, Cohen's energy levels were understandably not what they once were, so he penned a written appeal to American Jewry instead. In this letter, which was published in the *New Yorker Staatszeitung*, he condemned the British and French for being in cahoots with the Russians, before going on to extol Germany's role in shaping modern American-Jewish life. Without Moses Mendelssohn, explained Cohen, Jews would never have been able to enter the modern cultural world. For this reason, Jews in the western world needed 'to recognise, to revere and to love Germany as the motherland of their modern religiosity', he proudly argued.[73]

Germany's attempts to woo the United States never looked likely to reap diplomatic rewards. But they were torpedoed once and for all when a German submarine sent the Cunard liner *Lusitania* to the seabed in May 1915. The Germans had declared British territorial waters to be a war zone earlier that year, so when the *Lusitania* passed the coast of Ireland on its way to Liverpool, there seemed justification enough to attack. Almost 1,200 people lost their lives in the sinking, including 128 American citizens. News of the *Lusitania*'s sinking provoked a wave of public outrage across the United States. Graphic headlines in the press pointed to the 'murder' of prominent citizens, such as the millionaire philanthropist Alfred Vanderbilt, who had been on his way to Liverpool on business.[74] What most angered the public and the press was the manner in which this new weapon had been employed. Almost without warning, the submarine had sneaked up on its innocent prey from below the waves before unleashing its deadly weapons. According to the Philadelphia *Public Ledger*, the Germans had even employed 'high-powered torpedoes of [an] especially deadly type' to ensure maximum damage.[75]

Not surprisingly, most Germans viewed the use of this new technology very differently. If the government's propaganda to neutral nations represented a diplomatic means to tip the balance of the war in Germany's favour, then the submarine was the military version. The use of submarines provoked few dissenting voices from within German-Jewish communities. Indeed, far from it. In the wake of the *Lusitania*'s sinking Georg Bernhard even went on the offensive, declaring that Germany was 'free of all moral responsibility' for the sinking. As it had warned in advance that all shipping would be targeted, the British only had themselves to blame for the disaster, he argued.[76]

Another commentator on naval affairs was Albert Ballin. The Hamburg shipping director is often painted as something of a wartime liberal, but when it came to the subject of maritime policy he was anything but.[77] In an article for the *Frankfurter Zeitung*, he bemoaned the fact that Germany's navy was stranded in the 'wet triangle' of the North Sea. A way out, he believed, was for Germany to acquire naval bases in Belgium and France.[78] Theodor Wolff confessed to being slightly perplexed at Ballin's belligerence.[79] But as if to prove this was no aberration, Ballin went on to demand 'the most brutal execution of a submarine blockade'.[80]

By operating a policy of enhanced submarine warfare in British waters, Germany had dangerously changed the dynamics of the conflict. Ballin and Bernhard simply took this shift towards total war in their stride. The spring of 1915 also marked the war's first large-scale use of chemical weapons. Seeking to regain the initiative in the west, the German army released chlorine gas against the French lines at Ypres. Although presumably of less interest to a seafaring man like Ballin, this development once again showed Germany's willingness to push the boundaries of international law in order to bring about a military breakthrough.

The development of both gas and submarine warfare required a remarkable marriage of scientists and engineers with specialists in the military world. But whereas the submarine emerged from hundreds of engineers working in the shipyards of Kiel and Danzig, gas warfare owed its success to a small group of scientists working in the prestigious Kaiser Wilhelm Institute for Physical Chemistry and Electrochemistry.[81] Housed in an imposing building specially designed by the kaiser's chief architect, Ernst von Ihne, and situated in the leafy Berlin suburb of Dahlem, the institute seemed an incongruous setting for experimenting with mass killing techniques. Yet, under the guidance of its founding director, Fritz Haber, this is exactly the path it followed. Haber was a brilliant scientist; he later received the Nobel Prize in Chemistry for his pioneering work on the synthesis of ammonia. What became known as the Haber–Bosch process provided Germany with an alternative source of nitrates, an essential ingredient in both fertilisers and explosives. As nitrates had previously been imported across the Atlantic from Chile, Haber's work undoubtedly helped to prolong the German war effort.

Haber, though, was not only the leading chemist of his generation: he was also a rather vain man who revelled in the pomp and status of Prussian society. His godson Fritz Stern remembered Haber as a man who was 'German in every fibre of his being, in his restless, thorough striving, in his devotion to friends and students, in his very soul and spirit'.[82] Haber's adulation for all things German arguably encouraged his decision to convert from Judaism to Protestantism at the age of twenty-three, which also helped to ease his passage into the conservative world of academia.[83] When the war started, Haber followed his patriotic convictions and committed himself to Germany's 'defensive' struggle. Rejected from the military on the grounds of his age – he was already in his mid-forties – Haber had had to find other ways to serve Germany. He initially found a home in Rathenau's KRA, advising on the procurement of chemicals. However, after clashing with Rathenau during the winter of 1914–15, Haber turned his back on the KRA to concentrate on his chemical weapons research instead.[84]

For a scientist of Haber's standing, working at the coalface of chemical research undoubtedly offered more fulfilment than merely advising the administration. In any case, Haber made the leap back to the scientific world at just the right time. The military, fully aware of their lack of progress at the front, had already started to investigate the possibility of using chemical weapons during autumn 1914. Therefore, when Haber approached them at the end of the year with a proposal to use chlorine gas, the military agreed to his plans in principle. With this support in place, Haber set about putting together an expert group first to develop the weapon and then to install it. Quite by coincidence, many of the individuals Haber recruited also had a Jewish background. Chief amongst these were his closest assistants Friedrich Epstein and Friedrich Kerschbaum, as well as the two physicists Gustav Herz and James Franck, who both worked on the installation of the gas equipment out in the field.[85] For these scientists, their work was purely about the application of scientific innovation to resolve a technical challenge, which in this case was an efficient killing technique.

After months of experimenting, the first gas attack was arranged for April 1915 in the Ypres Salient. In the run-up to the assault, troops secretly installed thousands of gas canisters facing the French lines. After a tense few days waiting for the wind to blow in the right direction, the taps were finally opened on 22 April and the gas released. From the German lines, the gas cloud appeared innocuous enough. 'It looked beautiful', observed one German officer; 'the sun was already fairly low, which gave the gas a browny-yellow hue in the evening light.'[86] For the soldiers defending the enemy trenches, the gas cloud was far more horrific. The gas killed and wounded several hundred French and Algerian troops. The German army, though, failed to push home the advantage and the attack eventually petered out. Even the most chauvinistic of nationalists could find little to celebrate in these grisly scenes. Jewish communities gave no public comment on the development of chemical weapons, but then they had no real reason to respond. Georg Bernhard's *Vossische Zeitung* meanwhile firmly supported the gas attacks, arguing that 'our opponents have used this means of combat for months'.[87]

The international community saw the situation very differently. As far as it was concerned, Germany's use of chlorine gas ran counter to the Hague Conventions, which had outlawed chemical warfare. Like Bernhard, Haber never appeared particularly perturbed by such judgments. Even after the war, he continued to maintain that 'gas warfare is by no means as cruel as flying artillery shells'.[88] But this was merely symptomatic of Haber's uncompromising commitment to the use of chemical weapons. Throughout the development of this weapons programme, it was Haber, rather than the military, who pushed the technology forward. Haber arranged the experiments, won the backing of the army and even went to the battlefield to oversee the installation of the gas equipment. Such was his commitment to this new form of warfare that he put military success before his own family life. Soon after the first gas attack, Clara Immerwahr, Haber's wife of twelve years, shot herself with her husband's service pistol. The reasons for her suicide remain unclear. Nonetheless, looking back on events, it appears remarkable that the very next day Haber decided to travel to the Eastern Front to arrange further rounds of gas attacks.[89]

For Haber, it seems, a German victory achieved through the judicious use of chemical weapons had come to mean everything. In this equation, the moral dimension of gas warfare was an irrelevance. Many German Jews, though by no means a majority, shared the belief that Germany needed to apply unconventional means and new technologies to achieve a military breakthrough. From the frontline, Herbert Sulzbach praised the 'splendid work' of Germany's 'U-boats and Zeppelins'.[90] This was a sentiment that

Georg Bernhard and Albert Ballin propagated on the home front. However, this unstinting support did not bring an end to hostilities. Instead, the opposite was true. Germany's use of these new weapons, whether submarines or chemical weapons, not only served to sour world opinion but also brutalised the conflict, as other nations responded in kind. Despite Haber's belligerence, German Jews were never the main cheerleaders of this aspect of total war. Yet, like all other Germans, they gave their tacit backing through either quiet acquiescence or, on rarer occasions, direct support.

A New Fighting Machine

When looking back on Haber's wartime career from the distance of the 1950s, his former colleagues vividly remembered the great scientist's penchant for wearing military attire. Apparently, on visits to the front, he used to stand 'proudly' dressed in the uniform of an army captain, the rank to which he was promoted in 1915.[91] Haber was not the only German of Jewish descent to warm to the symbols of German militarism. Victor Klemperer also thought it worth mentioning when he visited a synagogue service in Berlin. 'The cantor stood in his field grey uniform at the pulpit', he commented. 'And in the tiny room, I counted twenty-eight uniformed men, including nine with the Iron Cross.'[92] The sight of German Jews in polished boots, with buttons glistening and jackets tightly pressed, was not entirely new. After all, Jewish soldiers had fought in previous German armies. Yet circumstances were very different come 1914. It would be going too far to call this a new army, for the German military still did its best to restrict Jewish access to the higher echelons of the officer corps. But under the pressures of a totalising war, it was forced at the very least to pay lip service to Jewish religious needs and customs.

Based solely on its pre-war composition and character, there is no doubting that the outbreak of the First World War radically changed the way in which the German army approached its Jewish members. There seemed to be a genuine determination within the ranks of the armed forces to respect Jewish soldiers' religious needs. It was important, suggested one internal letter, to avoid 'any sense that Jewish soldiers are treated worse than their Christian comrades'.[93] As a result of this guidance, army officers ended up discussing not just issues of recruitment and battlefield tactics but also the availability of kosher food and the intricacies of Jewish festivals. There were clearly differences in experience between those soldiers stationed at home and those serving under the pressurised atmosphere of the front, but on the whole the military reached agreement on both issues. In home garrisons, Jewish soldiers could eat kosher if they supplied their own food, while leave for the major Jewish holidays was granted 'as long as it fitted the military situation'.[94]

The medals and promotions that started to flow Jewish soldiers' way during the first weeks of the conflict also suggested that this was now a more open and democratic army. Perhaps the best-known Jewish officer was Hugo Gutmann, a regimental adjutant in the Bavarian Army and also the man who later recommended Hitler for the Iron Cross 1st Class. Outside Bavaria, German Jews also earned promotions.[95] As the army had been almost bereft of Jewish officers before the war, these promotions seemed to confirm the impression of an institution in the midst of internal reform. A similar view could be garnered from the large number of military decorations awarded to Jewish soldiers. When Fritz Herz received his Iron Cross during the Belgian campaigns, excitement got the better of him. 'I'm sending you the Iron Cross in this letter', he told his family. 'No, I've changed my mind', he joked, 'I'm going to wear it.'[96] Herz's excitement was shared by many other Jews during the first year of the war. Some indication of actual numbers comes from the Jewish students' group, the Kartell-Convent, which calculated that eighty-five of its members, both past and present, had been awarded the Iron Cross by the end of 1914.[97]

The Kartell-Convent's careful focus on statistics reflected German Jews' excitement for this new, supposedly more open, army, but were also a sign of widespread pride in the personal achievements of each individual Jewish soldier. In spring 1915, one young soldier from Munich secured a promotion to lieutenant of the reserve. Considering he had started his military career as an ordinary soldier, this was quite an achievement. His uncle Eugen Beer, one of the leading figures in Munich's Jewish community, clearly thought so too. Beer wrote to friends and acquaintances to share the news, including the Federation of German Jews (Verband der deutschen Juden) in Berlin. 'He was one of the very first to win the Iron Cross', Beer exclaimed proudly.[98] It is quite remarkable how quickly German Jews took on the language and symbols of the German army as their own.

For Jewish communities more generally, surely the greatest sense of pride came from the inclusion of rabbis within the German army. The resulting combination of military and Jewish religious values gave the impression, at least, that the German military had fully accepted its Jewish members. The Munich rabbi Leo Baerwald was one of eight rabbis to begin their military duties during the second month of the war. Baerwald, a tall, imposing figure with a crop of dark hair, looked every bit the part once he had been kitted out with uniform and frontline equipment. The army rabbis' basic uniform mirrored that of the Christian chaplains: a long grey coat with a Red Cross band on the arm, heavy riding boots and military cap, only with a Star of David badge rather than the Christian cross. To go with this, the rabbis were also each provided with a wagon, two horses and a coachman.[99]

It was not only in uniform that the rabbis mirrored the Christian chaplains; once at the front their army duties were also very similar. In a report back to the Federation of German Jews in Berlin, Baerwald gave a flavour of his first few weeks in Belgium and France. A good proportion of his time had been spent visiting wounded and sick Jewish soldiers, with the remainder being taken up in meeting individually and collectively with Jews in the field. A photograph of the Hamburg rabbi Jacob Sonderling holding a Yom Kippur service captures this spiritual role to the full (see Plate 8). Several hundred Jewish servicemen in full military uniform, heads covered with the Prussian spiked helmet rather than the kippah, have turned a field into a place of prayer. Uniformed and standing powerfully at the front of the group, Sonderling gives the impression of being both a religious and military leader.

Jewish religious services out in the field, such as the one held by Sonderling, also provided an opportunity for Jews to demonstrate that they too were at the front. Large gatherings of German Jews, impeccably turned out in their military clothing, were, as Leo Baeck suggested, of 'undisputed importance for the recognition of Judaism'.[100] As the visual face of the Jewish servicemen, therefore, it was crucial that the army rabbis' work was fully recognised. To do this, they bombarded their communities back home with frequent reports and perhaps more importantly also contributed on occasion to the soldiers' newspapers that circulated among the troops.[101] The rabbis also leapt at any opportunity for inter-confessional work with the other army chaplains, whether this was through shared religious services or through a joint presence at burials. Photographs of Jewish and Christian chaplains, serving together at the front, were particularly common (see Plate 9). The message to be taken from such images was obvious: Jews, for so long at the margins of the military and wider society, were now the equal of all other Germans.[102]

Baerwald and his colleagues were not the first rabbis to serve in the German army; four rabbis had previously volunteered during the Franco-Prussian War. Yet this is where the similarity ended. The most recent Jewish recruits took on their roles safe in the knowledge that Germany and its military had entered a new, more inclusive, age. Such was the rabbis' embrace of the military that one even turned up to a Rosh Hashanah service wearing his hard-won Iron Cross, seemly oblivious to the medal's Christian iconography.[103] Instead, it was the excitement of the early months of the war that appeared to be the biggest attraction for army rabbis. As with the thousands of young Germans who volunteered to fight at the front, the promise of new experiences, adventure and travel in foreign lands all proved a draw. Writing home, Rabbi Bruno Italiener excitedly described his journey to the Western Front, which had involved sharing a car with a wounded dragoon major, twelve hours on one train and encountering a machine gun post in Liège.[104] Once at the front, the excitement ratcheted up even further. His colleague Georg Wilde was so struck by the power of British bombs that he collected pieces of shrapnel as battlefield souvenirs; tending the wounded and comforting the living, it seemed, could wait.[105]

Yet the rabbis' excited embrace of German military life does need to be tempered somewhat. The army may have allowed rabbis to wear military uniforms and to serve near the frontlines, but it also placed numerous obstacles in their path. Until later in 1915, the War Ministry managed to avoid paying the rabbis a proper salary; effectively they remained unpaid volunteers. Therefore, although Leo Baerwald and his colleagues wore the same uniforms as the Christian chaplains and moved around the front using the same army equipment, their financial arrangements were very different. The chaplains received a salary; the rabbis by contrast had to rely on an allowance provided by Jewish communities back home. The financial outlay for the War Ministry should never have been that great; the thirty or so army rabbis paled in comparison to the 1,441 Catholic chaplains who served in the Prussian Army alone.[106]

The experiences of the army rabbis were emblematic of some of the wider difficulties with this supposedly new army. For example, although many Jewish soldiers celebrated decorations and promotions, others watched on in dismay as their military efforts were ignored. Victor Klemperer remarked on the fate of one unfortunate soldier who had served before the war and had been awarded the Iron Cross in the current conflict. Despite his vast experience, a promotion had continued to elude him, probably because 'of his strongly accentuated Jewishness', surmised Klemperer.[107] Going further, in all sections of the army it was possible to find German Jews who had suffered some form of discrimination. Reports of anti-Semitism in the military continued to land on the desks of the CV with regular frequency. One of the many complaints described how a group of soldiers on leave joked about sending Jews to the very front, 'so that they can be shot first'. Another report concerned overly aggressive officers, who had specifically targeted Jews when putting the new recruits through their paces. Possibly overstating the pleasures of military service, the CV moaned that such practices 'completely exorcised the joy of being able to serve the fatherland'.[108]

On this evidence, any suggestion that anti-Semitism was no longer a part of the wartime German army is surely wide of the mark.[109] The army had certainly changed with the outbreak of war, but discriminatory practices were still commonplace. This particular disjuncture reflected the war's shifting dynamics. With attrition rates high and rising, the War Ministry had little option but to promote and reward its Jewish members. And therein lay the problem. The Jewish soldiers were integrated into the German army out of necessity, rather than out of a genuine and heartfelt desire to reform the military's institutions. Not that any of these structural faults particularly concerned German Jews during the first year of the war. The army may still have had its faults, but it looked at long last to be on the right path. Safe in this knowledge, German Jews continued to give their full backing to the conflict, willingly helping to lay the foundations for Germany to fight what was becoming an increasingly total war.

4

ANNEXATIONS

In a friendly letter to Albert Ballin, Max Warburg, the leading man of Hamburg banking, made what on the face of it seemed a remarkable proposition. He suggested that Germany should establish a new set of colonies in the Baltic territories of Latvia and Courland. In building up the German Empire in the east, Warburg envisaged a complicated scheme of population movements. The Latvians currently living in the region 'would be easily evacuated', he claimed. In their place, the area would be repopulated with 'peoples who are of German descent'.[1] Objectionable as Warburg's comments now sound, they merely reflected commonly held imperial ambitions. With Germany losing its toehold in Asia and Africa, territorial aggrandisement on the European continent seemed a far more achievable proposition. Germans Jews, like Warburg, were often at the forefront of these colonial fantasies, motivated not only by the thought of increasing German power but also by the opportunity to rescue Jews from the Russian yoke.[2]

At the start of 1915, talk of colonising the Baltic could easily have been dismissed as nothing more than a pipe dream. The military situation in all theatres of the conflict offered the Central Powers little reason for optimism. On the Western Front, the impasse of trench warfare showed no sign of abating. After gas warfare – the new wonder weapon – had failed to break the deadlock, the Germans seemed content to sit tight and repel wave after wave of assaults from the British and French. Initially, the military situation was little better in the east. Walter Wolff, a Jewish businessman from Hamburg who was ensconced to the northwest of Minsk in Maladzyechna, recalled the misery of the campaigns against the Russians. With little movement at first, he and his comrades sat tight as the bitter cold of winter eventually made way for 'the horrible Russian mud'.[3] Even the war at sea provided the Germans with little respite: presumably out of fear of further riling American public opinion, the German government decided to scale back its submarine campaigns during 1915.

Military shortcomings, however, did not stop many Germans from planning territorial aggrandisement. Heinrich Claß and his Pan-German League once again led the way in this respect. In May 1915, Claß, together with six leading industrial and agricultural organisations, produced a memorandum on war aims for the chancellor, Bethmann Hollweg. All the signs of Claß's characteristic bombast were there. It called for extensive annexations both in the east and west while also demanding the seizure of raw materials for German industry. However, the real significance of the memorandum lay in the consideration it gave to the governance of conquered territory. In Eastern Europe, Claß suggested that 'disenfranchised German farmers living in Russia' could be resettled in a new 'German territorial and economic area' formed from parts of the Baltic lands.[4] As 1915 rolled on, then, the focus was not just on expanding the German Empire, but also on constructing a set of German colonies in the east.[5]

Annexationists could find plenty of reasons for fixing their territorial gaze on the east. Not only did it offer a vast expanse of land ripe for agricultural settlement, but it also housed a diverse, but largely poor, population that looked as if it would benefit from a European civilising mission. The region that German annexationists had their eyes on just happened to be home to the majority of Russia's Jewish population, some 4.9 million people in total. The area's large Jewish population was a consequence of Russia's nineteenth-century policy of forcing Jews to live within the so-called Pale of Settlement, an area that stretched from the Ukraine in the south through Russian Poland and up to the Baltic states in the north. With German annexationists themselves eyeing up these lands, the Pale, complete with its economically poor Jewish population, came to be at the heart of Germany's territorial ambitions. What this meant, therefore, was that German annexationist plans and the fate of the Eastern European Jews became intricately entwined. For German Jews, the war now offered two potential benefits: Germany could increase its territorial reach, while at the same time removing the Eastern European Jews from the Russian sphere of influence.

From Annexation to Colonisation

In June 1915, the political right's annexationist agenda gained a modicum of respectability when Reinhold Seeberg, a professor of Christian theology in

Berlin, waded into the debate. Encouraged by colleagues from Germany's right-wing political scene, Seeberg agreed to issue a petition on war aims. Echoing the rhetoric of the Pan-German League, Seeberg called for both large-scale annexations and the Germanisation of land in the east. As far as Seeberg was concerned, this new territory would house 'some of our growing population' as well as offering 'a new homeland in the old homeland' for German re-migrants.[6] Seeberg's petition attracted the signatures of some 1,341 intellectuals, including 352 university professors. Hidden in this long list of names were the signatures of several German Jews. Putting their names to the motion were, amongst others, the art historian Adolph Goldschmidt, Max Pappenheim, a legal historian in Kiel, and Walther Rathenau's cousin, Fritz Rathenau.[7]

Goldschmidt, Pappenheim, Rathenau and of course Warburg were not the only German Jews sympathetic to the colonisation of the east. The conservative publicist and academic Adolf Grabowsky was particularly vociferous in his support of eastern expansion. Grabowsky's background was interesting but by no means unique. He had been born into a Berlin Jewish family in 1880, later converting to Protestantism. In the pre-war years he edited the *Zeitschrift für Politik* and the young conservative newspaper, *Das neue Deutschland.*[8] No sooner had the first salvos in the conflict been fired than Grabowsky started to advocate German territorial expansion. In his mind, the issue was simple: 'regardless of the cost, our continental territory has to be extended during this war'.[9] Following the trend set by Claß, Seeberg and others, Grabowsky's mind soon turned from merely advocating expansion to actually planning the logistics of imperial rule. The key to Germany's future as a world power, he argued, was to turn areas of the east into agricultural land that could serve the existing economy. At the same time, the spread of Germany's 'culture [and] its language' would help to cement the country's position on the world stage.[10]

As a conservative publicist enlivened by the war, Grabowsky's stance was easy to comprehend. Far more surprising was the fact that other German Jews occupying very different social and political milieux also began to plan the parameters of a future German colonial empire. Chief amongst these was Davis Trietsch, a lesser-known Zionist originally from Dresden. Until the outbreak of hostilities, Trietsch was perhaps best known for a bitter spat he had had with Theodor Herzl during the Sixth Zionist Congress over the location of a future Jewish state.[11] But by 1915, Trietsch's mind was elsewhere. Increasingly he dedicated his time to working on, and then promoting, a set of expansionist war aims which in many ways reflected his own deep attachment to Germany.

In comparison to the belligerence of Claß and Seeberg, Trietsch's language sounded far more reasonable. He expressed admiration for the British Empire, sympathised with the French and cautioned against 'outright annexations'. Dig below the surface, however, and Trietsch's actual message could be just as aggressive as that of his right-wing compatriots. In the west, he demanded the seizure of France's border regions for defensive reasons and proposed splitting Belgium between Germany, the Netherlands and Luxembourg, though naturally the Belgian Congo would fall into German hands alone. In the east, where Russia was 'the most dangerous' opponent, the Baltic states would have to be annexed, while Lithuania, the Ukraine and Russian Poland would be placed under the stewardship of Germany and Austria. These territorial changes, Trietsch explained somewhat optimistically, will bring about 'a new empire' as the basis for 'world peace'.[12]

However, for every Trietsch or Grabowsky dreaming of colonial expansion, there were also many more German Jews trying to moderate such claims. One of the most radical voices in this respect was that of Rosa Luxemburg. Born in 1870, the youngest of five children, her Polish-Jewish parents had first lived in rural Zamosc before resettling in bustling Warsaw. Her Marxist politics had started to take real shape once she had left Poland to study in Zurich; a move to Berlin in 1898, where she joined the SPD, helped to crystallise her political beliefs still further. Never far from controversy, Luxemburg was imprisoned several times during the 1900s and again in February 1915. She used this enforced period of wartime solitude particularly productively, drafting a critical attack on her own party. 'The Crisis of Social Democracy' ('Die Krise der Sozialdemokratie'), or the Junius pamphlet as it is more commonly known, not only condemned war and militarism, but also the SPD's silent acquiescence to the conflict. 'Nowhere [other than Germany] is a proletarian organisation so totally subservient to imperialism', she angrily wrote. Luxemburg was already an outsider in mainstream socialist politics and as such her critical views could be pushed to the margins.[13]

Far more dangerous for the SPD as a party were the criticisms of the Jewish politicians Eduard Bernstein and Hugo Haase, and their colleague Karl Kautsky. In June 1915, the trio published a short manifesto rejecting outright any talk of annexations and imperial expansion. Under the title 'The Demand of the Hour' ('Das Gebot der Stunde'), they robustly criticised the government's apparent move from fighting a defensive to an expansionist war. 'A genuine and permanent peace', they argued, 'is only possible through an open agreement' and thus not through force.[14] Heartfelt it may have been, but the main effect of the trio's manifesto was to provoke the ire of others in the SPD. While the party stayed together for now, criticism of Haase, the party's co-chairman, pointed ominously to dangerous splits opening up within the German left.

By the summer of 1915 anyone who was anyone was freely offering their views on Germany's international future. Theodor Wolff, whose criticism of the conflict was growing by the day, attached himself firmly to the moderate war-aims camp.[15] He encouraged Hans Delbrück, the Berlin military historian, to draw up an anti-expansionist petition, which he then duly signed. 'The annexation of politically independent peoples and those used to independence must be rejected', demanded Delbrück's petition.[16] The campaign itself proved something of a damp squib, garnering a mere 141 signatures in total. One name missing from the list was that of Albert Ballin, who had doggedly resisted Wolff's calls to sign. As far as Ballin was concerned, Delbrück's petition, in renouncing all annexations, was a step too far. Put simply, Ballin believed the opposite; the war had to strengthen Germany economically and to a certain degree territorially too. He hoped the conflict would end with both the port of Zeebrugge and the Belgian Congo safely in German hands.[17]

Ballin may have wanted to hold out for gains from Belgium but the immediate opportunity for territorial aggrandisement occurred not in the west but in the east. During the first half of the year, Hindenburg and Ludendorff managed to strengthen their forces in preparation for a spring advance. Looking on from the army's eastern headquarters, Ismar Becker from Berlin believed the 'decisive battle' was just around the corner. 'The piercing sound of our trumpets, which call us to attack and lead us from victory to victory, will very soon be announcing peace', he observed confidently.[18] Becker's hope for peace proved elusive for now but his optimism was not entirely misplaced. The German forces alongside their Austrian allies began a combined offensive in May that reaped immediate rewards: 150,000 Russian soldiers were taken prisoner in only six days of fighting. The attacks continued through the summer, only ending in September, by which time the Russian army had retreated some 400 kilometres.[19]

As Germany's leaders had been starved of good news stories for longer than they cared to remember, they were determined to reap the rewards from the army's 'great advance' against the Russians. Best placed to fulfil this propaganda task was a select group of war correspondents whose frontline reports were only supposed to confirm the army's own interpretation of the military situation.[20] Fritz Wertheimer, a German-Jewish journalist with the *Frankfurter Zeitung*, took his duties seriously, writing a series of glowing articles about the German army's eastern advance. The impression his reports gave was one of growing momentum. No matter what force the Russians offered, they were now powerless to stop the well-drilled German war machine. Thus, the South Army charged through the Carpathians with 'the sound of victory rebounding from the first, back to the very last man', then broke through the Russian lines at Stryi like an 'unstoppable tidal wave' and finally pushed its way across the River Dniester. All this had been achieved, Wertheimer proudly noted, with only '50 dead and wounded, and less than 100 missing'.[21] If Wertheimer's reports were to be believed, dreams of colonial aggrandisement no longer seemed so far-fetched.

New Colonial Pioneers

Accounts of Hindenburg and Ludendorff's latest successes in the east provided welcome copy for German-Jewish newspapers. With considerable pride, the Zionist *Jüdische Rundschau* described the army's eastern push as 'an unstoppable triumphal march' that had seen 'one important town after the other' falling into Germany's hands.[22] What made the eastern advance so important for Jewish communities was that it combined German military superiority with the rescue of Eastern European Jews from Russian brutality. Tsarist Russia's long history of persecuting its Jewish minority had only worsened as the war gathered pace. In the town of Zurawno, Fritz Wertheimer witnessed first-hand how the Russian army had vented its rage on the Jews during its great retreat. From a population of over 1,000, only around 50 Jews remained, living squalidly amongst piles of smouldering houses. 'Whenever the Russian takes flight', he lamented, 'he still finds the time to reach for a match so as to play the firebug.'[23] The arrival of the German army, warmly welcomed by both the German-Jewish and Eastern European Jewish communities, may have ended the immediate threat of persecution, but the long-term future of Jewish life in the east remained unclear.

One small group of German Jews came up with their own rather drastic solution to this 'problem'. The Committee for the East (Komitee für den Osten, KfdO), as it came to be known, suggested that the Eastern European Jews could head up a colonial mission to Germanise the east. In effect, Germans with their new Jewish partners would work together to dominate the entire region. The plan was similar to a number of nineteenth-century

schemes which had proposed using Eastern European Jews to colonise swathes
of South America, only in this later incarnation of the idea Jews were to colonise the areas in which they already lived.[24]

Surprisingly for a group working towards such a radical agenda, the KfdO
enjoyed support from across the Jewish political spectrum. Its main spokesmen,
Max Bodenheimer and Franz Oppenheimer, both from the first generation of
German Zionists, were joined by members of the CV and other liberal associations. Yet the KfdO's plans, perhaps because of their Jewish national focus,
were never to everyone's taste. And in autumn 1915 a second Jewish group
came into being, also with the aim of assisting the Jews of Eastern Europe.
The German Association for the Interests of Eastern European Jewry
(Deutsche Vereinigung für die Interessen der osteuropäischen Juden) favoured
improving conditions in the east through education rather than by promoting
nationalism, an approach that proved far more palatable to liberal Jews.[25]

The KfdO proved fairly immune to the waves of internal Jewish criticism
directed its way. As far as its members were concerned, the group's real legitimacy came not from other German-Jewish organisations but from the German
state itself. In its literature and correspondence, the KfdO reminded anyone
who cared to listen that it was working in partnership with the German
government. According to Oppenheimer and Bodenheimer, the KfdO only
came into existence after the 'Foreign Office and the General Staff' had agreed
that its 'activities were desirable'.[26] The two veteran Zionists offered a rather
generous rendering of events, as the KfdO never truly operated at the behest
of governmental officials. It was just that a series of fortunate encounters
served to give this impression.

The first of these meetings with senior officials occurred in August 1914
prior to the KfdO's actual formation. Operating at this time under the name of
the German Committee for the Liberation of Russian Jews (Deutsches Komitee
für die Befreiung der russischen Juden), Bodenheimer and Oppenheimer
worked with the Foreign Office to draft a pro-German leaflet to be distributed
to Polish Jews. The plan was that on marching into the east, the German army
would bombard the local Jewish population with a message of liberation. 'The
despotic [Russian] government has been forced to flee', the leaflet assured its
recipients, before going on to paint a picture of a brave new world: 'Our flags
are bringing you justice and freedom, equal citizenship, religious freedom and
the autonomy to exist undisturbed as you wish in all areas of economic and
social life.'[27] Arguably the leaflet itself did far more damage than good as it only
confirmed the idea of Jewish treachery in Russian minds.[28] Yet for Bodenheimer

and Oppenheimer, the project's dubious success paled into insignificance when compared to their new-found contacts in the Foreign Office.

Once the leaders of the KfdO had gained the ear of state officials, they were determined to make the most of their new contacts. During the winter of 1914–15, representatives from the KfdO managed to engineer a series of further high-level meetings with government representatives. Undoubtedly the group's biggest coup came when they received an invitation to meet with Hindenburg and Ludendorff in their eastern headquarters. Getting there necessitated a complex overland journey deep into freshly conquered territory. Bodenheimer recalled that he and Oppenheimer, who accompanied him on the adventure, felt like colonial explorers dressed 'as though for a journey to the North Pole'. After driving around bomb craters, dead horses and the general detritus of war littering the roads, the pair eventually arrived at the army's eastern headquarters. They first met with Ludendorff who was sympathetic to their project, but as Bodenheimer put it, there was something about his disposition that 'betrayed calculation and a cold heart'. 'We were for him only insignificant pawns on the chessboard of war', he added.[29]

In stark contrast, Bodenheimer's and Oppenheimer's view of Hindenburg could not have been more different. His features exuded 'self-confidence, calm assurance and kindness', recalled Bodenheimer. No doubt this impression was strengthened by the fact that Hindenburg invited the members of the KfdO to dine with him at the Hotel Rome in Radom. Over their meal they chatted about the state of the military campaign and the peoples of the east. Yet aside from finishing off 'several bottles of wine from the Rhineland and champagne', the pair left having made little real progress with their plans for the east.[30]

Presumably for this reason, once home they followed up their meeting with Hindenburg with a letter that sketched out their designs for a future German colonial mission in much greater detail. The KfdO's plans, they explained, rested on the German army destroying 'Russian rule' and then 'planting the German flag in Warsaw, Vilna, Minsk, Kiev and Odessa'. The army's victory in the east would help to bring about the KfdO's first overarching aim which was to free Eastern European Jews from the Russian Tsarist regime. In essence, the KfdO viewed the German army as a liberating force that would rescue Eastern European Jews from decades of persecution, oppression and neglect at the hands of the Russians. The group's second goal, as Bodenheimer and Oppenheimer explained, was to secure the Jewish population's long-term future in the east. Amongst the different groups of people inhabiting Eastern Europe, it was 'the Jewish population in West Russia', the KfdO argued, who should 'take on a leading role'.[31]

It must have required quite a leap of faith for Hindenburg to conceive of the Eastern European Jews heading up a new German colonial mission. After all, even Wertheimer observed that the 'overwhelming mass' of the Jewish population consisted of 'poor, starving proletarians'.[32] Yet it was in their inherent foreignness that their Germanness was apparently to be found. According to the KfdO, the cultural and linguistic values of the Eastern European Jews were closely aligned to those of Germany. This could be most closely observed in the Eastern European Jews' use of the Yiddish language which the KfdO repeatedly called 'medieval German'. After a few years living under 'the German sphere of influence', the group insisted, Yiddish would evolve to become a 'modern German language'. On this basis, the Jews would act as a 'German-speaking element caring for German culture, while forming a living wall against the Poles' separatist aims'.[33]

The KfdO may have been rather too buoyant in its assessment of Eastern European Jews' loyalties, but the idea of linguistic convergence attracted considerable sympathy amongst German Jews. Even the KfdO's nearest political rival, the German Association, worked on the assumption that Yiddish was 'an undeveloped form of German', which ensured that the Eastern European Jews were tightly 'connected with Germany'.[34] However, it was again Davis Trietsch who went furthest in his pronouncements. Fresh from his calls for German territorial aggrandisement, Trietsch went on to publish a pamphlet outlining the basis for a Jewish German-'language community'. Like the KfdO, Trietsch maintained that Yiddish needed to be seen as a strand of the German language. Once people had overcome this mental hurdle, he explained, they would find that there were some 10 million Jews worldwide who could understand Yiddish and thus German. The importance of this linguistic relationship was of critical importance to 'the supporters of German expansionism', who like him wanted to see a greater Germany.[35]

If the KfdO's pronouncements were to be believed, the German army and German Jews shared almost identical colonial aims in the east. On this point, Bodenheimer was fairly emphatic. 'The Committee for the East owes its existence', he asserted, 'to the conviction that during the military involvement, the interests of the Jewish population in the east – particularly in Russian Poland – are identical to those of our fatherland'.[36] It would be easy to dismiss such pronouncements as simply overblown rhetoric designed to curry favour with Germany's military and civilian leaders. Yet this would be to miss the point.

The KfdO was entirely sincere in its assertions. It was just as determined to see Germany's colonial realm spread farther towards Russia as it was to rescue the Jews of Eastern Europe. Indeed, the committee argued that giving the Jews greater autonomy would be 'the best way to Germanise the east'.[37]

Employing the Eastern European Jews as German pioneers in the east seemed to offer a satisfactory solution to a tricky problem. On the one hand, the Jews would be liberated from Russian despotism, while on the other Germany could extend its influence further into Eastern Europe. Unfortunately, neither the KfdO nor the German government had troubled to ask the Eastern European Jews if they wanted to take on the role of German colonialists. Instead Germany's Jewish communities were content to make sweeping judgments about the region and its people based almost entirely on their background as Germans rather than as Jews.

A Sobering Reality

Once the dust had settled on the German army's 'great advance', the major cities of Warsaw, Bialystok, Vilna and Brest-Litovsk were under its control. Each of these cities had large Jewish populations. Vilna had even been dubbed the 'Jerusalem of the east' on account of its vibrant Jewish culture. To all intents and purposes, it looked as if the KfdO's time had come. With the Jewish populations of the east in German hands, the group could now move from theory to practice. However, as the KfdO was soon forced to admit, it was much easier to talk about colonial plans than to implement them. During the first months of occupation, the German army and its Jewish supporters gradually began to realise the sheer size of their task. They discovered a region of wildly different peoples, languages and cultures, all badly torn apart by war and poverty. Far from being pioneers of German culture as the KfdO had claimed, the Eastern European Jews turned out to be just as exotic as the other ethnic groups inhabiting the region.

Jewish transmigration during the pre-war years had already opened German minds to the idea of Eastern European Jewish cultural distinctiveness. Once Jews and other Germans entered the east their worst fears were only confirmed. In rather ungracious terms, one German-Jewish soldier described crossing the Russian border as akin to having 'come from a good lounge to a dungheap'. On one side of the border, well-maintained 'two-storey stone homes' lined the streets, while on the other there was little sign of 'well-ordered lives'.[38] The military leadership's concerns, however, lay elsewhere. Their main priority was to move the German troops eastwards so as to keep the Russian forces at bay, a plan that was hindered somewhat by the woeful condition of the existing infrastructure. Hindenburg and Ludendorff's deputy, Max Hoffmann, described 'the roads, the filth and the vermin' in Poland as being 'beyond belief'.[39] Leopold Rosenak, who at this time was serving as an army rabbi with the German South Army, would probably have agreed with these sentiments. He experienced even worse conditions in the Carpathians. Along some tracks, the mud was so deep that the army's horses were sucked in and simply drowned. In these circumstances, it is not surprising that Rosenak struggled to reach the Jewish soldiers who were themselves scattered over a wide area of the front.[40]

Transport problems merely hinted at the grinding poverty of the region. Russia's western fringes boasted patches of prosperity, mainly in the larger urban centres, but for the most part were economically deprived. The Russian army's retreat during 1915 made an already difficult situation much worse, for as the troops marched eastwards, they destroyed much that was in their path. Entire villages were wiped from the map, while roads, railways and bridges were all severed.[41] Despite claims to the contrary, the advancing German army did not always help matters either. Eugene Kent, a fresh-faced soldier from a Berlin Jewish family, remembered with slight embarrassment that once in Russia, the 'watchword was now requisitioning'. As they passed Russian homes, he and his comrades marched in and looted anything and everything they could lay their hands on.[42] For locals who had to live between the two warring armies, the consequences were devastating. 'The misery is so boundless', complained Rabbi Emanuel Carlebach on a visit to a Jewish orphanage, 'so wretched, so dreadful'.[43]

However, poverty was not the only shock the German invaders faced. As they quickly discovered, where there was extreme depravation, there was often also disease. For the German soldiers, used to Western European standards of hygiene and health care, the biggest threat was typhus. Poor sanitation and overcrowding provided the ideal circumstances for infected lice to transmit the disease from human to human. By March 1915, 27,500 cases of typhus in Russian POWs had been reported.[44] It was not just Russians or Eastern European peasants who proved susceptible to typhus; German soldiers and even doctors treating those infected came down with the disease themselves. As the number of typhus cases continued to rise, so too did German fears of infection. Alfred Friedemann had only one piece of advice for his friend and colleague in the KfdO, Max Bodenheimer: before travelling to Poland, he urged 'get yourself . . . immunised against typhus, if possible twice'.[45]

As they picked their way through the dirt, disease and destitution of the east, German soldiers and their civilian entourage uncovered a mixture of different peoples, from Lithuanians and Latvians through to Poles and Baltic Germans. It was the Eastern European Jews, however, who were the most visible presence. This can partly be explained by the size of the Jewish population in Eastern Europe, but it was also a consequence of the particular trades they pursued. Many of the Eastern European Jews earned their living in the cattle markets, as traders or as street sellers. This last role, in particular, put them in direct contact with German troops who could often be seen trying to barter down Jewish hawkers. Indeed, if the newspaper of the German 10th Army was to be believed, Eastern European Jews stood waiting at every corner ready to dupe the German occupiers: 'Every time we walk through the town, a Jewish trader, with crowing voice touting his wares, latches on to us.' Yet there were no real bargains to be had, the article warned. These Jewish street sellers hunted out their 'victims', 'flogged' them goods of poor quality, before making off.[46]

Should the German soldier manage to avoid being ensnared by street hawkers, he still then had to run the risk of Jewish prostitutes. Long before the war's outbreak, Jews had been publicly linked to crimes of sexual promiscuity and deviance, primarily through their supposed involvement in the transport of young women from Eastern Europe to brothels in North and South America, what was rather brutally dubbed the 'white slave trade'. Indeed, Bertha Pappenheim, the redoubtable president of the JFB, dedicated much of her energy to combating this miserable trade. During the First World War, the white slave trade declined. There was no need to send women abroad when business – in the shape of German soldiers – came to the east instead. The Jewish population in these areas certainly played a significant role in wartime prostitution. In Łódź, for example, estimates suggested that 60 per cent of prostitutes were Jews. Whether or not this statistic was accurate, prostitution and – as many soldiers found – venereal disease came to be directly associated with Eastern European Jews.[47]

German soldiers, then, discovered – sometimes at very close quarters – an extremely poor Jewish population, living at the margins of a depressed society. There was very little to suggest that these impoverished individuals were German pioneers, ready and waiting to colonise the east as the KfdO had promised. Instead the Eastern European Jews became something for German soldiers to gawp at or even photograph, as if they were some kind of exotic oddity. In their reports, army newspapers published for the frontline troops frequently made reference to the Eastern European Jews, not always negatively, but certainly in terms of cultural difference. 'They are all unwashed and uncombed', one article explained, 'and emanating from all of them, the smell that gives this whole city its atmosphere.'[48]

Germany's military leadership, however, was not particularly concerned about cultural sensibilities. They had already decided that the Jews in the east were responsible for spreading dirt and disease which threatened to undermine the fighting strength of the German army. A report from the German administration in Warsaw suggested that Jews made up 90 per cent of those infected with typhus. The report explained that this was largely due to the poor hygienic standards of the Jewish population: 'The unspeakable dirt in the narrow and dark homes; the inclusion of scoundrels and rogues on a large scale; all types of vermin and the disgusting levels of personal cleanliness offer shocking evidence for the spread of contagion amongst the poor Jewish section of society.'[49]

The German-Jewish soldiers' view of the Eastern Jews did not differ wildly from that of the wider army. Most appeared genuinely appalled at the prevailing conditions which from a western perspective were akin to 'returning to a cultural world that lay several centuries in the past'.[50] Robert Ehrmann, a Jewish soldier who served in the east, captured the abysmal conditions that reigned there in a photograph of two women and a man scavenging for salt (see Plate 10). Surrounding them lies a barren landscape of rubbish and ruined buildings. In recording this scene, however, he – like many of the German-Jewish soldiers – was actually looking to put distance between himself and the Eastern Jews. These were 'poor Jews' as he wrote underneath the image, not educated, western Jews, fully acculturated into a modern society like himself. No one articulated this desire for distance more powerfully than Victor Klemperer, who concluded that under no circumstances did he 'belong to these people'. 'I belonged to Europe, to Germany', he continued. 'I thanked my creator that I was German.'[51]

However, it proved impossible for the German-Jewish soldiers to close their eyes entirely to their Jewish co-religionists in the east. They may have been suspicious, critical or even fearful of the Eastern Jews, but the Jewishness of these people was irrefutable. Despite the influence of the Hasidic movement, it was still clear that German, Polish and Russian Jews shared a similar religious heritage and followed the same calendar of religious festivals. Therefore, when the soldiers required kosher food, when they needed reading material or even a place to celebrate the Sabbath, they often sought out the local population. For example, on arriving in Chełm, Arnold Tänzer, who served as the rabbi to the Bug Army, managed to gain permission to take over the town's main synagogue for the day. After removing the local Jewish population – for fear of disease – Tänzer held his own service for the German troops based on the theme of 'sense of duty and faith in God'.[52]

Pragmatism seemed to be the key to surviving in the east. As one of Tänzer's colleagues sagely advised, living here meant 'leaving behind Western European assumptions about form and beauty'.[53] For those German Jews able or willing to follow this advice, the first months abroad became a time of cultural discovery. Amidst the dirt and despair, there was certainly religious beauty waiting to be unearthed. Even Tänzer himself, who never warmed entirely to the Eastern European Jews, managed to find much to admire in his new surroundings. In an article he penned for the Bug Army's own newspaper, he eulogised the art that adorned the main synagogue in Brest-Litovsk. 'On the east wall, surrounding the Torah ark', Tänzer explained, stood 'a lovely wooden carving that stretched some 20 metres and about 6 metres across, which depicted different moments of synagogue ritual.'[54]

While it was possible to uncover evidence of a vibrant Jewish life in the eastern territories, the local population still remained something of a frustration. Max Bodenheimer recalled, for example, how locals disrupted a military synagogue service in the town of Skierniewice. The service was apparently in full flow when suddenly some 'completely undisciplined' Jewish youths stormed through the main door and into the ladies' gallery. Order was only restored when the army stepped in to discipline the interlopers.[55] Bodenheimer's experiences in Skierniewice went to the crux of the KfdO's difficulties. It had arrived in the east on the back of the advancing German army determined to employ the existing Jewish population as colonial pioneers. What the KfdO discovered instead was a group of Jews who were not only very different to those in Western Europe, but who also resented the arrival of their German co-religionists. The local population, it seemed, did not necessarily want to be colonised.

Modernising the East

In 1915, the Viennese journalist Nathan Birnbaum, renowned for his invention of the term Zionism, published his own retort to the KfdO's colonial plans. He rejected any suggestion that the Eastern European Jews were somehow culturally German. 'The Eastern Jews are not Germans, just as they are not Russians or Poles', Birnbaum maintained. 'They are a people, similar to and commensurate to other peoples.'[56] Like Birnbaum, other writers gradually came to this conclusion. Adolf Grabowsky suggested that there was a strong distinction between German and Eastern European Jews. While the former were undoubtedly 'part of a German cultural community', the latter 'lived solely in a Jewish cultural community'.[57] If the Eastern European Jews were not going to help colonise the east, then a new role for them needed to be urgently found. The German army's response was one of pragmatism. Rather than viewing the Eastern Jews as potential partners, they instead sought to reform and civilise the Jews within their grasp.

The size of the German army's civilising mission, however, was immense. By the time the Eastern Front had stabilised in late 1915, the Germans occupied some 160,000 square kilometres of Russian territory, bringing several million Eastern European Jews under their direct control. This vast expanse of territory left the German military with plenty to deal with, even though Rathenau mischievously suggested that the German army really needed to march on to St Petersburg and 'if possible to Moscow' too.[58] To help rule the vast region now under German control, a decision was taken to form different administrative districts. Russian Poland was split into a German and an Austrian part, while Lithuania, Courland and Bialystok-Grodno remained under direct military control, to be administered as the Ober Ost ('Oberbefehlshaber der gesamten Deutschen Streitkräfte im Osten') district.[59]

In both Poland and Ober Ost, the German occupiers faced a massive task of reconstruction and repair, but it was not just the physical infrastructure that needed to be coaxed back to health; the local people too required urgent help. The upheaval of war combined with a harsh winter hit the Eastern European Jewish population particularly hard. In the town of Kobryn, members of the local synagogue community were so ravenous that they scrambled for any food they could find, including in one instance mouldy bread: 'They yanked it out of our hands; they gathered the crumbs on the ground', observed the Russian-Jewish writer, S. Ansky.[60]

Helping these civilian victims of the war largely fell onto the shoulders of Jewish relief organisations. From the United States, the American Jewish Joint Distribution Committee, which had been established in November 1914, provided funds and direct aid for the war's Jewish victims. Demonstrating a transnational concern for Jewish suffering, the Joint also provided the Aid Association of German Jews with finance so that the group could assist Jews on the ground. At the same time, the Aid Association launched its own fund-raising campaigns within Germany, in which it urged German Jews to show 'sympathetic human love'.[61] Much of the money raised through such fund-raising efforts went towards providing emergency food for an estimated 700,000 malnourished and starving individuals. Ninety soup kitchens and twenty-five tearooms were initially established in the occupied regions. Kovno's Jewish soup kitchen even bore the name of General Ludendorff, ironically as a symbol of his 'lasting sympathy for the Jews'.[62]

Rebuilding lives and reconstructing infrastructure was only the first stage towards creating a more permanent German presence in the east. With both Austro-Hungarian and Polish nationalists eyeing up the occupied Polish lands, Ober Ost rather than Poland seemed to offer greater scope for a German colonial project. Ludendorff was certainly of this view. He saw the German military's task as being part of an ongoing process of 'civilization at which the Germans had laboured in those lands for many centuries'. Placing himself at the heart of this mission, Ludendorff established his headquarters in the Lithuanian city of Kaunas in October 1915. There, amidst the 'low, mean, wooden houses', the German military requisitioned two large villas for its purposes.[63] From these modest beginnings, the staff of the Ober Ost administration grew at a remarkable rate, numbering some 18,000 by 1918.[64]

One of the most remarkable aspects of the German occupation, both in Poland and in the Ober Ost district, was the number of German Jews who took up administrative posts. In German-occupied Poland, the liberal Reichstag politician Ludwig Haas was appointed as the first adviser on Jewish affairs. Haas had already proved his military capabilities on the Western Front, where he had received the Iron Cross 1st Class for bravery. In this new role, Haas was charged with ensuring that Polish Jews' religious and cultural needs were respected. His appointment was not to everyone's taste, however. One member of the Interior Ministry, whose anti-Semitic sympathies were clearly visible, complained that employing a Jew could 'be detrimental to the reputation of the administration'.[65] From a very different perspective, the theologian Hermann Strack dismissed Haas as 'religiously liberal and completely without knowledge of the Eastern Jews'.[66] Strack certainly had a point. Haas, a smartly dressed law graduate and politician from Baden, with a penchant for collecting fine soaps, cut a rather incongruous figure amongst the Jews of Eastern Europe.[67]

Haas embodied a larger clash between Western and Eastern European values that defined much of the German occupation. Yet the precise dynamics of this cultural chasm did not seem to be of great concern to Germany's leaders. Jesko von Puttkamer argued forcibly for the use of German-Jewish intermediaries in the east. 'Obviously these cannot be natives', he pointed out, but rather they should be 'Imperial German Jews with trustworthy views'.[68] Based on this logic, a large number of German Jews started to take on roles in the Ober Ost administration. Victor Klemperer, Arnold Zweig, Hermann

Struck and Sammy Gronemann all found work in the press section, where they were responsible for translations, censorship and propaganda. This did not necessarily mean they were qualified for the task at hand. Gronemann was employed as a translator for Yiddish texts, but struggled even to read the language, which somewhat undermined Jewish attempts to call Yiddish a German language.[69] Nonetheless, with so many leading German-Jewish intellectuals gathered in Ober Ost, at times it almost seemed as if the vibrancy of Berlin had been transplanted 900 kilometres further east.

Most of those who moved into the Ober Ost administration had already seen frontline military service. Klemperer and Zweig, for example, had both survived close encounters with death on the Western Front before their transfer to Ludendorff's personal domain. After the mud of Flanders, it was an undoubted relief to have proper beds in which to sleep, regular meals and time to enjoy leisure activities. The artist Magnus Zeller, therefore, was not far off the mark when he called Ober Ost 'a life raft for the remains of an intelligentsia, slowly bleeding to death'.[70] Understandably, as word spread of the cosy arrangements in the east, other German Jews sought to scramble aboard the lifeboat before it filled up. Friends of Bertram Stern, a Zionist recently called up into the army, sought to pull strings to get him a posting in the east. Stern is 'an exceptionally feeble person and as such . . . really suffers in active service'.[71] Stereotyping the male Jewish body as weak and effeminate had long been the preserve of anti-Semites looking to keep German Jews from public service. In Stern's case, these same ideas could be drawn upon to attain a posting behind the lines.

Seeing out the war in Ober Ost was an undeniably more pleasant proposition than risking life and limb at the front. This was not to say, though, that those stationed in the east viewed their work as any less valuable than that of the fighting troops. Indeed, the Jews and other Germans working in the Ober Ost administration generally approached their mission with considerable pride. As befitting a military occupation, all members of the administration conducted their business in uniform. In his memoirs, Sammy Gronemann included a revealing sketch of himself and Hermann Struck visiting the offices of the Lithuanian newspaper *Dabartis* (see Plate 11). The pair are seen bedecked in neatly pressed German army uniforms; Gronemann even has his bayonet on display, hanging loosely from his belt. Once they were in uniform, the German Jews in the Ober Ost were just as capable of playing the part of victorious occupier as any other German soldier. Gronemann recalled a conversation between two German Jews in a Jewish restaurant in Vilna. One of the diners suggested to his guest that he might want to put his cigar away; it was the Sabbath and he was keen to avoid offending local sensibilities. With a shrug of his shoulders, his partner replied: 'why do I need to take account of people's feelings; we're the victors here'.[72]

This sense of moral and cultural superiority trickled down to shape the way German Jews approached their work in the east. Being part of an all-conquering army gave legitimacy to Western European Jewry's longstanding claims to Jewish leadership. Their mission, as the theological scholar Ismar Freund expounded, was to cast aside 'the decay of Russian corruption', thereby allowing the Jews to 'be transformed into useful citizens and fully fledged members of human society'.[73] With Freund's message ringing in their ears, German Jews joined in with the occupying regime's attempts to reform the existing structures of society. Education quickly came under the microscope. In comparison to the high standards of the German system, schools across Eastern Europe were deemed woefully inadequate, with too few classes and poor levels of teacher training. In an attempt to remedy these deficiencies, Yiddish instruction came into the firing line, as it suited neither Polish nationalists nor the German occupiers. German Jews, some more vociferously than others, stood up for Yiddish, but even then there was a general belief that German would eventually dominate as levels of education increased.[74]

Civilising the Eastern European Jews also meant civilising their cultural activities. Ever since Gershom Scholem first popularised the term 'the cult of the *Ostjuden*' in the 1970s, historical writing has obsessed over the German-Jewish soldiers' encounter with Eastern European Jewish culture.[75] One of the keenest examples of this phenomenon was Franz Rosenzweig, at this time a young Jewish soldier serving in the Balkans, but later to be better known for his masterful work of Jewish philosophy, *The Star of Redemption*. Stationed in the Balkans for much of the war, Rosenzweig spent his spare time soaking up his surroundings. In Skopje, he admired the 'Jewish life' of a Sephardic Jewish community, while later in Warsaw he watched in awe as Hasidic children prayed and sang. 'I have never heard anything like it', he marvelled.[76] Rosenzweig was far from alone in his admiration of the Eastern European Jews. Many of the German Jews stationed in the east, whether on the frontline or in the Ober Ost administration, explored the simple lives of the Jews in their midst, often recording their impressions with a sense of anthropological curiosity. As a highly educated German doctor, Theodor Rosenthal was shocked at the 'illness, misery and dirt' of the Jewish homes. Nonetheless 'a feeling of belonging' drew him back time and again to visit poorer Jewish quarters in Poland.[77]

Yet this cult, if indeed it ever truly existed, was never merely about revel-
ling in the authenticity of Eastern European Jewish life: it was also about
reframing this culture, thereby making it comprehensible to a Western
European audience. Yiddish theatre, which before the war had mainly been
confined to Central Europe's Jewish immigrant communities, offers a perfect
example of this repackaging in action. In Ober Ost, the German authorities,
presumably in a fit of enthusiasm for their surroundings, actively encouraged
previously closed-down troupes to re-form. Yiddish performances proved
popular amongst German officers, with advertisements and reviews even
appearing in army newspapers.[78] The key to the theatre's success was its acces-
sibility. A visit to the Yiddish stage pre-occupation would have meant battling
to understand a group of amateur actors speaking in a range of accents, while
the whole time forced to sit amongst a loud, boisterous crowd. Under the
watchful eye of German-Jewish members of the occupying army, new Yiddish
theatre groups, such as the popular Vilna Troupe, staged professional produc-
tions that were accessible to Jews and other Germans alike.[79]

Entertaining as Yiddish theatre was, the Jewish world from whence it came
still remained largely incomprehensible to the German public. In an attempt
to break down these barriers, Hermann Struck, together with the poet Herbert
Eulenberg, published a collection of intimate sketches that were designed to
familiarise a German readership with the people and cultures of the east.
Skimming through the pages of the book, readers would have been confronted
with Struck's detailed sketches of Eastern European landscapes alongside
portraits of Jews, Poles and Lithuanians. In one picture, an elderly Jewish
baggage porter is captured carrying a large, and presumably heavy, case on his
back; in another, a ragged coachman, whip in hand, stands ready to transport
goods across the city (see Plate 12). The book's message was clear: these were
hardworking, industrious people, now enjoying the freedom brought by
German rule. There was certainly no attempt to follow in the footsteps of the
KfdO by suggesting that the Eastern Jews were somehow German. That
moment had passed. Instead this was a land and people being civilised, thanks
to the 'dedication and strength' of the German occupiers.[80]

Raising the Barricades

Hermann Struck's book was a passionate elegy to the people and landscapes of
the east, but also to the wider goals of German occupation. Like other Germans
working in the Ober Ost administration, German Jews enjoyed being part of

a colonial mission designed to bring order and certainties to what seemed to be an underdeveloped part of the world. Being members of a victorious army also brought considerable personal satisfaction, particularly with battles still going on elsewhere. As Victor Klemperer reflected, food was plentiful, the accommodation was good and his shaving water was even delivered to his bedside each morning.[81] Yet for all the tangible benefits of Germany's colonial project, one unintended consequence continued to play on German minds: what if the population of Eastern Europe, particularly the Eastern European Jews, were to exploit Germany's generosity and move to the west? Fearing a wave of poor, diseased migrants, Jews and other Germans sought to build a barricade between Germany and its new colonial possessions in the east.

What heightened public fears was the fact that the pattern of Jewish immigration from Eastern to Western Europe had a long and rather thorny history. In the four decades before the outbreak of the First World War, some 2 million Eastern European Jews had travelled westwards. The majority continued their journeys on to the United States, though a smaller number remained in Central Europe. With the memory of these movements still fresh, conservative groups wasted no time in revisiting their earlier concerns. The conflict was only three weeks old when the economists Ludwig Bernhard and Leo Wegener penned a polemical memorandum on the state of Germany's eastern border. Buried in between proposals to repopulate the border region with ethnic Germans was a damning attack on the Eastern Jews, who were deemed 'culturally too low' and only good for 'emigration further east or overseas'.[82] Although no one had invited him to respond, Georg Fritz, a government bureaucrat from the same political and cultural milieu as Bernhard and Wegener, went a stage further. He painted a picture of a veritable flood of 'foreign-raced, Judaised Mongols whose admission en masse would negatively and unilaterally alter the entire character of the German people'.[83]

Towards the end of his polemic, Fritz made a direct appeal to Germany's Jewish population. He warned them that a sudden wave of Eastern European Jewish immigrants 'would lead to an intensified resurgence of the Jewish question' in Germany.[84] Uncomfortable as this thought was, German Jews could recognise the logic behind Fritz's argument. After all, the organised Jewish communities had faced a similar dilemma during the late nineteenth century when an influx of Eastern European Jews had threatened to destabilise German Jews' relationship with wider society. Some thirty years later, the big fear for Jewish communities was that the arrival of poor immigrants from the east would undermine all their efforts towards full integration. Franz

Oppenheimer expressed this very concern in private. The arrival of '200,000 *schnorrers* from the east' would not be in '[German-]Jewish interests', he reportedly remarked. Oppenheimer's criticism of the 'caftan Jews' as he called them, reflected a sense of German-Jewish superiority combined with an evident wish to avoid association with other, apparently lesser Jews.[85]

At first glance, German Jews' apprehensions about Eastern European Jewish immigration appeared entirely self-serving; they were determined to protect their hard-won position within Germany. Yet look closer and it becomes clear that many German Jews actually shared the prejudices articulated by Fritz and other conservatives. Large sections of the German-Jewish community viewed the Eastern Jews as a fundamentally un-German group: poor, uncivilised and lacking even the most basic understanding of Western European cultural norms. Willy Cohn, a teacher and historian from Breslau, put it bluntly when he declared that the 'average Jew from the east is not on the same cultural level as a Jew from the west'. As soon as an Eastern European Jew comes into money, Cohn added, 'he seeks out the big German and western cities', even though he has yet to develop into a 'fully civilised person'.[86] This notion of a cultural deficit was picked up by Kurt Alexander, a prominent CV activist. Viewing things through the same Western European lens as Cohn, Alexander explained that people from this lower 'level of civilisation' could not simply be integrated into German society. They need to experience 'a century of German cultural work' to become fully German, he added.[87]

There was never complete unanimity on the issue. Nonetheless, the thought of increased immigration from Eastern Europe left both Jews and other Germans with a distinct sense of apprehension. Groups on the German right came up with a simple solution to the problem: Germany's eastern border should be sealed. In effect, no unauthorised individuals would be allowed to cross the closed border (*Grenzschluss*) between the German Empire and the occupied lands of Eastern Europe. The idea itself originated in the late nineteenth century, when anti-Semites proposed sealing Germany's border to Eastern European Jews, but it came back onto the political agenda with a vengeance during the war. After Georg Fritz had given the whole issue momentum with his proposal to seal the border, other groups on the right soon followed his lead. The Wirtschaftliche Vereinigung, a political faction of conservatives and anti-Semites, took the issue to the very top, when they demanded Bethmann Hollweg take action to close 'the existing German Reich borders to Jewish immigration'.[88]

Sealing the border was only one possible solution to the apparent problem of Jewish immigration. A different school of thought coalesced around the idea of creating some form of border strip (*Grenzstreife*) in the east. The basic idea was a simple one. Land would be carved out along Germany's eastern borders which would then be populated by ethnic Germans, clearly a reliable population group. This new German territorial strip would serve two functions. It would provide a buffer zone to Russia, thus protecting Germany from future invasion from the east, while at the same time it would stop the westward migration of 'the great crowd of bedraggled and destitute Jews', as Edgar Jaffe put it. Jaffe's description of the Eastern European Jews reflected the view of many Germans. But considering that Jaffe was an economics professor at Munich University and had himself converted from Judaism in his youth, his choice of language was inappropriate at best.[89]

As Jaffe's comments demonstrated so well, there was something deeply unpleasant about the language employed in the Jewish immigration debate. The Eastern European Jews were branded as 'unproductive', a 'danger', 'inbred' and 'feeble'.[90] No one gave them an opportunity to defend themselves against such resolute attacks. This was perhaps to be expected. What was more surprising, though, was the paltry defence mounted by the existing German-Jewish communities. The CV complained about Fritz's racist world view that singled Jews out for particular attention, while the Zionist *Jüdische Rundschau* mocked these proposals as nothing more than an attempt to build a new 'Great Wall of China' in the east.[91] But other than this sniping from the sidelines, there was little direct condemnation of the right's plans to block the eastern border or indeed any real attempt to counter them.

Instead of shielding their co-religionists from the worst of this anti-Semitic discourse, many German Jews appeared to accept the underpinning idea of cultural and even racial difference. This stance was plain to see from the response of the KfdO. It agreed that the last thing Germany needed was a sudden 'deluge of Poles, whether Christians or Jews'.[92] This was almost a given. However, as far as the KfdO was concerned, this was not the end of the story. It continued to argue the case that the Eastern Jews could be reformed and turned into productive members of society. In a special edition of the increasingly conservative monthly *Süddeutsche Monatshefte*, leading members of the KfdO took turns to explain how education, social improvements and retraining would help to raise the self-image of the Eastern Jews. Somewhat optimistically perhaps, Max Bodenheimer declared that if these measures were taken, Germany 'need no longer fear the danger of a mass migration from Russian Poland'. As full citizens, the Jewish population in the east would be content to remain where they were.[93]

The only time that the KfdO and other Jewish groups went to the barri-
cades over the plan to seal the border was when it seemed that an exception
was being made of the Eastern European Jews. If the Jews from Eastern Europe
were to be banned from entering Germany, then other immigrant groups
needed to be too. It was an all or nothing approach, as far as the KfdO was
concerned. The group could accept a complete ban on Eastern European
immigration, but it 'would fight with all its might any special law' targeting
only Jews.[94] The German Association for the Interests of Eastern European
Jewry, the KfdO's rival for the affections of German Jews, had a similar take
on the situation. It agreed that, for now, freedom of movement for the Eastern
Jews should 'not just be granted'. Such restrictions were acceptable as long as
the 'Polish population' was 'subjected to the same restrictions'. Failure to
apply border controls equally would turn the Eastern Jews into 'second-class
citizens', the group warned.[95]

The strategy of the German Association and the KfdO was clearly designed
to ease pressure on the beleaguered Eastern European Jews. By drawing other
potential immigrant groups into the debate, in particular Polish Catholics,
matters would no longer hinge on a question of Jewish difference, but on
immigration more generally. However, underpinning these defensive moves
was always an implicit sense of ethnic superiority. The KfdO seemed genuinely shocked that the German military could even contemplate favouring
Poles over Jews. After all, the group had consistently made the argument that
the Eastern European Jews were linguistically and culturally German and as
such the most 'intelligent group' in the east. Closing the border to Jews while
still allowing for the entry of 'Polish peasants' was thus regarded as preposterous.[96] The KfdO refused to countenance the idea that the Poles could ever
be regarded as the ethnically superior group.

Despite the growing calls for a ban on the entry of Jews, Poles or both,
officially Germany's eastern borders remained open, in the short term at least.
The reality on the ground, however, proved very different. German businesses
that wanted to tap into the vast labour pool in the east often struggled to bring
their new workers into the country. It proved one thing to recruit Eastern
European Jews, quite another to set them to work. The plight of one small
group of Jewish workers followed a fairly typical pattern. Mannesmann, which
like many German firms used agents to recruit Eastern European workers,
had taken on Jews and Poles to work in its Gelsenkirchen steel factories. The
transport taking them into the west, though, never got any farther than the
German border. Officials allowed the Poles to continue their journey but

barred the Jewish workers from entry, leaving them stranded and penniless on the wrong side of the border.[97] Fears that Germany's eastern borders were about to be stormed not by Russians, but by Eastern European Jews, effectively debarred Jewish workers from jobs in Germany.

What German Jews found hardest to swallow was the realisation that Jewish workers from Eastern Europe were being treated very differently to all others. Actual sympathy for the plight of those stranded the other side of the border, however, was less forthcoming. Even Bertha Pappenheim, whose Jewish Women's League was supposed to be fighting anti-Semitism, struggled to see beyond the otherness of the Eastern Jews. Privately she complained about the influx of Russian Jews into German society. 'It doesn't make much difference if you go to Eastern Europe, or if Eastern Europe – unfortunately – comes to Germany.'[98] The word 'unfortunately' betrayed Pappenheim's view of the Eastern European Jews, which was based on an unbridgeable gap between the cultures of Germany and Eastern Europe. Many German Jews, like Pappenheim, wanted imperial possessions, even welcoming the move towards colonialism in the east. They were less thrilled, however, when their new colonial subjects threatened to travel westwards, bringing their ways and mores into the very heart of Germany.

5

CELEBRATING DESTRUCTION

A feverish atmosphere gripped the industrial city of Bochum on 3 June 1916. People thronged the streets while above them the national flag fluttered from public buildings and the bells rang out across the city. Later that evening, Bochum's long-serving rabbi, Moritz David, addressed the crowd that had by now converged on the central Wilhelmsplatz. Placing the sober, religious language of his usual sermons to one side, David instead spoke in highly patriotic terms. He celebrated Germany's 'colossal hammer blow against the English dragon, which had been ruling the waves' and then praised the kaiser and Admiral von Tirpitz for their military leadership. 'There was once the song: Rule Britannia, Britannia rule the waves', David joked, 'but now and in the future, the only refrain is: *Deutschland über alles*.' This was the just the prompt the crowd had been waiting for; David's speech ended with nationalist songs ringing through the streets.[1]

The catalyst for these scenes was the first and only significant naval clash of the war, the battle of Jutland (or in German mouths, the *Skagerrakschlacht*). On paper this was a clear German victory – six British capital ships (and only two German) had been sent to the bottom of the North Sea – hence the celebrations in Bochum and other towns. However, as the German High Seas Fleet would spend the remainder of the war once again docked in port, it can hardly be described as an overwhelming victory. The battle itself was far more gruesome than the carnivalesque crowds in Bochum may have initially suggested. In less than two days of fighting, 8,645 men lost their lives. Although David would not have known this, the dead included Jewish sailors serving in both the Royal Navy and Germany's Imperial Navy.[2] Numbered amongst these was

Karl Weißkopf, a medical doctor aboard the cruiser SMS *Wiesbaden*. In April, Weißkopf had written home excitedly about life at sea, which was apparently far more exhilarating than catching 'the tram to work for a few pennies'; one month later he and almost the entire ship's crew were dead.[3]

David's response reflected the type of war that Germany was now engaged in. By 1916, the conflict had mutated into a brutal fight for survival that pitted not only soldiers and modern weaponry, but also entire societies, against one another. In this context, the deaths of more than 8,500 people in a matter of hours no longer came as much of a shock. Germans, both at home and in the field, had become desensitised to the tremendous scale of death and destruction. At home, newspaper obituaries, black-clad mourners and military funerals became the norm rather than the exception. For those fighting on the frontline, death also became entirely routine. Recalling the piles of bodies that littered the front, the Jewish lawyer Max Hirschberg, who later became famous for his courtroom clashes with Hitler, remarked simply: 'People get used to everything.'[4]

This nonchalant attitude towards mass death formed a central part of Germany's wartime culture. Had someone suggested before 1914 that men would die in their thousands and that towns and cultural artefacts would be lost, most Germans would have been simply aghast. But once the war had set in, the untold scale of human and physical destruction became something not to lament, but rather to celebrate. The inversion of previous social values initially focused on military targets, the defeat of enemy troops or units. However, very quickly the targets grew. Crushing enemy businesses, homes and property, even civilians themselves, became worthy of celebration. The language of militarism, the celebration of destruction and the embrace of violence were not unique to Germany's war culture. The French press, for example, dedicated much of its energy to condemning the Germans as barbarians whose racial characteristics attuned them to selfish violence, while British intellectuals proved as adept as their German counterparts in extolling the virtues of wartime violence.[5]

As Moritz David's excitement at Germany's 'victory' at Jutland demonstrated all too clearly, members of Jewish communities also found it relatively easy to embrace Germany's new 'dynamic of destruction'. Max Liebermann's regular contributions to the journal *Kriegszeit* captured this sentiment. In one issue, he sketched an image of menacing zeppelins on a bombing raid over Britain; in a later issue, another of his images depicted German soldiers lined up, ready and willing to shoot the enemy.[6] Elsewhere, many German Jews were quick to praise the destruction of Germany's enemies, to justify the crushing of Belgium and to mock the cultural achievements of Britain and France. The renowned German-Jewish sexologist Magnus Hirschfeld, best known for his scientific reflections on same-sex relationships, took time out from his research to condemn the Entente in racial terms. On one side stood German discipline and order, he explained, and on the other 'savage and semi-civilised peoples' from the most distant of lands.[7]

The Brutality of Warfare

The willingness of people to accept the brutality of the conflict as a necessity made it extremely difficult for the country to move towards peace. Not even the ever-rising death toll proved enough to force those in power to reject the war. Despite falling living standards, the number of Germans who actually came out against the war at this stage remained tiny. The socialist Karl Liebknecht continued to condemn the war and government, setting himself on a path that only ended with his murder during the revolutionary skirmishes of 1919. For now though, his anti-war stance resulted in a prison sentence on charges of treason after he had spoken at a May Day demonstration in Berlin. While Liebknecht's opposition to the conflict was based on Marxist principles, the young Gershom Scholem's stemmed from a belief in Jewish nationalism. In a series of barbed attacks on Martin Buber, who continued to support the conflict, Scholem criticised the older Zionist's use of mystical language to justify the ongoing hostilities. As far as Scholem was concerned, the war was purely a German issue, one in which the Jews had no reason to ensnare themselves.[8]

The problem for those who, like Scholem or Liebknecht, desired peace was twofold. First, theirs were scattered, disunited voices, and second, they were very much in the minority. Their calls for peace simply vanished amidst the din of the German right. Emboldened by the military's successes in the east, their demands for further territorial expansion grew ever louder. One new and particularly noisy voice was that of Wolfgang Kapp, a government official from East Prussia. Putting his career in the bureaucracy of East Prussian agriculture to one side, Kapp rose through conservative circles during the pre-war years. As the war ground on, Kapp, who had a keen eye for populist rhetoric and public agitation, led calls for Bethmann Hollweg to step down. In spring 1916, he challenged the chancellor directly by issuing a pamphlet calling for Germany's supposedly most potent weapon, the submarine, to be unshackled. Kapp followed up this attack with other populist stunts, such as challenging Bethmann Hollweg to a duel over the war's future direction.[9]

As had been the case from the very early days of the war, it was not just figures on the German right who pushed for expansion. More moderate sections of society, including many German Jews, also hoped to see the war end with an expanded Germany. Arthur Schlossmann, a leading physician specialising in children's health in Düsseldorf, summed up this line of thinking in one of his many essays. 'There is simply no question', he began, 'that after the war, the new Germany will be a much bigger Germany.'[10] Many of Schlossmann's Jewish contemporaries in the liberal political scene agreed with such sentiments. Slightly unhelpfully perhaps, the Prussian parliamentary member Robert Friedberg suggested that Belgium had to remain in German hands. After all, 'Belgium had never been the neutral country . . . [that] it appeared to be on 4 August 1914'.[11] Turning his attention to the east, another German-Jewish parliamentarian, Otto Landsberg, suggested that annexations were a matter of national defence: 'If the annexation along the line of the River Narew is needed to improve the defence of the east, then how can any German really disagree?' This plan may have secured the existing borders, but it would have permanently placed Polish, Lithuanian and Russian territory into German hands.[12]

Whether coming from political moderates, like Schlossmann, Friedberg and Landsberg, or from right-wing agitators in the mould of Kapp, territorial expansion still remained a central war aim for many Germans. The question of annexations, then, amounted to small degrees of difference between liberals and the political right rather than a gaping ideological chasm. With the discourse of expansionism continuing to simmer, Germany's military leadership saw no real need to bring the war to a sudden end. Falkenhayn, as the current chief of the German General Staff, believed that Germany could grind out a favourable result in the west. Rathenau, whose views on the war oscillated between all-out support and deep resignation, seemed to agree with Falkenhayn's analysis of the situation. In a letter to Ludendorff, he explained that 'a result in our favour in the west' was urgently needed.[13] Rathenau and Falkenhayn's western strategy made sense in principle, but it was much harder to execute in practice.

With little prospect of an immediate military breakthrough in the west, Falkenhayn devised a more meandering route to victory. He intended to manoeuvre the British to the negotiating table not by force of arms but through staying power. Once Britain's leaders realised the war could not be won,

Falkenhayn believed, they would seek a way out of the impasse. Georg Bernhard was similarly minded. Under his stewardship, the *Vossische Zeitung* argued repeatedly that Germany needed to focus its attention on Britain rather than Russia.[14] In early 1916, Falkenhayn began to put this strategy, so favoured by Bernhard and others, into action. He proposed joint land and sea campaigns in the west. At sea, the German submarine fleet would be unleashed to deadly effect against Britain's trade routes, while on land the French army would be hit so hard that it would lose the will to fight. Without its ally, Falkenhayn argued, the British would have no choice but to sue for peace, or this at least was the plan.[15]

Falkenhayn's approach cannot be faulted for optimism. Unfortunately for him, the final plan failed to take account of the realities of Germany's military and political situation. The sea campaign never really got beyond the drawing board. Still fearful of provoking the wrath of the United States, Bethmann Hollweg only agreed to a limited submarine campaign regulated by strict rules. Submarine commanders, for example, had to check the weaponry of merchant ships before attacking, which as the Admiralty argued rather nullified the raison d'être of this silent killer. The land campaign, however, did not have to walk such a rigid political tightrope. Drawing on all his knowledge of French military tactics, Falkenhayn plotted a thunderous campaign to welcome in the New Year. The historic city of Verdun, the target of this assault, had more psychological than military value, which is why Falkenhayn hoped its loss would weaken French resolve. The resulting battle of Verdun, which rumbled on for much of 1916, became emblematic of the unending slaughter of French and German troops with almost no strategic gain to show for it.

Germany's Jewish soldiers also found themselves thrown headlong into the ravenous blades of Falkenhayn's 'Meuse mill', not just as victims, but also as killers. Indeed, there was only one reason for their presence on the battlefield and that was to kill, maim or injure as many Entente soldiers as possible.[16] Twenty years after the battle, K. Wachsner, by then a civilian in Breslau, recalled his memories of fighting at Verdun. The operation started with a 'hellish barrage' of the French positions, Wachsner remembered. This bombardment managed to flush out many of the 'frogs' who ran 'ashen-faced' towards the German positions to surrender. A few hours later, Wachsner's battalion advanced cautiously towards the French lines, unnoticed at first until suddenly bullets started to rain on them from behind. Wachsner immediately sent 'two groups to clear them out', by which he clearly meant 'shoot them'. This took care of most of the resistance, but for good measure 'a hand grenade lobbed into the trench finished off' the rest.[17] Battle, as Wachsner described it, was a cold-blooded affair: either you killed your enemies, or you and your comrades were killed yourselves.

For most Jewish soldiers, Verdun would not have been their first experience of killing. Those who had fought from the start of the conflict would have already faced the unnerving experience of shooting, bombing or bayoneting the enemy to death. When soldiers had to kill for the first time, the experience was almost always deeply harrowing. After all, for the most part these were civilians who had gone from the comforts of home to the battlefield in a matter of weeks. One month, their lives revolved around work, friends and family; the next they were in a foreign land killing other men. The German-Jewish officer Julius Marx first encountered death during the campaigns along the French border in August 1914. Lying on the side of the road, he discovered the body of a young French soldier, his back broken in two by a shell: a 'wax figure, pale, yellow'.[18] Stefan Westmann's first glimpse of a dead body was that of a man he had killed himself. During an attack on the enemy trenches, he forced his bayonet through the chest of a French corporal. After the adrenalin of battle had passed, Westmann 'felt giddy', his 'knees shook' and then he 'was actually sick'.[19]

The initial shock at having taken someone's life did not last. Very quickly, most German Jews grew accustomed to the ubiquity of death, becoming very accomplished killers along the way. After a time, Westmann, whose background was in medicine, appeared almost to relish the dangers of fighting. He later recalled in gruesome detail how he had bludgeoned a Frenchman to death in face-to-face combat. The soldier had been about to throw a grenade, when Westmann reached for a spade, whacking it down so hard on the poor man's neck that he had 'difficulty in extracting it'. After this bloody incident, Westmann found the sight of death and act of killing fairly tolerable. 'I no longer cared that I had blood over my uniform', he remembered. 'I had become hardened.'

In Westmann's memoirs, beating the enemy to death was nothing more than a necessary part of military life, of being 'a good soldier'.[20] Other Jewish soldiers imposed different narratives onto their frontline experiences. The nephew of Henriette Fürth, a women's rights campaigner, justified his attack on the enemy with guns and bayonets in rather black and white terms. It was a case of 'him or me', he remarked.[21] Martin Feist, by now based in the Picardy region of Northern France imposed a similar friend-versus-fiend dichotomy onto his experiences. After he and his comrades had used their machine gun to mow down a row of advancing French soldiers, he remarked simply: 'our task was, and still is, to defend this position'.[22] For Feist and the other German-Jewish soldiers, the precise details of the enemy were irrelevant. What was crucial in this situation was simply to repel those seeking to attack them.

It may have been easy to justify killing, but the task itself still remained brutal and bloody. On the Western Front, stinking corpses littered the battle-field; some were used to patch up trenches or floated away during periods of heavy rain.[23] There was nothing pleasant about this type of warfare. A slightly cleaner encounter with wartime death came in the skies. Jews and other Germans who served in the newly formed German air force tended to take much more pleasure in the actual act of killing than those on the ground. Strapped in several thousand metres above the carnage below, airmen utilised the latest technology to hunt down the enemy. Aerial combat pitted one pilot against the other in dramatic duels to the death. The outcome of these clashes came down to technology and to the individual pilot's skill, which was very different to the arbitrariness of death in the trenches.[24]

The number of German Jews serving in the air force was relatively small but far from negligible. In the early 1920s, Felix Theilhaber, a Berlin physician and committed Zionist, produced a book commemorating the Jewish pilots' wartime exploits. Across the pages of this slim volume, he noted the names of a hundred or so German-Jewish airmen, which gives a reasonable estimate of the number who served. These men embraced the marriage of technology and war, revelled in the thrill of aerial dogfights and generally enjoyed the close-knit camaraderie of the air force. Without question, the most famous German-Jewish pilot was Wilhelm Frankl, who by 1916 even ranked as one of the country's most successful air aces (see Plate 13). Frankl's decision to convert to Christianity in 1914 was evidence, if any were needed, that anti-Semitism also defined the chances of Jews in the air force. Before being killed in combat in April 1917, Frankl won both the Iron Cross 1st Class and the exceedingly rare Pour le Mérite. Conforming to heroic type, Frankl played down his achieve-ments as nothing more than a boys' own adventure: 'Things didn't always go so smoothly', he joked; 'my plane, which has about fifty bullet holes down it, can tell a tale or two – recently a button was even shot right off my jacket'.[25]

German Jews' combat experience made a mockery of the anti-Semitism that Frankl and other fighters faced. As the Jewish soldiers demonstrated time and time again, they could kill just as effectively as any other German. Jews fighting at the front or in the air also went into combat with the same steely-eyed determination that characterised many of the most hardened killers. To Julius Marx's astonishment, one of the most ruthless fighters in his division turned out to be Jewish. What shocked him most was 'the cold-bloodedness of this man', who repeatedly risked his own life for his men and also berated anyone who stepped out of line.[26] Marx, though, should not have been surprised at this revelation. Whether Jew or non-Jew, men were rapidly turned from civilians into ruthless killers. As the events of 1916 showed, there was no better classroom for honing the art of killing than the battle of Verdun.

Frontline Heroes

The bloodletting at Verdun was still ongoing when the Entente powers launched the next major offensive of 1916. On 1 July, the British sent eighteen divisions and the French five into action against the Germans on the Somme. Their aim was to draw German troops away from Verdun, thereby regaining the initiative on the Western Front. The strategy, though, ended in failure. Three months later, 1.1 million men from all sides had either been killed, captured or wounded. Hans Senft, ensconced in a dugout with British shells falling around him, recorded something of the ferocity of the fighting in his letters home. 'A terrible time', he wrote, 'so many losses, so many dead.'[27] One of his German-Jewish contemporaries at the front, Georg Luft, described how much of his regiment had been wiped out on the Somme. Only half of the men actually made it to the frontline proper: 'the other half were killed or wounded on the way there'.[28] As Senft's and Luft's letters back to Berlin demonstrate, Germans on the home front had a reasonable idea of the horrors of frontline fighting. They received updates from friends and family in arms, who described battles, losses and their often awful daily conditions.

However, one glaring absence from much of this correspondence was any mention of soldiers' own participation in the killing process. Both Senft and Luft openly discussed the loss of their own comrades in the fighting on the Somme, but, when it came to their participation in the deaths of British and French soldiers, they remained silent. Theirs was a fairly typical response. Understandably perhaps, in their conversations with civilians, soldiers very rarely delved into the precise role they themselves played in the slaughter of the enemy.[29] In this one area in particular, then, there existed a fundamental disconnect between the home front and the frontline. Many of those in the army, though by no means all, had to kill. Those on the home front did their best to overlook this aspect of the war. It was one thing to live with the knowledge that their brothers or sons might die at the front, quite another to imagine them as trained killers.

Sidestepping the thorny issue of killing required nothing more than a judicious reframing of war stories. Instead of discussing the brutality of frontline life, Germans at home emphasised a vaguer set of fairly indisputable values: the soldiers at the front were brave and heroic patriots, certainly not bloodthirsty killers. Prayers given by Rabbi Nehemiah Anton Nobel in Frankfurt's Börneplatz Synagogue were fairly typical in this respect. Nobel spoke of the 'bravery' of the German soldiers at the front, who were simply fighting for 'freedom and justice'.[30] Abraham Glaßberg, a communal official in Berlin's Jewish community, went further in his own wartime prayer collection, though he still managed to avoid any direct descriptions of killing. 'Punish our wanton enemies and sentence them for their arrogance', he appealed to God.[31] The Jewish students in the Kartell-Convent drew from a similar set of innocuous idioms. When the organisation introduced an illustration for the front cover of its wartime journal, it settled on a classically styled sketch of three men striding into battle (see Plate 14). The figures might have been armed, but their weapons of choice – daggers rather than machine guns – harked back to an earlier, more innocent age. With their naked bodies and rippling muscles, these were supposed to be heroic warriors, not brutalised killers.[32]

The militaristic values in which the Kartell-Convent revelled held a similar allure for other German Jews. Nahum Goldmann, who later rose to become the president of the World Jewish Congress, declared German militarism to be a positive value worth celebrating. In a lengthy essay that the government distributed widely, Goldmann maintained that a 'Spirit of Militarism' had helped to shape modern Germany. Military values, such as duty and obedience, provided a framework around which the nation could coalesce. Pitted against Germany's militaristic culture were the weaker values of individualism and self that prevailed in France. In Goldmann's eyes, there could only be one outcome of this clash: 'militarism will lead the struggle and will be victorious', he concluded.[33] Goldmann's essay made such an impression on the officials in the Foreign Ministry that they recruited him for propaganda work, quite a result for a Polish-born Jew who had yet to attain full German citizenship.[34]

The public celebration of heroism and military values helped to blind people to some of the worst horrors of the war. It proved far easier to focus on rather trivial items related to the war than on mass killings at the front. For this reason, wartime Germany witnessed a boom in kitsch war memorabilia that encompassed humorous postcards of soldierly life, frivolous souvenirs for the home and special wartime board games.[35] J.W. Spear in Nuremberg, which was owned by a local German-Jewish family, produced a series of war-related games. Puzzles adorned with the heads of Hindenburg and the kaiser or board games that pitched German soldiers against a dastardly enemy all proved bestsellers.[36] Like many other Germans, Theodor Wolff's family failed to escape this commodification of the conflict. One Christmas, Wolff's young sons received toy soldiers' uniforms and military hampers as presents. Although Wolff disapproved, it did at least mean that his sons could play 'trenches' with the other children of Berlin.[37]

There was surely no greater symbol of wartime kitsch than the 'Iron Hindenburg' statue in Berlin. In September 1915, Princess August Wilhelm unveiled this monumental wooden sculpture of the revered general to a crowd of over 20,000 onlookers. Towering some 12 metres into the sky, the figure of Hindenburg dominated the neighbouring Victory Column that had been dedicated in the wake of the nineteenth-century Wars of Unification. The new structure stole some of the allure from its more illustrious neighbour to hint at a victory still to come, while in the meantime serving as an important fundraising tool. For the cost of one Mark, the public could purchase a nail to hammer into Hindenburg. Those with more disposable income were invited to buy a golden nail at the cost of 100 Marks. Smashing nails into this wooden effigy of Hindenburg was apparently a sign of the public's affection for the general, rather than an act of malice. All funds raised went towards supporting Germany's growing number of war widows.[38]

Such was the popularity of these 'nail figures' that examples sprang up all over Germany. An iron eagle in Frankfurt joined an iron lion in Düsseldorf, which itself followed Kiel's iron submarine.[39] Unperturbed by the trivialisation of the horror of war, German Jews joined the hammering crowds across Germany. In the Franconian city of Bamberg, Emma Hellmann, a local charity activist, even gifted the statue of a large wooden knight to the city. Holding a lance, sword and shield, the figure helped to place Germany's current fight within a longer line of defensive struggles. During 1916, the figure became something of a focal point for local clubs and societies who would gather on the central Marxplatz to hammer in nails.[40] Elsewhere, the Viennese Hilfskommission für Palästina sought to apply the spirit of these nail figures to a synagogue setting. As a means to raise funds for poverty-stricken Jews in Palestine, it urged communities to place a wooden Star of David in their synagogues. The congregation could then buy nails to hammer into the sculpture.[41]

The Hilfskommission's rather incongruous plan may have been for a specifically Jewish cause, but nonetheless, it demonstrated particularly clearly the spread of Germany's wartime culture. The process of trivialising war seeped into every pore of German society, from its more extreme fringes through into Jewish communities themselves. However, none of these examples of wartime culture, whether the published lists of medals or Hellmann's iron knight sculpture, should be seen as a direct celebration of frontline militarism, death and destruction. Any hint of the brutality of war and the act of killing had been filtered out to leave vaguer representations of the war's harsh realities behind. In this sense, then, these objects provided an easier way for people to digest the ongoing conflict without the need to choke on the true horrors of modern industrialised warfare.

The Cult of the Fallen

The combined death toll for the battles of Verdun and the Somme was staggering. German losses alone stood at some 833,000. Herbert Hirsch at first managed to avoid having his name added to this horrific roll-call of death. Sadly, however, just as his family back in Mannheim were presumably toasting their good fortune, catastrophe struck. Hirsch was killed in fighting near the Somme, a few weeks after his twenty-second birthday. A letter from another member of the regiment gave Hirsch's mother further details of her son's untimely death. Apparently Hirsch's death was instantaneous: 'he fell silently to the ground'. A short time later, the letter explained, Rabbi Martin Salomonski presided over an elaborate frontline funeral, which saw Hirsch buried in a proper coffin and his grave covered in fresh flowers.[42] This letter contained all the basic ingredients of a veritable cult of the fallen that took hold in Germany and elsewhere during the First World War.[43] Fallen heroes, families were told, received honourable burials after suffering at worst a gentle, painless death. Unfortunately, the reality tended to be very different.

Death at the front took many forms. Falling shells sliced through flesh, ripping soldiers into pieces. Where a man stood one minute, a muddy crater occupied the spot the next. Others ended their days mown down by machine gun-fire or taken out by a sniper's bullet. Sometimes aeroplanes swooped down, smashing men's bodies into bloody pieces with bullets and bombs.[44] One poor individual – a Jewish soldier from the Rhineland – took his own life, like many others. Seeing his legs had been blown off by a shell, the soldier picked up his revolver and fatally shot himself.[45] The claim, therefore, that Hirsch 'fell silently' to the ground presumably overlooked the sheer horror of his death. He had actually died after shrapnel from an exploding landmine tore into him. The raw metal fragments ripping through Hirsch's body would have resulted in a horrifically painful death set against the backdrop of a noisy battlefield environment. Certainly, this would have been very different to the peaceful slipping away described in the letter to his mother.

The military leadership was not particularly concerned to know how individual soldiers lost their lives. Once dead, they could no longer fire a weapon and as such were of no further use to the war effort. Nonetheless, something still had to happen to the soldiers' remains, presuming at least that there was a body to bury. Those killed were fortunate if they received a burial at all, let alone a dignified one. At the front, where disease prevention was paramount, mass graves often had to be used. Even further behind the lines, burials could be swift, impersonal and clinical. One German-Jewish nurse looked on appalled as three dead German soldiers were put to rest in a military cemetery. The priest eventually turned up, 'blessed the dead with a few words . . . and then disappeared'. After that, the coffins were simply buried in the ground 'without any great ado'. There was nobody else in the cemetery to bear witness and nobody seemed to care. 'Seen close-up, a hero's death is not quite as beautiful', she reflected afterwards.[46]

The burials that this frontline nurse witnessed were at least conducted in the presence of a military chaplain. This was not always the case. Rabbis were spread so thinly at the front that it proved impossible for them to reach every Jewish serviceman killed. Instead, they often had to rely on their Christian colleagues for assistance. Whenever Rabbi Emil Kronheim knew that he would be unable to get to a funeral on time, for example, he generally managed to find either a Protestant or Catholic chaplain to officiate on his behalf. In return, he occasionally ended up standing in at funeral services for Christian soldiers.[47]

Just as the Jewish war dead were fortunate to receive a dignified funeral officiated by a rabbi, they were also lucky to receive a suitable grave marker. Given the suddenness of frontline death, burial parties dealt with the dead as swiftly as possible, generally placing a Christian cross atop burial mounds before moving on.[48] This is not to say that other forms of grave marker were completely absent. Where time and space allowed, a Star of David sometimes appeared above the graves of the Jewish dead. After fierce fighting around the Aisne in early 1914, two of the German-Jewish casualties were buried under small stone headstones bearing the common Hebrew burial inscription: 'May his soul be bound up in the bond of eternal life.' Surrounding them a sea of Christian crosses for the other German dead stretched into the distance.[49]

The choice of headstone turned into a central issue for German Jews. There was understandably considerable concern that the Jewish soldiers' sacrifice was being forgotten in death. 'For the joiner making a cross', remarked one frontline soldier, 'it is no more effort . . . to carve a simple plaque or a Star of David.' He urged the army rabbis to take steps to ensure this practice was adopted across all fronts.[50] In actual fact, the rabbis had already started to address these very concerns. In September 1916, rabbis on the Western Front agreed that 'a cross over a Jewish fighter's grave is unacceptable', although the Iron Cross was deemed to be 'acceptable'.[51]

Not all German Jews approved of this policy. The soldiers fighting at the front, in particular, often failed to see any problem with the use of a cross over Jewish graves. For them, the cross represented military pride and unity; in battle it had apparently been shorn of its previous Christian symbolism.[52] One family even had their son's body exhumed and moved from the Jewish to the Christian cemetery, so that he could lie next to his comrades. This was something of a snub for the army rabbi who had gone to great lengths to arrange the original Jewish funeral. Somewhat aggrieved, the rabbi suggested that from now on he would 'ask every sick person where exactly he wants to be buried!'[53]

This relatively minor disagreement between a bereaved family and an army rabbi went far beyond the issue of headstones. Their discussions also reflected a much deeper divide as to how the home front and the frontlines understood wartime death. Death in battle was always a messy and rather chaotic affair. Yet when mediated back to the home front, death took on a cleaner form. This mismatch formed part of the grieving process. The mother of Herbert Hirsch, for example, had nothing to gain from learning that her son's reportedly quick, painless death had actually been a long-drawn-out affair clouded in screams and blood. Coming to terms with mass death required a workable narrative of individual loss that masked the gruesome details of wartime death.

The narrative that Germans at home increasingly settled upon focused on the heroism of military death. Jews embraced this 'cult of the fallen' with no less passion than any other German. Newspapers brimmed with black-bordered obituaries mourning the loss of individual Jewish soldiers who had suffered a 'hero's death for the fatherland' or had made a 'sacrifice for the fatherland'.[54] Similarly vague euphemisms reappeared during home front funerals. On one chilly November morning in Hamburg, a crowd gathered in the main Jewish cemetery to mourn David Wolff, an army doctor who had lost his life in Flanders. After Wolff's coffin had been carried into the service, resplendent with his Iron Cross, helmet and sabre, the mourners were told to take comfort in the knowledge that Wolff had 'experienced the most beautiful death, a death for the fatherland'.[55] Over the space of this short ceremony, what must have been a truly gruesome death was transformed into something far more poetic. The extravagance of Wolff's funeral continued into the actual landscape of Hamburg's Ohlsdorf cemetery, where a special area was set aside for the war's Jewish 'heroes'.[56]

This fascination with the trappings of military death also provided Jewish communities with a means to assert publicly their commitment to the war. There was perhaps no more poignant rejoinder to anti-Semitic sniping than the long rows of Jewish soldiers' headstones in home-town cemeteries, lined up one after the next as if the men were still on parade. For this reason, Jewish communities were always keen to send out a long list of invitations to remembrance events.[57] Guests at Wolff's funeral included prominent academics who had previously worked with him, as well as members of the Hamburg parliament. Yet convincing local dignitaries of Jewish loyalties was never the main catalyst for German Jews' ready immersion in the wartime 'cult of the fallen'. Instead, their acquiescence in these popular narratives was about transcendence. If the horrors of military death were to be overcome, then each individual war victim's sacrifice for the nation needed to be publicly venerated.

The Wounds of War

Handling the dead proved far easier than dealing with the living. The dead could be quickly buried and their relatives comforted with tales of heroic daring. In contrast, the conflict's other casualties were not so easily silenced. The missing and the war-wounded hovered around the military's campaigns, casting a dark shadow on proceedings. Yet the conflict's 'living war memorials', as Joseph Roth sagely called them, could not simply be ignored.[58] In the First World War, these other categories of wartime casualties far outnumbered those actually killed. Touring one of many military infirmaries, Rabbi Georg Salzberger discovered German Jews with a whole range of injuries and illnesses. Some of the injuries also came from German rather than enemy hands. One soldier had held onto a hand grenade for too long; another had been kicked in the body by a startled horse; and yet another had accidentally shot himself.[59] Jewish community organisations within Germany took on much of the physical burden. Healing the wounded and also seeking out those who had been captured turned into a major wartime activity.

In the wake of battle, medical orderlies rounded up the casualties the best they could. The lightly wounded could be patched up there and then in frontline dressing stations and field hospitals. Unfortunately these facilities could not always offer the wounded much of a refuge from the dangers of war. Rosa Bendit, a Jewish nurse who served in both the east and the west, noted the hazards facing frontline medics. From her hospital, she could catch sight of troops passing through the ruined landscape on their way into battle, while her ears grew accustomed to the sound of 'terrible shooting'.[60] What Bendit's diary entries highlight is how close women actually were to the fighting. The notion of an impenetrable divide separating the male frontline from a female home front certainly no longer holds true.[61]

Many of the wounded who ended up in the care of Bendit and others spent only a brief time in the field hospitals. Hospital trains, which were equipped with a team of doctors, nurses and medical supplies, shuttled back and forth between Germany and the frontline transporting those with the most severe wounds back home for more intensive treatment. The B'nai B'rith Lodge raised some 150,000 Marks to fund and equip one of these trains, which proudly bore the lodge's name on its side.[62] One Jewish soldier who returned to Germany after an operation on his colon had nothing but praise for the lodge's new facility. It was 'better than the first-class compartment of an express train', he wrote proudly. 'The train travelled so quietly, even the stopping and departing were done in almost complete silence.'[63] Due to the logistics of the railway system, the hospital trains generally arrived in urban centres, from where the patients were distributed to specialist hospitals depending on the severity of their wounds.

These destinations included the Jewish hospitals in Hamburg, Munich and Fürth, as well as the Berlin Jewish community's new medical facility in Gesundbrunnen. In early 1916, 41 of this hospital's 225 patients were from the armed forces.[64] The less seriously wounded could be returned quickly to the army or to a role on the home front. But for others their stay in hospital was only the start of a much longer journey of recovery. Amputees, whose numbers ran into the thousands, received crude artificial limbs from special advisory centres, while some of the war-blinded ended up in Berlin's new school for the blind, which had been established in November 1914. Its directors, the optometrist Paul Silex and the German-Jewish singer Betty Hirsch, who was herself blind, fought resolutely to help these men rebuild their lives. Silex and Hirsch's work was as much about helping the soldiers to come to terms with their new status as it was about actual training. Those who eventually left their care gained jobs as factory workers, cigar-makers, machinists or even as masseurs.[65]

In Berlin, a small group of German Jews, led by the cancer specialist Carl Lewin, were confident that they had found their own solution to the growing number of Jewish wounded. The Aid Association for Jewish War-wounded Soldiers (Hilfsbund für Kriegsbeschädigte jüdische Soldaten), as the group named itself, put forward plans to build a Jewish recovery centre deep in the hills of central Germany. If the war-wounded were ever to recover fully, the Aid Association argued, then they needed to escape the constraints of daily life. It was only out in the countryside that both a 'psychological and physical recovery' could occur. While the authorities accepted this argument, they were less convinced by the specifically Jewish character of the centre. They questioned why a home for Jewish soldiers was required, when the German Red Cross already provided kosher food to the wounded on request.[66]

In any case, the Aid Association's proposals painted a rather optimistic picture of the war-wounded soldiers' long-term prospects. Fresh air in a rural setting was supposed to help each individual's 'healing, relief and recovery'. Yet, as the public realised only too well, many of the most severely wounded could never be turned back into healthy male citizens. Capturing the grim horrors of human destruction fell onto the shoulders of a small group of expressionist artists. Undoubtedly shaped by their own military experiences, these painters placed the human cost of war under a grim spotlight. Max Beckmann, Georg Grosz and Otto Dix, with their shocking depictions of the war-wounded (particularly those produced later during the Weimar Republic), are surely the best known of Germany's war artists.

However, it was the less prominent German-Jewish artist, Ludwig Meidner, who first sought to capture the deep, unhealable, wounds of war in ink. Meidner was a short, squat man with an intense stare. Although some straggly tufts of hair around his balding pate gave the impression of maturity, he had in fact only just turned thirty at the start of hostilities. Unlike many of his contemporaries in Berlin's expressionist scene, Meidner was staunchly opposed to the conflict from the very start. His pacifist ideals found dreadful confirmation when his closest friend, the poet Ernst Wilhelm Lotz, died at the front in September 1914. Anti-war themes had always run as a thread through Meidner's work, being present even during the pre-war years of peace. His 1911 drawing, 'Horrors of War' ('Schrecken des Krieges'), for example, depicted three naked warriors shorn not only of their clothes but also of various limbs. The bare stumps that remained testified to the brutal horror of conflict.[67]

With the outbreak of the First World War, Meidner's apocalyptic vision went into overdrive. The first months of the war saw him produce a series of paintings and sketches depicting the destructive potential of modern warfare. In 'Battle' ('Schlacht') from 1914, an exploding shell throws a series of limbs, bones and bodies spiralling around the centre of the canvas, before spilling over the very edges of the frame (see Plate 15). The clash between artillery and human flesh remained a theme in many of Meidner's early wartime drawings, including 'Canon (111)' ('Kanone (III)') and 'Explosion on the Bridge' ('Explosion auf der Brücke'), which also shows damaged bodies and burning buildings. The vision was even more apocalyptic in 'Judgment Day' ('Der jüngste Tag'), in which Meidner depicts a bloodstained landscape, inhabited by a few confused, maimed survivors huddling at the edge of the canvas.

Thankfully, Meidner's apocalyptic image had yet to become reality. But nonetheless, German society experienced increasingly large physical and financial voids as the number of men missing, killed or severely wounded continued to rise. Käthe Herzberg, a young Jewish woman from Westphalia, had lost two of her brothers in quick succession during 1915: Paul had been killed by a shell in France and Hermann later in Poland. With the screams of her mother still ringing in her ears, Käthe could only watch on as other pillars of her life started to crumble. Her father – the patriarch of both home and the local synagogue – died a few months after her brothers. Her sister, who had three young children, was unable to help, so suddenly the pressure of leading what remained of the family fell on Käthe. Her grandfather implored her to give up her job with the industrial firm, Miele: 'Your mother can't manage on her own', she was told. Although Käthe 'enjoyed the work' and even more so the income, piles of washing, ironing and a mother 'mit den Nerven herunter' (who was 'a bundle of nerves') induced her to quit. In this case, the war had brought not greater female emancipation, but less.[68]

Deprived of their main male breadwinner – or in the case of the Herzbergs, breadwinners – many households had to get by on a much-reduced income. As one Jewish social activist explained, small military pensions could never cover the needs of children, a mother and grandparents too. What was 'an old soul, perhaps bowed by illness, weakness and suffering' supposed to do, she asked.[69] The biggest fear amongst Germans was one of moral and social decline. Siddy Wronsky, another Jewish social campaigner, explained that the sudden loss of money for 'the better sections of the working classes and those self-employed' could mean a 'drop back into the proletariat'.[70] For some women, this scenario appeared very real. It became a common occurrence to see small advertisements in newspapers from war widows seeking an income. 'War widow seeks work in a solid Jewish household', ran one such notice in Cologne.[71]

In an attempt to avoid a breakdown of the existing social order, several private charitable organisations stepped in to fill the gaps in the state's provision. The National Foundation for the Relatives of Those Killed in the War (Nationalstiftung für die Hinterbliebenen der im Kriege Gefallenen), which had the backing of several wealthy German Jews including Albert Ballin, Max Warburg and Rudolf Mosse, came into existence during the early days of the conflict. Its express aim was to provide short-term financial support to war widows until they could earn enough money to support themselves and their families.[72] Jewish communities also took a role in the National Foundation's local fundraising activities. In the Rhineland town of Elberfeld, for example, German Jews staged an afternoon concert featuring the full synagogue choir, again with all funds going to the bereaved.[73] Unfortunately charitable funds on their own were not enough to rebuild the thousands upon thousands of destroyed lives. Husbands and fathers were not so easily replaced and for the wounded, with destroyed limbs and broken bodies, recovery was destined to be a long, difficult process.

In Prison with the Enemy

Like the severely wounded, the war's thousands of captured soldiers also faced an uncertain future. When the choice was between death or severe mutilation and capture, then being taken prisoner was clearly by far the most palatable option. Capture, though, was far from an easy option. Jittery soldiers on both sides had been known to kill men trying to surrender or in some cases even after they had been captured.[74] The first thing that Theodor Rosenthal knew about his surrender was when a grenade landed in his trench, followed by two 'Tommys' who stood before him holding revolvers. The British soldiers stole his silver watch, a bar mitzvah present, then sent him behind the lines to join other captives.[75] As Rosenthal immediately discovered, degradation, violence and fear were essential parts of the prisoner experience.[76] Being captured may have removed the daily threat of frontline death, but in its place new dangers emerged. Those interned were left with little option but to see out the conflict living amidst their enemy's hostile war culture.

Before they were officially listed as prisoners of war, many soldiers lived somewhere in limbo. The journey to one of the many POW camps could take anything from a few days to several weeks.[77] For families at home, still unsure whether their loved ones were alive or dead, this was a dreadful time. Theodor Rosenthal's wife had been left waiting so long for news that friends even advised her to forget him. 'She was still young; she would find another man in time', they counselled.[78] This sense of uncertainty and unknowing was one that Max Pinkus also experienced. Pinkus, the German-Jewish director of a large Upper Silesian textile concern, received news in the post that his son Hans had disappeared without trace while patrolling along the France–Belgium border. Unsure of how to proceed, Max sent a series of desperate letters to the military authorities and to Hans's fellow officers. Max eventually discovered that on the night of his son's disappearance, seven members of the twenty-man patrol had been killed outright; the remainder had possibly been captured.[79] A further week of uncertainty passed before confirmation came through that Hans had indeed been taken as a prisoner of war and was now being held in a French camp.[80]

These weeks of uncertainty left a deep mark on Max. Long after Hans had been located, Max continued to assist other families with missing sons. He wrote to the Danish Red Cross asking them to help locate one of his long-serving employees' sons; another set of letters beseeched the German navy to investigate the fate of a sailor missing in Tsingtau.[81] Finding the missing and caring for the POWs required an international effort. The International Committee of the Red Cross led the way in this respect, creating a sophisticated card system to list the millions of prisoners scattered across Europe.[82] The organisation also distributed food and aid to prisoners from both sides as well as maintaining an inspection system of the larger camps.

The work of the International Committee of the Red Cross and its regional agencies offered one small glimmer of light in a landscape otherwise bereft of humanitarianism. Once entrenched in camps, though, few POWs found much to cheer. Theodor Rosenthal's long journey into captivity finally ended in Colsterdale in North Yorkshire. As it was a camp specifically designed for officers, conditions in Colsterdale were generally of a higher standard than many of the other larger camps scattered throughout Britain. Nonetheless, life in Colsterdale very quickly took its toll. Boredom, cramped conditions and poor food – Chinese bacon and the occasional bits of 'meat of dead horses' – offered neither comfort nor calories. When the limited options for exercise and entertainment were also thrown into the mix, then it is easy to see why so many prisoners suffered from 'barbed-wire sickness' (*Stacheldraht-Krankheit*); this was a term devised by a Swiss doctor to describe the psychological impact of captivity.[83]

What surely would have helped to reduce incidences of 'barbed-wire sickness' amongst the Orthodox Jewish POWs was access to kosher food, prayer books and tefillin. On the Isle of Man, where the largest British camps were housed, provision for such Jewish prisoners was made. But in the smaller

1 At the start of hostilities, Willy Liemann, a young German-Jewish student, rides off for the front, as his friends Fritz and Emma Schlesinger run alongside.

Die Wiener Note.

Wie Serbien sie erwartet hatte —

und wie Österreich sie blies.

2 The German-Jewish illustrator, Walter Trier, sketches Serbia's shock at receiving Austria's ultimatum in July 1914. As Trier suggests, Serbia had hoped that the Austrians' mood music was going to be of a very different tune.

3 Max Liebermann, the Impressionist artist, captures the apparent mood of unity that gripped Germany at the start of hostilities. Here, the crowds outside the royal palace in Berlin blur into one whole, as they listen to the kaiser's famous words: 'I no longer recognise any parties …'

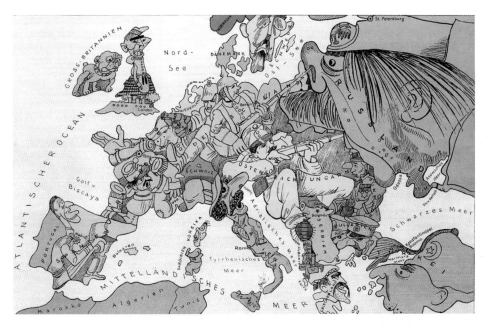

4 Walter Trier's 'Map of Europe in 1914' is one of many satirical takes on the geographical repercussions of war. In Trier's rendering, two neatly uniformed Germans defend their position in the centre, while all around a dishevelled group of enemies go on the attack.

5 According to Max Liebermann's sketch, the German military was striding off to battle ready to crush the enemy. The belligerent caption below reads 'Now we will thrash them'.

6 Louis Oppenheim, a successful German-Jewish graphic artist, refutes accusations of German barbarism in illustrative form. His poster places Germany ahead of Britain and France in spending on social insurance and schooling. It also leads in book publishing, patents and Nobel Prizes, whilst at the same time apparently having far lower rates of illiteracy.

7 Leopold Halberstadt, a Jewish soldier in a Hessian infantry regiment, sent his young daughter, Regina, a humorous postcard mocking British attempts to starve the Germans into submission. Surrounded by fresh meat, there is little sign that these hearty men were on the brink of starvation.

Jüdischer Gottesdienst im Felde
(Feldrabbiner: Dr. Sonderling, Hamburg)
Laut Armeebefehl S. M. des Deutschen Kaisers vom 29./30. September 1914

8 From early on in the war, the German military allowed rabbis to attend to the needs of Jewish soldiers at the front. In this postcard, Rabbi Jacob Sonderling, dressed in military uniform, holds a Yom Kippur service on the Eastern Front.

9 Rabbi Sonderling stands side-by-side with his Catholic and Protestant military colleagues. The image aims to give the impression that all faiths were equal in wartime Germany.

10 Robert Ehrmann, who fought on the Eastern Front, captures this scene of his Jewish co-religionists searching for salt amidst the ruins of battle.

11 For the German occupation army in Eastern Europe, life settled into a steady, and at times comfortable, routine. Magnus Zeller's sketch shows Hermann Struck and Sammy Gronemann visiting Hans Goslar, the editor of the Lithuanian newspaper *Dabartis*, in Kaunas.

12 Hermann Struck made a series of sketches of everyday life in occupied Eastern Europe. In this image, he depicts a hardworking Jewish coachman standing ready to hurtle down the potholed streets.

13 During the war, the Berlin firm W. Sanke produced a collection of postcards of German fighter aces. Wilhelm Frankl, one of a number of German-Jewish pilots, sits at ease with his medals clearly on display.

K.C.BLÄTTER
MONATSSCHRIFT·DER·IM·KARTELL·
CONVENT·VEREINIGTEN·KORPORATIONEN

Kriegsausgabe   März-April 1915   4. Heft

14 The Jewish students' organisation Kartell-Convent published a war edition of its newspaper throughout the conflict. A heroic picture of three classically drawn figures charging into battle was selected for the title page.

15 During the first year of the war, the German-Jewish artist Ludwig Meidner produced a collection of apocalyptic landscapes. As in this drawing, 'Battle' ('Schlacht'), Meidner focuses on the horrors of conflict, with bodies, limbs and explosions spiralling out of the picture.

16 Rudolf Marcuse, a prominent Berlin Jewish sculptor, was a frequent visitor to the prisoner of war camps that surrounded the German capital. His wartime work depicts the wide variety of people locked behind wire, such as this Scotsman dressed in a kilt.

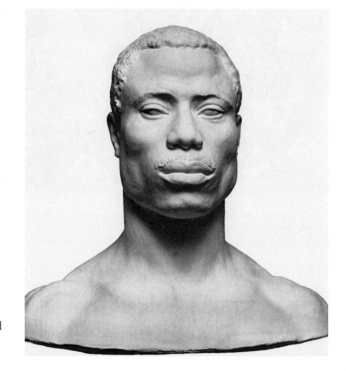

17 Another of Rudolf Marcuse's sculptures is simply titled 'Nigger from Liberia'. Minus torso and military uniform, this figure is simply a means to capture generalised 'racial' characteristics of an imagined West African.

18 Following the suicide of his first wife, the prize-winning chemist Fritz Haber married Charlotte Nathan in 1917. Here, the groom, proudly wearing his German military uniform, steps out of the Kaiser Wilhelm Memorial Church in Berlin, while his son, Hermann, looks on.

19 A light-hearted moment on the frozen Eastern Front as Robert Ehrmann play-fights with one of his comrades.

20 The setting was much warmer, but the picture of comrades relaxing was very similar. Max Haller, a German-Jewish submariner, dips his feet in the Adriatic during a break in the underwater campaign.

21 In the midst of the German spring 1918 offensive, the German-Jewish soldier Richard Schönmann sent this postcard home. A stern Ludendorff looks out, uttering the steely words 'Without sacrifice, there will be no victory! Without victory, there will be no peace!'

22 Another Louis Oppenheim poster focuses on German successes on the Western Front in 1918, highlighting the number of prisoners captured, the tanks, machine guns and artillery pieces taken, and the territory occupied.

Der erste Mona
deutsche Westoffensive!

127000 Gefangene

1600 Geschütze   ca 200 Tanks

Geländegewinn 4100 □Kilometer

Viele 1000 Maschinen= gewehre

Ungeheure Mengen an Munition u. zahlreiche Flugzeuge

23 Emphasising Jewish achievements in battle, the *Israelitisches Familienblatt* pictures the most recent recipients of the Iron Cross 1st Class.

24 Members of the Garde-Kavallerie-Schützen division enjoy a drink after murdering the communist politicians Rosa Luxemburg and Karl Liebknecht. It is unclear whether Rudolf Liepmann is in the image. Liepmann, a German-Jewish war veteran, increasingly aligned himself with reactionary forces after the conflict.

25 This poster – again from the hand of Louis Oppenheim – illustrates 'what we will lose' under the Treaty of Versailles. The different shading on the individual drawings shows in graphic form the percentage of German territory, population, coal, iron ore and food reserves to be sacrificed under the peace terms.

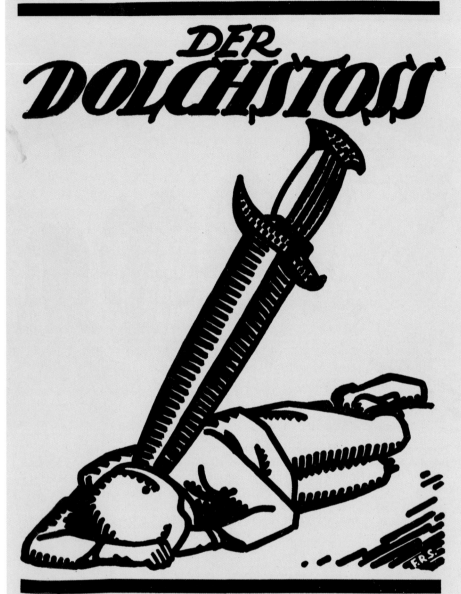

Süddeutsche Monatshefte
Heft 7. Jahrg. 21   April 1924

DER DOLCHSTOSS

Süddeutsche Monatshefte G. m. b. H., München
Preis Goldmark 1.10.

26 The title page of Paul Nikolaus Cossmann's *Süddeutsche Monatshefte* offers a provocative take on the 'stab in the back' myth. Although no hand holds the oversized dagger, the implication from within the journal is that the German military was undermined by socialists.

camps, such as Colsterdale or Handforth, south of Manchester, this was not the case. Jewish prisoners in Handforth could not even turn to Manchester's Jewish community for help, as its interest in the camp ceased when the last of the Jewish civilian internees left in late 1915.[84] In 1916, a National Federation for Jewish Prisoner of War Care (Reichsverband für jüdische Kriegsgefangenenfürsorge) was established in Berlin with the aim of filling some of these gaps in prisoners' spiritual care. Perhaps fearful lest it be thought that Jewish prisoners were gaining some kind of advantage over other German internees, the group was careful to stress that its care was 'not in addition to the normal food, but was rather a replacement'.[85]

In contrast to the situation in Britain, Jewish communities in Germany had a much closer, though not necessarily smoother, relationship to the POWs in their midst. By 1915, each of Germany's main POW camps had an assigned rabbi.[86] Responsibility for the Grafenwöhr POW camp in the Upper Palatinate district of Bavaria, for example, fell to Magnus Weinberg, who was a budding local historian, as well as rabbi to the community of Neumarkt. Weinberg diligently visited the Jewish POWs in Grafenwöhr on a regular basis, even though this meant several hours of extra travelling per week.[87] Caring for the ever-growing number of Jewish POWs not only added to Weinberg's and the other rabbis' already busy diaries, but also carried great financial costs for the German-Jewish communities. The rabbinates of Munich and Ansbach calculated that these duties cost the community an extra 13,000 Marks per year.[88] In Neumarkt, Weinberg appealed to the good nature of local German Jews for help. But in the midst of war, when food was scarce and inflation rising, it is not clear whether his plea met with any sort of success.[89]

The burden of caring for the Jewish prisoners was apparently alleviated by the knowledge that a shared sense of Jewishness improved the wellbeing of those held in captivity. In the East Prussian town of Heilsberg, a group of some 140 Russian-Jewish prisoners reportedly struck up a very strong relationship with the existing Jewish community, who donated food and cigarettes. The town's synagogue also became something of a shared spaced, with Rabbi Felix Perles holding services for both the local Jewish population and the Jewish POWs at the same time.[90] Elsewhere, Rabbi Max Simonsohn from Breslau was even more effusive about the new relationships that had developed between German Jews and Jewish prisoners. He explained how he had been overcome with a sense of 'pure joy' when two Jewish POWs had asked to meet with him: 'The happiness of being able to sit at a Jewish table after so many long months was plastered all over their faces', he explained. It 'almost robbed them of their voices'.[91]

Yet for all their successes at POW care, the German rabbis also encountered considerable difficulties. Often they went about their task with an innate sense of national superiority, looking down condescendingly at their defeated enemy. Many of the French-Jewish POWs were so incensed by this attitude that they simply chose to stay away from religious services altogether.[92] Magnus Weinberg's efforts at bridge-building, for example, badly collapsed when he explained to one unfortunate POW that the French had no chance of winning the war. 'He [the French POW] then covered his face and wept bitterly', remarked Weinberg.[93] On the surface, at least, the Russian prisoners seemed more forthcoming. They did actually manage to turn up for Jewish services at least. But then as one rabbi from Hanover complained, the Russian POWs were never that interested in the actual religious service. Instead, it was the promise of lining their stomachs with a hearty kosher meal that drew them into the arms of the visiting rabbis.[94] In another German POW camp, this time close to the Dutch border, it was a different group of Jewish POWs who failed to get on. Polish-Jewish prisoners, who apparently viewed themselves as 'culturally superior' to the Russian Jews, wanted nothing to do with these other co-religionists locked up in the camp.[95]

The German rabbinate viewed its care of the POWs as a sign of transnational Jewish identity. Russian, British and French Jews, who shared the same religious beliefs, found themselves alone in Germany, so it was almost a given that their co-religionists would step in to help. Yet the reality was often very different. The German rabbis' best efforts all too often failed, as the POWs were relegated to the role of vanquished foe. Rabbi Laser Weingarten from Bad Ems, for example, enraged the French-Jewish POWs by telling them that Germany was fighting a legitimate war, before giving the Russian Jews only the briefest of sermons. 'These people would never understand decent German', he complained, in a vain attempt to justify his actions.[96] This heady mix of chauvinism and national belligerence ridiculed the idea of wartime Jewish unity. Instead it only confirmed the way in which German Jews immersed themselves in the deadly dynamics of Germany's wartime culture. Many Jews celebrated the military's increasingly minor victories, revelled in wartime kitsch and mourned the dead as 'fallen' heroes. Even the slaughter of Verdun and the Somme failed to halt this momentum; mass killing, death and destruction had become an accepted part of Jews' and other Germans' daily lives.

6

THE 'OTHER'

From the earliest days of the conflict, definitions of 'friend' and 'foe' had been in constant flux. The Italians, for example, became a new foe in May 1915 when they joined the side of the Entente, while perceptions of Bulgarians went in the other direction after they allied themselves with Germany, Austria-Hungary and Turkey later in 1915. The constant shifting of wartime allegiances added to the uncertainty as to who exactly was the real enemy. In these circumstances, it became easier to turn inwards, to trust the familiar and to shun anyone or anything deemed to be foreign. The 'spy fever' of 1914, the popular campaigns against foreign words and then the start of civilian internment were all manifestations of these concerns. Within the German-Jewish communities, similar suspicions had been directed towards the Eastern European Jews, due both to their unfamiliarity and to fears of rising anti-Semitism.

Defining the precise identity of Germany's enemy, however, became harder the longer the war went on. By the winter of 1915–16, it was not just the external foe that needed to be identified, but also the supposedly far more dangerous internal enemy.[1] With no end to the fighting in sight, Germans – including many Jews – started to look around for an explanation for the military's failure to end the war. Rumour and suspicion of shirking or deception spread like wildfire. Individuals already at the margins of society – whether Jews, Alsatians, Poles or Danes – were increasingly saddled with the blame for Germany's wartime failings. Military reports that singled out Polish soldiers or units from Alsace-Lorraine for particular failings circulated widely. Friedrich von Loebell, the Prussian interior minister, for example, remarked knowingly that 'a large number' of Prussian soldiers of Polish background had deserted to fight in the enemy armies. Turning his attention to troops from Alsace-Lorraine, Ludendorff demanded that they stop singing French songs and refrain from communicating in French entirely.[2] The implication was clear: Polish and other national minorities made for second-rate German soldiers, whose questionable loyalties needed to be kept in check.

German Jews were also drawn into this toxic web of suspicion and fear. Yet the process of defining the enemy and of identifying the 'other' always ran in two directions. Therefore, while Jewish communities faced hostile questions over their commitment to the war, at the same time other German Jews willingly participated in the exploitation of non-Germans. In the German occupation zones, Jewish and other German industrialists took advantage of the local populations to the full. People were numbered, categorised and recorded before being forced to work in often appalling conditions for their German occupiers. POWs interned in Germany suffered the same fate. Some prisoners even became the subject of academic studies, as Jewish and other German anthropologists sought different ways to categorise their defeated enemy. The reduction of people to the status of material categories contributed to an atmosphere in which those at the margins could be listed and labelled, all in the name of the greater war effort.[3]

Suspicions on All Fronts

The increasing propensity for Jews and other Germans to seek out the 'other' stemmed from a number of impulses. One crucial factor was the fragility of national unity. In the short term, the 'civic truce' had managed to paper over some of the glaring problems with Imperial Germany's unequal structures of power, where old elites presided over a weak parliamentary system. However, even the seductive narrative of national unity espoused by the kaiser could not survive an increasingly long and brutal war. In this respect, then, the slaughter of Verdun and the Somme brought a lot of simmering tensions back to the surface. Sold by Falkenhayn as a means to end the conflict, the land campaigns of 1916 did the exact opposite; they led not to France's surrender and to peace but to untold bloodshed for little perceivable gain. As Germany entered the third year of the conflict in August 1916, the kaiser struggled to find any words of comfort. The best he could offer the German people was the promise of 'plenty more hard times still to come', which was hardly the message that most Germans wanted to hear.[4]

As even the kaiser had little positive to say, it should come as no surprise that the German people became increasingly disillusioned with the ongoing war. There was perhaps no better place to witness the population's disenchantment than in Germany's urban landscape. On the streets, down back alleys or in weekly grocery markets, women, who had to fend for both themselves and their families, moaned about the war, criticised rising prices and complained about food shortages. During 1916, the shelves of small shops, which had once been filled with bread, meat and vegetables, were now more often bare. In Frankfurt, an acute lack of flour even meant that matzos had to be rationed 'in the general interest of the fatherland and the city'.[5] Whenever new food supplies arrived, the crowds soon followed. In Cologne, the mere rumour of new food stocks saw a sea of bodies gather outside shops said to be selling fat in March and those allegedly with potatoes in June.[6]

Increasingly, the only way for people to ensure an adequate diet was by turning to the black market. This was the route that the Munks, a Jewish family from Munich, reluctantly took. Like other families, they travelled out to the countryside with goods to barter and returned with precious quantities of potatoes and meat.[7] Gerda Luft and her family in Königsberg, however, had far less success. They had no rural acquaintances, which put them at an immediate disadvantage. Adding to these woes was the fact that Luft's ill father was in no position to pack his rucksack every weekend and scavenge for food. Just as they were bracing themselves for a diet of 'artificial honey' and 'powdered eggs', Luft secured her own food supply. She met a young soldier who tried to win her affections with bags of flour. Grateful for any scrap of food, the family mixed the flour with salt and water to make something vaguely bread-like. 'Admittedly it wasn't that tasty or nutritious, but it did at least dampen the hunger pains', she recalled. Wartime shortages, in this case, had brought about a rapid generational change; the daughter now took care of the parents.[8]

Members of the public seemed to have their own suspicions as to who was responsible for Germany's ever-dwindling menu options. Like many people, the Jewish politician Charlotte Landau-Mühsam held the state responsible. After food shortages started to damage her own health, she wrote to the council of her hometown of Lübeck arguing for a fairer distribution of food, based entirely on a family's size.[9] The German-Jewish Social Democratic politician Emanuel Wurm, meanwhile, attributed much of the blame to farmers reportedly hoarding meat and crops for themselves. The only solution, as far as he could see, was for food distribution 'to be headed by a man who will be fairer to the cities than has been the case hitherto'.[10] Yet a glance towards rural Bavaria makes clear that the farmers there were not living a life of opulent luxury, but were themselves suffering from food shortages. According to many of these farmers the elites harboured much of the blame. 'As long as the kaiser and the other bigwigs have enough to eat, the war is not going to stop', proved a common complaint.[11]

When people tired of blaming the Entente's blockade, the state, greedy farmers or the kaiser for food deprivation, the finger of suspicion often fell on German Jews. Jewish communities became an easy target for Germany's increasingly disgruntled urban population. It was obvious to people that food supplies had not evaporated entirely. Both the local and national press continued to advertise a vast range of delectable foodstuffs that were available 'while stocks last'. The Tietz department store had everything from salmon and herring through to lemons and dates on offer, while its retail competitor, A. Wertheim, advertised its range of fine Dutch cheeses and fresh asparagus.[12] The fact that Jewish families owned the Tietz and Wertheim department stores only seemed to confirm suspicions that German Jews were hoarding goods, thereby dealing in other people's misery for their own profit. In Berlin, some members of the public reportedly accused Jews of selling the worst products, while keeping the best to sell later at a greater profit, whether this was eggs or poultry.[13]

Ideally the political establishment should have been above the petty grumbles and poisonous mistrust of the streets. But by 1916, the political arena proved little better than the public realm as both individual politicians and whole political parties struggled to fathom why an end to the conflict remained so elusive. Although it was the army that was floundering on the battlefield, much of the blame ended up being directed towards the chancellor. Bethmann Hollweg's failure to resume unrestricted submarine warfare and to push for greater annexations angered those on the right, while the left demanded the chancellor do more to reach a negotiated peace. The pompously titled German National Committee for an Honourable Peace (Deutscher Nationalausschuss für einen ehrenvollen Frieden), established in June 1916, supposedly occupied the more moderate ground on these issues. Its leading members, amongst them the Jewish industrialist Eduard Arnhold, generally supported Bethmann Hollweg by following the government's line. Officially at least, the National Committee also opposed further submarine campaigns, although in reality its individual members held widely differing views on this and all other matters.[14]

To give its campaign more credence, the National Committee managed to recruit a number of prominent figures from the world of politics and industry, including members of the Foreign Office and the firms of Krupps and Mannesmann.[15] Naïvely as it turned out, the committee also tried to win

Georg Bernhard for its cause. After long discussions, they eventually lined him up to speak on the anniversary of the war's outbreak at an event in Bochum. The National Committee must have hoped that a German-Jewish editor of a supposedly liberal newspaper would be sympathetic to their cause. Bernhard, however, continued to confound expectations and demonstrated once again that German Jews could be as belligerent in their views as any other Germans. When Bernhard took to the stage of the imposing Evangelisches Vereinshaus in Bochum, it quickly became clear that his message was not quite on cue. Far from outlining a framework for peace, as the National Committee had hoped, Bernhard actually insisted that the war could only end when Germany had received either 'land or money'. He then went on to condemn anyone pushing for an immediate peace:

> We have to protect ourselves from people who speak like this; they are the one bad apple that can spoil the entire barrel . . . As soon as our enemies realise that we are hoping for peace, their will to continue fighting will only be strengthened . . . We are fighting for our lives. We all know that it is a matter of our national being, which is why we are prepared to fight for as long as it takes.[16]

Bernhard's contribution was the kind of friendly help that the National Committee could have done without, particularly as it already faced strong competition from two opposing groups: the Independent Committee for a German Peace (Unabhängiger Ausschuss für einen deutschen Frieden) and the Bavarian People's Committee for the Rapid Overthrow of England (Volksausschuss für rasche Niederkämpfung Englands). The names of these two groups may have implied a desire for European stability, but their collective aims were anything but. Both groups not only demanded territorial gains, but also publicised their belief that the war should be won, which for the most part differed markedly from Bethmann Hollweg's approach. The Independent Committee favoured offensives in the east against Russia as a means of securing German domination of the continent, while the People's Committee set its eyes on defeating Britain through an intense campaign of unrestricted submarine warfare.

Reflecting the radicalisation of German domestic politics, the two committees also attracted anti-Semitic elements. The notorious British-born anti-Semite Houston Stewart Chamberlain, for example, was one of the People's Committee's many prominent sympathisers.[17] Surprisingly, this darkening anti-Semitic atmosphere was not enough to dampen some German Jews' enthusiasm for the more extreme war aims of these groups. In the Franconian community of Georgensgmünd, for example, three members of the Heidecker family followed Chamberlain and joined the People's Committee.[18] Further south in Munich, Paul Nikolaus Cossmann, who had converted to Catholicism the previous decade, placed his monthly journal, the *Süddeutsche Monatshefte*, firmly behind the political right's war agenda. This turned out to be a canny move: the shift to the right led to an increase in circulation, securing the journal's future for the medium term at least.[19]

However, the decision to reposition the publication was always more than just a cynical marketing ploy. Under Cossmann's editorship there was real conviction to many of the pro-war articles published. During the first half of 1916, the journal took an aggressive stance on some of the usual areas of wartime dispute: Britain's responsibility for the outbreak of hostilities and the need for Germany to expand its borders. Cossmann's editorials, in which he trained his eyes on internal affairs, were similarly belligerent. He bemoaned the resignation of Tirpitz – 'a dark day' – and in a clear dig at Bethmann Hollweg demanded the introduction of a 'creative [*schöpferische*] politics' as the only way 'to appeal to people's hearts'.[20]

The simmering suspicions occupying the German people and their politicians during 1916 were replicated, with just as much vehemence, within the highest echelons of the military. Hindenburg and Ludendorff, the commanders of the eastern armies, had never seen eye to eye with their nominal superior, Falkenhayn. While Falkenhayn favoured a western strategy, Hindenburg and Ludendorff believed the key to ending the war lay in defeating the Russians in the east, as victory there would free up forces to fight the British and French in the west. Falkenhayn's setbacks at Verdun and on the Somme added considerable weight to the duo's demands for an eastern strategy. Hindenburg and Ludendorff, who were well versed in Machiavellian plotting, readily used Falkenhayn's difficulties to their advantage. A letter to the chancellor penned by Ludendorff's devious adviser Colonel Max Bauer attempted to lay bare the problems with Falkenhayn's leadership. The letter warned that now 'only a strong-minded man can save' Germany, by which of course was meant the combination of Ludendorff and Hindenburg.[21]

Following Romania's declaration of war in August 1916, Falkenhayn's fate was sealed. The entry of this 'vile bunch', as one assistant army rabbi called the Romanians, made a mockery of Falkenhayn's earlier insistence that Romania would remain neutral, and he was dismissed.[22] With the existing chief of the

General Staff now out of office, the path was clear for Hindenburg and Ludendorff to take up the reins. Hindenburg, as the senior man, became chief, while Ludendorff, his long-term assistant, took on the role of first quarter-master-general. The decision to elevate the popular duo had as much to do with deflecting criticism away from Germany's civilian leaders as it did with military strategy. Albert Ballin, like many Germans, was delighted at the change. 'Thank God', he said simply to one political confidant.[23] From the front, meanwhile, the fighting troops seemed equally delighted at the news. One Jewish soldier exclaimed loudly that with 'these two supremely gifted leaders in charge' there was at last 'a fair promise of success'.[24] Yet any jubilation was short-lived. Far from drawing German society closer together, Hindenburg and Ludendorff's promotion only served to open up chasms between those deemed to be full members of the nation and those at its margins.

The Hindenburg Programme

Whereas Falkenhayn had concerned himself primarily with military affairs, Hindenburg and Ludendorff interpreted their brief much more widely. They swept into office determined to make dramatic changes to the structures of the home front, the political realm and military strategy itself. Their habit of intervening in all aspects of the war has led to the duo being labelled a 'silent dictatorship', although this language of authoritarianism is more of a nod towards Germany's later dictatorships than to the actual structures of power during the First World War.[25] Nonetheless in at least one area this terminology proved particularly apt. Under the duo's command Germany moved towards a policy of economic and human exploitation, most clearly seen in the willingness of some of the country's leading industrialists, including Walther Rathenau and Eduard Arnhold, to utilise forced labour. Identifying the 'other' in this respect meant exploiting individual lives and breaking international law in the pursuit of victory.

Hindenburg and Ludendorff set to work with a burst of energy. Determined to increase the availability of armaments for the fighting troops, the duo immediately laid out plans to make better use of Germany's existing resources. There was to be a doubling in munitions production as well as significant increases in the manufacturing of aircraft and field artillery. The duo's vision, which came to be known as the Hindenburg Programme, also saw non-essential industries closed, further state controls over raw materials and more restrictions on workers' freedoms.[26] Placed together, these changes immersed men and women at home into the full realities of the conflict, while also pushing Germany far closer to fighting a total war. Theodor Wolff was not far from the mark when he exclaimed that 'it seems as if the war is just beginning'.[27]

As military men, one of Hindenburg and Ludendorff's first directives concerned the army itself. In an attempt to strengthen Germany's fighting capabilities, they lowered the age of conscription to eighteen and recruited more older men into the army, measures which together brought in an extra 300,000 men. However, this sudden recruitment binge did little to alter the military balance, particularly as, physically, many of the new soldiers fell far short of the army's basic requirements. One Jewish soldier fighting on the Eastern Front proudly explained that, in stark contrast to most of the new recruits, he could march all day and still shoot distant targets with his rifle. 'There are men drafted who can barely see', he complained. 'People that you can tell suffer from some serious illness such that they struggle to keep up on marches. Yet despite all this, they aren't sent home.'[28] This soldier's musings were aimed principally at the military itself, but they also revealed a certain satisfaction at his own high levels of physical fitness. Many Jews had longed for just such an opportunity to demonstrate themselves as the physical equal of any other German, thereby refuting narratives of a weak Jewish body.[29]

Irrespective of their fighting qualities, the recruitment of each and every man had a knock-on effect on the home front. It left businesses short of workers, schools of teachers and farms of labourers. Jewish communities were particularly badly hit. In some areas, where membership levels were already low, the very future of some Jewish communal institutions was thrown into doubt. Two Jewish teacher-training colleges near Würzburg, for example, were pushed to the brink of closure as the war robbed them of their staff. Firing a warning shot to the local education authorities, the institutions' directors explained that the loss of any more teachers would result in 'the full closure of one of the two institutions'.[30] Perhaps even more pressing for some Jewish communities was a growing shortage of synagogue personnel. In some districts, shortages became so acute that teachers were even called on to stand in for rabbis during religious services held for the military.[31]

If individuals were unable to be recruited into the army, then Germany's new military leaders expected them to serve in a different way. Their guiding principle was simple: every member of the nation needed to help push for victory. To give these ideas a legal framework, the Reichstag passed the Auxiliary Service Law in December 1916. This deeply contentious piece of legislation made it compulsory for all males aged between seventeen and sixty to provide labour for the war economy. Where men worked in non-essential industries, they too could be directed to areas of greater need. Most controversially, workers no longer chose their place of employment; local committees assigned them an employer instead. Restrictions on the free movement of labour may have made economic sense, but it did little for already tense industrial relations. This same issue had already proved a lightning rod of discontent for the Eastern European Jewish workers whose employment was governed by contract, but now it threatened to disturb other sections of the German working class too.[32]

Those workers upset by the Auxiliary Service Law could not look to the political establishment for much support. In the Reichstag, the only real opposition to the law came from the extreme left of the SPD, whose German-Jewish politicians Hugo Haase, Oskar Cohn and Joseph Herzfeld voted against the proposals. Haase, whose scepticism of the war had grown by the month, even called the law a military 'monstrosity, never before seen in world history'.[33] As a sign of the diversity of Jewish wartime opinion, however, German Jews were just as prominent in their support of the legislation. Georg Davidson and Max Cohen-Reuß, for example, both voted with the government and supported the introduction of compulsory labour.

Women's organisations in Germany also took issue with the Auxiliary Service Law, but for very different reasons. They demanded not less but more compulsory labour. What most riled the women's organisations was that the law only targeted men – it made no provision for forcing women into work. After much debate, the Union of German Women's Associations (Bund Deutscher Frauenvereine), which represented many of the individual women's groups, including the Jewish Women's League, reluctantly accepted the government's stance. In a statement from its chairwoman Gertrud Bäumer and German-Jewish secretary Alice Bensheimer, the union explained that whilst it wanted equality for men and women before the law, its members would nonetheless do everything they could 'to strengthen German military power and to ensure economic resilience'.[34] The military took the union up on this offer and created a National Committee for Women's War Work (Nationaler Ausschuss für Frauenarbeit im Kriege) as a means to coordinate the activity of the different women's organisations. Through the efforts of the German-Jewish social reformer Alice Salomon, who represented the union on the committee, female volunteers took part in the general remobilisation efforts and were directed to areas of greatest industrial need.[35]

Larger firms, such as the German-Jewish Cassella chemicals company, found much to savour in the Hindenburg Programme. The expansion of the army inevitably meant more equipment orders which in turn promised greater profits for firms that like itself held military contracts.[36] However, it was in the occupied territories that the greatest opportunities lay. German heavy industrialists had been eyeing up Belgium's assets for a long time: they now seized the opportunity to strike. They formed three separate companies which enabled them to carve up Belgian and foreign-owned businesses in the region amongst themselves. Although Rathenau was not one of the main protagonists on this occasion, his AEG still managed to secure a seat at the top table, with a place on one of the supervisory boards. There, the firm was joined by Albert Ballin, who hoped to gain access to the port of Antwerp for his own shipping line.[37] Another major German-Jewish businessman involved in the three Belgian companies was Georg Solmssen. Born into the Salomonsohn banking dynasty, he had converted to Christianity in 1900 and shortened his name at the same time. In Belgium his interest lay not with the banks, but rather with the country's lucrative coalmining industry, to which he sought access.[38]

Taking control of Belgian industry, though, was just a starting point. Many of Germany's leading businessmen also cast an envious eye at Belgium's workforce too. With German firms struggling to find workers to fill their factory floors, this untapped body of labour sitting over the border appeared ripe for exploitation. There had long been discussion about making greater use of Belgian workers, but the plans had repeatedly foundered on the obstinacy of the German governor-general in Brussels, Moritz von Bissing, who wanted to avoid an international dispute over labour.[39] The Hindenburg Programme, with its emphasis on industrial efficiency, changed the dynamics of this debate. As Rathenau pointed out in another exchange with Ludendorff, to achieve 'the necessary increases in the munitions industry' required drawing labour from the army reserves and in particular from the occupied territories. He suggested that some 700,000 people could be recruited from Belgium alone. Rathenau was fully aware that such an arrangement would be in contravention of international law; he emphasised the need to 'ignore . . . international questions of prestige'.[40]

Lobbying by the likes of Rathenau and others for the recruitment of Belgian workers was merely the latest example of German industry's wilful exploitation of the occupied regions. German businesses, including many Jewish-owned firms, had already made considerable use of involuntary labour. The coalmining magnate Eduard Arnhold, for example, had no qualms about sending POWs to work in his mines. Indeed, as the labour situation within Germany worsened, he pushed repeatedly for the release of more prisoners and appropriate guards to work in his facilities.[41] Such was the success of his efforts that by the end of 1916, Arnhold could report that roughly 30 per cent of his 130,000 workers in Upper Silesia were either Poles or POWs.[42] Franz Oppenheimer, fresh from his campaigns to Germanise the east, proved to be another keen advocate for the use of POW labour. Seemingly unperturbed by the small matter of POWs' rights, Oppenheimer reminded people that Germany was currently home to 'three quarters of a million prisoners, mainly farmers and agricultural labourers, who will have to help us' to increase food production.[43]

The use of POW labour, therefore, very quickly became an accepted part of the German war economy. The plans of industrialists to recruit Belgian workers stemmed from these same exploitative practices but then extended them to an even more brutal level. Unlike the POWs forced to work in Germany, the Belgians were civilians, not members of the military. For the most part they made no decision to work for the Germans; they were simply rounded up off the streets of Belgian towns and herded into goods wagons heading across the border. Once in Germany, the workers were housed in abysmal camps, where regular beatings and a lack of food and heating marked their daily existence. Two Belgian workers, whose plight came to the attention of the SPD, described in vivid detail how they were 'forcibly deported to Germany' leaving their 74-year-old father at home alone. In Germany, it was only 'hunger and violence that forced them to work', they explained, particularly as they 'had never even signed a contract'.[44]

Everyone involved in the deportation of Belgian workers, whether the War Ministry, the government or even Rathenau himself, clearly knew that the operation was illegal. Yet Rathenau did not seem to be particularly concerned by this inconvenient truth. In another cosy letter to Ludendorff, he suggested 'a similar operation in Poland' to what had been proposed for Belgium.[45] In effect, this meant forcing another 100,000 to 200,000 workers across the eastern border and into German industrial concerns. The same basic logic that had led to the recruitment of Belgian workers also underpinned the approach to forced labour in Eastern Europe. The sole concern for German industrialists, like Rathenau, was to secure increased production levels which would be of benefit for their own businesses and the war effort more generally. Whether or not these people wanted to leave their homes and families in the east was of no great interest.

Yet recruiting workers from the east threw up two additional difficulties that had not been encountered with the Belgian case. First, the population diversity of Eastern Europe meant that the German authorities needed to pay

attention to local nationalist desires. The decision to promote Polish sovereignty, for example, brought Germany's policy of forced labour in the
Government General of Warsaw – the area of Poland under German control
– to a premature halt. As Ludwig Haas, Germany's Jewish adviser in Warsaw,
rightly pointed out, it was very difficult to pay lip service to Polish nationalism, while at the same time forcing Poles to work for the German war effort.[46]

A second difficulty in recruiting labour from Eastern Europe, which was also
of Germany's own making, concerned the large Jewish population in the region.
The German authorities had already banned unqualified Jewish workers from
taking up jobs in Germany the previous winter.[47] Even the dire labour shortages
that gave birth to the Hindenburg Programme failed to provoke a change in
attitude. Germany's industrial concerns, including Rathenau's own AEG,
returned time and again to existing stereotypes, arguing that the productivity of
Jewish workers was too low to warrant employing them in German factories.[48]

In the Eastern European Ober Ost district, the racial dimensions of
Germany's labour policies were far more evident. During the late autumn of
1916, the German authorities instructed both men and women to report for
work. Where the numbers were too low, the local police simply grabbed
people from the streets or even their homes. However, amidst this maelstrom
of violence and repression not all ethnic groups experienced the same treatment. While Poles, Lithuanians and Belorussians easily found a place in
Hindenburg and Ludendorff's plans and were deported to Germany, the situation for the Eastern European Jews was very different. Although some Jewish
workers ended up in labour columns heading to Germany, many more
remained in the east. German industrialists' scepticism over the value of
Eastern European Jewish labour, it seems, was simply too great.[49]

However, a deep-lying reluctance to recruit Jewish labour did not mean
that the Eastern European Jews were simply excused from work. This was far
from the case. In large parts of German-occupied Eastern Europe, Jews
suffered particularly badly from the military authorities' forced recruitment
policies. Men aged between seventeen and sixty were rounded up, placed into
labour battalions and then put to work in the east itself. The city of Vilna
provides a pertinent example of how this process functioned on the ground.
During the winter of 1916–17, Vilna's German mayor, Eldor Pohl, who was
himself apparently of Jewish heritage, ordered that all 'unemployed' men
report for work. When the number of volunteers fell short, Pohl instructed
the local police to grab men from the streets. Those rounded up, of whom the
majority were Jewish, were set to work in fields or on road-building projects.[50]

Against any discernible measure, it is clear that Germany's wartime labour policies treated the Jews living in Ober Ost and Poland particularly harshly. They were banned from entering Germany and then rounded up to work in forced labour battalions, in greater numbers than all other population groups. Yet the authorities' sheer disregard for the basic rights of Eastern European Jews was symptomatic of a much wider change in attitude. Hindenburg and Ludendorff's rise to power and the subsequent Hindenburg Programme blew a callous wind through the German military and civilian establishment. Plans to force Belgians and Eastern Europeans to work for the German war effort suggested a cruel and uncaring stance towards other population groups. A line had now been drawn between those identified as loyal German citizens and those at the margins. Crucially, both Jews and other Germans played a role in identifying the 'other'.

Other Prisoners

Walther Rathenau, who declared himself 'absolutely delighted' with Hindenburg and Ludendorff's changes, was not the only German Jew to show a cruel disregard for the treatment of non-Germans.[51] Eduard Arnhold and Franz Oppenheimer became firm advocates of POW labour, while Georg Solmssen jumped at the opportunity to exploit Belgian industry. Although the use of POWs and forced labour provided perhaps the most damning example of Jews' and other Germans' callous disregard for their vanquished enemy, these were not isolated incidents. The wartime exploitation of other population groups also occurred in a subtler fashion. During the conflict, Jewish and other German anthropologists started to take a new interest in exploring the ethnic and racial origins of the captured soldiers interned on German soil. What these projects had in common was that they were based on a distinct sense of national superiority. German anthropologists approached their specimens as though representatives of a conquering power determined to uncover every characteristic of their vanquished foe.

There were very few places where Germans' sense of national and cultural supremacy was more powerfully felt than the POW camp. In these ever-expanding enclosures – the majority of which were in Germany itself – soldiers from the Allied armies were forced to spend the remainder of the conflict behind barbed wire. The longer the war went on, the larger and more diverse the POW populations became. By 1916, the German authorities held more than 1.5 million men in a network of camps spread across Germany. When it seemed that there was political capital to be made, the German authorities divided their camps by both nationality and religion. Ukrainian soldiers often ended up in camps near Wetzlar, Rastatt and Salzwedel, while captured Muslim soldiers were held in Wünsdorf and Zossen in Brandenburg.[52]

The peculiarities of modern warfare meant, therefore, that a wide segment of the world's population suddenly resided on German soil. For German anthropologists, this state of affairs provided their research with a real boost. No longer did they need to travel to Africa or Asia to conduct their studies: a local train journey now sufficed. The Wünsdorf and Zossen camps, which lay less than 40 kilometres from the centre of Berlin, allowed anthropologists to spend the day examining a whole range of different ethnic and racial groups, before travelling home to the capital the same day. As one anthropologist was quick to point out, the source base in the camps was of the highest quality. 'A visit to the camps', he assured his audience, 'is almost as worthwhile for the specialist as a trip around the world.'[53]

What was perhaps most remarkable about this anthropological research was the enthusiasm that many German-Jewish academics showed for these projects. The artist and committed Zionist Hermann Struck teamed up with one of Central Europe's leading anthropologists, Felix von Luschan, to produce a book of sketches based on the internees in the camps. Rudolf Marcuse, a contemporary of Struck and renowned sculptor, applied his talents to producing a series of sculptures of the different peoples imprisoned in Germany. Finally, Adolph Goldschmidt worked with the Berlin-based linguist Wilhelm Doegen to record the voices of POWs. Goldschmidt was only supposed to be involved in an advisory capacity, but curiosity it seems got the better of him, and he started to visit the camps himself to take photographs of Doegen's different 'specimens'.[54]

Struck, Marcuse and Goldschmidt's excitement reflected their own place within a German intellectual community that had been a part of a wider European colonial discourse. In short, these Jewish anthropologists' ideas of the 'other' had been shaped by a German understanding of cultural superiority. Certainly, notions of 'race' and 'nationality' were rather fluid at this time, with the two terms often being used interchangeably.[55] Nonetheless, the fact was that many Germans, including Struck, Marcuse and Goldschmidt, approached the camps through a racial lens. The biggest draw in the camps, at least as far as Goldschmidt was concerned, were the colonial prisoners. His memoirs record a fleeting interest in the interned European soldiers; this was soon surpassed when he encountered groups of African POWs. No longer was he in a familiar and safe European world, but in the midst of a 'hostile society without any form of protection'. Betraying his own belief in the idea of racial difference, Goldschmidt imbued the black prisoners with 'animalistic' characteristics. Their accommodation block, he remembered, looked like a 'giant monkey cage', where the prisoners 'climbed down a pole' to get to the entrance.[56]

Like Goldschmidt, Struck also appeared to hold by racial categorisations. His work with Luschan was certainly no act of 'engaged anti-racism', as some historians have proposed.[57] While Struck's sketches were for the most part more restrained than Goldschmidt's photographic project, they still revealed a strong belief in the idea of race as a marker of difference. The first issue was one of selection. It was never the case of Struck simply entering a POW camp with sketchbook in hand and recording what he saw; he carefully chose his subjects to ensure that he recorded every 'racial' type, whether this was an interned Gurkha or a captured North African soldier. Second, and with the completed sketch in hand, Struck went on to categorise the origins of each of his subjects at the bottom of the page. Thus, his book with Luschan contained sketches of a Sikh from the Punjab alongside a Kabyle Algerian and a 'nigger from Senegal'. Third, Struck proved more than amenable to Luschan's demands that he extenuate 'racial' stereotypes in his drawings. He willingly 'enlarged the skull and ear' on a sketch of a Russian POW, while at the same time giving an African soldier 'pretty, frizzy Negro hair'.[58] The aim of these adjustments was to ensure that the POWs met preconceived ideas of how these different groups should appear.

The sculptures of camp prisoners that Marcuse produced followed a similar pattern to Struck's drawings in that he tried to identify 'types of people' (*Völkertypen*). The catalogue accompanying his sculptures identified a swathe of different groups interned in Germany, from Moroccans and Arabs through to Somalis and Romanians. Like Struck, the approach that Marcuse took in modelling each of his subjects is also particularly instructive. His sculptures of Europeans POWs, whether Scotsmen, Italians or even French soldiers, captured the individual's entire body, often clothed in full military uniform (see Plate 16). In his African or Asian studies, Marcuse took a different approach, focusing on the head profile alone, as if trying to highlight specific 'racial' differences. Shorn of their bodies and thus their military uniforms too, Marcuse's 'Nigger from Liberia' (see Plate 17) or 'Japanese man' became nothing more than examples of 'racial' types, rather than of living people.[59] Marcuse's sculptures, along with Goldschmidt's photographs and Struck's sketches, took full advantage of this unique opportunity to examine 'almost all peoples and races' in one place.[60] Collectively their studies highlight the prevalence of racial thinking in German society. But more significantly, these cultural products also demonstrate the extent to which German Jews participated in the process of categorising and recording population groups, even to the extent of classifying Jews as a distinct 'race'. Alongside his sketches of Russians and Tatars, for example, Struck drew images of a 'Jew from Lublin' or a fierce-looking 'Jew from Kiev'.[61] There was nothing fundamentally new about this fascination with the supposed 'racial' characteristics of different peoples. Europeans had long applied ideas of 'racial' difference to their colonial subjects. However, the war heightened these attitudes. Not only did the conflict provide an opportunity to explore Asians and Africans up close, but it also intensified ideas of European, though particularly German, superiority. These shifts were a sign of the narrowing of Germany's wartime culture, but also of a determination to categorise, list and record the peoples Germans encountered.

War Shirkers

The intensification of the conflict during 1916 not only thrust the racial 'other' under the spotlight, but also bred suspicions among Germany's own citizens. Men of military age not at the front suffered the most; at best they were shirkers, at worst spies. In Munich, a well-dressed young man, going by the name of Karl Weber, fell under the police radar during 1916. The doorman at the city's Kontorhaus had been seen passing letters to Weber each day, which as far as one local resident was concerned warranted 'further police investigation'.[62] What the police uncovered, though, was not a complex spy ring but rather a married man trying to cover up an affair. Getting post delivered to an intermediary ensured that Weber's wife remained unaware of his extramarital dalliances.[63] This exchange in Munich was just one example of the German population's growing distrust of anyone whose actions or appearance appeared to place them at the margins of society.

By taking accusations such as the one made against Weber seriously, the German authorities helped to harden an atmosphere of complaint and suspicion. The launch of the Hindenburg Programme in the autumn only served to deepen the population's sense of mistrust. If its basic aim was to maximise Germany's human and material resources, it meant by implication that many people had yet to contribute fully to the war effort. The state's job, therefore, increasingly became one of both detective and arbiter. It had to hunt out those individuals and businesses that had more to give, cajoling or forcing them to contribute where appropriate. A potent tool in this fight against apparent shirking and profiteering were the War Profiteering Offices (Kriegswucherämter), which several states established during the final months of 1916. The basic aim of these offices was to clamp down on black market activity and to punish anyone perceived to be making an excessive profit from the conflict.[64] Irrespective of their overall purpose, the message that once again came across from these offices was that some people had sacrificed themselves for the nation, while others were primarily interested in lining their own pockets.

As this discourse of war shirking gathered momentum, Germans became ever more adept at spotting those not doing their bit. In southern Bavaria, the target was female agricultural labourers. According to the local military authorities, rumours were rife that many women were living off state financial benefits, such as a widow's pension, rather than working in the fields, something that was obviously a dereliction of their duties.[65] In Düsseldorf, it was 'gypsy' families that fell under suspicion after the military uncovered an ingenious method of avoiding conscription. Whenever one of their members received his call-up papers, the families would travel to a nearby town where they were unknown and send a sick or infirm relative to the barracks in place of the real recruit. Once the inevitable happened and the replacement had been signed off as unfit for duty, the families returned to their original town.[66]

If these 'gypsy' families had truly sought to avoid conscription, then they were merely following in the footsteps of many other Germans. The history of the conflict is one of both willing fighters and reluctant recruits. Throughout the war, Germany's borders with its neutral neighbours – Denmark, the Netherlands and Switzerland – witnessed a constant trickle of men crossing over, hoping to avoid military service.[67] Many German Jews also demonstrated an understandable reluctance to become frontline cannon fodder. Viktor Klemperer's older brother Berthold suffered terribly when he was called up. The strains of drill alone proved enough to hospitalise him. At this news, the Klemperer family rallied round, made use of their contacts and eventually managed to get Berthold a desk job in the War Ministry.[68]

It did not matter that almost everyone pulled strings to secure the best possible posting: the finger of blame fell increasingly, and almost exclusively, on those deemed to be on the margins of society. Jewish communities, along with Germany's French, Polish and Danish national minorities, suffered particularly badly in this respect. Both the military and the civilian population more generally questioned the loyalty of these groups on numerous occasions. The case of an Alfred Cohen in Munich was typical of the suspicions that increasingly targeted German Jews. In summer 1916, an angry letter landed on the desk of Munich's military commander, demanding to know why an Alfred Cohen was working in the Tietz department store, which just so happened to have Jewish owners, instead of fighting at the front. Cohen had apparently been lightly wounded in 1915, but for some reason had never made it back to the front after his recovery. In case anyone should mistake his intentions, the anonymous complainant explained that these observations were not personal, but merely stemmed from his own deep 'patriotism for the fatherland'. The military investigated these accusations but found nothing amiss. Cohen, whose military record gave 'no cause for complaint', had actually been granted temporary leave to work for Tietz.[69]

Although nothing was said explicitly, it seems reasonable to presume that Cohen was targeted as a war shirker because of his surname. Not only was the name Cohen often used in a negative context to signify a Jew, but the attack on him also occurred at a time of rising anti-Semitism.[70] During the spring and summer of 1916, against a backdrop of social tensions at home and military setbacks in the field, German Jews had to fend off repeated accusations of traitorous behaviour and shirking. Many of the old anti-Semitic tropes resurfaced, often repeated by some of the country's most notorious anti-Semites. Alfred Roth and Theodor Fritsch, for example, bombarded members of the political elite with a memorandum that accused Jews of putting profit before national unity. 'The Ballin–Rathenau system', they argued, had led to 'Jewish infiltration of German economic life'.[71] In Berlin, meanwhile, it was the Eastern European Jews who became the target of vitriolic attack. These Russian-Jewish pedlars were 'undesirable', insisted the High Command of the Marshes (Oberkommando in den Marken), and they should be 'shoved off' as quickly as possible.[72]

Increasingly, anti-Semitism also pervaded daily life, with Jews blamed for many of society's wartime ills. Often German Jews found themselves placed in an unwinnable position. When one Hamburg printing firm launched a new series of postcards, under the imaginative title 'The German army', it hoped to capture a particular set of patriotic moments. One postcard depicted a group of strapping young men taking a dip in a river; another showed soldiers lined up in the trenches ready to perform their duty. However, on discovering the new postcard series on sale, one disgruntled gentleman from Landshut condemned the publisher in a sternly worded letter: 'On an artistic level, these postcards are simply dreadful kitsch', he moaned. The writer of the letter was not merely an art connoisseur determined to uphold the highest of artistic standards; his grievances went much deeper. Introducing the idea of the cunning war profiteer, the complainant developed an uneven dichotomy between the 'crafty Jewish blood' of the businessman selling the postcards and the 'good-natured, innocent Germans' gullibly buying them.[73]

What proved most dangerous for German Jews over the longer term was that this anti-Semitic wave also swept through the military establishment. Within the closed circles of privilege and tradition that made up the Prussian officer corps, grumbles could be heard about Jewish influence in the press and around the kaiser. It was hardly a surprise, therefore, when Jewish soldiers who had only just started to gain entry to this body were once again passed over for promotion.[74] The Prussian War Ministry, which had never been the most welcoming of places for German Jews, also stoked the flames of prejudice. In June, the ministry held a conference on ways to boost the fighting capabilities of the army by bringing in more reserves and by cracking down on shirking. During the day's discussions, two of the speakers made specific reference to Jewish soldiers. The combined thrust of their argument was that Jewish doctors connived to ensure that their fellow Jews found cushy jobs in offices on the home front.

The War Ministry's conference was a microcosm of much larger discussions taking place throughout Germany during 1916. The most pressing issue was how to make the country's scarce human and material resources stretch much further. But the search for more food, raw materials and fighting soldiers also led to the belief that the burden of fighting the war was not being shared equally. In short, while some people sacrificed everything in defence of the German homeland, others were simply out to profit from the good will of the majority. Jewish communities found themselves on the wrong side of this populist discourse. As the War Ministry's conference implied – and public opinion confirmed – German Jews were viewed as having made large profits from the war, while the whole time ensuring that they stayed away from the battlefield.[75]

The Count

The second day of November 1916 dawned damp and grey in Northern France. Julius Marx, who had already fought at Verdun and the Somme, was readying his men for further fighting when he was called to his commanding officer. 'I have to note down your personal details', Marx was told. When he asked the reason, the lieutenant replied rather apologetically that the 'War Ministry has been told that it needs to determine how many Jews are at the front'. Marx's angry response was completely understandable. 'What is this nonsense? Do they wish to degrade us to second-class soldiers and make us the laughing stock of the entire army?' he demanded.[76] Such exchanges were the first that many soldiers had heard of a decision taken by the War Ministry the previous month. On 11 October, it issued internal instructions for a Jewish census with the aim of counting each and every Jewish soldier. The German authorities had already blundered from one self-made crisis to the next, whether this was the sinking of the *Lusitania* or the execution of the British nurse Edith Cavell. But the Jewish census, which was directed towards Germany's own citizens, topped all of these and in doing so marked a new low.

Statistics form a central component of modern warfare. Statisticians can calculate numbers of available men, rates of attrition, economic productivity and the availability of essential resources. In wartime Germany, the state sought to capture statistics on everything it possibly could. The War Raw Materials Corporations, for example, collated detailed information on the firms they controlled.[77] One of the largest statistical projects in fact came from within Jewish communities. In early 1915, a new organisation, the Main Committee for War Statistics (Gesamtausschuss für Kriegsstatistik) came into being. Building on the earlier work of the Federation of German Jews, it sought to collect every piece of information relating to the Jewish soldiers, from age and rank through to decorations and service record. Reflecting an evident sense of nervousness, its aim was to create a comprehensive record of German Jews' contribution to the conflict so that any criticisms could be easily rebuffed.[78]

There did at least seem to be some discernible logic to these earlier statistical projects. After all, knowledge of business activity was essential for managing the war economy, while in the case of the Main Committee for War Statistics, the aim was to offer comprehensive evidence of German Jews' wartime participation. By 1916, the purpose of statistical surveys had fundamentally changed. As Germany's Jewish population discovered to its cost, statistics themselves had become a weapon. In June, Ferdinand Werner, a committed anti-Semite and later a leading Nazi functionary in Hesse, demanded precise statistics of the Jews' military contribution: 'How many people with a Jewish background are at the front? How many are behind the lines? How many in administrative or management roles at home? How many Jews have been the subject of complaint or been marked as unfit?'[79]

Later in the summer, the prominent Catholic Centre Party politician Matthias Erzberger asked that the War Raw Materials Corporations be subjected to a statistical investigation based on 'sex, military service age, income and religion'.[80] Erzberger may have made no specific mention of Jewish membership of the corporations, but 'religion' in this context meant in essence Jewishness. Like many prominent figures in German life, Erzberger could quickly switch from defence to attack. At the start of the year, he had publicly advocated the promotion of German Jews to officers; six months down the line his stance was very different.[81] His call for a survey of the corporations was in effect a tacit acknowledgment of the German right's claim that Jewish businessmen controlled Germany's wartime economy.

The War Ministry's census of its Jewish servicemen, when it came, stemmed from this same anti-Semitic discourse, effectively a belief that German Jews were shirking their military duties. However, while these precedents laid the foundations for the census, it was in fact a far more mundane change that eventually set the count in motion. Soon after Hindenburg and Ludendorff had taken charge, the deputy war minister in Berlin, Franz Gustav von Wandel, tendered his resignation. The significance of this move lay in Wandel's attitude towards Jewish communities. Although he had previously been quick to condemn the 'international Jews' interned in Ruhleben, he had shown far less interest in pursuing the right's attacks on Germany's Jewish soldiers.[82] His default approach seemed to be to ignore the matter entirely, leaving many letters unanswered or sending a tardy reply at best.[83] Wandel's superior and administrative successor, Adolf Wild von Hohenborn, proved more meticulous with the paperwork, however. His reputation as something of a jovial character clearly did not extend to Jewish communities, as in early October Wild von Hohenborn announced a count of German Jews in the military.[84]

What made Wild von Hohenborn's decision to hold a census all the more remarkable was the sheer bureaucratic folly of the enterprise. At a time of increasing scarcities, both of material and of men, administrating the count served only to deny the frontline of even more resources. The War Ministry issued each military unit with two questionnaires to be completed by 1 December 1916; the first asked for statistics on those at the front, while the second required details of all Jewish soldiers serving behind the lines. It also sought information on the number of Jewish volunteers, the number of Jewish-won Iron Crosses and the number of Jewish officers. A rash of documents landing at the feet of the military's commanding officers conjures up an image of a physical count, with each Jewish soldier being called out from the line and then marched back one at a time. In practice the whole affair was far more haphazard. The clerk of one battalion plucked the figures from thin air. It was easier to guess than 'to draw some precise conclusions by going through the muster rolls'. With German troops fighting continual battles in the west, most commanding officers clearly had more pressing matters on their minds.[85]

This slightly haphazard process of data collection was made all the worse by the fact that many soldiers were out of position at the time of the count. And as the census could only capture one particular moment of the conflict, if a Jewish soldier happened to be away from the front on the day the count was conducted, he suddenly went from being a frontline fighter to a 'rear-area pig'. There were a host of good reasons for an individual's absence, leave or injury being the most obvious. Jewish soldiers who had been wounded and then confined to desk jobs, for example, were marked as non-combatants. As one such soldier complained, no one was 'bothered by the fact that we had already done our bit at the front until we could no longer be used'.[86] A far more sinister reason for Jews being absent from the frontline emerged, when in a few isolated cases commanding officers put them on other duties during the census.

As historians have repeatedly pointed out, the Jewish census was fundamentally flawed. The War Ministry's failure to consider the particular circumstances of each individual soldier meant that the statistics they gathered were fragmentary at best.[87] However, to spend too much time decrying the choice of methodology is to give the process far more credence than it deserves. More significant than the statistical failings is the fact that the Jewish census took place at all. The kaiser's oft-cited words in August 1914, which ushered in the 'civic truce', had been about national unity, about Germans coming together to fight a common enemy. The Jewish census was the exact opposite; it involved one section of the population attacking another.

It is hardly surprising, therefore, that many Jewish soldiers expressed their complete dissatisfaction at the census, often discussing their complaints with the army rabbis in the field. Rabbi Siegfried Klein, who spent almost the entire war on the Western Front, reported the high degree of 'indignation and exasperation amongst the Jewish soldiers' singled out by the count.[88] The atmosphere appeared to be very similar in the east. In a report back home, one of Klein's fellow army rabbis, Leopold Rosenak, explained how the census had had 'a thoroughly depressing effect on the Jewish members of the army'. After 'giving everything for the fatherland', he complained, these loyal soldiers had now been 'betrayed'.[89] These complaints were not just the preserve of the Jewish soldiers. According to Jacob Sonderling, army rabbi for the German 8th Army, some of the non-Jewish servicemen in his area were equally annoyed at the military's actions. They reportedly reacted with considerable 'disconcertment' as the news of the census spread.[90]

Once the immediate shock of the census had passed, what most irritated German Jews was the War Ministry's almost complete lack of remorse for its actions. As far as the military was concerned, the census had been a logical response to external complaints and therefore required no apology. The aim had merely been 'to collect statistical material' which it would later check; there were certainly no 'anti-Semitic intentions', the military insisted.[91] However, the fact that the results of the census were never released rather undermined these claims.

Despite the seriousness of the situation, the overall response of the main Jewish organisations to the military census was rather muted. The CV made the obvious point that the army had decided to target the very people who had given their 'blood and life to defend the fatherland', while the Zionist *Jüdische Rundschau* complained that the census was 'a flagrant abuse of the honour and the civic equality of German Jewry'.[92] Thereafter, the two organisations returned to the census on occasion, but never with any real conviction of enacting change. With the war ongoing, it once again appeared easier to keep complaints to a minimum for fear of drawing even further attention to the German-Jewish communities.

The timidity of the CV and the Zionists left space for other critics to come to the fore. Surprisingly given its general feebleness so far, it was the Reichstag that initially witnessed the most fulsome display of public defiance. On 3 November, parliamentarians gathered in the chamber to debate a range of military issues, from food supplies through to soldiers' leave. The most impassioned speeches, though, were saved for the Jewish census, with Ludwig Haas's gaining the most plaudits. Clearly keen to play on the chamber's emotions, Haas pulled out all the theatrical stops. In military uniform and wearing his Iron Cross 1st Class, Haas, who represented the liberal Fortschrittliche Volkspartei, explained how the bravery and loyalty of the Jewish soldiers had been abused. As he pointed out, the count was not just an insult to German Jews, but also damaging at a time when 'we still desperately need . . . internal unity'. Haas ended with a patriotic crescendo: 'now above all, [let us have] unity and harmony in the interest of the fatherland'.[93]

Once the heat of the parliamentary debate had faded, it was obvious that very little had actually changed. German Jews remained aggrieved, while the military doggedly stuck to the line that they had conducted the census only with the very best of intentions. At this point, Oscar Cassel and Max Warburg made the issue their own. Cassel, a liberal politician and lawyer from Berlin, had long been involved in Jewish defensive work; Warburg, in contrast, was more at home in Hamburg's banking and business circles than with Jewish community matters. Throughout the winter, the pair fought a concerted campaign in the hope of drawing a full apology from the War Ministry.

Individually, Warburg and Cassel sent letter after letter to high-ranking officials in the War Ministry and Reich Chancellery; Warburg even managed to
engineer a face-to-face meeting with Max Hoffmann as he sought to push the
military to explain its actions.

By the following February, neither Warburg nor Cassel had much to show
for their efforts. Cassel managed to extract a begrudging line of apology from
the latest Prussian War Minister, Hermann von Stein. 'I have established that
the behaviour of the Jewish soldiers and fellow citizens during the war gave no
reason for my predecessor's order', Stein insisted. There was 'never any form
of prejudice against the Jews', he claimed. 'On the contrary they wanted to
acquire evidence to counter the complainants'. This was hardly a resounding
statement of faith in the Jewish soldiers. Stein neither condemned the basic
principle of counting, nor offered any basis for restoring Jewish communities'
badly tarnished reputations. Nonetheless, Cassel – perhaps by now weary of
the whole affair – accepted Stein's apology and stopped his personal campaign.
Warburg, on the other hand, was less easily pacified and continued to fight
almost a lone campaign against the census throughout 1917.[94]

Warburg was entirely right to demand a fuller apology. After all, the Jewish
census represented an attack by one group of Germans against another. It was,
however, not the only example of internal discord. Just before their count of
German Jews, the military also increased its surveillance of its soldiers from
Alsace-Lorraine. Commanders were instructed to tighten the censorship of
post, to ensure that men only utilised German in their conversation and to
keep tabs on the number of these soldiers in their division.[95] On one level, the
military's love of counting reflected the breakdown of inner unity; the warm
glow of the 'civic truce' had all but faded by late 1916. On quite another level,
though, these discriminatory measures were also a sign of Germans' increasingly reckless attitude towards ethnic and national minorities. In the west,
Rathenau pushed for the deportation of Belgian workers; in the East Pohl
arranged forced labour; and in Germany itself Goldschmidt and Struck set
about recording the racial characteristics of the ever-growing number of
POWs. German Jews, therefore, became both target and marksmen: victims
of the military census, but also quite willing to subject those at the margins to
forced labour or anthropological examination.

7

BREAKDOWN

Ernst Simon, the prominent Israeli educator and philosopher, was a young, rather green, volunteer at the time of Verdun. Unlike 143,000 other Germans, he survived the intense fighting, but only just. Suffering a severe leg wound, he went first to a military hospital before being moved to Berlin to recuperate during the winter months.[1] Simon's injuries eventually healed, but the horrors of the battle of Verdun and the subsequent Jewish census left a much deeper mark. In many respects, these two moments had a seminal influence on his very identity. Being first wounded and then counted killed off any of his earlier enthusiasm for the conflict and left him pondering where he truly belonged. For Simon, answers to his existential questions only started to emerge when he joined a Zionist youth group in Berlin. As he later put it, after the census 'we were now all Zionists'.[2]

The 'we' that Simon spoke of was actually not as all-encompassing as he implied. It has become almost a given that the military's census permanently altered German Jews' relationship to Germany. Some Jews, like Simon, became Zionists; others apparently deepened their Jewish identity and distanced themselves from Germany's war.[3] However, while there is certainly evidence of a deepening of 'Jewish consciousness', this was the exception rather than the rule. The students in the Kartell-Convent, for example, continued to publish their wartime newspaper; each edition proudly listed members who had died a 'hero's death' or who had won the Iron Cross in battle.[4] Rabbi Martin Salomonski also seemed to have lost little of his earlier support for the conflict. Moments of particular patriotism continued to capture Salomonski's imagination. When the kaiser turned fifty-eight in January 1917, for example,

Salomonski revelled in the large military celebrations held in Saint Quentin. 'We want to thank the kaiser', he noted with no sense of irony, 'for promoting our armed forces and creating the wonderful German fleet.'[5]

What actually occurred in the wake of the military's Jewish census was not so much a clearer sense of Jewishness, but rather new and deeper divisions. While some individuals like Ernst Simon turned inwards to seek community support, others, such as Martin Salomonski, remained firmly behind the conflict. The divisions opening up within the German-Jewish communities mirrored those in wider society. During 1917, Germany as a whole began to split along ever-more regional, social, political and religious lines. Not even the front was immune from such splits. Where Victor Klemperer was stationed, the talk was no longer of the German army, but about the fighting qualities of its different components. 'The Prussians lose ground; the Bavarians then have to win it back', went one common complaint.[6] As Germans would discover in the interwar years, once wounded, it proved very difficult to heal these divisions, to sew society back together again.

Jewish Solidarity?

Aside from Ernst Simon's utterances, the strongest expression of a change in German-Jewish self-understanding came from the writer Arnold Zweig. In his eloquent but damning short story 'Jewish Census at Verdun' ('Judenzählung vor Verdun'), the German military humiliate and castigate not only the living but also the dead. The Jewish war dead are called up one by one from their final resting places and are forced to declare whether or not they were Jewish in life. This ghastly roll-call brings various mutilated bodies back to the surface: 'Bullet holes through their heads, half their skulls ripped off by grenades, missing arms and legs, broken ribs poking out of shredded uniforms.' In Zweig's unflinching take on the Jewish census, the promise of national unity had gone; even the sanctity of military death was no longer free from anti-Semitic attack.[7]

More personal, but no less angry, angles on the post-census position of German Jews came from Julius Marx and Rabbi Georg Salzberger. In his oft-cited war diaries, Marx recorded the telling line: 'So that's why we're risking our necks for this country.'[8] From this point on, Marx struggled to contain his disillusionment with the German military and the conflict: 'Cold feet, trenches and shells, how much longer?' he groused.[9] Salzberger, whose familial background was similar to that of Zweig, painted an even bleaker picture of

German-Jewish life. To Salzberger, it seemed that the conflict was not bringing Jews and other Germans together, but remarkably pulling them apart. 'The cleft between Jews and Christians', he wrote, 'which had been bridged, has now opened up again. The Jew sees himself as marked', Salzberger concluded bitterly.[10]

Yet, in the case of Zweig, Marx and Salzberger, their consciousness of their Jewishness deepened gradually; the military's census might have hastened their journey, but it was certainly not the sole catalyst. Long before the fateful count of autumn 1916, all three already despaired of the horrors of war and had started to seek out an alternative future. The count merely confirmed the veracity of decisions already taken. Zweig may have entered the conflict with such high hopes in 1915, but as with so many other soldiers, his hopes were quickly subsumed by the realities of frontline life.[11] After his company had been transferred from the Eastern to the Western Front, the horrors of the war – and his own loneliness within it – appeared to hit home. He complained openly about the cold and damp, 'the dirt and grumpiness' eating away at his health, as well as the waste of his talents as an 'academic' at the front.[12]

Like Zweig, Georg Salzberger and Julius Marx had also already expressed their doubts about the war and the position of Jews within it. Marx recalled a story from earlier in the conflict, when a new commander had ranted that the Jews were 'cowardly dogs'. In response, he looked longingly at the other armies fighting, in which he believed no one saw any difference between Jews and non-Jews. For Salzberger, it was the growing number of Jewish casualties killed or wounded by the 'murderous weapons of war' that had ground him down.[13] As an antidote to this misery, Salzberger praised services and gatherings that allowed the Jewish soldiers to come together 'as a single community'.[14]

When the deep-rooted despair of Salzberger, Marx and Zweig mixed with the humiliation of the Jewish census, it is hardly surprising that all three started to question their relationship to Germany. Although born and educated in Germany, Zweig in particular no longer knew if he truly belonged. His emotional torment came flooding out in a letter to Martin Buber in which he powerfully described 'Germany's pain and our pain'. The result, as far as Zweig was concerned, was that he was no longer a German, but 'a captured civilian and a stateless foreigner'.[15] Salzberger similarly spoke of the 'deep internal change' that he and the Jewish soldiers experienced after the census. 'The Jews were viewed as a different form of human being', he reluctantly observed.[16]

If Germany rejected its loyal Jewish soldiers, then the obvious place for this dejected group to turn to should have been Jewish communities. There, in theory, they could hope to find comfort and support from a group of like-minded individuals. Unfortunately, in practice organised religion – both Christianity and Judaism – often failed to provide the answers to war, mass death and political upheaval that people sought. At the start of the conflict, there had been a belief that religious observance would rise markedly, but to the despair of priests, ministers and rabbis the exact opposite proved true; church and synagogue attendance often dropped.[17] Ever the optimist, Salzberger still hoped that a stronger sense of Jewish identity would emerge as a result of frontline fighting and the disappointment of the military's census. 'Where we Jews can take some comfort', he commented, 'is in the fact that our Jewish soldiers have become more Jewish.'[18] When Salzberger wrote these words, he had clearly not heard the views of the philosopher Julius Goldstein. After attending one of Martin Salomonski's synagogue services in Northern France, Goldstein left complaining of 'the banality and emptiness'. 'My poor Judaism!' he lamented. 'And people like this get sent out to represent us.'[19]

The one real sign of strengthening Jewish community came with the launch in April 1916 of Martin Buber's long-planned periodical, *Der Jude*. According to Buber, the journal was firmly rooted in the way that German Jews had experienced the war. The conflict represented 'the most difficult test for the Jewish people', he explained, but it also marked 'the start of genuine [Jewish] collection and unity'.[20] *Der Jude* undoubtedly sparkled with self-confidence, which was fitting for a journal that desired a new Jewish cultural renaissance. From the bold title – *The Jew* – through to its line-up of leading writers – Franz Kafka, Arnold Zweig and Gustav Landauer – this was a journal that sought to make an impression. However, its success also needs to be contextualised. *Der Jude*'s print run of 3,000–4,000, which was not even enough to cover its costs, meant that it was a rather marginal phenomenon, reaching only a small percentage of Central Europe's Jewish population.[21]

Thumbing through the pages of *Der Jude*, readers would have found only one, relatively short, article on the military's census. Martin Buber wrote a few paragraphs urging Jewish communities not to protest against the count, for this was the job of 'upstanding Germans', not 'upstanding Jews'.[22] The brevity of coverage in *Der Jude* should not be taken as a sign of lack of interest in the census and its wider impact; this was far from the case. Nonetheless, *Der Jude*'s rather fleeting discussion is in itself instructive. When looking back at the course of twentieth-century German history, the census has gained the unenviable reputation of having been a seminal event, permanently changing the relationship between Jews and other Germans from 1916 onwards.[23] While this may well have been the experience of Zweig, Marx and Simon, for many other German Jews the impact of the census was far from clear. Willy Cohn, who much later joined the Zionist movement, rightly remembered how the military's count did not suddenly change people's identities 'from one day to the next'. Developing a deeper Jewish consciousness or even a specifically Zionist outlook was a much more complex process that required a 'very long and serious mental struggle'.[24]

Holding the Line

In late January, the Jewish Women's League staged its fifth annual conference in Berlin. Some eighty members from across the country gathered in the capital to hear what their colleagues had achieved over the past year. The Leipzig group outlined its work to help Jewish refugees from Russia and Galicia, while the Breslau branch of the organisation discussed its new children's home for destitute orphans. As proceedings were drawing to a close, Bertha Pappenheim gathered the delegates to agree one final resolution: 'The delegates' conference of the Jewish Women's League as the representative body of 44,000 women . . . wishes to express how deeply painfully Jewish women – mothers, wives, fiancées and sisters – have experienced the German army's Jewish census.'

In her next breath, however, Pappenheim declared to her audience that all members of the organisation would continue to 'fulfil their duties to the fatherland' and to fight 'for German victory and greatness'.[25] This final line was more than mere rhetoric. It reflected the very real fact that, with the conflict still ongoing, it was difficult for any group to completely disengage itself from the war. And in short, this in itself was the reason why the military's census changed very little for most German Jews. Bullets whizzing past at the front or the deprivations at home meant that they, like all Germans, had little option but to continue to live their lives in the midst of war. Pragmatism, therefore, ruled the day.

Had German Jews wished to withdraw from the conflict, they would have found this an almost impossible task. During the winter of 1916–17 not only was there no let-up in the conflict, but the intensity of the war both on the frontlines and at home deepened significantly. On the Western Front, Hindenburg and Ludendorff reversed Falkenhayn's ill-fated offensive strategy and dug in for defence. As part of their new approach, the duo withdrew one section of their forces to the heavily fortified Hindenburg Line. In the east, in contrast, the military situation suddenly appeared far more favourable, although this turn was not entirely of Germany's own making. Street protests in the Russian capital, Petrograd, over food shortages turned rapidly into a full-blown revolution that eventually led to the abdication of Tsar Nicholas II in March 1917. This dramatic turn of events did not bring the conflict to a sudden end but it brought its conclusion much closer. After the revolution, the Russian soldiers seemed to lose the appetite to fight. As one German-Jewish soldier later recalled, the Russians frequently shouted out across the lines: 'We want peace.'[26]

At home, Germans had little choice but to continue to live their own lives in the shadow of war. There was no escaping economic turmoil, material shortages and the horror of mass death. Although Hindenburg and Ludendorff had opted for a defensive strategy in the west and the Russian army was buckling under the strain of the revolution in the east, Germany's casualty rate crept ever higher. During 1917 alone somewhere in the region of 335,000 soldiers lost their lives. Newspaper obituaries and special prayers spoken in both the Christian churches and Jewish synagogues may have become the norm, but there was still nothing routine about individual grief. In August, Maximilian Horwitz, president of the CV, joined the ranks of the bereaved. His only son, Hermann Horwitz, who had served in the army since the start of the conflict, lost his life in skirmishes near the Aisne. Hermann Horwitz may have been just one of many soldiers killed on that day and in that month, but this was of no comfort to his distraught family. It is unclear whether the news of his son's death hastened Horwitz senior's own journey to the grave. But two months later, he too found his final resting place and was buried amidst much emotion in the Jewish cemetery in Berlin-Weißensee.[27]

By this stage of the conflict, the threat of wartime death was no longer confined just to the battlefield. Food shortages caused by the Allied naval blockade, crop failures and poor distribution of available supplies saw people's daily calorific intake drop to below 900 in comparison to a normal diet of roughly 1,985 calories.[28] When the cold, wet winter of 1916–17 caused the failure of much of the potato harvest, the state promoted the virtues of the humble turnip in its place. The motto for housewives was simple: 'turnips instead of potatoes'.[29] Though these slogans were snappy, converting people to this tough and tasteless root vegetable proved a hard sell. The 'turnip winter', as it came to be dubbed, contributed to a significant rise in civilian mortality rates. By the war's end, 700,000 Germans had died from malnutrition alone.[30]

Margarete Sallis, a young Jewish student, just about managed to avoid going the same way. Living in a cold Berlin flat – no coal remained to heat it – left her with a terrible cough, which rapidly turned into a bout of whooping cough. Sallis needed an extended period in a Heidelberg sanatorium to regain something of her health.[31]

Shortages at home and death at the front almost always focused people's minds. Demoralising as the Jewish census was, mere survival remained the overriding priority. At the time of the count, many soldiers were in the midst of battle or, as was the case with Herbert Sulzbach, just about to return to the front. When Sulzbach's unit eventually made it to the Somme, the sight of 'dismembered houses' and the sound of 'humming and quaking' shells overhead hinted at the intensity of the battles that had already happened as well as those still to come.[32] Like many Jewish servicemen, Sulzbach made no reference to the military's census in his wartime diary.[33] Historians have sought to explain such absences by highlighting the shame of the count; soldiers apparently found it easier to ignore the event than to play the embarrassment of the count over and over in their minds. Of equal importance, however, was the issue of time and space. Soldiers ensconced in battle, as one army rabbi observed, were generally more concerned with the ongoing fight than with the military's count.[34]

Some 2,000 kilometres further east from where Sulzbach was fighting, Rosa Bendit, an experienced nurse from Stuttgart, was also embroiled in the travails of war. She had begun her wartime journey in August 1914 on the Alsatian Front, but by the time of the Jewish census had moved east to the Romanian town of Sibiu. Like Sulzbach, her greatest concern at this time was with the scenes of devastation and destruction that surrounded her. Heavy fighting around Brasov during the autumn of 1916 meant that up to 500 wounded landed in Bendit's hospital each day. By this stage of the conflict, some of those hospitalised were men well into middle age who had fought in battle for the first time. For Bendit and her fellow nurses, exhaustion simply became another part of their daily routine. They went to bed 'dead tired', she wrote wearily, but in the morning 'we wake up no better at all'.[35]

Bendit's battles against exhaustion were indicative of why so many German Jews allowed the military's census to pass them by. Simply put, amidst the bloodshed of war, people's energies were focused on more pressing matters of life and death. For many German Jews, then, the military's count initially changed very little; they remained as soldiers, nurses and home-front patriots. Adding to this sense of continuity was the fact that German Jews still received official recognition for their commitment to the war effort. In autumn 1916, just one month after the census, the Austrian Knight's Cross (*Ritterkreuz*) was bestowed on Rabbi Arnold Tänzer in recognition of his ongoing service to the Bug Army. A few months later, the Ottoman Empire awarded Arthur Oppenheimer the prestigious Iron Crescent medal as a reward for his efforts to secure grain supplies for the Central Powers.[36]

Iron Cross decorations also continued to flood in. The numbers awarded to Jewish servicemen actually went up rather than down during the second half of the war. Admittedly part of the reason for this rise was a general devaluation in the currency of the decoration. Where in 1914 the medal was only issued for the most heroic of acts, by 1917 participation in a few skirmishes could be enough to earn an Iron Cross 2nd Class. One joke that did the rounds, as Julius Goldstein recounted, was that while it was 'hard to earn the Iron Cross, it was very easy to be awarded it'.[37] Nonetheless, the very fact that German Jews continued to win the Iron Cross helped to reinforce the picture that the Jewish soldiers remained active participants in Germany's military struggle.

A similar sense of continuity could be discerned from the promotions process. The Jewish census did not radically alter German Jews' chances of being promoted. Indeed, in the six months following the military's census, a further 137 Jewish soldiers rose to become reserve officers. Sulzbach fell into this category, being promoted to second lieutenant soon after the count.[38] The impression of continuity here, however, came not just from those promoted, but also from those rejected. As had been the case earlier in the war, the military authorities remained quick to find reasons not to promote German Jews. One long-serving Jewish soldier, Max Maier, a member of the prestigious Hussars, was encouraged to apply to become an officer. His forms and references were approved without question, but in order to proceed any further the regimental adjutant demanded he be baptised. 'I want to remain a Jew', Maier responded, and that was the end of his officer career before it had even started.[39]

Ultimately, though continuing to restrict the promotion of Jewish soldiers was a strange way of going about it, the German authorities wanted the country's Jewish population to remain committed to the war. In early 1917, Frankfurt's police president, Riess von Scheurnschloss, expressed his fears that the city's Jewish communities would disengage from the conflict. His concern was not driven by any form of altruism, but rather stemmed from a fear that Jewish communities, who he rather brazenly presumed to have financial influence, would stop paying into the next round of war bonds.[40] Riess need not have feared; German Jews backed the campaign with gusto, once again contributing large financial sums. If there were any doubts whether Jewish communities would continue to back the war in the wake of the military's census, then the answer was clear. The vast majority of German Jews remained committed to the war, not out of compulsion, but out of choice.

Unleashing the Weapons of War

With little in the way of military success to cheer, Germans had to find other events to celebrate instead. Hindenburg's seventieth birthday on 2 October 1917 provided just such an occasion. In Bonn, a celebratory event was held in the town's main theatre, while further east the *Coburger Zeitung* printed an image of a stern-looking Hindenburg alongside a German and an Austrian soldier.[41] Ernst Lissauer, clearly unfazed by the furore surrounding his 'Hymn of Hate', penned his own elegy in honour of the venerable general. Homing in on all the characteristics that apparently made Hindenburg such a formidable figure, Lissauer praised his 'mannerisms and speech', and noted his 'massive sense of calm' and ability to carry 'responsibility like a mountain'.[42] Lissauer's swooning paean to Hindenburg represented his own genuine and sustained commitment to the conflict, but it was far more than just a nod of support. Lissauer, like many German Jews, went beyond pure pragmatism and also demonstrated a steadfast and unflinching passion for the war and Germany's military cause.

Public enthusiasm for the conflict had plummeted dramatically by 1917, but despite this there was no shortage of German Jews still willing to help Germany achieve victory. Young people, who clearly occupied a very different demographic to Lissauer, were among the most committed. Those born between 1900 and 1908, who had grown up, attended school and pursued their leisure interests in the midst of a society at war, seemed to display a carefree attitude towards authority. Concerned pedagogues viewed this wartime generation with considerable anxiety. Like other German communities, the Jewish school board in Berlin witnessed 'a frightening increase in different crimes' committed by young Jews. In its view, in the absence of strong father figures their young people were running wild.[43] A more compelling reason for the younger generation's unruliness, however, was their desire to escape the tedium of home life for the excitement and adventure of the fighting front.[44]

The War Office (Kriegsamt), which had been formed under the Hindenburg Programme, sought to tap into this well of youthful enthusiasm by increasing the number of civilians employed in auxiliary roles. By utilising young people behind the lines, men would be freed up for the fighting front. In the face of some protest, women also received permission to assist the military, serving just behind the lines as rear-echelon helpers (*Etappenhelferinnen*). The Jewish social reformer Alice Salomon visited some of these new recruits during a tour of occupied Eastern Europe. Although she tried to put a positive gloss on the women's new roles, Salomon viewed the entire enterprise with suspicion. She looked on aghast at the 'primitive' conditions and was also sceptical of the men who lived without females for so long. Salomon warned that only women 'from an educated background, with good skills, good principles and a strong character' should consider applying.[45]

Salomon's scepticism reflected the fears of wider society. Women may have been accepted in the nursing profession, but mobilising women as rear-echelon helpers was a different matter. Such a move went against people's understanding of existing gender roles. Lion Wolff, a rabbi in the twilight of his years, certainly shared these concerns. The men 'fight, suffer and die' to protect the female space of 'home and hearth', he explained forcibly.[46] Many of those in the military shared Wolff's concerns and seemed to take great pleasure in finding a reason to send female helpers back home. One woman was dismissed for allegedly staying out all night and then trying to creep back into her accommodation 'disguised as an infantryman'; another female helper was sent home for damaging 'the reputation of German women'. For good measure, the report added that she was also poor on the telephone.[47]

Grumbles from those at home and at the front dampened the atmosphere but did nothing to stop women volunteering. From less than 5,000 in July 1917, the number of females serving in the occupation zones rose month on month to stand at over 17,000 by the war's end.[48] Jewish women, who were as keen as other young German women to travel overseas and to earn a proper wage, certainly made up some of this figure. Sophie Hellmann, for example, had begun the war working as a nurse in her home city of Nuremberg. It was not long, though, before the lure of foreign adventure took her to occupied Brussels, where she was employed as a military secretary. By all accounts, her new position proved a personal triumph; promotion, a pay rise and even the Merit Cross for War Aid (Verdienstkreuz für Kriegshilfe) all followed in quick succession.[49] Another Jewish civilian, Helene Klascher, remained closer to home, but no less involved in the military. Klascher, who was fluent in French, put her language skills to good use, serving as a military translator in one of the POW camps surrounding Stuttgart.[50]

The history of the First World War by 1917, however, was not just one of new, more youthful faces taking up military positions. In many cases, the enthusiasm of older figures, involved in the war from the very start, remained undimmed. Fritz Haber, for example, appeared to be as enthralled by the conflict as ever. When he married his second wife Charlotte Nathan that autumn, he appeared at the ceremony in full military uniform. In a photograph taken on the day, Haber's broad grin, which shines out from under his spiked *Pickelhaube*, exudes a sense of quiet contentment (see Plate 18). Aside from his new marriage, he had many reasons to smile. Haber appeared to have arrived at the very heart of the German state; he could dash off letters on War Ministry-headed notepaper or rush off to the war zones in east and west to attend to urgent military business.[51]

It was not just the general accoutrements of the military that had Haber in their grip; the scientist also retained a blinkered attachment to chemical warfare. During 1917, Haber and the War Ministry colluded over plans to establish a new gas institute to be housed in the Kaiser Wilhelm Institute. Both sides had much to gain from the enterprise. The War Ministry wanted to develop Germany's expertise in gas warfare, while Haber was keen to secure new sources of funding for his own research activities.[52] In pitching his proposals to the senate of the Kaiser Wilhelm Institute, Haber played down the future importance of gas weapons, emphasising instead civilian applications for chemical technology. Nonetheless, his report still looked back proudly at how his work had helped to 'revive' the technology of chemical weapons and how he hoped 'to strengthen the connection between national defence and science'.[53] Haber, then, remained an unreformed enthusiast for gas warfare. Neither international outcry over this tactic nor the German state's increasingly belligerent attitude to its own citizens dented his commitment to the war and the way it was being fought.

Davis Trietsch was another prominent German-Jewish figure who seemed unperturbed by the direction in which the war was going. Trietsch remained a fierce advocate of an expansionist war-aims policy, which he hoped would ultimately bring Germany a spate of new colonial possessions. Having already carved up parts of Europe in his previous publications, Trietsch now turned his gaze to Africa. Along similar lines to Naumann and Rathenau's idea for a German-dominated Central Europe, Trietsch made the case for a new German Central Africa (Mittelafrika). 'Our goal', he stated in no uncertain terms, 'has to be to form a large African colonial empire, which stretches from the south-west to the southeast . . . connecting areas which were once French, Belgian or even English.' As Trietsch's writing implied, possession of this central belt of Africa would help to end the Entente's dominance of the continent, while at the same time providing Germany with its own strategic and economic base in Africa.[54]

Eugen Mittwoch, a German-Jewish Orientalist based at the University of Berlin, understood the desire of Trietsch and others to expand Germany's colonial influence, but his approach relied more on soft power than outright coercion. From spring 1916, Mittwoch headed up the Information Office for the Orient (Nachrichtenstelle für den Orient), which had been founded at the start of the war by the archaeologist Max von Oppenheim. Mittwoch's organ-isation, which was technically under the auspices of the Foreign Office, spear-headed German propaganda efforts in the Middle East and in parts of Africa. If the Muslim world could be won over to the German cause, then the hope was that Britain and France's colonial dominance would be nullified. With this goal in mind, the Information Office supported Arab and African nation-alists, presenting them with published materials and financial aid.[55]

Bethmann Hollweg, who did his best to keep both annexationists and more moderate figures on side, sought to play down the demands for exten-sive expansion in Europe, the Middle East and Africa. But by the winter of 1916–17, Bethmann Hollweg had a second, far more dangerous, dispute on his hands: unrestricted submarine warfare. Germany had already employed submarines throughout the conflict with rather mixed results. To their credit, the country's leaders had just about managed to avoid provoking the United States to enter the war, but in the debit column, the submarines rarely managed to sink more than 200,000 tons of merchant ships a month. As far as the Admiralty was concerned, this poor statistic confirmed that their powerful weapon had been effectively neutered. Instead of adhering to inter-national rules of engagement, as had hitherto been the case, the Admiralty demanded the introduction of a policy of unrestricted submarine warfare which would allow their boats to torpedo enemy shipping without warning. It dismissed any suggestions that this policy could hasten American entry – Bethmann Hollweg's biggest fear – by reassuring the doubters that the subma-rine would soon bring Britain to its knees and as a result the war to a swift conclusion.[56]

The Admiralty's confidence was not entirely unfounded. A small group of civilian experts, headed by the Heidelberg professor of economics Hermann

Levy, who had converted to Protestantism in his youth, gathered a body of statistics that appeared to confirm the Admiralty's claims. The material that Levy and his colleagues put together was based more on wishful thinking than hard evidence, but nonetheless it offered a path to victory in which both the Admiralty and the general public were more than happy to believe.[57] Support for unrestricted submarine warfare gathered momentum through 1916 and into 1917 with both conservative and more moderate politicians backing the weapon. Georg Bernhard, who Theodor Wolff mockingly labelled the 'raging U-boat hero', frequently used the *Vossische Zeitung* to promote the wonders of submarine warfare.[58] Other less high-profile German Jews followed a similar line to Bernhard. The Berlin lawyer Wilhelm Loewenfeld, for example, wrote a forceful letter to the Foreign Office arguing for the use of submarines as the only means 'to push England towards peace'.[59]

After months of debate, Germany's military leaders finally got their way in early 1917 when the kaiser agreed to a campaign of unrestricted submarine warfare to start on 1 February. In a retrospective defence of his own position, Bernhard suggested that almost all Germans had welcomed the new submarine campaign. 'In public, aside from the extreme left', he recalled, 'there were almost no voices of opposition to this type of naval warfare.'[60] Presumably Bernhard's otherwise sharp mind must have been rather hazy on this particular point, as there were a great number of Jews and other Germans who responded to unrestricted submarine warfare with great alarm. Theodor Wolff, already a critic of Germany's wartime methods, expected nothing more than 'America's declaration of war'. Expressing a similar sense of resignation, Max Warburg branded the decision to unleash the submarines as 'a mad step'.[61]

Despite these concerns, once the submarines had slipped their moorings and entered the war zone, Jewish communities generally gave the campaign their public backing. A mix of patriotism and politics – the need to be seen backing the war – encouraged the communities' (at times somewhat sceptical) support. In private, Ballin, like Rathenau, was deeply pessimistic, seeing little chance of the submarines forcing the British to make peace.[62] Yet in public, he put his concerns to one side and helped to establish the U-Boot-Spende, which was the latest in a long line of fundraising appeals for servicemen and their families. Other prominent German Jews to join Ballin in putting their names to the appeal were Eduard Arnhold, Arthur Salomonsohn and Max Warburg. In Bochum, meanwhile, Rabbi Moritz David, who remained an ever-enthusiastic supporter of the conflict, urged the local population to reach into their pockets and to donate money for Germany's submarine 'heroes'.[63]

The U-Boot-Spende appeal proved a massive success, bringing in over 20 million Marks for submariners and their families.[64] Public support for their undersea heroes was clearly welcome, but it did very little to make life on board any easier. Being crammed into a hot, airless steel tube with forty other sailors for company quickly took its toll on a ship's crew. Adding to these almost unbearable conditions were limited supplies of food and water, as well as the constant threat of death. During 1917 alone, seventy-five German submarines were lost, many with no survivors.[65] As was the case with the navy more generally, only a small number of German Jews served on the submarines. One Jewish sailor who did see active service under sea was the young Silesian Max Haller. Moving from the surface fleet to submarines in 1916, Haller went on to spend the remainder of the war on *UC-22*, a 400-ton mine-laying vessel.[66] His wartime notebook, although irregularly kept, gives some sense of the routine on board, which seemed to swing between 'bad weather', boredom ('*nirgends was zu machen*') and moments of action: 'steamer torpedoed. Large explosions.'[67]

The rigours of life on board did little to deter Haller and his comrades in their fight against enemy vessels. In February, *UC-22* attacked several armed merchant ships in the Mediterranean, while in June its crew sunk a French submarine, the *Ariane*, before sending the French troop carrier, the *Golo II*, to the seabed in August 1917 with the loss of 125 lives.[68] The fate of these men warranted little more than an aside in Haller's wartime notebook. 'Golo II torpedoed', he recorded. 'There were some 300 men on board and several high-ranking officers. We took 4 captains on board.' What happened to the remaining men went unsaid. 'On arriving back in dock', he continued, 'we discovered that our very first captain had won the Pour le Mérite.'[69] Haller's dogged hunting down of the enemy matched Haber's unswerving enthusiasm for gas warfare and Bernhard's chauvinistic editorship of the *Vossische Zeitung*. When these different strands of Germany's war effort were placed together, it was clear that many German Jews still retained much of their appetite for the conflict. The Jewish census of 1916 and the growing hardships on all fronts may have wiped some of the lustre from the fight, but their desire to see Germany emerge victorious was undiminished.

A Political Implosion

In a letter to General Hans von Seeckt in March 1917, Rathenau expressed his fears for the unrestricted submarine warfare campaign. His worries had nothing to do with the actual tactics employed, but instead concerned the likelihood of a British capitulation. 'So far the evidence doesn't point in this direction', he observed sagely.[70] Rathenau was right to be apprehensive. Although the submarines increased their strike rate, the tonnage sunk was still too low to have any real effect on the British war effort. A far more ominous sign of the strategy's failure, however, came not on the high seas but across the Atlantic in Washington. On 2 April, Woodrow Wilson, the Democratic president of the United States, stood up before a joint session of Congress to deliver one simple message: 'I advise that the Congress declare the recent course of the Imperial German Government to be in fact nothing less than war against the government and people of the United States.'[71] Four days later, Wilson's request was granted and the United States entered the conflict on the side of the Entente. Instead of forcing the British to sue for peace, as originally promised, the reverse had happened: Germany had added another powerful new foe to its growing list of enemies.

The advocates of unrestricted submarine warfare – among them many German Jews – achieved their goal of unleashing Germany's submarine fleet, but it came at a high cost. Militarily, America's entry tipped the balance in favour of the Entente, while domestically, the failure of the submarine campaign fatally damaged public morale. German Jews now found themselves in the middle of a maelstrom of political debate as German society started to tear itself apart. Bernhard's *Vossische Zeitung*, which remained as belligerent as ever, did its best to raise spirits. The newspaper dismissed the American threat as nothing but a minor irritation. 'We will continue to follow our preordained path', it optimistically declared, 'confident that even America's alliance with our enemies will not alter the outcome of this war to our disadvantage.'[72] Georg Arnhold, head of the Gebrüder Arnhold banking concern, tried a different tack. He suggested that Britain's food supply problems were in fact 'growing from week to week' and thus Germany was close to making a major breakthrough.[73] Despite Bernhard's and Arnhold's best efforts, public scepticism continued to rise. It was not victory that they could see on the horizon, but rather more enemies and fewer military options.

The failure of submarine warfare to end the conflict gave renewed impetus to a growing strike movement on the home front. During 1917, Germany experienced some 561 separate strikes, a massive increase on the 136 incidents that had occurred only two years before.[74] These earlier strikes had stemmed from a familiar set of complaints: wages, working conditions and hours. By 1917, a further set of disgruntlements had been added to this mix. The continuation of the war, the lack of adequate food supplies and further reductions to bread rations all combined in April to send thousands of disillusioned workers, starving housewives and children spilling on to the streets in protest. 'A new general strike appears to be brewing', observed the German-Jewish historian Gustav Mayer.[75] The protests themselves, which mainly affected Berlin and Leipzig, never quite reached the level of a general strike, although reports of smashed and looted shops certainly pointed to a scene of some devastation.[76]

Broken windows and looting were bad enough, but of even greater concern for the authorities was that politics also intruded into the April strikes. Those on the streets were calling not just for food and better working conditions, but also for peace and a fairer franchise. With recent events in Petrograd fresh in their minds, Germany's leaders could ill afford their own revolution. The military and the police, therefore, acted swiftly to quash any signs of left-wing agitation. Rosa Luxemburg, the Polish-Jewish leader of the Spartacus League, was already locked up in prison on charges of treason alongside Karl Liebknecht, the league's co-founder. Those still at liberty, such as Oskar Cohn and Hugo Haase, who sought to politicise the strike movement, faced the threat of incarceration. One of their contemporaries, the young Jewish socialist Rosi Wolfstein, was herself marked for arrest after she was caught distributing political pamphlets in the industrial Ruhr region.[77]

The involvement of Wolfstein, Cohn and Haase in the April strikes, along with Adolf Cohen – a leader of the Metalworkers' Union – gave ammunition to a popular discourse connecting Jews with socialist agitation. Heinrich Claß, as ever at the forefront of anti-Semitic campaigns, sensed an international Jewish conspiracy designed to seize world power.[78] A disastrous split within the SPD that same month provided further evidence for those seeking it that German Jews had abandoned the war effort for a socialist and pacifist future. An extreme left-wing faction of the SPD, which was already separate from the main party, finally broke away in April 1917 to form a new party, the Independent Social Democratic Party of Germany (Unabhängige Sozialdemokratische Partei Deutschlands, the USPD). After their acrimonious divorce, there were now two parties claiming to speak for Germany's working class. The USPD, though, went a stage further and also positioned itself in opposition 'to the war policy of the Imperial Government', which the SPD in contrast continued to back.[79]

Out of the USPD's eighteen founding members, six were Jewish, including the party's first leader, Hugo Haase, who had relinquished his role as chairman of the SPD the previous year. The preponderance of Jewish members in the

USPD did not pass unnoticed. Conservative politicians and those on the extreme right, whose own politics were clearly at odds with those of the USPD, referred to the new party as the 'Haase group' or the 'party of Herr Cohn'. The label of choice conveniently always managed to encompass the name of one of the USPD's Jewish members. Reinhard Mumm, a follower of Adolf Stoecker's anti-Semitic ideology, took this labelling to the extreme when he referred to the new party as the 'Cohn, Herzfeld, Stadthagen, Bernstein' group. It was no coincidence that all four had a Jewish family background.[80]

As had been its general approach in the past, the CV hoped the entire furore would simply fade away with time. The Jewish defence organisation, though, had clearly not counted on the response of Oskar Cohn, one of the USPD's more outspoken parliamentarians. When Cohn entered parliament in 1912, he quickly gained a reputation as a powerful orator, which no doubt was partly due to his previous career as a lawyer. In May 1917 – less than a month after the USPD's founding – Cohn put these skills to good effect when he took to the floor of the Reichstag to deliver an extraordinarily provocative speech. He attacked Hindenburg, branded Germany 'a military autocracy' and declared the war unwinnable. With the jeers of the right ringing through the chamber, Cohn ended by reciting the refrain of the socialist 'Internationale'; making the matter even worse, Cohn chose the French rather than the German lyrics.[81] The CV looked on aghast as a German Jew attacked 'the feelings of a large part of the German people'. In an attempt to calm the situation, it assured the public that 'German Jewry has nothing in common with the politics or the talk of Dr Cohn'.[82]

Unfortunately for the CV, over the weeks that followed, Germany's political landscape became even more fraught. But rather than the USPD, it was now the majority SPD that placed German Jews back under the spotlight. In July, after unrestricted submarine warfare had failed to make a breakthrough, Matthias Erzberger, the leader of the Catholic Centre Party, proposed a resolution calling for a 'new orientation in internal as well as external affairs and peace without annexations or indemnities'.[83] In his endeavours, Erzberger was ably supported by the German-Jewish parliamentarian Eduard David. As the SPD's representative in discussions over the peace resolution, David took a hand in drafting the final text. When this 'spectacular act of parliamentary defiance' passed through the Reichstag on 19 July, it represented a decisive break between the more moderate parties and Germany's conservative forces, which remained determined to achieve a victorious peace.[84]

The liberal press was full of plaudits for the peace resolution, as it appeared to mark the start of a new, more democratic 'parliamentary system'.[85] While David and Erzberger basked in the warm glow of success, Haase popped up, like an uninvited guest at a wedding, not to praise their achievements but to highlight the pair's failings. He complained that on one level the resolution was unlikely to bring an immediate peace, while on another it was also filled with a lot of empty rhetoric. The resolution may have called for a peace without 'territorial annexations by force', but, as Haase pointed out, it made no mention of territory that had been acquired without force, where Germany was trying to extend its economic and political influence using more informal methods. David simply rejected Haase's contentions as being 'dishonestly reasoned'.[86] What was most significant about this spat was that it pitched the USPD against the SPD, but also German Jew against German Jew.

Haase's and David's public involvement in the peace resolution, albeit on opposing sides, further riled the German right. Already enraged at the temerity of elected politicians to undermine the military campaign, Heinrich Claß and his supporters went on the attack. Konstantin von Gebsattel, a longstanding member of Claß's Pan-German League, dismissed the parliamentary resolution as nothing but a 'Jewish peace' threatening a true 'German peace'.[87] This, though, was only the start. In September, the German right coalesced around a new nationalist movement, the German Fatherland Party (Deutsche Vaterlandspartei). Led by Wolfgang Kapp and the redoubtable Alfred von Tirpitz, the party grew rapidly to become a haven for disgruntled Germans of a nationalist persuasion. Part of the group's appeal to the right was that it promised a 'Hindenburg peace', which unlike the parliamentary peace resolution meant ending hostilities with territorial conquest.

With Germans angry and divided over the failure of unrestricted submarine warfare and then the peace resolution, there was a certain inevitability to Bethmann Hollweg's fall from power. The chancellor was wise enough to know that the end was coming, so in a vain attempt to save himself he promised to reform Prussia's antiquated electoral franchise. But as Ballin wittily pointed out, this was a case of too little, too late. 'Bethmann is like a bankrupt banker', he observed, 'who wants to enjoy another few days in the stock market and theatre, and in order to do this robs a bank vault.'[88] Once Bethmann Hollweg had finally filed for proverbial bankruptcy and retired to his Hohenfinow estate, few Germans shed a tear. Haase's main concern, for example, was that the new chancellor, Georg Michaelis, was nothing but 'Ludendorff's mouthpiece'.[89] Bethmann Hollweg's departure may have been generally accepted, but it was nonetheless a damning indictment of the strategy that Germany had followed during 1917. Instead of the promised end to hostilities, the submarine campaign had only served to highlight the country's political, social and military shortcomings.

Blurred Dividing Lines

Bethmann Hollweg's resignation did nothing to calm German domestic politics. While the Reichstag peace resolution gave the more moderate parties a much-needed boost, the German right continued to seethe at parliament's actions. During the summer, the Pan-German League turned its attention to what it called the 'Jewish press'. It accused the *Berliner Tageblatt*, the *Frankfurter Zeitung* and the SPD's organ *Vorwärts*, which all had Jewish editors or owners, of conspiring against the right's annexationist plans.[90] Such attacks could have given the impression that German Jews had been pushed to the very margins of society, but this was never entirely the case.[91] Against a backdrop of rising anti-Semitism, some German Jews continued to sympathise with the right's annexationist agenda. Georg Bernhard, for example, may have been a member of the increasingly vilified 'Jewish press', but he had little time for the Reichstag's peace resolution. Under his editorship, the *Vossische Zeitung* questioned the 'point' of the resolution and urged parliament to avoid destroying 'internal unity' and damaging the country's 'defensive will'.[92] By 1917, German society was clearly deeply divided. However, this was not a clean break; these fractures ran in multiple directions.

Bernhard's criticisms proved fairly mild in comparison to some of the attacks launched against the peace resolution by other German Jews. Most vociferously, Adolf Grabowsky vented his own anger at recent events through his stewardship of *Das neue Deutschland*. What Grabowsky feared was that a peace without annexations would send out a dangerous signal to Germany's enemies. If Germany stopped pursuing territorial expansion, it would 'have to forgo [its] place with the other great powers', he predicted. Paul Nikolaus Cossmann, one of Grabowsky's contemporaries as editor of the *Süddeutsche Monatshefte*, held a similarly disingenuous view of the peace resolution. Cossmann emerged from his office, habitually filled with the acrid smoke of strong cigars, to republish one of Claß's own articles. In this short piece, Claß condemned the peace resolution as a 'denouncement and denigration of Bismarck's great achievements', a view that Cossmann presumably shared.[93]

As Cossmann and Grabowsky's responses clearly demonstrated, the warm glow of German nationalist politics continued to seduce some German Jews even during the latter stages of the war. More remarkably perhaps, a small number of Jews actively sought a home in Tirpitz's new German Fatherland Party. Arthur Salomonsohn and Georg Solmssen, both directors of the powerful Disconto-Gesellschaft, signed up as party members, as did Louis Hagen, the influential banker and investor in many Rhineland industrial concerns. Solmssen appeared to be so taken by the new party's nationalist policies that he even gave the movement financial support.[94] No German Jews, though, went quite as far in their support of the Fatherland Party as the journalist Clemens Klein, who was a recent convert to Christianity. With smart suit, clipped moustache and pince-nez spectacles, Klein looked every bit an upright German citizen. Klein must have given the right impression, as in spring 1918 he rose to become the party's press secretary, a position which allowed him to place his journalistic talents at the service of the party's annexationist agenda.[95]

Klein's rapid elevation to press secretary was met with considerable bewilderment from within the Fatherland Party. Some members struggled to conceive of how Klein would ever be able to rally the movement against 'Judaism and the Jewish representatives of the press'.[96] This attack on Klein was certainly no isolated incident; the Fatherland Party very quickly established a reputation for harbouring anti-Semites and for giving voice to anti-Jewish rhetoric. With anti-Semitism growing inside the movement, the CV decided to take their concerns directly to Tirpitz, who in a brief letter reassured the group that the Fatherland Party welcomed all confessions as members. 'I deeply regret' the occasions where 'the name "Fatherland Party" has been misused by anti-Semitically orientated individuals', he added. Although the CV remained highly sceptical of the movement, it was forced to acknowledge that a small number of German Jews, like Klein, identified with Tirpitz's party and therefore could not be discouraged from joining.[97]

For its part, the German Fatherland Party managed to perform a difficult juggling act; it accepted Jews into the movement, but at the same time did very little to curtail the anti-Semitic tendencies of its wider membership. Notwithstanding Tirpitz's assurances to the CV, his party was dogged by anti-Semitic incidents throughout its short existence.[98] The Fatherland Party, therefore, displayed some of the common characteristics of historic anti-Semitism. It projected its fears onto an imaginary Jew, someone who embodied all the worries of a modern, capitalist society. In contrast, real, existing Jews, who might be friends or neighbours (or in the case of the Fatherland Party its own members), were spared some of the most damning criticism.[99]

Nowhere was the phenomenon of this imaginary Jew more visible than at the fighting front. In the latter half of the war, pressures on Jewish soldiers started to grow. Frustrations at the lack of military progress, combined with internal divisions and sinking morale, led to an increasing number of anti-Semitic incidents. Erich Schlesinger, a Jewish legal specialist, complained bitterly about the inflammatory remarks he heard at the front. 'As I have personally observed', he wrote, 'anti-Semitism is stronger than ever.' On the Romanian front, the situation appeared to be just as bad. Nurse Rosa Bendit recounted how a senior military doctor had made an openly anti-Semitic comment in front of her and her colleagues. 'Anti-Semitism is very widespread here', she noted despairingly.[100] However, for every Bendit or Schlesinger there were just as many German Jews who experienced little day-to-day discrimination. One Jewish soldier remembered that he 'never experienced any unpleasantness at all' that could be put down to 'anti-Jewish tendencies or views'. Another Jewish soldier, who happened to be serving with his brother on the Eastern Front, wrote that 'we never heard a derogatory word, never an anti-Semitic utterance'.[101]

The striking difference in these soldiers' experiences of the frontline can be put down to the distinction between imagined Jews and actual Jews. Where soldiers lived and fought side by side, relationships tended to run deep. Friendships sometimes developed, but more often than not a sense of 'group solidarity or comradeship' at least pervaded at the micro level.[102] In their small fighting units, where Jews and other Germans fought closely together, anti-Semitism was rarely directed internally towards Jewish members. The Bavarian List Regiment, for example, which counted fifty-nine German Jews as well as a young Adolf Hitler in its ranks, showed few signs of harbouring any form of anti-Semitic spirit.[103]

Jewish soldiers' wartime photo albums typically paint a very similar picture. On the Eastern Front, Robert Ehrmann's only clashes with comrades appear to have been of the light-hearted variety. One image captures an icy scene of Ehrmann play-fighting with another soldier (see Plate 19). As Ehrmann dives in, clutching an icicle in each hand, his comrade dodges back out of the way, while drawing back his own icicles, ready to strike. Admittedly the climate was markedly different, but Max Haller and his comrades aboard *UC-22* also shared very similar moments of joviality. In the midst of the unrestricted submarine warfare campaign Haller and two other crew members stripped down to their shorts to enjoy the sun, sea and sand of the Adriatic (see Plate 20). This 'holiday snap' recorded not tensions between Jews and other Germans but rather what on the surface appeared to be very friendly relations.

Ehrmann and Haller, like most other Jewish soldiers, ended up living between two worlds: the familiar environment of friends, family and close comrades on the one side and then the increasingly hostile world of German wartime society on the other. However, it was not just German society that started to split and fracture; Jewish communities also found themselves in the midst of internal strife. The main lines of debate revolved around the war and Jewish identity more generally. Hermann Cohen, the unofficial spokesman for the liberal camp, followed the older line, advocating the unity of Jewishness and Germanness. In the opposite corner stood the formidable figure of Martin Buber, who spoke of a form of cultural Jewish nationalism, which placed the idea of Jewish identity firmly to the fore.[104] Unlike Cohen, Buber also turned against the war. Conveniently forgetting his earlier fervent support for the fight, Buber attacked those Jews who continued to back the conflict. Chief amongst these was the nationalist poet Rudolf Borchardt, who had once controversially suggested that 'we will crush Russia'. 'I have affinity neither with this "we" nor with crushing', declared Buber defiantly.[105]

Divided over both the war and the question of German-Jewish identity, a clash between Buber and Cohen appeared almost inevitable. When it happened in late 1916, the two intellectual heavyweights ended up fighting over the necessity of a future Jewish state. Cohen set the debate rolling when he very publicly dismissed the Zionists' goals in Palestine as a distraction for German Jews who were firmly tied to German culture. Buber responded by claiming first that Cohen had ignored the very real problems that German Jews faced, and second that he had also misinterpreted the dimensions of a new Jewish state. Palestine was not a nationalist dream, Buber argued, but was instead about humane ideals for mankind as a whole.[106]

Just as the debate between Buber and Cohen appeared to be dying down, another contentious issue – this time in the shape of the Balfour Declaration – emerged to sow further discord within Jewish communities. While German Zionists had clearly long desired the promise of a Jewish national home in Palestine, receiving this gift from Germany's wartime enemy, Britain, had never been part of their calculation. Arthur Hantke, chairman of Germany's principal Zionist movement, recognised that the Balfour Declaration, although far from ideal, was a moment to celebrate. 'It would make a terrible impression in the wider world', he remarked, 'if German Jews were to protest against the idea of a Jewish Palestine.'[107] However, while the Zionist movement basked in the warm glow of international recognition, other sections of German-Jewish life were more circumspect in their response. Most strikingly, the German national periodical *Liberales Judentum* reminded its readers that Judaism was first and foremost a religion, rather than a nation as the Zionists believed. 'It is this that separates us', it added.[108]

Debates over the future direction of German-Jewish life were always more than a mere intellectual pursuit. Local and national Jewish organisations, even entire families, split over the direction in which the war was going, and over German Jews' role within it. In Mönchengladbach, a young Hans Jonas angered his father by becoming the only family member to turn to Zionism; the Scholem family were similarly split. The younger brother, Gershom, was drawn to Zionism, while the older brother, Werner, was active in left-wing anti-war politics. Their father, a proud German patriot, threw the pair out in disgust. He paid me 'one hundred Marks on 1 March and that was it – end of story', remembered Gershom.[109] The national stage magnified such splits several times over. Very few German Jews were as committed to the idea of peace as Hugo Haase and Oskar Cohn of the USPD; instead far more Jews remained sympathetic towards the wider war effort and – in the case of Bernhard and Loewenfeld – even clamoured for unrestricted submarine warfare. For a society that had entered the war in August 1914 apparently united, the journey to division and acrimony had been rapid. As Jews and other Germans quickly discovered, once society was divided, recreating some form of unity proved exceedingly difficult.

8

MYTHS OF DEFEAT

For Arnold Tänzer, the winter of 1917–18 proved to be one of his busiest. Not only was he constantly on the move as an army rabbi on the Eastern Front, but in his spare time he also managed to research and write a history of the Jews of Brest-Litovsk. The Polish (later Belorussian) city, which had been home to a thriving Jewish population, was badly damaged during the Russian retreat of 1915. Under the 'yoke of the Muscovites', as Tänzer labelled the Russians, buildings were destroyed and the city's Jewish inhabitants attacked. Thanks to the 'bravery of the allied armies' who had recaptured Brest-Litovsk, he hoped that Jewish life would bloom once again.[1] Tänzer's book struck something of a chord with Germany's ruling classes, who clearly welcomed his description of the German army as a benevolent force for good. The kaiser, Ludendorff and Hindenburg all sent letters of congratulation to Tänzer on the publication of his book.[2]

The timing of Tänzer's book, which he completed in October 1917, also encouraged this warm reception. Two months after he had finished writing his history, a Russian and German delegation based themselves in Brest-Litovsk – the very setting of Tänzer's study – to discuss bringing hostilities in the east to an end. With Russia all but defeated, Germans were finally able to dream of peace. This was certainly the impression that the kaiser tried to give. In his 1918 New Year's message, he celebrated the 'hefty blows' that had brought 'massive successes' in the east and looked forward 'to new achievements and new victories' in the year ahead.[3]

However, less than six months later this bravura was dead; faith in a German victory, particularly amongst the soldiers, petered out during the summer and

Germany then stumbled towards an ignominious defeat. If this dramatic and sudden shift in Germany's wartime fortunes was perplexing enough, then what made defeat even more confusing was the fact that at the war's end no enemy soldiers stood on German soil and the army itself still appeared to be intact. The question that cast a dark shadow over the German people was an obvious one: how had Germany moved from euphoria to defeat in less than twelve months? Simplistic answers in response to this most baffling of questions flourished at the war's end. The seeds that gave rise to these myths, however, had been sown much earlier, amidst the bursting of euphoria in 1918.

A Winter of Discontent

One of several dangerous narratives to take hold during the latter half of the conflict was the idea that Germany's chances of victory were proportional to the amount of effort its citizens put in. A successful end to the war, according to this thinking, was in the German people's own hands. Hindenburg and Ludendorff had first initiated large-scale propaganda programmes designed to boost the morale of their fighting troops; it was the home front equivalent, however, that proved most dangerous. For if victory could not be achieved, a ready culprit – in the shape of Germans at home – was already in place. Whether it was Louis Oppenheim's graphic posters or Moritz David campaigning for war bonds, German Jews played a significant role in these propaganda campaigns. In Berlin, Rahel Straus was also called upon to do her bit. Speaking as a medical doctor, she gave authoritative talks on how to live off a war diet. 'We had to explain to housewives', she remembered, 'that during peacetime people had eaten too much and thus the body could survive on a lot less.'

It proved very hard to convince a starving family that their hunger pains stemmed from pre-war gluttony rather than wartime hunger. As Straus herself admitted, most people already knew that 'it made more sense to travel out to the countryside [to find food] than to listen to us [talk]'.[4] Although Straus's propaganda efforts may have had little chance of success, they did nonetheless add to the notion that a strong-willed, highly motivated population could shape the outcome of the war. It was, therefore, all the more shocking to the authorities that instead of showing the expected self-discipline, many city dwellers openly bartered on the black market or simply helped themselves to food wherever they could find it. At Munich's main railway station, when a policeman tried to arrest a man with a suspicious package of food, the crowd turned on him, allowing the smuggler to escape. 'Catch the big black-marketeers', they shouted, and leave the little man alone.[5]

It was against this backdrop of social discord and weakening state power that Germany suffered its worst public order crisis of the war. On 28 January, 200,000 workers downed tools in Berlin, calling for 'more and better food', peace and democratic reforms. Over the days that followed, thousands more men and women went on strike in the capital; across Germany the picture was similar as workers in the country's main industrial centres left their factories and took to the streets. In total, around a million people are estimated to have joined the strike movement, drawn to its key demands of democratisation, food and a role for the workers in peace negotiations. German Jews were fairly prominent among the strike leaders. In Berlin, Hugo Haase, who excitedly called the January strike 'one of the greatest events in working-class history', sat on the action committee, while further south in Munich, another USPD politician, Kurt Eisner, directed the city's own strike movement. Fearing a repeat of the recent Bolshevik uprising in Russia, the authorities moved swiftly to break the strike, arresting large numbers of workers and sending them to the front. Eisner himself was rounded up and imprisoned for the remainder of the war.[6]

The role of Eisner and Haase in the January strike seemed to provide further evidence for those who believed that German Jews were somehow inextricably linked to revolutionary, unpatriotic behaviour. In Berlin, for example, flyers appeared blaming German Jews, such as Eisner and Haase, for the strike and accusing them of national betrayal.[7] Yet Jewish involvement in the strike movement was actually the exception rather than the rule. Jewish industrialists whose firms had suffered walkouts, such as the AEG and Ludwig Loewe armaments factories in Berlin, were understandably opposed to the strike movement.[8] Rathenau himself recommended that the 'misguided movements' behind the strikes be 'fought'.[9] If Rathenau's response was perhaps to be expected, then a commentary in the *Allgemeine Zeitung des Judentums* was more of a surprise. The newspaper, which had the largest reach of any Jewish weekly, complained of 'unfortunate disturbances' in some cities that had damaged Germany's war effort. It urged 'the naïve masses to come to their senses' and to recognise that their actions 'only played into the hands of our enemies'.[10]

Coverage of the January strikes in the *Allgemeine Zeitung des Judentums* was certainly explosive. The implication of the article was clear: the striking workers had undermined the brave efforts of the frontline soldiers at the very time when all Germans needed to hold together. The newspaper was not alone in holding this view. As had been the case throughout the conflict, Georg Bernhard stepped in to pour even more oil onto the flames of this debate. In a lengthy leader, he explained forcefully how the failure to produce just one shell 'represents a weakening of the army's military clout'. With even more polemic rage, Bernhard concluded that the workers at home were 'stabbing the frontline army in the back'.[11] The 'stab in the back' myth tends to be seen as a postwar narrative that developed to explain Germany's inglorious defeat, but Bernhard's unfortunate choice of language highlights the idea's wartime origins.[12]

The discourse of internal treason and betrayal encouraged by Bernhard and the *Allgemeine Zeitung des Judentums* seemed to strike a chord with many of the troops fighting at the front, who had little sympathy for the workers' complaints. Writing from occupied Warsaw, the young Victor Ehrenberg also expressed his 'considerable disappointment' at recent events and declared the strikes to be 'inexcusable'.[13] What drew the anger of those at the front was the fact that the January strike contravened the military's well-honed propaganda message. If Hindenburg and Ludendorff were to be believed, an end to the fighting would come as long as all Germans held strong and showed a firm will to victory. By going on strike, the home front, and in particular the working classes, had shown themselves to be at odds with this simple message. In expressing their anger at this turn of events, Jews and other Germans began to draw the boundaries for the later myths of defeat. The home front, and not the military itself, had proved incapable of uniting for victory.[14]

Peace in the East

Like many frontline troops, Herbert Sulzbach's anger at the strikes came down to its actual timing. 'If the people at home could only hold out', he wrote. 'We have a huge job to do in the west after getting our hands free in the east!'[15] As Sulzbach implied, most German soldiers viewed the situation on the Eastern Front with renewed optimism. Peace talks between Bolshevik Russia and the Central Powers had been under way since December 1917 in Brest-Litovsk. Negotiations between the two sides proved to be as ruinous as this once great city. While Leon Trotsky, who headed the Russian delegation, did his best to stall for time, the Germans argued amongst themselves as to whether to agree an immediate peace or to push for territorial gains too. When the treaty was finally signed on 3 March 1918, it was clear that the annexationist spirit had once again won through. Russia lost 34 per cent of its population and 54 per cent of its industry, as the Baltic states, Belorussia, Russian Poland, the Ukraine and Finland all came into the German sphere of influence.[16]

Ludendorff expressed his satisfaction at the final treaty, dismissing any criticism of the settlement as being 'invented by hostile propaganda'. He aimed this comment in two directions. First in his sights were foreign politicians like Britain's former prime minister Herbert Asquith, who had labelled the treaty a 'humiliating peace'.[17] Ludendorff's second target was the USPD, the only political party to vote against the Treaty of Brest-Litovsk and its associated agreements. The USPD's opposition, as Haase explained, stemmed from the military's decision to seize vast swathes of Russian territory. In his view, annexations would not end the war, only lengthen it. Oskar Cohn, who had been given the unenviable task of justifying the USPD's position to the Reichstag, developed Haase's original criticisms. But in doing so, he bore the brunt of the attacks coming from the treaty's many supporters. When Cohn retook his seat at the end of his speech, mutterings could be heard spreading through the chamber: 'It is only Cohn, not a proper German!'[18]

Haase and Cohn's criticism of the Treaty of Brest-Litovsk gave the unfortunate (and wholly false) impression that German Jews were opposed to a victorious peace. Max Cohen-Reuß's decision to add his own voice to those critical of the settlement only served to confirm this view. Together with Ludwig Quessel, Cohen-Reuß led the SPD's opposition to the treaty. As had been the case with the USPD, Cohen-Reuß had reservations about the sustainability of an annexationist peace that went against his own conception of a future Europe.[19] Seeing Cohen-Reuß, Haase and Cohn all speak out against Germany's great moment of triumph in the east further provoked anti-Semites back to life. *Auf Vorposten*, a publication with an unhealthy obsession with Jewish and freemasonry conspiracy theories, for example, took Cohn's opposition to be evidence that revolutionary Bolshevism was about to spread its web across Germany. The idea that Bolshevism and Judaism were intricately connected now started to gain a dangerous momentum.[20]

What these attacks failed to acknowledge was the fact that most German Jews were far from unhappy with the Brest-Litovsk settlement. It was not opposition but reserved scepticism that defined the Jewish response to the treaty. For example, while Cohen-Reuß urged the SPD to reject the agreement with Russia, his colleague Eduard David proved to be far more supportive. Speaking in the Reichstag, David confessed that he had reservations about the way the peace talks had been conducted, but he was nonetheless pleased that 'murder and destruction' had come to an end and that the POWs held in the east would soon be released.[21] The SPD fraction appeared to be closer to David's position than Cohen-Reuß's as they agreed to abstain from the vote, rather than to reject it outright. Like David, Rathenau welcomed an end to the war in the east, but was also sceptical as to whether it would bring about a lasting peace. In his judgment, it was nothing but 'a massive temporary solution'.[22]

While neither Rathenau nor David was stringing out the bunting, they were nonetheless genuinely relieved to see the fighting in one theatre of the conflict come to an end. For Jews and other Germans, both at home and at the front, the Treaty of Brest-Litovsk provided some glimmer of hope. It was a 'happy day', as Victor Klemperer expressed it.[23] The conflict may not yet have been won, but after so many months bereft of any positive news at all, Brest-Litovsk gave Germans a reason for optimism. People could at the very least begin to conceive of an end to war, in all likelihood in Germany's favour.

Not all of this optimistic spirit, it should be stressed, was based on pure altruism. Ludendorff, as ever, set the tone. In his view, Brest-Litovsk provided the ideal opportunity to spread Germany's influence further east into the Crimea and towards Scandinavia; both regions were rich in raw materials and foodstuffs, two things that the German military badly needed. Davis Trietsch, whose passion for German expansionism continued to burn brightly, seemed to share much of Ludendorff's vision for Eastern Europe. As general secretary of the recently founded German–Georgian Society, Trietsch welcomed any attempts to weaken Russia's influence in the Caucasus, arguing that everything had to be done 'to limit [it] to the [borders of] Greater Russia in the narrowest sense'. In newly independent Georgia, Trietsch saw a country ripe for German exploitation. Its manganese ore industry warranted 'our fullest attention', its copper mines could export to Germany instead of Russia and the entire country had the potential to supply Germany with 'Peaches, apricots, apples, pears, oranges, lemons, figs and a host of other fruit'. 'All in all', concluded Trietsch, the Caucasus region 'would appear to be an incredibly important region for the economy of the Central Powers.'[24]

Trietsch did an excellent job of opening people's eyes to the material riches of Eastern Europe, but he was in no position to exploit the region himself. Instead it was German industrialists who swooped in to seize the rewards of Russia's defeat. Just as they had earlier in Belgium, Jewish and other German firms signed off a string of exploitative economic agreements. The Disconto-Gesellschaft of Arthur Salomonsohn and Georg Solmssen seemed to be at the forefront of many of these lucrative deals. In Romania, the bank was part of a consortium that signed a thirty-year agreement to take sole control of the country's oil reserves. Not content with exploiting Romania, the bank then joined forces with Max Warburg's banking concern and representatives from heavy industry to secure control of the most productive elements of the Ukraine's economy. Finally, the two banks collaborated on a project to carve up railway lines in the east that could be used to transport goods back to the Central Powers.[25] As Germany's economic elite quickly discovered, the Treaty of Brest-Litovsk not only appeared to bring a German victory a step closer, it also opened up new business opportunities in the vast hinterlands of Eastern Europe.

Russia's defeat and the reconfiguration of Europe's eastern borders after Brest-Litovsk also gave Germany's Jewish communities reason to cheer. After all, destroying Tsarist despotism and rescuing Russia's Jewish population from servitude had motivated many German Jews to enter the war in the first place. The *Allgemeine Zeitung des Judentums* set the tone in its report on the treaty. 'At last we are able to begin with some pleasant news', commented the newspaper. However, the end of hostilities on the Eastern Front brought with it new questions about the future of the entire region and the sustainability of Jewish life more generally. As the newspaper article itself rightly pondered, 'nobody would like to predict how things will further develop'.[26]

The main source of uncertainty lay with the successor states along the Baltic, in Poland and the Ukraine. Germany's Zionists were particularly concerned by the thought that local nationalisms would destroy the tight-knit structures of Jewish life in Eastern Europe. 'Apart from in Russia, there is no other country where in the last century genuine Jewish culture has developed', lamented one prominent Zionist. He feared that once Jews were placed into separate nation states, then not only would this rich culture be lost but the chances of promoting a national Jewish future would also be jeopardised.[27]

Of far greater concern for the German-Jewish communities was the very real threat of increased anti-Semitism in the east. Amidst the rising nationalist passions in the new states, the existing Jewish populations found themselves pushed to the margins. Cohen-Reuß pointed out how Jews in Poland and Lithuania were being silenced, while his colleague in the USPD, Oskar Cohn, spent over half an hour explaining to the Reichstag the dangers facing Romanian Jewry. He argued that the Romanians had long persecuted their Jewish population and so there could be no justifiable reason for Germany to agree any form of peace treaty with the country.[28] Jewish communities were sufficiently concerned about the situation in Eastern Europe that they demonstrated a rare moment of unity and formed a new organisation, the snappily titled Association of Jewish Organisations in Germany for the Protection of the Rights of the Jews in the East (Vereinigung jüdischer Organisationen Deutschlands zur Wahrung der Rechte der juden des Ostens, the VJOD).

Reflecting its broad constituency, it pursued a mixed set of aims, from protecting religious freedom and ensuring political equality through to campaigning for the right of settlement in Palestine.[29]

To mark the signing of the Treaty of Brest-Litovsk, the kaiser attempted once again to rouse the German population behind the war. A royal decree ordered public buildings to fly the imperial flag and all schools were to close for one day in celebration of this major peace treaty.[30] Presumably many schoolchildren were happy with this decision, but beyond this group, the kaiser was always going to fail to recreate the excitement of August 1914 or even of the battle of Jutland. By 1918 other fears dominated, whether for loved ones in the field or – in the case of the VJOD – over the future of Jewish life in Eastern Europe. Peace in the east could never bring back the enthusiasm of the early days of the war, but it did nonetheless build hope. It gave people the chance to dream of a future end to the conflict, even of a German victory. This was certainly how one German-Jewish soldier interpreted Brest-Litovsk. 'What do you make of the fact that peace with Russia has finally come?' he asked his parents rhetorically. 'You could say thank God, at least it's finally gone quiet on one of the frontlines.'[31]

The Spring Offensive

Once the guns had fallen silent on the Eastern Front, German attention turned to the west. All that was required was a successful campaign against the Entente powers and the war would finally come to an end. During the spring, public optimism began to grow; the end, it seemed, was at last within sight. Many of the Jewish soldiers at the front were only too willing to share in this confidence. Richard Schönmann had been an avid letter writer throughout the conflict, frequently finding time to pen another note to his sister, Mariele, in the Bavarian town of Landshut. His choice of postcard in the spring, however, was particularly revealing. The image on the front of the card captures a rather stern-looking Ludendorff staring impassionedly into the camera lens (see Plate 21). The general's message at the bottom of the postcard declares simply, but defiantly: 'Without sacrifice, there will be no victory! Without victory, there will be no peace!' Schönmann, like other Germans, wanted to believe Ludendorff's words: that after Brest-Litovsk the war could also be won in the west.

Ludendorff's plan, for what he called 'the biggest task in history', was fairly straightforward. He chose to launch an all-out attack against the British forces north of the River Somme, thereby cutting off the army's main supply route; once Britain had been knocked out of the war, the French, he believed, would soon follow suit. In preparation for what was dubbed 'Operation Michael', Ludendorff built up his forces in the west from 143 to 191 divisions.[32] Most of these men came from the Eastern Front, where Russia's defeat had allowed numbers to be slightly reduced. There were plenty of Jewish soldiers who joined the steady stream of trains heading from the east through Germany to the Western Front. After so many months, even years, stationed in Poland or in the Baltic states, the sense was of an era coming to a sudden end. In Kaunas, Sammy Gronemann had been waving people off since the end of 1917; colleagues went west, while many Russian Jews returned east. In early April, it was Gronemann's turn to depart. He just had time to celebrate one final Passover with members of the local Jewish community before he too headed to the railway station to take his leave from Kaunas for good.[33]

There could be no doubting that Gronemann wanted to see peace. But like many Germans, he would have preferred to watch the conflict come to an end from the relative safety of the east, rather than have to travel west to the epicentre of the fighting. Fortunately for Gronemann, luck was on his side. When he reported for duty in Brussels, he was sent not to the front but to a civilian press department. And with that decision he recalled, 'my glorious military career . . . came to a sudden and surprising end'.[34] Other people found it much harder to avoid being sent back into the heat of battle. The Swiss Zionist David Weinbaum pleaded with the German consulate to have his son, Fritz, excused from frontline military service. Weinbaum's other son, Herbert, had already been killed in battle, and he had no wish for his only surviving son to suffer a similar fate.[35]

For those on the home front, the weeks leading up to the spring offensives were mixed with frantic anticipation and then deep melancholy. Like Weinbaum, many people feared the scenes of blood and carnage that were to come; others, though, attempted to rally friends and family, confident that the war would soon be over. Germany's urban centres reverberated to a new optimistic beat. In Freiburg, the talk was once more of victory. Flags fluttered, bells rang out and crowds gathered at the city's Victory Monument.[36] Elsewhere Jews and other Germans made what preparations they could for the army's final push. In Berlin, the Jewish Women's League joined with their Protestant and Catholic sister organisations to distribute nappies and supplies for new mothers.[37] Further east, in Upper Silesia, Ernst Fränkel, showed his commitment to the war effort by donating a further 70 Marks' worth of jewellery to the Reichsbank.[38]

On a much larger scale than Fränkel could offer, 6.5 million people dug deep into their pockets to subscribe to Germany's eighth war bonds issue in March 1918. This was a considerable feat as the previous war bonds campaign in autumn 1917 had recorded a drop in donations. Some of the success of the March campaign must have been down to the hard work of Jews and other Germans who promoted the bonds both locally and nationally. In Stuttgart's Jewish communities, for example, the rabbis took the lead, advertising the bonds to their congregations and organising collections in clubs and societies.[39] On a national level, the young German-Jewish filmmaker Julius Pinschewer directed a short advertisement promoting war bonds. Putting his pre-war work making advertising films for Maggi to good use, Pinschewer produced a short film – *Jung-Siegfried* – that sold not herbs and spices, but a German victory. Clearly based on the *Nibelungenlied* epic, the film depicts Siegfried drawing his sword to slay a marauding dragon, representing – as contemporary cinema-goers would have known – the Entente. To defeat the dragon once again, Germans needed to sharpen their 'cutting sword' and 'buy war bonds', the film explained.[40]

With anticipation growing at home and at the front, Ludendorff finally gave the instruction to launch the German offensive on 21 March. By all accounts, the first days of 'Operation Michael' were an unprecedented success. In only one week, the German army had advanced 60 kilometres into enemy-held territory, thereby turning the war of attrition on the Western Front back into a war of movement. Seemingly inspired by Pinschewer's *Nibelungenlied* analogy, Bernhard hailed the army's advance as 'the victory of the sword'.[41] Should any Germans still have had doubts as to the scale of the army's advance, then Louis Oppenheim was on hand to calm their nerves with a graphic illustration of Germany's success. Under the imposing title of 'The first month of the German western offensive', Oppenheim sketched out details of the bounty now in German hands: '127,000 prisoners', '1,600 artillery pieces', 'some 200 tanks' and so on (see Plate 22). For those who preferred factual images over statistics, Oppenheim placed a map at the bottom of the poster depicting a vast red splodge of new German territory.

The optimism engendered from such propaganda gained momentum through into the late spring. Newspapers, including the German-Jewish press, published snippets of news that suggested the army's advance was surging forward. The CV's main organ joined in the excitement, celebrating how 'the German hammer' had struck down on 'the truculent heads of the English, French and Americans'. The conflict had not yet been won, it admitted, but 'the anticipation of the coming peace' was growing.[42] One of the most uplifting stories at this time came from the German-Jewish soldier Richard Adler. After surviving two long winters in Russian captivity, Adler undertook an audacious escape in late 1917. Once beyond the barbed wire of the POW camp, Adler experienced the kind of adventures that Arnold Zweig would later popularise in his Great War novel, *The Case of Sergeant Grischa*; he acquired a Russian military uniform on the black market, jumped from moving trains and trudged through snow-covered landscapes, before finally reaching the German lines. As the press reported, after recuperating at home, Adler then re-joined his battalion in the west; the implication was that as victory neared, the German soldier was prepared to march halfway across Europe to share this moment.[43]

When he was reunited with his battalion on the Western Front, Adler may well have pondered whether he had in fact been rather hasty in escaping the Russians. The German advance was still striding forward, but the actual fighting was bloody and brutal. Walter Foerster, a young Jewish soldier from Thuringia, explained how his company had had to use both artillery and machine guns in order to force 'Tommy' back. In writing home, Foerster somehow managed not to dwell on the horrors of hand-to-hand combat and instead concentrated on the progress being made. 'Every battery commander, indeed every single person, had only one goal: "Forward!"' It was this sense of movement that kept the German soldiers going; every sacrifice, they hoped, brought them closer to ending the conflict. Another Jewish soldier, Alfred Baruch, expressed a similar sentiment of the fighting so far. 'Too much blood has again flowed', he wrote, but he managed to comfort himself with the thought that this was 'the final battle'.[44]

Sadly for the German soldiers at the front and for those making sacrifices at home, the powerful sense of progress that everyone thought they were witnessing proved to be something of a mirage. The German advance had actually been built on very shaky foundations. While the army had managed to push the British and French back by at least 60 kilometres, in reality it had merely retaken the land it had lost the previous year when the German forces had withdrawn to the Hindenburg Line. Unperturbed, Ludendorff launched a series of further offensives through the early summer, but again these did little more than capture swathes of strategically insignificant territory. Moreover, seizing back these battle-scarred landscapes had come at great human cost, some 500,000 casualties for little perceptible gain.[45] Richard Adler, whose heroic exploits in escaping from Russian captivity had reached the national press, was one of those killed during the military's offensives that year. His reward for fleeing the Russians was death in the final months of the conflict and a lonely burial spot in Belgium.

When the French launched their own counter-attacks in mid-July, there could no longer be any question that Ludendorff's spring offensives had spectacularly failed. Many Germans, though, had already been sceptical as to the chances of success. Politicians, such as the chancellor Georg von Hertling and the foreign minister Richard von Kühlmann, had tried hard to convince Ludendorff that instead of seeking a total victory, he should seek a negotiated peace. But this was not what the great general had wanted to hear.[46] Many of the soldiers had realised that there was something amiss with Ludendorff's plans at a much earlier stage. When they stormed into the British and French positions, expecting to find an army in disarray, they discovered the exact opposite. 'The British were well cared for', noted one Jewish soldier with considerable surprise. 'We're now sleeping in large British tents, using British leather jackets to protect us from the evening chills and wearing British coats when it rains.' Useful as these material comforts were, they did rather betray the fact that the Entente was nowhere near collapsing. A Nuremberg soldier, Ludwig Hirsch, made a similarly depressing observation about the French troops: 'they look so well fed, so well clothed and excellently equipped!'[47]

Once confidence had started to drop at the front, it did not take long for a similar pessimism to set in at home. Letters from loved ones in the field often revealed a mixed picture of German progress, challenging the more upbeat reporting in the press. After surviving Ludendorff's ill-fated attack on the Marne in July, Victor Ehrenberg committed his thoughts on the army's chances to paper. The offensive, he wrote, had 'completely failed'. He still hoped that something would give the Germans back the initiative, but 'nonetheless, everyone is depressed', he concluded despairingly.[48] Even the kaiser, who was as desperate as anyone for some good news, could no longer ignore the scale of the military's difficulties. 'The kaiser was in very low spirits at lunch', reported one of his advisers. He 'ate nothing but a chocolate mousse'.[49] In the spring, Jews and other Germans had had high hopes of following their success in the east with victory in the west, but their faith was quickly dampened. Once the British and French troops had turned from retreat to attack in July, all anyone was left with was despair. The kaiser could comfort himself with chocolate mousse, but nothing could satiate the disappointment of Germany's starving population.

Searching for Answers

Only a matter of months separated the German military's resounding victory in the east from its devastating reversal in the west. This rapid shift in Germany's wartime fortunes provided fertile ground for the country's powerful myths of defeat to take root. Most worryingly over the longer term, the failure of the spring offensive added the element of culpability to these nascent myths; someone had to be responsible for this sudden spiral of despair. In the summer of 1918, there was no single target for people's anger. Like petulant children, Germans lashed out at a whole range of different targets. Some people criticised the authorities for mismanaging food supplies, others laid the blame at the feet of rich capitalists, while a few held Germany's military leaders culpable. As the hunt for suitable scapegoats gathered pace, the sense hardened that Jewish communities must also take some of the responsibility. In the popular imagination, German Jews were military shirkers, while Eastern European Jews had done little but spread disease and weaken the national body. This connection between Germany's military struggles and its Jewish communities hardened during the second half of 1918, leaving German Jews dangerously entangled with the country's impending defeat.

Throughout the conflict, accusations of Jewish shirking had ebbed and flowed with the tide of military success. The army's difficulties in the west set off a new wave of anti-Semitism. The experience of Siegfried Marx, a cattle dealer from Landshut, exemplified the vindictiveness of this latest spate of attacks. In mid-July, just as the German advance was grinding to a halt, an anonymous letter arrived on the desk of the deputy commanding general in Munich. The sole subject of the letter was Marx and how he had apparently spent the entire war at home in Landshut rather than where he should have been, which was on the military frontline. The only reason he had managed to avoid the battlefield, explained the writer, was that Marx had paid his sergeant major a bribe. Not content with making such a sweeping judgment of Marx's character, the author then went on to belittle Marx with a shower of vitriolic language. Marx, the letter writer claimed, was 'lippy', a 'shirker', a 'good for nothing' and also extremely 'cocky'. Compared to this 'Jewish fool', the author added, 'thousands of family fathers have to give their lives out in the field'.[50]

The spitefulness of this attack on Marx, and the sheer ferocity of the language used, came to characterise anti-Semitism in the later stages of the war. Around the same time that Marx was suffering slander in Landshut, another writer launched a more widespread assault on Jewish communities.

On this occasion, the author, who similarly hid under a cloak of anonymity, produced a bitter little poem entitled 'The Jews in the World War' ('Die Juden im Weltkriege'). Its main refrain ran: 'their smirking faces are everywhere / but just not where the trenches are' ('*überall grinst ihr Gesicht / nur im Schützengraben nicht*').[51] Judging by the weakness of the verse, the potency of this attack came not from the quality of its rhyming couplets, but rather from the way it was distributed. The anonymous author arranged for the poem to be printed and then circulated both within Germany and at the front. As the CV complained, copies of the poem then started to appear in public houses at railway stations and were even pasted to advertising pillars in the street.[52]

Despite the CV's protests that the poem was damaging the spirit of the 'civic truce', the authorities proved unable or perhaps unwilling to halt its spread. Of course, what made the poem so difficult to censor was the fact that it had been written by an unknown poet from the safety of the shadows. Yet there was also a growing suspicion within the CV that the military lacked the appetite to eradicate anti-Semitism in its entirety. From the CV's discussions it was clear that the organisation's leaders had lost faith in the military. They were, however, keen to find a way to rebuild 'some sense of trust between representatives of the War Ministry' and themselves.[53]

But it was not just established Jewish communities that came under more pressure. As the military's problems mounted in the west, public and official antipathy towards the Eastern European Jews working in Germany also increased. Since the start of the conflict, some 30,000 Jewish workers had come to Germany, mainly to fill labour shortages in the essential war industries.[54] Wherever the Eastern European Jews settled, criticism and complaint was never far behind. The authorities proved themselves particularly adept at uncovering incidences of Jewish involvement in the black market and other illegal trades. In Stuttgart, the police apprehended a Russian Jew, Isaak Bernstein, for selling sardines without a licence and for inflating prices by dealing with shadowy middlemen (*Kettenhandel*). After investigating Bernstein's personal circumstances, the police decided that he should be imprisoned in Ulm for the remainder of the conflict. What was most concerning about this punishment was the subjective attitude of the police. As far as they were concerned, Bernstein was nothing but a 'brazen foreigner', by which they meant a Jew, 'who had flouted the law'. Locking him up, therefore, would protect the German economy from external damage.[55]

Sensing public disquiet at the presence of Jewish workers from Eastern Europe, the political right seized the opportunity to push once again for stronger border controls. Writing in Heinrich Claß's *Deutsche Zeitung*, Georg Fritz suggested that a 'deluge of morally inferior aliens' posed a danger to both German society and the economy. The only solution, Fritz craftily argued, was to 'close the Reich's borders to the immigration of foreign Jews'.[56] In a roundabout way, one of Fritz's comrades in the Pan-German League, Wolfgang Heinze, came to the very same conclusion. Rather than banning Eastern European Jewish immigration outright, he called for a restriction on certain categories of people: 'poor and unemployable, large families', those carrying 'infectious diseases' and people 'below a certain level of education'. Conveniently, it just so happened that most Eastern European Jews could easily be slotted into one of these categories.[57]

Fritz and Heinze had first called for Germany's eastern borders to be sealed in 1915. But in the early months of the war, their arguments failed to gain traction; three years later the door to discrimination swung open more easily. In late April 1918, the Prussian Interior Ministry closed the state's borders to Eastern European Jews under the flimsy pretext of preventing the spread of typhus. The difference between 1915 and 1918 was clearly the state of the conflict. With the German army's struggles in the west creating very real fears of defeat, it proved much easier to lash out against anyone deemed to have undermined the war effort. Over the longer term, the decision to close the border had a deleterious impact on Germany's own Jewish communities. It legitimised a popular belief that Jews – whether German or Eastern European – had not given their all, thereby undermining the wider war effort.

However, the more immediate effect of the border closure fell directly onto the shoulders of Eastern European Jewish workers. During the summer, as the war drew to a gradual close, a steady stream of Jews were removed from their place of work and sent back across the eastern border. From Berlin alone, between fifty and seventy people suffered this fate each week.[58] Other Eastern European Jews were caught out by a different piece of legislation. In May, the Polish general government suddenly decreed that if Jewish workers returned home – possibly on leave or to visit friends and family – then they would not be allowed back across the border to Germany. Again, the rather spurious justification for this decree was to prevent the spread of typhus.[59] Moses Zitron was one of many who found himself caught out by this order. He had left his job as a metalworker in Posen for what he thought would be a few days back home in Warsaw. However, things turned out very differently. Banned from returning, not only did Zitron have to forgo his job, but he also lost a 50-Mark police deposit as well as his 'spare clothes, laundry, suitcase and pocket watch' which were still in Germany. For people already on the poverty line, these were devastating losses.[60]

German Jews looked on with considerable concern as their co-religionists suffered at the hands of German officialdom. Yet their actual response to the border closure, particularly on the part of the liberal Jewish communities, was fairly restrained. The CV's only comment was a nine-line article that described the closure of the border as a 'provocative issue'.[61] This was a thoroughly underwhelming response, particularly given the fact that the organisation was fully aware of the damaging effects of the border closure. One businessman had written to the CV in late May about two Jewish workers now stuck in Poland. By closing the border, he complained, the authorities had demonstrated that they still treated Jews 'as second-class citizens'.[62] The Zionist *Jüdische Rundschau*, in contrast, took a far more assertive line on the whole issue. Reflecting its Jewish national outlook, it viewed the authorities' actions as an attack on all Jews, regardless of whether they were from Germany or Eastern Europe. 'We request that this humiliation be scrapped immediately . . . and that this insult be ended right now', the newspaper demanded.[63]

The relative timidity of the CV's response when compared to that of the Zionists stemmed from the fact that the liberal organisation was able to rationalise the decision to seal the border. When the authorities claimed that the Eastern European Jews represented a health danger, many German Jews agreed, albeit quietly for fear of further stoking the flames of anti-Semitism.[64] There was a similar level of acceptance to the authorities' claim that the Jewish immigrants made poor workers. Rathenau's AEG, for example, had long refused to employ Eastern European Jews on this basis, a position which the Orenstein & Koppel (O&K) locomotive firm also appeared to share. Commenting on its experience of Jewish workers, the management of O&K complained simply: 'A bad experience – in general not suitable for heavy labour.'[65] Even the VJOD conceded on this point. In a report, which was supposed to be defending the status and qualities of the Eastern European Jews, it admitted that industry's experiences with these workers 'have been unfavourable'.[66]

Yet, hard as they tried, the liberal Jewish organisations repeatedly came unstuck on the issue of singularity. It was all very well to restrict immigrants on the basis of skills or hygiene, but to issue a blanket ban on one single group, based solely on ethnicity or religion, was a very different matter. Franz Oppenheimer, for example, noted privately that he could understand the need for immigration restrictions either on 'cultural grounds' or to restrict the influx of 'a mass of lowly workers'. What he refused to accept was the idea of a ban solely targeting Jews.[67] It was something of a shock, therefore, when it emerged that Ludwig Haas, who was responsible for Jewish affairs in German-occupied Poland, had actually attended the very meeting where the decision to ban only the Jewish workers had been taken. To the annoyance of other German Jews, Haas had sat passively by as Eastern European Jews were described as being 'a serious danger for public order' and posing 'a health danger to our fatherland'. Rather than challenging this consensus, Haas appeared only too willing to accept the sweeping judgments of those around him.[68]

Haas was not alone in playing down the seriousness of the authorities' decision to seal Germany's eastern border. Hermann Struck, who occupied a similar administrative position to Haas only further east in Ober Ost, also managed to turn his attention to other matters. During the summer of 1918, Struck attended a meeting in Copenhagen of the American-funded Jewish Emergency Committee (Jüdisches Hilfskomitee), which sought to supply food and medical supplies for the Jews of war-torn Eastern Europe. With the furore over the border closure still ongoing, it would have been easy to imagine Struck placing this high up on the agenda. But instead of delving into recent events, Struck launched into a more general defence of the German occupation. When questioned on German policy and conditions in the east, Struck reportedly became 'very annoyed'. His mood only worsened when the subject turned to food costs. 'I don't know the prices', he replied, 'I didn't bring my cook with me.'[69] At this stage of the war, many German Jews, even Zionists like Struck, managed to compartmentalise anti-Semitic incidents; they ignored the severity of rising anti-Semitism and instead focused on more positive aspects of Germany's wartime struggle. Unfortunately, other Germans were not quite as quick to dismiss the connection that was forming between impending defeat and the Jews.

Fighting to the End?

Debates on the sealing of the eastern borders were rapidly overtaken by events on the Western Front. In late September, Ludendorff, his nerves shot, suddenly recognised the scale of the military's task. 'Victory is out of the question', he told Paul von Hintze. 'The situation the army finds itself in demands an immediate armistice, if we are to avoid a catastrophe.'[70] With these few lines, Ludendorff had effectively conceded defeat, after which the end came rapidly. During the final desperate weeks of the conflict, interwar myths of defeat took an even firmer hold, spreading their roots more deeply into the public's consciousness. It was the physical state of the army that encouraged their growth. Although the German army was clearly defeated by the war's end, it managed to give the outward impression of still being very much intact. A small number of German Jews contributed – unwittingly for the most part – to this false image by urging the military on, when all the indications were that the war was lost.

Ludendorff later attempted to retract his scathing assessment of the military's fighting capabilities. In late October, he and Hindenburg suggested that the army remained strong and thus there was now no need to sue for peace. The reality, though, was different.[71] Ludendorff's original analysis of the German army, although exaggerated, was far closer to the mark. From mid-July onwards, the German forces found themselves entirely on the back foot. Assisted by fresh American troops, the Entente's forces charged forward through August and September, retaking much of the territory they had lost earlier in the summer. Ludwig Hirsch, who had just celebrated his twentieth birthday at the front, experienced the full force of this onslaught. In September, the anti-tank battery he was commanding came under a direct French attack. It left two of his men dead and the remainder of them stuck in their gas masks for the next ten hours. 'I caught a bit of gas myself', he remarked casually. Seven days later Hirsch had succumbed to the effects of this gas attack, joining the ranks of the German-Jewish war dead.[72]

During the final months of the war, the German army came under attack not just from bullets and bombs but also from illness and disease. The most devastating outbreak occurred in mid- to late 1918, when the influenza pandemic, commonly known as Spanish flu, wreaked havoc on the armies of both sides. Poor sanitation, closely quartered – often malnourished – troops who were continually on the move, all provided the ideal conditions for the virus to spread. Helmut Freund, a Jewish military doctor stationed in Belgium, at first noticed a few isolated cases of the disease, but soon he was dealing with between thirty and forty new patients a night. 'Their body temperature got up to 39, 40, even 41 degrees', he recalled. 'Some of them shivered and trembled, convulsing with fever, while others were delirious and had no idea where they were.' The young German-Jewish soldier Heinrich Buxbaum had not even completed his basic training when he was struck down by the pandemic. One day he was feeling weak, the next he was barely able to move. The influenza itself eventually passed, but a secondary kidney infection left him stranded in hospital for the next nine weeks; by the time he was discharged the war was over.[73] Germany lost some 500,000 soldiers in this fashion, at the very time when its forces were already under terrible strain.[74]

A resurgent enemy, rampant disease and the failure of the spring offensives hit the morale of the German army particularly hard. One commander gave a withering assessment of his division: 'The men give the impression of being completely exhausted and worn out', he wrote bluntly.[75] From the front, a long-serving Jewish soldier looked on grimly as the morale of those around him slowly collapsed. 'I don't know what you have heard in Berlin about the mood out here', he wrote, 'but one thing's for sure, a change in our military fortunes is never going to happen with such broken morale and discipline.'[76] As was hinted at in this exchange, one of the biggest problems towards the end of the war was the indiscipline of the soldiers. Estimates suggest that somewhere in the region of 385,000 German soldiers surrendered during the final four months of the war, while many more simply disappeared in the other direction.[77] When desertions were added to the other problems facing the German army, it was little wonder that Ludendorff had decided the war was lost.

Yet despite all these problems, the army did not simply collapse in 1918. It may have been dangerously weakened, but it just about remained intact. Military orders continued to be followed and most soldiers stayed at their posts, albeit reluctantly.[78] There was, therefore, a severe disparity between the actual fighting capabilities of the army, which were increasingly limited, and its public persona. The consequences of this mismatch reverberated throughout the postwar years, giving credence to nascent myths of defeat. If the army was still intact, then the question people wanted answers to was why the war had been lost. Mostly unintentionally, during the last months of the conflict Jews and other Germans helped to disguise some of the military's worst problems, thereby building up a false impression of the army's strength.

From reading Jewish communities' public pronouncements of summer 1918, it would have been difficult to believe that the German army was actually in a state of considerable turmoil. As had been the case throughout the conflict, the main community newspapers continued to print lists of their newly decorated members and to name those who had suffered a 'hero's death' at the front.[79] The *Israelitisches Familienblatt* offered the same information but in a far more accessible format. Right until the very end of the war, it regularly published full-page spreads of those German Jews awarded the Iron Cross 1st Class. Not only did the newspaper list the details of the newly decorated, but it also reproduced a photograph of each recipient smartly dressed in military uniforms (see Plate 23). There was clearly a defensive element to this exercise, as it offered visual proof of German Jews' loyal service. But at the same time, this celebration of military paraphernalia also gave the impression that the German army remained fundamentally intact.

Even the fulfilment of straightforward administrative tasks spoke of order when all around was chaos. Nowhere was this clearer than with the organisation of the Jewish festival of Rosh Hashanah in September 1918 for those stationed at the front. Despite the obvious logistical difficulties facing a retreating army, the War Ministry gave permission, as it had done on previous occasions, for army rabbis to stage religious services to mark the festival. The commander of the 3rd Army, for example, allowed Jewish soldiers, where 'militarily possible', to attend services being held by Rabbi Reinhold Lewin in a cinema building in Sedan.[80] Although the line 'militarily possible' gave commanders a get out clause, many German Jews still managed to leave their positions to celebrate the festival. Rabbi Siegfried Klein estimated that some 1,400 soldiers came to his Rosh Hashanah service and he hoped for similar numbers during Yom Kippur later in the month. The military even laid on extra trains for the occasion and assisted with the organisation of the necessary ritual fare.[81] Looking on from afar, the celebration of Rosh Hashanah in September 1918 certainly gave little indication of being one of the final acts of a broken, almost defeated military machine.

From the home front too, German Jews also helped to give the impression that the German army remained a strong, fully intact force. In October, the Union of German Women's Associations came up with a plan to boost the army's resilience. As Alice Bensheimer, the organisation's secretary and a Jewish women's rights campaigner, explained, what was required was greater recognition of the army's achievements. She urged all women's groups to back a public declaration of 'faith and thanks' in the army which she believed would help to strengthen public morale. At first glance, this may have looked like a perfectly reasonable attempt to secure the home front. The approach taken, however, only served to obscure any sense of the military's real predicament, focusing on the army's achievements rather than its current difficulties.[82]

In the final weeks of the conflict, two prominent German Jews – Georg Bernhard and Walther Rathenau – trumped Bensheimer's petition with their own rather grandiose plans for the military. It is not clear how the pair could make judgments over the fighting capabilities of the army from the safety of Berlin, but this is exactly what both men managed to do. Bernhard confidently stated that the German soldiers at the front had the capacity not only to keep fighting, but also to make gains. 'For every month the war goes on', he suggested optimistically, 'Germany's respective position will also be improved.'[83] Rathenau followed a similar line of argument. In his view, the army could keep going for another six to nine months, particularly if another 1 to 1.5 million men could be recruited.

If the army was still ready and able to fight, then in Rathenau's and Bernhard's view, Ludendorff had made a fatal mistake in suing for peace. His decision may have been brought on by a 'nervous breakdown', but the general's mental health, complained Rathenau, 'did not offer the slightest excuse' for his actions.[84] What most annoyed the pair was the fact that as a result of Ludendorff's impetuosity, Germany had been forced into negotiating peace from a position of weakness rather than strength. It was clearly easy to be wise after the event; this, though, did not stop Bernhard from going on the attack. 'A government that requests an armistice as a starting point for peace negotiations shows that it has already lost any faith in the ability of its troops to secure a final victory', he pompously opined.[85] Rathenau and Bernhard were not alone in holding this view. Max Warburg, a close confidant of the new chancellor, Max von Baden, had urged him to defy Ludendorff's call for an armistice and to continue the fight. 'I know that my only son . . . will be in the trenches in four weeks', he is reported to have told the chancellor, 'but I beseech you, do not stop now!'[86]

There was, however, one crucial difference between Warburg's concerns and those of Rathenau and Bernhard. Whereas Warburg confided quietly in the chancellor, they announced their fears with great fanfare to the wider German public. In early October, Rathenau published a romantic, though ill-conceived, call to arms. It was 'a cry from the heart [Herzensschrei] of a great patriot', suggested Max von Baden.[87] With a nod to the French revolutionary idea of levée en masse, Rathenau called on the German people to rise up in defence of their land. Rather than meekly succumb to unrealistic peace terms, 'the defence of the nation, an insurrection of the people' needed to begin immediately. Max von Baden's cabinet gave the suggestion serious consideration. However, they realised very quickly that a war-weary, demoralised population was unlikely to rise up in the way that Rathenau desired.[88]

It was no coincidence that Rathenau's passionate appeal appeared on the very front of the Vossische Zeitung under the apocalyptic title 'A Dark Day'. After all, Rathenau's fears about the impending peace neatly dovetailed with those of the newspaper's editor, Georg Bernhard. Over the coming weeks, Bernhard used his editorship to air his own concerns with Woodrow Wilson's 'peace diktat' (Friedendiktat), as he termed it; at one stage, he even threatened to call

all of Germany's forces to 'the national struggle' if Wilson did not treat the country with more respect.[89] What made Bernhard and Rathenau's pronouncements so dangerous was the fact that they aired their concerns in the public arena. The pair gave people the impression that there was a genuine alternative to the armistice terms that were on offer. If the army fought on, then Germany could negotiate a different end to the war than the one Wilson had proposed. However, with the German people's morale flagging, the idea that Germany had an alternative was nothing but wishful thinking. All Bernhard and Rathenau did, therefore, was to mask the grim reality of Germany's predicament.

The end, when it finally came, was nothing like Rathenau, Bernhard or any other German could have imagined. Ludendorff's time as first quartermaster-general came to an inglorious end in late October when the chancellor effectively conspired to have him dismissed. Theodor Wolff, like most liberal-minded Germans, shed few tears at the news. 'Ludendorff believed in himself and that was perhaps his biggest problem. Indeed, he had so much faith in himself that his gestures took on the shape of a dictator's', Wolff observed perceptively.[90] Shorn of its strategic leader, the army limped on for another couple of weeks, until the signing of the armistice on 11 November finally brought this futile resistance to a close. In the intervening period, the kaiser had abdicated and fled to the Netherlands, as Germany itself was engulfed in revolution.

The year 1918 proved to be one of remarkable transformations. It had opened with genuine hope and optimism that the war could be brought to a favourable conclusion. After putting Russia to the sword in the east, the military looked to achieve a similar outcome in the west. However, the failure of the spring offensives left people's dreams of victory dead; all that remained was the gloom of defeat. The big question that emerged from this dismal situation was simple: how and why had Germany's fortunes been transformed so dramatically in less than a year? The obvious place to find answers would have been with the military leadership and the precarious state of the army. Yet in postwar Germany, people looked elsewhere and managed to pin the blame for defeat on the home front, on the socialists and Jews who had apparently stabbed the army in the back. The myths of defeat that emerged were not simply plucked from thin air, but rather stemmed from the actions of Jews and other Germans during the final months of the conflict. Once the seeds of defeat had taken root, eradicating these poisonous mythic weeds proved almost impossible.

9

THE END

The armistice agreement signed between Germany, the Entente and its allies on 11 November 1918 finally brought the first day of peace after more than four years of grim fighting. On the streets of London and Paris, vast crowds celebrated the cessation of hostilities. People made merry 'by the ringing of handbells, the hooting of motors, the screaming of whistles, the rattling of tin-trays, and the banging of anything that could be banged', reported *The Times* in London.[1] In stark contrast, few Germans could find much reason to let out a cheer or even to rattle a tin-tray. Joseph Levy, an Orthodox Frankfurt cantor, watched glumly as the conflict stuttered to an end. When the news of the armistice came through, Levy recalled, he 'almost fell over in shock'. It was not just Germany's defeat that sent Levy into a pit of despair, but the fact that this also represented the death of Imperial Germany. Levy had dedicated himself to the German Empire and its war, waving his eldest son off to the front and joining the military reserves himself at the ripe old age of forty-five. His synagogue congregation had even got used to Levy leading prayers dressed head to toe in full military uniform. But the events of November 1918 put an end to all this. With tears in his eyes, Levy exclaimed, somewhat apocalyptically, of the fatherland itself: 'It is lost.'[2]

The general despondency of November 1918 was far removed from the apparent excitement that had originally greeted the war's outbreak in August 1914. A humiliating defeat was not the occasion for flag waving and patriotic songs. The world was different and Germany had changed. Few Germans even wanted to talk about the enthusiasm for war that had engulfed the country four years previously. Theodor Wolff, who had been one of a small number of sceptics from the start, remembered slightly mockingly the 'war-enthusiasm hype of August 1914', but that was about it.[3] The metaphor of the 'spirit of 1914', however, was not completely dead; one element of the 'August days' still made the occasional fleeting appearance. The idea of social unity, which people had so powerfully embraced in the early months of the war, remained a goal for some politicians, even if the chaos of postwar Germany made the idea of any form of togetherness seem but a distant dream.[4]

Yet while the 'spirit of 1914' lay largely dormant in the immediate postwar years, other wartime legacies remained very much alive. The effects of total war, a brutal culture of destruction and of widespread annexations continued to make themselves felt. Added to this, Germany remained deeply divided, minority groups continued to be castigated, and myths of defeat became even more powerful. Jews and other Germans may have collectively helped to shape the way that Germany conducted itself in the First World War, but once the fighting had stopped, Jews played only a minor role in disseminating the legacies that remained. Instead, the war's many dangerous legacies were increasingly turned against their co-creators, the German Jews, as anti-Semitism and social problems deepened.

Seeking Peace

At the war's end, German Jews not only faced the difficult task of unpicking the legacies of total war, but they also had to face the challenge of rising anti-Semitism. The first stage on the long road back to peace for all Germans was military demobilisation. Under the terms of the November armistice, the German authorities had fourteen days in which to remove their troops from the Western Front. Fritz Beckhardt, who had spent the final two years of the war in the skies, had little trouble in evacuating. But his speed should not be taken as a sign of acquiescing to the Allies' demands. Beckhardt, as a young, headstrong fighter pilot, disregarded instructions to surrender his aircraft to the French and instead flew his precious machine to the safety of Switzerland. Upon landing near the town of Rapperswil by Lake Zurich, Beckhardt was arrested and sent back across the German border.[5] Otto Meyer, like Beckhardt a Jewish serviceman, had a much more arduous journey home. His unit, which had been stationed in the Ardennes, started the long march back to Germany on 13 November. After dragging themselves through a landscape marked by victorious Belgian flags and the detritus of war – downed aeroplanes, crashed cars and abandoned equipment – Meyer and his men eventually crossed the

German border on 21 November. From there, they spent a further nine days barracked in Koblenz waiting to be demobbed.

The last line in Meyer's war diary reads simply: '9 December 1918. Midday, arrival in Rheda.'[6] These final words were clearly an attempt to demarcate the war years from the new world of peace. However, the obvious relief of making it home unscathed – of surviving the conflict – often proved short-lived, as soldiers were quickly confronted with the realities of postwar Germany. Meyer, for example, returned to Rheda to find the family's once profitable clothing factory extant, but struggling to turn a profit. Friedrich Rülf, a young assistant army rabbi, who had been discharged from his military post in November, also found himself in dire financial straits. Seemingly in terrible need of money to finance a return to his studies in Breslau, Rülf resorted to chasing the Federation of German Jews for a missing 100 Marks, which he believed he was still owed for his military chaplaincy work.[7]

A perilous lack of food and basic materials during the first postwar winter only added to people's woes. It was one thing to starve during the conflict, remembered Rahel Straus, but it was quite another when 'the war had finished [and yet] the hunger remained'.[8] The Allies' decision to leave their naval blockade of German ports in place worsened an already difficult situation. Recognising the severity of the food crisis, one of Germany's most prominent feminist campaigners, the German-Jewish journalist and politician Jenny Apolant, took the fight directly to the Allies. Showing typical doggedness, she drafted a petition of protest demanding that the Allies allow food and goods to flow back into Germany. Her plan was for the text to be circulated to women's groups across the world, in the hope that female solidarity would change Allied opinion.[9]

Unfortunately for Apolant and other Germans, protests against the armistice terms fell on deaf ears. Individual families, therefore, faced a double bind; they struggled with continued food shortages, while at the same time trying to reintegrate men back into the home. As people all too quickly discovered, erasing the scars of conflict involved much more than simply removing a uniform. Many returning soldiers had seen and experienced too many horrors, while a lot of women had also enjoyed greater independence. 'It is not going to be easy for married couples to settle back with one another', observed the social reformer (and cousin of Walther Rathenau) Josephine Levy-Rathenau. 'As soon as the joy of returning has passed', she added, 'potential points of friction will be massive.'[10] Sadly, Levy-Rathenau's predictions proved correct. Rates of alcoholism, domestic violence and divorce all rose in postwar

Germany.[11] Max Sichel, a prominent Jewish psychologist and medical practitioner from Frankfurt, observed similar patterns in Jewish communities. To Sichel's surprise, after the war alcoholism turned from being a disease of the 'lower cultural circles' to one that also afflicted other social groups, including middle-class Jews.[12]

If the transition was difficult for families whose loved ones actually made it home, then the process was even harder when the soldier remained absent, whether hospitalised, in captivity, or dead. The Joseph family (mother Fanny, sister Eva and brother Otto, all members of Berlin's Jewish Reform community) must have thought they had survived the conflict unscathed. But then on 9 November – two days before the armistice – a letter arrived in Berlin informing them that Otto had been missing since early September. 'I delayed telling you this news', wrote Otto's commander, 'because I was hoping that he would find his way back to the battery.' Unfortunately, this never happened, and Otto joined the massed ranks of the German-Jewish war dead, some 12,000 by the war's end.[13] Jewish communities did what they could to offer comfort to the bereaved. *Memorbücher*, a traditional way of recording the dead, were produced in some Jewish communities especially for those killed in the conflict. And across the country, war memorials sprang up in synagogues and Jewish cemeteries in quick succession.[14]

The tremendous scale of wartime death was a reminder of the devastating legacy of total war. Like the Josephs, millions of families across Germany were forced to rebuild their lives around a gaping absence. In some cases, particularly with the most severely war-wounded, this turned out to be a living absence. While the majority of wounded veterans returned to their families, though not necessarily to their old professions, a small minority of severely disabled veterans never managed to find a route home. There was some suggestion that Jewish communities should follow the Christian churches in setting up specialist centres for the war-wounded. Arthur Kahn, a Jewish doctor from Berlin, dreamt of a series of rehabilitation centres in rural settings, where the Jewish war-wounded could, if possible, be retrained as agricultural workers. Sadly for Kahn, his plan never really got off the drawing board.[15]

At the war's end, it was not just individuals who had to master the return to civil society; businesses too had little option but to attempt to unpick the legacies of conflict. As military orders for barbed wire, shells and guns dried up, factories needed to return to peacetime production. Albert Ballin, the great shipping magnate, was certainly aware of the enormity of the task facing his own company. During the war, HAPAG had lost its position as the world's largest shipping line and shrunk into a mere skeleton of its former self; many of the company's great liners were either sunk, confiscated or in port. The thought of rebuilding HAPAG from scratch proved too much for Ballin. On 8 November, the director had spent the afternoon in business meetings; not long after, though, he felt faint, dizzy and generally unwell. The next day, 9 November, Ballin was reported dead. The suddenness of his demise encouraged speculation; at first the talk was of a heart attack, then a stomach ulcer and then later suicide.[16] Whatever the cause, one thing remains certain: Ballin, like other business leaders, could see no way back after Germany's defeat.[17]

Other German-Jewish businesses fared slightly better amidst the turmoil of the postwar transition. Bonn's premier flag-making company – the Bonner Fahnenfabrik – which had been owned by the German-Jewish Meyer family ever since its founding in 1866, continued to expand its business. The political shifts in the postwar years, which resulted in a sudden demand for new national flags, no doubt provided a much-needed financial boost. Walther Rathenau's AEG also made the leap from total war to the very different demands of the postwar world. The AEG's success lay in the firm's strategy of long-term planning. Even when the conflict was still ongoing, the AEG's management had begun preparing for the war's end, for example by investing some of the company's considerable profits into non-military machinery.[18]

However, the economic success of the Bonner Fahnenfabrik and the much larger AEG came at a considerable cost. Both the general public and at times other businesses viewed with suspicion any firms deemed to have profited from the war. Meyer's flag business was rebuked in the press when rumours spread that the company had delivered wagonloads of 'French, Italian, English, American, Belgian and even Russian flags' to the people of Lille. Fraternising with the enemy was one thing, but the accusation here was that the French then used the flags to celebrate Germany's recent defeat. Rudolf Meyer, head of the Bonner Fahnenfabrik, took to the local press to dismiss the charge as a 'crass untruth' and 'a web of lies'. He explained rather exasperatedly that as there was an export ban covering former enemy countries, 'there was never any possibility of sending wagons full of enemy flags!! to Lille'.[19]

The accusation of illegal war profiteering, underpinned by an unhealthy dose of anti-Semitism, present in the rumours about Meyer's flag factory, also surfaced in a series of attacks on Rathenau. Reinhard Mumm, a conservative politician and notorious polemicist, accused Rathenau of 'rampant capitalism' that had led to Germany being 'controlled by the Jews'.[20] The War Raw Materials Corporations that Rathenau had helped to establish in the early months of the conflict became the focus of much of this vitriol. Speaking in the Reichstag, Wilhelm Bruhn, a short, rather plump politician in his early fifties, produced a spectacular, if well-rehearsed, piece of political theatre. In a debate on the workings of the corporations, Bruhn outlined the age and alleged salary of some of those who managed them. After each description, Bruhn's colleagues in the German National people's party (Deutschnationale Volkspartei, DNVP) shouted in unison: 'So what's his name?' In answer to which Bruhn shouted out a recognisably Jewish-sounding surname: 'Meyer with a "y"!' And so the play went on.[21]

Rathenau and the main Jewish organisations fully refuted the discourse of war profiteering and also did their best to defend the War Raw Materials Corporations from criticism. In a sober tome on the issue, the CV calculated that a mere 11 per cent of those in the corporations had been Jewish; Rathenau meanwhile explained to Mumm straightforwardly that the War Raw Materials Section had always 'distanced itself from contractual and financial matters'.[22] Yet in an era of uncertainty, upheaval and change, the German right continued to find fertile ground for its anti-Semitic attacks.[23] What many people desired was a return to the certainties of the pre-war world, to a time before war. Instead, what they had ended up with was a very different Germany, one that had been permanently shaped by the stresses of fighting a total war. German Jews, who had been falsely branded as the war's financial winners, ended up saddled with some of the blame.

Revolution

The discourse of war profiteering that swept through war-torn Germany was a reflection of the deep chasms that divided German society. As the war dragged on, people increasingly split along class, religious, political and regional lines. The Bavarians turned on the Prussians, the SPD attacked itself, splitting into two competing factions in 1916–17, while city dwellers directed their anger towards landowners for apparently hoarding food. German Jews experienced all of these rifts as Germans, but at the same time also suffered as Jews, with rising anti-Semitism and the military's Jewish census being the most obvious examples. The German revolution made matters much worse, further dividing an already fractured society. German Jews received much of the blame for the tumultuous revolutionary period, but they themselves were actually as divided as the rest of German society.

The revolution itself had started in earnest in early November, when sailors in Kiel protested at plans to send them into one final – and in their minds futile – battle against the British. From this North German port, street demonstrations rapidly spread further south to Hamburg, Cologne, Frankfurt and Munich before finally reaching Berlin on 9 November. The high point of the revolution occurred that very same day, when the kaiser was forced to abdicate, a move that paved the way for the declaration of a new German republic. Considering the massive changes it unleashed, this first phase of the revolution passed relatively peacefully. In Berlin, Theodor Wolff was even confident enough to take his children, 'who absolutely [had] to see the revolution', out onto the streets.[24] It was almost as if the fall of the Hohenzollerns was nothing more than free family entertainment.

Wolff had clearly been swept along by the emotion of the revolution. This 'greatest of all revolutions', he wrote in the *Berliner Tageblatt*, had ripped apart 'a deeply rooted' system: 'Yesterday morning everything was still there . . . Yesterday afternoon nothing remained.'[25] Yet not all German Jews shared this same exuberance. It was not so much that German Jews had a deep-seated loyalty to the kaiser, although some certainly did, but more the case that the revolution which had forced his abdication represented uncertainty for the future. Max Liebermann did his best to bury his head in the sand. He threw himself into his painting, simply as a way to avoid 'having to think about all the misery'.[26] The *Allgemeine Zeitung des Judentums* did a better job of capturing people's fears when it stressed that 'difficult years, even difficult decades' lay ahead.[27] German Zionists found themselves in a similar quandary, praising the fall of a discriminatory system, but at the same time fearing the future. We 'cannot predict which successes it will achieve and how it will continue to develop', explained the Zionists' *Jüdische Rundschau*.[28]

The question of the revolution's direction was not only the source of many people's fears; it also provided the basis for deepening divisions. After the kaiser's downfall, a sizeable majority hoped to build a new stable, democratic Germany, thereby firmly crushing any thoughts of a full-blown socialist revolution. The main vehicle for achieving this goal was the new Council of People's Commissars, which held power until a new national government could be elected. Out of its six members, two – Hugo Haase (USPD) and Otto Landsberg (SPD) – were Jewish. The pattern was similar on a regional level, where a number of German Jews took on leading roles in the new governments. Paul Hirsch entered the Prussian state government, Charlotte Landau-Mühsam was voted into Lübeck's parliament, while Ludwig Haas, who had recently returned from advising on Jewish affairs in Poland, took on the role of interior minister in Baden.[29] Like Hirsch and Landau-Mühsam,

Haas was a moderate in revolutionary affairs. During the November uprisings, he had donned his hat, grabbed a walking stick and run to the grand duke's palace in Karlsruhe to ensure the royal family's safety. Haas clearly feared, more than encouraged, a socialist revolution.[30]

In stark contrast to these moderate voices, an initially much smaller group, which also included many Jews, hoped to push the revolution forward in a more radical direction. Having only recently been released from prison, Karl Liebknecht and Rosa Luxemburg, the two leaders of the Marxist Spartacus League, played only a limited role in the initial events of November 1918. Liebknecht may have declared a German Soviet Republic on 9 November, but this was more a gesture than a serious basis for a new Germany. Luxemburg was even more adrift of the revolution, only arriving in the capital on 10 November, by which point events had already taken their own path. Despite their slow start, it did not take them long to get up to speed. By December, both Liebknecht and Luxemburg were desperately calling for a full-blown socialist revolution. 'Proletarians arise! To battle!' they urged.[31]

While Liebknecht and Luxemburg had been somewhat sidelined in Berlin and Breslau respectively, Kurt Eisner had already managed to set a socialist agenda in Munich. Eisner played the left-wing radical role to a tee. Even his friend, the Munich lawyer Philipp Loewenfeld, mockingly suggested that Eisner 'could be mistaken for Karl Marx' on account of the bushy grey beard that flowed down over his chest.[32] On 7 November, Eisner started and the same day concluded the Bavarian revolution almost single-handedly. After addressing a large crowd in the afternoon in central Munich, he led a procession to the barracks, where the soldiers joined the revolutionary movement. That night, with the city effectively in Eisner's hands, a republic was declared; before the sun had even risen, Eisner – a Jewish Berliner – had also been appointed Bavaria's first republican prime minister.[33] Everything happened so quickly that many people only learned of the new republic when they awoke the next day. 'I could not believe it. Had I actually slept through a revolution?' quipped the German-Jewish academic, Moritz Bonn.[34]

Bonn may have dozed through the Munich revolution, but there was little chance of sleeping through the events that took place in Berlin at the start of 1919. On 5 January, large crowds gathered in central Berlin to protest against the removal of Berlin's chief of police, who was a committed USPD member. During the day, the demonstration exceeded all expectations, growing in size and ferocity. By the late afternoon, some of the protesters had broken away and seized control of government buildings and the main press offices; later

Berlin's central railway stations also fell into the rebels' hands. Georg Bernhard, who was clearly perturbed at having his newspaper offices occupied, condemned the left-wing rebels as 'a mob of deserters and the rubbish from prisons and jails'.[35]

The Spartacist uprising, as the revolt was commonly called, threw Germany's Jewish population fully into the glare of the revolutionary spotlight. Not only was Rosa Luxemburg, co-head of the Spartacist movement, Jewish, but other prominent members, such as Leo Jogiches and Paul Levi, also came from Jewish families. The extreme right, which needed little excuse to go on the attack, complained that a revolution 'of the people' was nothing more than a 'dictatorship of the Jews'.[36] But this rather ignored just how divided Jews and other Germans actually were. The politics of the extreme left found little traction with German Jews, who in the main at most sympathised with the moderates. Indeed, the CV was so determined to distance itself from the socialist revolutionaries that it tried to remind people of Liebknecht's Protestant heritage. Under the rather loaded headline of 'Liebknecht's Aryan Ancestry', it printed copies of both his birth and baptism certificates.[37] The extreme right, though, cared little for the finer detail; it had already decided that Jews, 'in the pay of the Entente', had organised the entire revolution.[38]

A Culture of Violence

Emil Julius Gumbel, a headstrong Jewish academic who brimmed with self-confidence, had enjoyed a brief and undistinguished military career. Discharged from the army in 1915 on medical grounds, Gumbel spent the remainder of the war studying mathematics and dabbling in the anti-war movement.[39] In 1921, Gumbel put his pacifist beliefs to good use when he published a short pamphlet entitled 'Two Years of Murder'. His stark conclusion was that not only had right-wing sympathisers committed 326 more murders than those on the left, but also that the majority of the killers had escaped justice.[40] The following year Gumbel reissued his pamphlet under a revised title of 'Four Years of Political Murder'; he now upped his calculations to show 354 political murders on the right and only 22 on the left.[41] Gumbel never published 'Six Years of Political Murder', although there would have been justification enough to have done so. Just as had been the case during the war, a culture of destruction also saturated the immediate postwar years. Yet this was never a simple continuity of violence and destruction. There were subtle differences both in terms of the perpetrators, who were now generally much younger, and in terms of the enemy, which was no longer the Entente, but communists or in some cases even Jews. For the extreme right, the terms became interchangeable.[42]

The German revolution entered a deadlier phase during the Spartacist uprising. The Spartacists, who stormed into the centre of Berlin armed with machine guns and artillery, clearly showed violent intent. But this merely marked the start of a violent cycle. In an attempt to restore order, Germany's provisional government approved the establishment of volunteer military formations, known as the Freikorps. These heavily armed bands of youths and seasoned soldiers then went on the rampage through Berlin, crushing the Spartacists as they went. Finally, on 15 January 1919, members of the Freikorps captured Luxemburg and Liebknecht before taking them to the Hotel Eden for questioning. The pair were never seen alive again: Liebknecht was shot in the back, while Luxemburg's corpse was later dragged from the Landwehr Canal after her execution. The following month, Kurt Eisner suffered a similar fate in Munich, when an aristocratic young nationalist gunned him down in the street.

There was widespread condemnation of all three murders, even from the likes of Georg Bernhard, who had previously criticised the revolutionaries in the sternest fashion. Without necessarily sympathising with the victims themselves, the newspaper resolutely condemned the method of their passing as nothing more than 'mob justice'.[43] The families of Liebknecht and Luxemburg appointed Siegfried Weinberg and Kurt Rosenfeld, two Berlin-based lawyers, to investigate their relatives' sudden deaths.[44] The fact that Weinberg and Rosenfeld happened to be Jewish has the danger of giving the wholly false impression of a simple perpetrator–victim dichotomy, with German Jews on the victim side of the fence and a violent, rampaging German right on the other. The reality was very different: during Germany's increasingly violent revolution, German Jews were both victims and perpetrators.

One of the most notorious perpetrators in this respect was Rudolf Liepmann, or 'the murderer Liepmann', as the communist newspaper *Die Rote Fahne*, called him.[45] He may or may not appear in an image that surfaced soon after the murder of Luxemburg and Liebknecht – the killers sit around a table with drinks, as if at an after-work party – but he was certainly involved in their deaths (see Plate 24).[46] Like his co-conspirators, Liepmann had fought in the war, rising to the rank of lieutenant, but unlike the others, he came from a middle-class Jewish family. During a rather farcical trial, staged by the military itself, Liepmann acknowledged his involvement in Liebknecht's death, admitting that he had fired a shot, but only because this 'highly dangerous enemy' had tried to escape.[47] Like the other defendants, Liepmann got off with a mild sentence of six weeks' house arrest. Seemingly unperturbed by events, Liepmann went back to fighting left-wing revolutionaries on the streets, until he himself was shot and badly wounded in the leg in spring 1920.[48]

Liepmann may have been an extreme case, but he was far from being the only German Jew to be involved in the violence of the early postwar years. Bernhard Kahn, a Jewish relief worker in Berlin, recalled how he had been threatened by another German Jew at this time. Kahn fell under suspicion, simply for having been a good friend of Liebknecht. Opening his door one morning, Kahn was confronted by a group of soldiers led by 'a very arrogant, boisterous and aggressive Jewish sergeant'. The man demanded money from Kahn or else his 'wonderful collection of ceramics . . . [would] be broken in the search'. One thousand Marks proved enough to send the soldiers on their way.[49]

Outside the capital, plenty of other German Jews signed up for the Freikorps and became involved in its reign of anti-Bolshevik violence. In South Bavaria, Fritz Dispeker, who had recently returned from the front, joined a Freikorps group in Landsberg, while in Bochum another Jewish veteran, the lawyer Dr Koppel, helped patrol the streets during the height of the Spartacist insurrections.[50] Those who joined the Freikorps came from a variety of backgrounds and the Jewish members were no exception.[51] It was not just war veterans like Dispeker, Koppel and Liepmann who signed up. A younger generation of German Jews, not old enough to have experienced the violence of the front themselves, also joined the group. In Munich, 17-year-old Alfred Neumeyer fell into this category, enlisting in the Freikorps Epp at the start of 1919. What motivated him, he later explained, was 'eradicating the power of the reds', but like other young Germans 'seeing uniforms and witnessing [street] battles' also opened Neumeyer's eyes to the excitement and adventure of conflict.[52]

Life in the Freikorps could actually be fairly dull for much of the time. However, the Freikorps' notoriety stemmed from the occasions where routine tedium was replaced by torrents of violence against the extreme left. Their brutal suppression of the January uprising in Berlin was replicated in the spring when the Freikorps moved on Munich. The target on this occasion was the newly formed Bavarian Council Republic (Räterepublik), which proved to be a remarkably short-lived socialist state. As in Berlin, German-Jewish revolutionaries again played a leading role in this left-wing experiment. At first, it was the tall, wiry anarchist Gustav Landauer whose name appeared on the new republic's proclamations. Joining Landauer in the main intellectual clique were other German Jews, such as the playwright Ernst Toller and his fellow anarchist Erich Mühsam (brother of Charlotte Landau-Mühsam). After the first week of the republic, Eugen Levine, a Russian-born Jew, and according to Moritz Bonn a 'rather sinister person', attempted to bring the Munich government under the control of the communists.[53]

German Jews were not just present in Bavaria's revolutionary government; they also appeared in the ranks of those lined up to overthrow the Council Republic. When a Freikorps regiment was founded in the Franconian city of Würzburg, for example, Jews and other Germans, including several Jewish university students, volunteered for action. Before departing for Munich, the group lined up at the main station to be photographed, as if they were going on some kind of leisurely day trip. Bruno Hellmann and Eugen Kürzinger, casually standing at the back, are joined by another Jewish volunteer, Fritz Ruschkewitz, sporting a German uniform steel helmet at the very front.[54] However, by the time the Freikorps Würzburg had made it down to Munich, the Bavarian Council Republic had already been brought to a premature end. Other Freikorps formations rampaged through the city and its environs leaving more than 550 people dead, including Gustav Landauer, who was beaten to death in custody, and Eugen Levine, who was put before a firing squad.[55]

In the wake of the violence that swept first through Berlin and then through Munich, the extreme right had little problem in finding the culprits. The *Münchener Beobachter*, mouthpiece of the virulently anti-Semitic Thule Society went into propaganda overdrive, publishing articles, pamphlets and speeches that blamed Jews for the recent violence and disorder.[56] One flyer, produced by an anonymous source, stated plainly that 'the Spartacists are nothing more than Jewish nonsense'.[57] The simple dichotomy that emerged through these repeated attacks pitted Jews and Bolsheviks against those in the Freikorps, supposedly defending order.

On the ground, the reality was very different. German Jews could be revolutionaries, but they could also be Freikorps fighters. Jewish victims of this wave of violence also spanned the divide. While Luxemburg and Landauer fell victim to Freikorps mobs, in the case of Ernst Berger, the reverse was true. Berger, a Jewish professor of art, had been rounded up along with seven members of the Thule Society; all were held hostage in Munich before being executed by supporters of the Bavarian Council Republic.[58] Postwar violence, therefore, cut both ways. Jews may have been labelled Bolshevik revolutionaries, but they themselves could be both perpetrators and victims of left- and right-wing violence. Just as had been the case during the war, a culture of destruction ensured that violence, brutality and murder could be justified, if not celebrated.

The Shadow of Annexations

The violence of the revolution and the Spartacist uprising failed to stop Germany's gradual move towards parliamentary democracy. Elections held in January 1919 led to the creation of a new national assembly, which replaced the temporary Council of People's Commissars. The national assembly, headed by the Social Democratic president Friedrich Ebert, had one main task: to draw up a German constitution. However, shadows of the recent past loomed over its work from the very start. Not only did it have to deal with ongoing violence, it also inherited the Allies' plans for peace as well as the legacies of wartime expansion.

The national assembly and the German public came face to face for the first time with the Allies' peace plans in the spring. On 7 May, a solemn procession of cars took members of the German peace delegation in Paris the short distance from their base in the Hotel des Reservoirs to the Hotel Trianon. After receiving his guests, Georges Clemenceau, France's victorious prime minister, rather soured the atmosphere by presenting a draft of the final peace treaty. Reeling with shock at the terms, the German delegation returned to their hotel to plan their next move.[59] Carl Melchior, who had been in the room for Clemenceau's speech, decided very quickly that Germany's only course of action was to reject the treaty. Max Warburg, Melchior's business partner in Hamburg, who was also present in Paris, was in full agreement. The proposals, he complained to his wife, 'will kill off any hope of a better future'.[60] Disgusted and appalled at the terms, Melchior and many of the other delegates left Paris for home, but not before they suffered a second humiliation. En route to the station, an angry mob threw stones and sand at the German delegation's cars, slightly injuring Melchior in the process.[61]

In an apparently helpful attempt to make the peace terms more comprehensible to those at home, Louis Oppenheim put them into visual form. Under the heading 'What We Will Lose!' the poster he produced highlighted the potentially devastating consequences of the peace treaty: 20 per cent of productive land and 10 per cent of the population were to go; colonies, coal, iron ore and food reserves were also to be lost (see Plate 25). Oppenheim's graphics – an ordinary worker, a poor, emaciated family and a simple factory building – suggest that the Treaty of Versailles intended to devastate an innocent hardworking population rather than to target a warmongering nation as claimed by the peacemakers in Paris. What made the terms of the peace treaty all the more difficult to swallow was the fact that the previous year Germany had imposed its own devastating peace on Russia, at Brest-Litovsk. Under the proposed peace terms, Germany faced losing not only these gains, but also parts of its existing territory. The legacy of wartime expansionism, therefore, left an inflated understanding of Germany's continental position, very much at odds with the postwar peace settlement.

As news of the peace terms filtered back from Paris, the overwhelming response of German Jews was one of despair. The influential *Allgemeine Zeitung des Judentums* repeated the popular nationalist cry of 'a brutal peace based on might' (*Gewaltfrieden*); even the Zionists called this a 'severe peace'.[62] Understandably perhaps, the sense of outrage went much deeper among those German Jews who had previously demanded German expansionism in the east, whether in an economic or a territorial form. Georg Bernhard, who as ever showed little restraint in exercising his thoughts, branded the draft treaty 'a shameful document' and then for good measure added that it had 'no precedent in the previous thousands of years of human history'.[63] Despite Bernhard's anger, this was not quite a call to arms. It was instead left to Rathenau to invoke once again a more radical option. In an impassioned piece of writing, he suggested that Germany's president, ministers and entire national assembly should hand in their resignations. If the Allies wanted to destroy any chance of peace, Rathenau argued, then they could also pick up the pieces and care for 60 million people. It is about the 'protection of our honesty and conscience', he added.[64]

The righteous indignation of Bernhard and Rathenau raised the public temperature against the proposed peace treaty, but did very little to alter the Allies' plans. On 28 June, Johannes Bell and Hermann Müller, representing the national assembly, signed the Treaty of Versailles on Germany's behalf. Its main clauses were almost identical to the original draft. Germany suffered territorial losses, mainly in Eastern Europe; its colonial possessions were removed; the military was reduced in size; and reparations were imposed, although the final figure was only set in 1921.

It was somewhat ironic that Rathenau, in his attempts to prevent this state of affairs from happening, had published his blistering attack on the peace treaties in *Die Zukunft*, which had been edited by the German-Jewish journalist Maximilian Harden ever since its founding in 1892. Harden, a passionate actor turned journalist, had firmly backed the war in 1914. 'We

Have to Win' was *Die Zukunft's* uncompromising demand at the start. But as the conflict drifted into its second year, Harden's enthusiasm turned to pessimism and *Die Zukunft* was repeatedly banned.[65] In 1919, he was one of a small group of Germans who appeared to accept the Treaty of Versailles and its much-derided war guilt clause. 'The constant assertions of Berlin's innocence' are 'false' and 'damaging', argued Harden.[66] Such frank views on the treaty were guaranteed to win him few friends in postwar Germany. Indeed, one conservative commentator suggested that Harden acted 'as if he is a paid-up agent of the Entente' and thus no longer 'backs his own nation'.[67] Harden's open acceptance of the peace treaty certainly made him something of an outlier. Aside from Oskar Cohn, who kept pointing out Germany's own injustices at Brest-Litovsk, few Jews publicly approved the Allies' peace terms; the general consensus was one of condemnation, not of acquiescence.[68]

However, amidst the deep gloom of the Paris peace conference, Germans could still find a few small glimmers of hope. According to the terms of the final treaty, the ownership of territory along Germany's northern and eastern borders was to be decided by plebiscite, with the population voting either to remain German or to join Denmark in the north or the new Polish state in the east. There was a tangible sense of relief when the plebiscites were confirmed. Germany's Jewish organisations, which were rightly fearful of anti-Jewish excesses in Poland, saw in the referendums a means to save Jewish lives. Keeping the eastern borderlands German, argued the Zionists, would protect Jews from a Polish state 'where anti-Semitism has penetrated through to its very core'.[69] But German Jews had other good reasons to hope that Germany's eastern borders would remain intact. Like their fellow Germans, many Jews wanted to see Germany retain a foothold in the east; at the very least a presence in this area offered the prospect of securing German territorial ambitions in the region. Jews and other Germans, therefore, launched a dogged campaign to keep hold of the country's threatened borderlands.

Perhaps the most hotly disputed region to be determined by plebiscite was the economically prosperous province of Upper Silesia. The vote itself was set for March 1921, which left little more than eighteen months for the Poles and Germans to stake their claims to the region. In the intervening period, both sides fought an increasingly bitter paramilitary and propaganda campaign. The Freikorps, fresh from fighting the Bolshevik threat within Germany, now moved to the eastern borderlands. Kurt Joseph, a highly patriotic Berliner, was one of many German-Jewish fighters to take part in the Polish border clashes. As Joseph himself recalled, the fighting was often fierce. On one occasion,

Joseph and his men came under 'heavy [Polish] infantry and machine gun-fire' which left about 20 per cent of those under his command dead or wounded.[70] Violent clashes in the east, such as the one Joseph described, achieved little in terms of territorial gain, but the Freikorps' actions did none-theless signal the extent of some Germans' disgruntlement with the Treaty of Versailles.

While the Freikorps laid physical claim to the disputed territories in the east, the new republican government in Berlin attempted to do the same through an expensive propaganda campaign. Motivated no doubt by the fact that his coalmining empire lay in Upper Silesia, the German-Jewish industri-alist Eduard Arnhold smuggled state funds into the region for the secret prop-aganda war.[71] Most other German Jews in the border regions followed Arnhold and also backed the pro-German camp. As patriotic Germans, they had no wish to abandon their own country for Poland. It was not just Polish anti-Semitism they feared; it was also the thought of being thrown in with the Eastern European Jews. Speaking as the regional head of the Jewish CV, Berthold Haase explained the situation in stark terms. 'The Jewish commu-nity in Posen', he explained, 'differs not only in language but also on a cultural level . . . from the Jews living in Congress Poland and Galicia'. To emphasise the point, he added that 'the thought of being turned into Eastern European Jews . . . fills us with horror'.[72]

Happily for Haase and his borderland compatriots, Jewish communities elsewhere in Germany seemed to agree with his analysis. For example, 1,100 Marks flowed in from Berlin's Reform community to help the German cause in Upper Silesia.[73] The depths of Jewish support came to the fore in the days running up to the plebiscite. Under a contentious clause buried in the Treaty of Versailles, those Germans born in but living outside Upper Silesia had full voting rights. The German government sought to take every advantage of this by petitioning all eligible voters to travel east. As had almost come to be expected at any significant moment, an Oppenheim poster – this time showing a train steaming to the ballot – again whipped up support. Encouraged by such propaganda efforts, German Jews from almost every political and religious persuasion flocked to the east in time for the vote. Even Cohn, the voice of moderation when it came to the peace treaties, made the journey.[74] Once in the plebiscite zone, people often bumped into friends and family whom they had not seen for years. Emanuel Kirschner, who had left Upper Silesia for Berlin in the 1870s, met up with his seven brothers, one sister and numerous cousins, all of whom had travelled east to vote for Germany.[75]

Unfortunately for those involved, these family reunions often turned into one long goodbye. When the votes were counted, the German campaign received a small majority. Yet in their final deliberations, the Allies decided to reduce the size of German Upper Silesia by carving off some of the most industrialised areas, which would become Polish. Unsurprisingly, many Germans, particularly those who had invested time and money in the plebiscite campaign, were indignant at the final settlement. Speaking in his capacity as Reichstag president, Paul Löbe captured the views of many when he called the agreement a 'heavy, perhaps insurmountable, blow'.[76] The shock was even greater for German Jews; they ended up suffering the fall-out as both Germans and Jews. Eduard Arnhold, for example, lost control of much of the Caesar Wollheim coalmining concern, which had mainly operated on the Polish side of the newly redrawn border. Worse was to come for another German-Jewish business owner, Felix Haase from Rybnik. Haase, who owned a major leather factory in the town, had to look on as his 15-year-old son Rudolf was arrested on suspicion of anti-Polish activities. Rudolf's body was later returned to his parents with a gunshot wound in the back.[77]

Rudolf Haase was murdered because he was too German. But at the same time other German Jews suffered: apparently they were not German enough. The anti-Semitic tendencies of the Freikorps, in particular, became more pronounced as their mission to defend Germany's eastern borders turned sour. The local Jewish population, who were viewed as a potential Bolshevik enemy, experienced abuse, discrimination and violence. On one occasion, a German officer and his men whipped a local Jewish man 'over his crooked nose', beating him 'half dead' in the process.[78] Not content with just attacking civilians, the Freikorps movement even turned on some of its own Jewish members. Kurt Joseph, who led a Freikorps unit based at the Polish border, was singled out by another section who 'did not want a Jew amongst the Freikorps'. Rightly fearing for his life, Joseph fled to Berlin where he signed up with a home guard group instead.[79] The gloom and despair of post-plebiscite Germany only added to Jewish communities' fears. Anti-Semites, complained the CV, 'write and scream that the Jews are working to sell Upper Silesia to the Poles'.[80]

Despite being saddled with the blame for territorial loss, many German Jews still retained a deep attachment to the east. This was particularly true of Max Naumann's newly formed Association of National German Jews (Verband nationaldeutscher Juden), which was firmly situated on the political right. The movement as a whole was active in campaigns against the Versailles settlement, while many individual members could be found in nationalist Heimat associations.[81] For other right-wing Germans, however, reversing the peace treaties and re-establishing a German foothold in the east was to be a project excluding German Jews. The newly formed National Socialist movement, for example, which at a very early stage adopted the idea of gaining 'living space' (*Lebensraum*) in Eastern Europe, understood this in purely racial terms. During the First World War, members of Germany's Jewish communities had done as much as any other sections of German society to fuel interest in the east as a space ripe for colonisation. But after revolution and the imposition of a crushing peace treaty, German Jews came to be viewed as the opponents of territorial expansion, rather than its proponents.

Creating Outsiders

Josef Lange had worked for many years as a synagogue cantor and teacher in the West Prussian town of Culmsee, which under the terms of the Treaty of Versailles was due to become the newly Polish town of Chełmża. Despite holding a deep attachment to the community, the thought of becoming a Polish citizen left him cold. Realising that 'one could not stay much longer in Culmsee', Lange and his extended family decided to move westwards to Berlin. The transition, though, proved to be exceedingly difficult. Lange suffered personal loss – the death of his wife – loneliness and then eviction, after his landlord denounced him to the housing office. His difficulties, as Lange recognised, were also about personal identity and belonging.[82] Like other Germans, Lange suddenly found himself rootless in his own country, without old friends or even his own regional heritage to lean on for support.[83]

Lange came to Berlin as a German refugee, one of approximately 850,000 former German citizens who opted to start afresh in the Weimar Republic, rather than to live their lives in the new Polish nation.[84] If acclimatising to a new home was difficult enough for Lange and other Germans, then it was even trickier for the other groups that entered postwar Germany. Amongst the largest was a new wave of Eastern European Jews and, on a more temporary basis, thousands of soldiers who entered Germany as part of the Allies' occupying army. Both groups found themselves the target of considerable public enmity. This partly reflected the continuation of wartime hostilities towards apparent outsiders, whether these were 'enemy aliens', prisoners of war or foreign workers. However, the destabilising impact of defeat and revolution only served to harden attitudes towards foreigners and social outsiders still further.

Allied troops were deployed in both the east and west of Germany. In the eastern borderlands, where the British, French and Italians served, public complaints were often of fraternisation. Relationships between a number of the Italian officers and local women – including the daughter of the grain merchant Moses – initially provoked some resentment.[85] On the western side of Germany, public anger towards the occupying troops was much fiercer. The main cause of complaint concerned the French decision to deploy some 25,000 black soldiers, mainly from North Africa, in the German Rhineland. At Versailles, the German delegation had demanded that no 'coloured troops' be used in the occupation, but as the vanquished power, the Germans were never in a position to choose their own occupiers. The public's impotence in such matters made the black troops a lightning rod for popular resentment. Above all, though, this was about racial fears. The soldiers whom German anthropologists had so carefully examined in the wartime POW camps were now keeping guard over the (supposedly more advanced) German people.[86]

Once roles had been reversed and the black soldiers had become wardens in the Rhineland rather than internees in POW camps, German imaginations ran wild. Germans made sensationalised allegations, accusing the black soldiers of criminality, intimidation and sexual violence. Determined apparently to uphold German morality and civility, a number of women's organisations came together in spring 1920 to form a protest group: the Rhenish Women's League (Rheinische Frauenliga). The Jewish Women's League, which had already expressed its shock at events in the Rhineland, quickly signed up to the new Women's League, where it joined its Catholic and Protestant sister organisations. The new association led a passionate propaganda campaign designed to inform other Germans as well as the outside world of the 'black humiliation' (*Schwarze Schmach*) in the Rhineland. Interpreting the occupation in racial terms, the Rhenish Women's League juxtaposed German culture with the supposedly lesser standards of 'black savages'. The Jewish Women's League appeared to have few qualms in associating itself with such racist attacks, willingly signing up to many of these degrading propaganda campaigns.[87]

The fight against this apparent horde of invading black soldiers occurred at the same time as Germans were experiencing a new wave of Eastern European Jewish immigration. Since the closure of Germany's borders to Jewish workers in April 1918, the authorities' policy had been one of restriction and repatriation. As a result, by the turn of the year the number of Eastern European Jews employed in Germany had dropped; only 239 remained in Frankfurt, for example.[88] Yet it proved impossible to remove all of the wartime Jewish workers. Put simply, there was nowhere to send them. It was not only that the new Eastern European successor states refused to take many of the Jews back; they were also busily trying to extradite the Jewish populations they already possessed. Pogrom-like violence, particularly in the context of the Polish-Ukrainian war, saw Jews robbed, beaten and murdered in more than 100 Polish and West Galician villages.[89] With little option but flight, Eastern European Jews started to move westwards; some 70,000 had arrived in Germany by 1921. Where the Eastern Jews had once come as workers, they now entered as persecuted refugees.[90]

With the number of new arrivals mounting, Joseph Roth produced a wonderfully vivid sketch of the Eastern European Jews. As was his journalistic trademark, Roth wandered through Berlin's Scheunenviertel, where many of the poorest Jews settled, recording the lives of those he encountered. A 'shrivelled-up old lady' selling shoelaces appeared in Roth's sketch alongside a Russian businessman downing schnapps 'as if it were a bowling ball', and a man 'muttering to himself' as he prayed in the corner.[91] However, not everyone shared Roth's mix of curiosity and affection. Where Roth viewed a vibrant religiosity, other German Jews saw only regression and decay. These contrasting viewpoints came to a head over plans to establish a new rabbinical court, or beth din, an institution that the mainly Orthodox Eastern European Jews deeply desired. The liberal section of the Berlin community fought a robust campaign against the proposal. For them, a beth din represented an unnecessary intrusion into their established way of life. Creating 'an organisation only for the Eastern European Jews', complained one liberal Jew, will 'set back our development by 50 to 100 years'.[92]

The debate over the beth din was ostensibly about the internal workings of Jewish communities, but it also concerned external perceptions. Just as had been the case during the war, the immigration of large numbers of Eastern European Jews forced the existing Jewish population to reassess their own public profile. Felix Goldmann, Leipzig's fiercely patriotic community rabbi, was not alone in suggesting that there was a strong correlation between levels of anti-Semitism and the rates of Jewish immigration. 'There is no mistaking this connection', he explained. The solution, as far as Goldmann could see, was for the refugees to settle in other countries, rather than in 'a poor country' like Germany.[93] Other German Jews agreed. Unsurprisingly, Max Naumann's Association of National German Jews made it clear that they had nothing in common with the Eastern European Jews. To us they are 'foreign', stressed Naumann, 'nothing more than foreigners'.[94]

Goldmann, Naumann and other German Jews certainly had good reason to cast a wary eye at this new wave of Jewish immigration. Continuing where they had left off during the war, groups on the political right attacked the Eastern European Jews with ever-greater venom. They accused these Jews of stealing precious resources which were already in desperately short supply. Food and housing shortages, two issues that resonated loudly with many Germans, were at the centre of these attacks. The anti-Semitic Deutschvölkischer Schutz- und Trutzbund, for example, circulated millions of leaflets suggesting that Jewish immigrants had made themselves comfortable, while Germans were left to live in 'dog kennels'. Elsewhere, the political right drew on a common litany of complaints. The Eastern European Jews, they claimed, not only threatened to infest Germany with disease, namely cholera and tuberculosis, but at the same time posed a sexual danger to the pure, innocent German female.[95]

Hostility towards the Eastern European Jews and the black soldiers had broad roots, going back to a deep-seated history of anti-Semitism in one instance and to the culture of European imperialism in the other. Yet in both cases the conflict, which Jews and other Germans had fought as a war of cultural and moral superiority, had only served to deepen these pre-existing attitudes. During the war, non-German nations and peoples had gradually been reduced to nothing more than a dangerous 'other'. Once denigrated in this way, it proved very difficult to restore a more liberal understanding of human difference, particularly as Germany itself descended into postwar chaos.

The 'Stab in the Back' Myth

The defining image of the infamous 'stab in the back' myth appeared on the *Süddeutsche Monatshefte*'s title page in April 1924 (see Plate 26). An oversized dagger protrudes from the neck of an incapacitated soldier, presenting the clear message that the German army had been betrayed at the very point when victory seemed within grasp. The *Süddeutsche Monatshefte*'s editor, Paul Nikolaus Cossmann, who must have agreed to the image, had long accused the socialists on the home front of bringing about Germany's defeat. His own Jewish heritage may explain why he resisted laying the blame more openly at the doors of Jewish communities. However, Cossmann's illustrator's unfortunate decision to draw no hand holding the dagger meant that people could sketch in their own perpetrator of choice. More often than not, this shadowy figure turned out to be Jewish.[96]

Rather disingenuously, the Munich Jewish lawyer and war veteran, Philipp Loewenfeld suggested that 'the Jew' Cossmann had invented the 'stab in the back' myth.[97] Loewenfeld, though, was wrong on both counts. First, Cossmann had converted to Christianity in his mid-thirties. And second, he was never the inventor of this myth of defeat, even though he readily propagated it. The idea that the army's fighting capabilities had somehow been undermined from within had first emerged in 1917 in the wake of the Reichstag's peace resolution, when Major-General Hans von Seeckt complained that 'the home [front] has stabbed us in the back'.[98] Rathenau, Bernhard and Warburg then built on these foundations with their rather fanciful attempts to keep Germany fighting in the final months of the war.

At the heart of the diagnosis that Rathenau, Bernhard and Warburg offered was their firmly held belief that the German army had had the capacity to fight on. In short, the military was far from defeated in autumn 1918. Ironically, when the armistice brought the fighting to an end that November, their argument appeared to be confirmed. German soldiers returned home not as a bedraggled mess, as might have been expected of a defeated army, but in formation, in uniform and to all intents and purposes as an intact fighting force. To his astonishment, Sammy Gronemann witnessed just such a sight in Brussels. A retreating German infantry battalion marched past him on the street to the tune of the 'Watch on the Rhine'. It was 'as if there had been no revolution and as if nothing had changed since August 1914', he remarked.[99]

If these 'unconquered' heroes, as Friedrich Ebert rashly called them in December 1918, could return home intact, then the question remained: why had they been defeated in the first place?[100] Max Bauer, Ludendorff's former military adviser, knew exactly where to find the answer. Despite the odd regrettable mistake, mainly by his former master, Bauer concluded that the army itself was free from blame. Logically, therefore, the weak link had to lie elsewhere. 'The war was lost', he concluded in no uncertain terms, 'singly and exclusively due to the failure of those at home'.[101] As other figures weighed into the debate, including several prominent German Jews, the general consensus hardened around the idea that the revolutionary left had caused the home front to collapse. Ludwig Haas should have known better when he opined that Germany had been 'stabbed in the back' by those 'prepared for any kind of peace'.[102] The intervention of the converted Jewish banker, Georg Solmssen, however, was far more in character. In a speech in Cologne, Solmssen continued to espouse the nationalist themes that had served him so well during the war. He happily apportioned all blame for Germany's defeat to the SPD, which had apparently 'destroyed Germany's national honour' and 'stabbed the brave German army in the back'. Solmssen's populist themes seemed to appeal to the crowd in the 'packed-out' hall, who by all accounts left satisfied.[103]

Neither Bauer nor Solmssen made any mention of Jews in their polemical interpretations of defeat. Even Hindenburg and Ludendorff left them out when they appeared before a parliamentary select committee in November 1919. Before a packed audience of politicians, journalists and diplomats, the pair offered their take on Germany's collapse the previous year. However, neither had any interest in probing too deeply; their main aim was to exonerate themselves. Hindenburg – the embodiment of 'a living corpse' according to Moritz Bonn – and Ludendorff – 'the choleric manager' – gave long scripted answers that contained pointed digs at both the home front and the revolutionaries. Hindenburg concluded his ramblings with the only line that anyone really remembered from the day: 'As an English general rightly said: The German army was stabbed in the back.'[104]

Without specifically blaming Jews for Germany's defeat, Hindenburg and Ludendorff had done enough to sow further seeds of doubt. Not only did the pair's testimony give the 'stab in the back' myth their own stamp of approval, but they also managed to drop in small nuggets of information that might have implied some form of internal betrayal, whether from the home front, revolutionaries or even particular personalities. Ludendorff, for example, 'reluctantly' repeated a remark which he attributed to Rathenau: 'The day when the kaiser and his entourage victoriously march through the Brandenburg Gate on their white horses will be the day when world history loses its meaning.'[105] With far less subtlety, other members of the defeated military began to offer more pointed attacks on the Jews. Major-General Ernst von Wrisberg specifically criticised Jews for their role in all aspects of the revolution. By this stage, Max Bauer had also given up on any civilities, suggesting that Jews had planned the revolution and Germany's downfall since at least the conflict's midpoint.[106]

The political right, which also counted former members of the military amongst its ranks, also concluded that the Jews must have thrust the dagger into the army's back. Yet, while Ludendorff, Bauer and others stumbled to this view, the extreme right reached this conclusion with a disturbing level of calculation. In February 1919, Heinrich Claß and other members of the Pan-German League gathered in the Franconian city of Bamberg for their first postwar convention. As was perhaps to be expected, the main agenda items for this fiercely nationalist group were defeat and revolution. Claß made it very clear to his attentive audience that 'Jewish influence' had been the 'driving force' behind Germany's military collapse. What was most astonishing about the meeting was not this juxtaposition of Jews and defeat, but rather the group's cynical anti-Semitism. In effect, the Pan-German delegates coolly decided that their movement would attack the Jews to further its own political interests. The 'Bamberg Declaration', which emerged from the meeting, stated simply that the Jews represented 'a foreign element' in the country.[107]

Considering that thirty-nine Bamberg Jews had lost their lives in the First World War, the Pan-German League's choice of conference venue was provocative to say the least. But the Pan-Germanists were never likely to be overly concerned by such considerations. Instead, the group launched its own vicious attack on German Jews' contribution to the war, with the aim of proving that they had shirked their military duty. One of the Pan-German League's leading lights, Alfred Roth, who often wrote under the pseudonym Otto Armin, published his own set of service statistics, which allegedly stemmed from the 1916 Jewish census. According to Roth's dubious data set, for every Jewish soldier killed in the war over 300 non-Jewish Germans had died. Therefore, 'the notion of selfless devotion to the people and the fatherland has no place among them [the Jews]', he argued.[108] What followed was a virtual battle of statistics, as Jewish statisticians and anti-Semitic polemicists traded their own competing figures.[109]

The reason why people expended so much energy on this futile statistical exercise was the 'stab in the back' myth. If Germany had been defeated by traitors from within, then it was crucial for German Jews that their fingerprints were not to be found upon the dagger. At the same time, it proved equally important for the German right to wash the blood of defeat from their own hands: pointing to a different perpetrator proved a convenient distraction. This frighteningly simple explanation for Germany's wartime loss had been encouraged by both Jews and other Germans during the dying days of the conflict, but in the midst of the revolution the German right managed to turn the narrative firmly against the Jews. Other dangerous legacies of the conflict developed in a similar fashion. Total war, a culture of destruction, territorial ambitions and a denigration of the 'other' had all marked a shared German war experience. After defeat, revolution and Versailles, however, German Jews were gradually excluded from the legacies that they themselves had earlier helped to shape.

EPILOGUE

In 1949 the German-Jewish medieval historian Ernst Kantorowicz made what at first glance seemed to be an extraordinary claim. Reflecting on his military service in the German army of the First World War and then in the Freikorps, he stated that his activities may have inadvertently helped Hitler to power. 'Fighting actively, with rifle and gun', he explained, had 'prepared, if indirectly and against my intention, the road leading to National-Socialism.'[1] Kantorowicz had never been afraid to state his mind, whether in his academic writing on the thirteenth-century emperor Frederick II or indeed in his disputes with university administration.[2] And the same was no doubt true of this critical appraisal of his own personal biography.

The key to Kantorowicz's comments is the word 'indirectly'. Kantorowicz never believed for one moment that Jewish soldiers, such as himself, had intentionally contributed to the rise of National Socialism. After all, the success of the Nazi movement came down to a whole host of reasons, from economic depression and effective propaganda, through to a public desperate for change. Nonetheless, at the back of Kantorowicz's mind was clearly the nagging thought that the First World War had not only provided the foundations for the emergence of the National Socialist movement, but had also shaped the fortunes of the postwar Weimar Republic. And in this more general respect, he was absolutely right to express concern.

The Weimar Republic lived and died almost entirely in the shadow of the recent conflict.[3] This, though, is not to suggest that Weimar was a failed system from the start. Many of the crises that apparently dogged the republic during its short life exist more in the writings of critical commentators than in the realities on the ground.[4] Far from being permanently on the brink of collapse, the Weimar Republic actually enjoyed a degree of authority that allowed its supporters to shape state and society in their image.[5] It was this confident optimism that provided the space for some of the republic's most celebrated achievements to emerge, whether in the aims – though not always implementation – of its social welfare system, the apparent sexual freedoms of its capital or the period's cultural vibrancy.[6] The Weimar Republic may well have come to a dramatic end with the rise of Nazism, but this certainly did not mean that the republic itself should be regarded as a failure.[7]

Yet, while Germany's postwar republic was never preordained to collapse, it was nonetheless beset by the problems of a difficult birth. Indeed, even the most visible and celebrated achievements of the republican period were themselves often a response to the experience of war and defeat. The cultural highs – whether Otto Dix and Max Beckmann's expressionist art, the literature of Arnold Zweig and Erich Maria Remarque, or Walter Gropius's path-breaking Bauhaus design school – emerged as these artists worked through their years of military service.[8] The same was equally true of the social welfare programme. It developed out of an urgent need to take care of the thousands of war-wounded and war widows who faced a desperate future in postwar Germany.[9] Similarly, more contested developments, such as Hindenburg's election as president in 1925 or ongoing debates over gender relations, all stemmed from the upheaval of war.[10]

As Ernst Kantorowicz was all too aware, the inability of the Weimar Republic to move beyond the First World War stemmed from the way in which Jews and other Germans had originally approached the conflict. Kantorowicz's regrets, though, lay not with the way in which the war saturated the republic's cultural, social or political life; rather his concerns lay with the war's deeper and far more dangerous legacies. One set of these – annexations, an aggressive wartime culture and total war – ensured that the conflict remained ever-present, and as such stopped Germany from becoming a truly postwar society.[11] A second set of legacies – war enthusiasm, divisions, scapegoating of the 'other' and the 'stab in the back' myth – fundamentally weakened the position of Jewish communities in Germany.

When placed together, both sets of legacies ensured the fragility of postwar Germany, therefore laying the foundations upon which the National Socialists built. Understandably, this is what Kantorowicz most lamented. If German Jews had been ambivalent towards the war or had even been its disgruntled opponents, as is so often implied, then there would have been no need for regret. As it was, though, many German Jews had taken a leading role in shaping Germany's approach to the conflict or, as in case of Kantorowicz, had thrown themselves headlong into some of the bitterest of fighting. It was this knowledge that proved so discomforting for Kantorowicz and other German Jews when they looked back to interwar Germany.

A Distant Peace

Defeat and revolution, of course, were the source of much instability, but so too was the first major wartime legacy: total war. As discussed earlier, the real turn towards fighting a total war had come in autumn 1916, when the kaiser had taken the plunge and installed Hindenburg and his assistant Ludendorff to head up the army. However, long before this point had been reached, Jewish communities, along with other sections of German society, had started to lay the foundations for the militarisation of society. At home, German Jews offered buildings for the war effort, donated money and valuables for war bonds and gave up huge chunks of time to volunteer in hospitals or at railway stations. Just as daily life was gradually subordinated to the needs of the military, so too was the wider economy. Under Walther Rathenau's sure-footed leadership, essential resources were centralised and economic production turned towards serving the needs of the military.

The all-encompassing nature of total war made it very difficult to unpick once hostilities had ceased. This was most obviously the case with the conflict's human casualties. Almost 2 million Germans had been killed, including some 12,000 Jewish soldiers; millions more had been permanently maimed or wounded. Mimi Marcuse's brother Paul, who was reported captured in 1915, never resurfaced. 'I'm often wondering whether we will finally hear something from Paul', pondered Mimi's husband repeatedly, but sadly no news would ever be forthcoming.[12] Life for the family of 20-year-old Max Waldmann was no easier. Waldmann had been shot through the head in 1918; he survived but was left partially blind and deaf.[13] In Hamburg, meanwhile, the parents of Moritz Hesse, who had been killed in 1915, never recovered from the loss of their only son and died soon after from 'grief and sorrow'.[14]

The bitterness that the victims experienced never completely faded; instead pain and anger gnawed away at many survivors throughout the interwar years. Kurt Wolff, a Jewish soldier who had been hit by an exploding grenade, could never completely escape the conflict. 'Replacements for the lost parts of his face' ensured that he remained visibly 'marked' long after the war was over.[15]

The continued suffering of war veterans could also be seen in Jewish news-papers, where personal notices from the war's victims were common fare: 'war-blinded man' looking for a 'quiet room' and 'war-wounded' seeking a suitable wheelchair were but two of many examples.[16] Like other German war veterans, many Jewish ex-servicemen ended up blaming state and society for their permanent injuries.[17] Hans Hamburger is a case in point. With one arm amputated and the other rendered almost immobile, he was offered a basic war pension, but this was not enough to cover his daily care. Hamburger, therefore, was forced to take the state to court to ensure that he received adequate help.[18] Such petty disputes caused unnecessary distress, while also frustrating the already difficult task of moving beyond total war.

However, it was not just the war's frontline casualties that were left deeply aggrieved. Fighting a total war had required all Germans – not only those in the army or with loved ones at the front – to contribute to the war effort. These sacrifices had come in many forms, from the pensioner donating the last of her savings for war bonds through to the women who gave up their time to run soup kitchens or to staff military hospitals. In postwar Germany, the reward for these sacrifices was often hard to find.[19] To make matters worse, women often ended up being held responsible for many of Germany's postwar ills. Everything from social degeneration and loose sexual mores through to problems of juvenile delinquency were blamed on female behaviour.[20] Even Jewish intellectuals, such as Martin Buber, joined the attack, arguing that German-Jewish women should follow Eastern European Jewish practices and dedicate themselves to maintaining patriarchal structures.[21]

If the legacies of total war hampered women's efforts to return to peace-time society, then the same was true of the German economy. During the conflict, Jews and other Germans had worked hard to mobilise the economy for total war. One consequence of their efforts, however, was that German finances remained wedged in an inflationary spiral, which reached a dangerous peak with the hyperinflation of 1922–24. During this period, people who had donated the last of their money for war bonds discovered that these invest-ments were now virtually worthless. What made these financial losses so hard to bear was the fact that this money had originally been donated for a patriotic cause, a debt that the state could no long repay.[22] Joseph Levy in Frankfurt, like many other Jews, also suffered badly at this time. After his wages had failed to keep pace with rocketing inflation, he and his wife supplemented their income by opening their house to American guest students, who paid their way with the more stable dollar.[23] Total war, then, left two – almost insurmountable – problems. On the one side were structural difficulties, whether economic or social. On the other side, all Germans – both civilians and veterans – struggled to make sense of a war that had demanded from them four years of pain, suffering and death.

The legacy of Germany's destructive wartime culture made it even harder for people to escape the clutches of total war. During the conflict both Jews and other Germans had shown few inhibitions when it came to denigrating Germany's enemies. The Belgians were condemned as crafty saboteurs, the Russians as uncivilised barbarians, while the physical destruction of the enemy, whether at the battles of Tannenberg or Jutland, was celebrated with great fanfare. Although some Germans, such as the Jewish academic Emil Julius Gumbel, had been early converts to pacifism, it took much longer for an internationalist spirit to replace the wartime 'dynamic of destruction'.[24] Even then the right often continued to employ aggressive, militaristic language in defence of the German army's achievements.[25]

It was not just at the extremes that elements of Germany's wartime culture continued to surface. This was most obviously the case with commemorative practices for the country's war dead. A 'cult of the fallen', which imposed heroic, militaristic values onto the war dead, survived the conflict largely unscathed. When several of Germany's right-wing student fraternities erected a memorial in Coburg in May 1926, for example, there was little hint of a new, more reflective, take on the war. The structure, which featured three powerful, muscular figures holding a sword aloft, bore the unwavering phrases – 'fatherland', 'honour', 'friendship' – around its base.[26] Even war memorials erected for the Jewish war dead were not immune to such strongly German nationalist tendencies. Some were adorned with images of pistols and bayonets; others contained the bold symbol of the army's steel helmet. In the town of Guben, in rural Brandenburg, the local Jewish community erected a memorial for their six members killed at the front. The focus of the small sandstone memorial was not so much the Star of David on the front of the structure, but rather the steel helmet, represented in almost life-size proportion, on its very top.[27]

However, it was the rapid growth of war veterans' organisations during the Weimar Republic that most readily revealed the continued draw of Germany's wartime culture. Republican ex-servicemen's associations, such as the SPD's Reichsbanner Schwarz-Rot-Gold, might have found less to admire in the nationalist 'cult of the fallen', but they still drew upon miltaristic symbols and language. During remembrance events, the Reichsbanner's members marched in formation, sang songs and relived the ideals of comradeship.[28] The same was true of the Reich Association of Jewish Frontline Soldiers (Reichsbund jüdischer Frontsoldaten, the RjF). Founded in 1919, the RjF, which grew rapidly to encompass some 40,000 veterans, placed the war experience at the very centre of its activities. Its members staged commemorative events, invested in war memorials and often revelled in heroic stories of military valour. The RjF's fortnightly newspaper, *Der Schild*, frequently contained tales of daring and fortitude in battle. In one issue, an Erich Wittner recalled his memories of the 1918 spring offensive: an 'honourable defeat', as he put it. In another edition, the heroic deeds of a Lieutenant Unger, who had been killed while patrolling on the Western Front, formed the main feature.[29]

Entangled with Germany's destructive wartime culture, the legacy of annexations also hindered attempts to move towards a full peacetime society. Jewish communities' original interest in the east had stemmed from an understandable concern for the Eastern European Jews who had suffered so horrendously under Russian rule. But far too often, German Jews had gone beyond the lines of this basic objective and advocated far more sweeping territorial plans. Albert Ballin, the Hamburg shipping magnate, had sought to justify seizing African colonies as well as parts of Belgium as a means of strengthening Germany's economic interests. Similarly, Davis Trietsch, Zionist, journalist and publicist, had proposed German annexations in Eastern Europe and Africa, while Max Warburg, Walther Rathenau and other prominent German-Jewish businessmen advocated economic dominance.

Although these expansionist dreams had been crushed with Germany's defeat, the general principle of territorial aggrandisement refused to die. During the interwar years, the main focus of these ambitions was again on the lands beyond Germany's eastern borders. What kept German interest in this region alive was the sense of unfinished business. First, as a result of the territorial changes ushered in by the Treaty of Versailles, a German minority – and within it a German-Jewish minority – continued to live in the east. The German population in the west of Poland in particular viewed the postwar settlement as temporary and pursued a policy of border revision.[30] Second, some 2 to 3 million German soldiers had been part of the wartime occupying armies spread across Eastern Europe. After the war, many of these men continued to meet through veterans' organisations or they published diaries and memoirs of their wartime experiences. The picture that emerged from these activities was of a backward region that still required some form of 'civilising' mission.[31] Sammy Gronemann's 1924 war memoirs fitted this category. His intensive account may have expressed strong sympathies for the Eastern

European Jews, but there was still no escaping the contrast between the German occupiers and the economically poor local population.[32]

Tapping into the vast potential of the east remained a dream for many Germans during the interwar years. To bring this aim a step closer, the academic discipline of *Ostforschung* established itself during the 1920s. The main aim of *Ostforschung* was to prove the Germanness of territory in Eastern Europe, thereby strengthening the claims for future German expansion.[33] One difficult side effect of this research was that it planted deep anti-Semitic roots. Confirming the ethnic identity of people in the east meant by implication also defining those groups – including Jews – who did not fit these definitions of Germanness.[34] Nonetheless what *Ostforschung* demonstrated more generally was the lasting legacies of a conflict that Jews and other Germans had initially helped to shape. The way Germany had approached war had opened people's eyes to new lands and new possibilities. Defeat reduced these horizons, but it certainly never closed them completely. Throughout the Weimar Republic, the cultural, social, political and even spatial legacies of war were always firmly alive.

War's Revenge

The centrality of the First World War to the Weimar Republic undoubtedly added to its frailties. A more damaging effect of this situation, however, was that it repeatedly confronted Germans with the depressing reality that the country had not been victorious in the conflict, but had actually been vanquished. This unwelcome realisation added potency to the conflict's four other deep legacies: war enthusiasm, divisions, the 'other' and the 'stab in the back' myth. These legacies, when placed alongside the Weimar Republic's failure to become a peacetime society, had a negative effect on the position of German-Jewish communities, making them less secure and far more susceptible to anti-Semitic attack.

War enthusiasm was certainly the least visible of the conflict's multiple legacies. In the wake of defeat, neither Jews nor other Germans wanted to celebrate their earlier excessive support for the conflict. The demise of the narrative of war enthusiasm was made patently clear in August 1924, on the tenth anniversary of the war's outbreak. To mark the occasion, the government planned to hold the republic's first Day of National Mourning (*Volkstrauertag*). However, far from reliving the excited unity of 1914, the whole event quickly descended into a farce. Jewish communities rightly protested that no rabbi had been invited to speak alongside the Christian chaplains, while pacifists denounced the event's militaristic tone and conservatives maintained that Friedrich Ebert, the republic's Social Democratic president, was incapable of staging a suitably dignified ceremony.[35]

However, it was the very absence of war enthusiasm that gave this legacy of the conflict its greatest strength. Once people recognised that the 'spirit of 1914' was gone, then they started to seek ways to fill the void. Some conservative politicians, for example, pushed for the creation of a new national idea based on shared cultural values. The National Socialist movement, meanwhile, put their own racial spin on the notion of a new 'people's community' (*Volksgemeinschaft*), which served as a convenient vehicle for their anti-republican, racially driven ideologies. At first glance, the National Socialists' idea of a 'people's community' hinted at the kaiser's 'civic truce'. It drew a clear dichotomy between the nation and a defined enemy. Only in the National Socialists' rendition of August 1914, the enemy was not the external Entente, but Jews and other outsiders. In effect, it was about uniting one section of society, while excluding the remainder.[36]

One of the appeals of Hitler's 'people's community' was that it spoke of unity at a time of considerable disunity. The war had opened up old wounds in German society as well as causing a whole series of new divisions; all of these remained an active legacy for the postwar Weimar Republic. A major source of wartime division had come from the question of the war's endpoint. Davis Trietsch, Clemens Klein, Georg Solmssen and a small number of other German Jews aligned themselves with the nationalist right and championed a peace that was to come through victory (*Siegfrieden*). In stark contrast, Hugo Haase and Theodor Wolff were among a second group of German Jews who led the call for a negotiated peace, without significant territorial gains. Diminishing food supplies and falling fuel stocks only aggravated the tenor of these debates over the war's wider purpose, cementing divisions as a result.

Sewing a divided postwar society back together proved difficult. Political splits widened rather than narrowed. The socialist movement, for example, which had entered the conflict as one party, exited the war divided between the majority SPD and Haase's minority USPD. These fractures remained throughout the life of the Weimar Republic, only that with the formation of the Communist Party (KPD), the divide was between the SPD and the younger KPD. Wartime splits between rural communities and the cities also continued. Debates, which during the war had been about food supplies, now increasingly revolved around perceived differences between the wages of urban workers and agricultural labourers.[37]

Betraying the suggestion that the 1920s witnessed a strengthening of Jewish community was the fact that German Jews were themselves also badly divided.[38] In one ideological corner stood the RjF, with its German-nationalist outlook and belligerent take on the war; occupying the other corner were the Zionists, whose small membership had doubled to 20,000 by 1920.[39] Thus, while the RjF marched onto the scene declaring defiantly that it would defend its members' 'patriotic actions in the war', the Zionists publicly declared that the war had been nothing but an unremitting disaster for Jews.[40] The continued presence of a large Eastern European Jewish population in Germany's major cities only added to these divisions. Far from bringing German and Eastern Jews together, the war had only served to confirm the cultural and political divide.

For German Jews, however, it was the legacy of wartime 'othering' that proved most dangerous in exacerbating divisions. The conflict itself had demanded the clear identification of Germany's external and internal enemies. Early on in the war, some German Jews had joined in with this process of identifying and then classifying the enemy 'other'. Adolph Goldschmidt and Hermann Struck's studies of the 'racial' characteristics of Germany's POW population or Walther Rathenau's calls to use forced labour had gone the furthest in breaking recognised international norms. As the war dragged on past its second and third years, Jewish communities had also found themselves increasingly targeted in this reckless wartime desire to define the 'other'. Rising anti-Semitism, the military's discriminatory Jewish census and repeated attempts to close the border to Eastern European Jews were the most visible examples of this trend.

Accusations of Jewish profiteering and shirking, as seen through the military's destructive census, persisted throughout the life of the republic. In 1922, for example, the extreme right took their revenge on Walther Rathenau, whose role in establishing the KRA at the start of the war had condemned him in their eyes as both a profiteer and a traitor. Rathenau, by then the republic's foreign minister, stepped into his open-topped car on 24 June, ready to be whisked to his ministerial office. The car had travelled little more than 1 kilometre when it was forced to a halt on the edge of the tree-lined Königsallee. Three men then approached the vehicle, launched a burst of machine-gun fire at the minister and threw in a grenade for good measure. Rathenau died instantly. Clearly his patriotic work to create Germany's wartime economy failed to protect him; if anything, these associations only accelerated his demise.[41]

The following year it was the Eastern European Jews who came under concerted attack. Their numbers in Germany had swelled postwar, as Jews fled pogrom-like violence in many of Eastern Europe's successor states. Berlin's desperately poor Scheunenviertel became the first port of call for many of these new refugees. Seemingly for this reason, the district became the setting for two days of extensive rioting in early winter 1923. Rumours first started to spread on 5 November that Eastern European Jewish immigrants were hoarding government money destined for the unemployed so that they could loan it out again themselves at higher rates of interest. The falsity of the story failed to stop groups of unemployed workers from storming into the Scheunenviertel on the hunt for Jewish extortionists. The crowds smashed up Jewish-owned shops, looted goods and attacked anyone who 'looked Jewish'. One man, the owner of a kosher butcher's, died after being beaten senseless; another narrowly escaped with his life after being repeatedly stabbed in the mêlée.[42] For all their brutality, the riots died down almost as quickly as they had started. Indeed, by 8 November, the press was able to report that 'Berlin's population has now more or less returned to peace'.[43]

The police may have managed to restore order in Berlin, but anti-Semitism persisted. Serving to deepen divisions and to heighten prejudice was the war's final major legacy: the 'stab in the back' myth. Although it became a rallying point for those on the political right during the Weimar Republic, the myth had actually first been propagated by a broader spectrum of Germans, including several German Jews, during the war. Georg Bernhard, Walther Rathenau and Max Warburg had all added elements to the 'stab in the back' myth with their response to the strikes of January 1918 or to the armistice later that same year.

When Bernhard, Rathenau and Warburg had first laid the foundations for the postwar myth, Jewish communities obviously played no role in the narrative. Instead, their criticisms were levelled variously at those on the left for supporting industrial strikes and at Germany's military leaders for contemplating an armistice. But after defeat, revolution and the Treaty of Versailles, all this had changed; a perpetrator now needed to be found. It did not take long for German nationalist politicians and those high up in the military to identify their suspects: Jews and socialists.[44] Both of the accused groups did their best to refute this storm of allegations. The SPD offered humorous rebuttals as well as accounts from ordinary soldiers that highlighted the realities of the front.[45] Jews also vigorously fought this toxic legend. On one occasion Dietrich Eckart, editor of the National Socialist *Völkischer Beobachter*, offered to reward anyone who could name a Jewish mother who had had three sons at the front for more than three weeks. Rabbi Samuel Freund from Hanover found twenty mothers meeting the criteria; armed with these details, he took Eckart to court and won.[46] Yet, no matter how vociferously the SPD or German Jews protested their war record, fighting a simplistic, one-dimensional narrative of betrayal proved almost impossible.

National Socialism and War

The persistence of aspects of the war into peacetime should not in itself have proved that dangerous for Jewish communities. After all, during the war, German Jews had played a full role in shaping Germany's approach to the conflict. The danger came, therefore, not from the fact that the war spread into peacetime, but rather that Jewish voices were largely absent from its multiple surviving legacies. When the German right discussed the apparent national unity of August 1914, for example, they never cared to mention that Jewish communities had also thrown themselves behind the conflict. Likewise, when attention turned to Germany's territorial ambitions, there was never any discussion of German Jews' own ideas for annexations or for the use of forced labour. Instead, as far as the extreme right was concerned, the war was a simple dichotomy between honourable Germans on the one side and traitorous Jews and socialists on the other.

The National Socialists' plans and policies could well have remained rather inconsequential had the country not descended into political and economic crisis at the end of the 1920s. Unfortunately though, the movement was given a huge boost by the Wall Street crash that gave way to the Great Depression. The economy stagnated, unemployment rocketed and the basic workings of democracy started to disintegrate. Against this gloomy backdrop, fierce debates about the war and its aftermath returned to centre stage. Germany witnessed a new wave of war commemoration, violent clashes between paramilitary groups and an increasingly militarised political culture.[47] Even the centrist chancellor, Heinrich Brüning, could not resist making repeated reference to his time as a frontline machine gun captain. With the economy crashing down around him, references to the recent war provided an easier way to demonstrate his credibility.[48] All this rhetoric proved, though, was how the stale legacies of war refused to abate. The Weimar Republic had always struggled to become a peacetime society; by the early 1930s, it had all but given up trying.

Attempting to capitalise on Germany's devastating economic turmoil, the National Socialists sought to make the multiple legacies of the First World War their own. They campaigned fervently around memories of the First World War, from the plight of the war-wounded and the injustices of Versailles through to the creation of a new Germany, centred on the idea of a 'people's community'. During the 1932 presidential elections, for example, posters produced for Hitler's campaign portrayed him as a simple frontline soldier who had valiantly risked his life for Germany, for which he received the Iron Cross.[49] German Jews, of course, never featured as positive actors in National Socialist narratives of the First World War. Their sole purpose was to act as a symbol for all that had gone wrong with Germany's wartime struggle. Anti-Semitism and a more direct attack on the role played by Jews in the First World War may not have directly raised the Nazis into power, but collectively they certainly pointed to the horrors that were to come.[50]

The National Socialists were rewarded for their dedication to the war's contested legacies when, on 30 January 1933, Hindenburg appointed Hitler to the chancellorship. That very evening, thousands of Brownshirts from the Nazis' paramilitary wing joined members of the Stahlhelm veterans' association in Berlin to show their support for the new government. In long columns, they marched through the centre of the capital singing the German national anthem and the National Socialists' 'Horst-Wessel-Lied', as if the two were now interchangeable. Watching on from the second floor of the Reich Chancellery, Hitler raised his arm to salute the parade as the men below marched past.[51] Joseph Goebbels, the National Socialists' chief propagandist, had instigated the event in an attempt to depict the new government as the outcome of a popular movement. The impression he tried to give was of a revolution, sweeping away the existing order. The parade itself harked back to the war enthusiasm of August 1914, when crowds had lined the streets apparently to celebrate the start of hostilities. Should anyone have missed this connection, Hermann Göring made sure to tell radio audiences that the crowd of 'hundreds of thousands' could 'only be compared with that of 1914'.[52]

Despite these allusions to the events of the First World War, January 1933 was not a return to August 1914, not least because it was a largely orchestrated parade. One witness noted that after a period of time, the same Brownshirts passed by once again; they had merely been marching around the block to give the illusion of strength.[53] Nonetheless, Hitler and other members of the party also had little wish to return to Imperial Germany's earlier conflict, to rerun the First World War, but with a different outcome. Their ideological aims were far more wide-ranging. They desired a war of conquest that would leave Germany heading up a new racial empire as the world's dominant power. In working towards this radical goal, the legacies of the First World War served a dual purpose. First, they gave legitimacy to a movement that depicted itself as the 'political embodiment' of the 'front generation'.[54] Second, the National Socialists turned the legacies of the conflict into a series of lessons; these needed to be fully digested to avoid the mistakes that had led to defeat in 1918.[55]

All of Hitler's thinking on the First World War came back to the same point: how Germany could avoid repeating the same mistakes in a second conflict.[56] According to the 'stab in the back' myth, which Hitler internalised very early on, the revolution had brought the war to a sudden and undignified end. If Jews and socialists, who were themselves in the pay of 'world Jewry', had caused the revolution, as Hitler firmly believed, then the diagnosis was simple. The decisive reason for Germany's defeat in 1918, concluded Hitler, had been 'the failure to recognise the problem of race and in particular the Jewish danger'.[57] This distorted mode of thinking clearly had an impact on Hitler's plans for a future war. According to Hitler's logic, for Germany to pursue a Second World War successfully, Jews in Germany and beyond needed first to be removed.

Once in power, Hitler and his supporters moved first with small steps, but then with increasing violence against German Jews, with the aim of neutralising the 'danger' that they themselves had identified. On 1 April, a boycott of Jewish businesses, including those owned by Jewish war veterans, was held throughout the country. Rightly appalled at the action, Richard Stern, a shopkeeper and Jewish war veteran, stood guard outside his business, proudly wearing his Iron Cross. Later that month, the regime introduced its first pieces of anti-Semitic legislation when it imposed restrictions on the number of Jews working in universities and in the civil service. Unlike the business boycotts, these new laws did include exemptions for war veterans and their families, even if these clauses were not always so closely followed. However, after the introduction of the Nuremberg Laws in September 1935, which stripped Jews of German citizenship, any exemptions for Jewish war veterans disappeared.[58] From this point on, the old soldiers, like all other German Jews, faced a spiralling tumult of anti-Jewish legislation and violence.

Another major lesson that the National Socialists took from the First World War was how best to fight a total war. There was a strong consensus among those on the right – from Ludendorff through to Hitler – that a future conflict would again have to be fought as a total war.[59] This meant reforming the German state and society along with the military in readiness for war. Ridding Germany of a democratic system in favour of a one-party state embodied in the figure of Hitler himself was one aspect of this.[60] Hitler had long maintained that a strong leader, rather than a parliament, was required to enforce the people's will.[61] Once in power, he was in a position to fulfil this prophecy. Rearming and reforming the military took slightly longer to implement, as the new regime needed to avoid immediately inflaming international tensions. Nonetheless, by 1936, rearmament was well under way with new weapons, aircraft and ships all in production. Going hand in hand with this process was the announcement of the four-year plan, which directed the economy fully towards military need.[62] It seemed that the regime, without recognising it, had taken some inspiration from Rathenau's economic central planning in fighting the previous total war.[63]

Imperial Germany's attempts to annex land in Eastern Europe during the 1914–18 conflict provided the National Socialists with a further major lesson. Although Hitler had fought his war on the Western Front, he was still well aware of events in the east. Germany's occupation and cultural domination of vast swathes of territory had clearly struck a chord with him. As early as 1921, he had spoken in effusive terms about the Treaty of Brest-Litovsk, which had apparently secured Germany's future 'by the acquisition of land and soil, [and] by access to raw materials'.[64] In Hitler's world view, the east became the site for future German living space (*Lebensraum*). An advance into the east also had the advantage of crushing the threat of Bolshevism, which in Hitler's mind was part of a wider Jewish conspiracy. This new war for living space, of course, was to occur solely at the expense of the existing 'racially inferior' population groups, whose supposed backwardness had already been identified during the First World War.[65]

At home, the National Socialist regime wasted little time in its attempts to militarise German society. This was a reminder of how the National Socialists drew on Germany's destructive war culture as they prepared for a second world war. The regime recognised the importance of drawing civilians into a militarised culture, for in a total war the lines between the home front and the frontlines would again be blurred. Very quickly, therefore, efforts were made to induct the German people into the values and ideals of militarism and war. Universal military conscription returned in March 1935 for men. Boys were catered for in the Hitler Youth, which provided them with pre-military training and war games.[66] For the older generation, who had fought in the previous conflict, the regime introduced a host of special privileges. Children were supposed to salute the war-wounded on the street, while on public transport or in the theatre veterans received subsidised tickets.[67] Even the dead soldiers of the previous war (excluding the Jewish war dead) were given a role in reinvigorating Germany's 'dynamic of destruction'. In 1934, the regime changed the names of the Weimar Republic's annual Day of National Mourning to Heroes' Remembrance Day (*Heldengedenktag*). Germans were no longer to mourn the dead; instead, they were to celebrate them as heroes who had willingly sacrificed their lives for the nation.[68]

The National Socialists' pursuit of a 'people's community' also showed how lessons had been learnt from the previous war. If Imperial Germany's war effort had been blighted by divisions and internal strife, then in a future conflict unity had to be paramount. To avoid a repeat of the divisions that had led to 1918, the regime made great efforts to pacify the working classes. On the one hand, trade unions were banned and their leaders arrested. In their place, the regime created the German Labour Front (Deutsche Arbeitsfront). This new formation was supposed to represent an idealised class-free 'people's community' that recognised no difference between an unskilled labourer and a trained engineer. On the other hand, the National Socialists introduced a series of material benefits, whether in the form of paid holidays or better leisure facilities. Being part of the 'people's community', then, may have meant fewer rights, but the promise of a better standard of living was supposed to cancel out any negatives.[69]

For German Jews, however, the establishment of this new racial state meant that they were to be permanently banished from the nation. During the mid-1930s, anti-Jewish violence increased and the scale of new legislation targeting Jews ratcheted up. In all spheres of daily life, legal measures and also at times public pressure combined to separate Jews from other Germans.[70] Ernst Kantorowicz discovered this darkening atmosphere to his cost. After returning from an honorary fellowship at New College, Oxford, his home institution – Frankfurt University – terminated his contract, forcing him into retirement as a result. Unable to publish and increasingly isolated from the academic community, Kantorowicz struggled on in Germany, living in Berlin until late 1938; he eventually managed to escape to the United States.[71]

As discussed earlier, what later most perturbed Kantorowicz was the thought that his wartime actions might have somehow contributed to the National Socialists' policies. He did not necessarily regret that he and other Jews had dedicated themselves to Germany's wartime struggle, even when this had involved participating in some of the more extreme aspects of the German war effort. After all, in a modern state German Jews saw little problem in aligning themselves with a wide variety of Jewish and German identities.[72] Instead, Kantorowicz's anger was directed towards the way in which the National Social movement combined an obsession with the First World War with both virulent anti-Semitism and preparations for a second major conflict.

This deadly triumvirate was firmly on display in January 1939, when Hitler made a doom-laden speech to the Reichstag in Berlin. After speaking for a good two hours in a self-congratulatory way about the party's rise to power, he shifted topic briefly to discuss the position of Jews in the state. Returning once again to the 'stab in the back' myth, he declared that 'if the international Jewish financiers', as he called the Jews, 'should succeed in plunging the nations once more into a world war, then the result will [be] . . . the annihilation of the Jewish race in Europe!'[73] The 'stab in the back' myth had evolved steadily during the 1920s to leave German Jews firmly blamed for Germany's failings during the First World War. On the eve of a Second World War, Hitler again reached for this lesson – only on this occasion he managed to blame Jews for any difficulties before a bullet had even been fired.

For all its genocidal tones, this threat occurred at a time when the National Socialists' plans were still firmly set on enforced Jewish emigration.[74] Nonetheless, Hitler's speech did highlight two interconnected ideological beliefs. First, it looked forward to a future conflict, one that would combine war with genocide. Second, Hitler's use of the pointed phrase 'once more' showed how the Nazis continued to take inspiration from the First World War. Ernst Kantorowicz and thousands of other German Jews had fought – and all too often died – in the German armies of the First World War. In a second world war, as Hitler was starting to make more and more clear, their role would be solely that of victims: they would either be forced into emigration or be murdered, as the Nazi regime sought to construct a new racial empire, thereby for ever obliterating the defeat of 1918.

ENDNOTES

Introduction

1. Fritz Schlesinger to Franz Josef Strauß, 1 April 1961, BArch MA, BW1/21634. Although Schlesinger himself named the soldier as Willy Liemann, the Jewish Museum in Berlin ascribes the name of Ludwig Börnstein to the figure: Ingke Brodersen and Rüdiger Dammann, *Geschichten einer Ausstellung: Zwei Jahrtausende deutsch-jüdische Geschichte* (Berlin: Jüdisches Museum Berlin, 2002), p. 140.
2. Jacob Rosenthal, *'Die Ehre des jüdischen Soldaten': Die Judenzählung im Ersten Weltkrieg und ihre Folgen* (Frankfurt: Campus, 2007); Werner Angress, 'Das deutsche Militär und die Juden im Ersten Weltkrieg', *Militärgeschichtliche Mitteilungen*, 19 (1976), pp. 77–146; Brian Crim, *Antisemitism in the German Military Community and the Jewish Response* (Langham: Rowman & Littlefield, 2014).
3. More generally, see: Todd Endelman, *Broadening Jewish History: Towards a Social History of Ordinary Jews* (Oxford: The Littman Library of Jewish Civilization, 2011). And for a defence of the Jewishness of Jewish history: Moshe Rosman, *How Jewish is Jewish History?* (Oxford: The Littman Library of Jewish Civilization, 2007), pp. 1–15.
4. Helmut Walser Smith, 'The Vanishing Point of German History: An Essay on Perspective', *History & Memory*, 17 (2005), pp. 269–95.
5. Anne Lipp, *Meinungslenkung im Krieg: Kriegserfahrungen deutscher Soldaten und ihre Deutung 1914–1918* (Göttingen: Vandenhoeck & Ruprecht, 2002), p. 239.
6. Janet Watson, *Fighting Different Wars: Experience, Memory and the First World War in Britain* (Cambridge: Cambridge University Press, 2006).
7. For the origins of this term, see: George Mosse, *Freud, Jews and Other Germans: Masters and Victims in Modernist Culture* (Oxford: Oxford University Press, 1979).
8. Marline Otte, *Jewish Identities in German Popular Entertainment, 1890–1933* (Cambridge: Cambridge University Press, 2006); Till van Rahden, *Juden und andere Breslauer: Die Beziehungen zwischen Juden, Protestanten und Katholiken in einer deutschen Grossstadt von 1860 bis 1925* (Göttingen: Vandenhoeck & Ruprecht, 2000).
9. On the difficulties of fitting German Jews into more problematic aspects of the past, see: Christian Davis, *Colonialism, Antisemitism, and Germans of Jewish Descent in Imperial Germany* (Ann Arbor: University of Michigan Press, 2012), pp. 3–6.
10. Steven Aschheim, *In Times of Crisis: Essays on European Culture, Germans, and Jews* (Madison: University of Wisconsin Press, 2001), pp. 86–92.
11. Peter Appelbaum, *Loyal Sons: Jews in the German Army in the Great War* (London: Vallentine Mitchell, 2014); David Aberbach, *The European Jews, Patriotism and the Liberal*

State 1789–1939: A Study of Literature and Social Psychology (New York: Routledge, 2013), pp. 54–63; Michael Berger, *Eisernes Kreuz und Davidstern: Die Geschichte Jüdischer Soldaten in Deutschen Armeen* (Berlin: Trafo, 2006), pp. 159–70.

12. Stéphane Audoin-Rouzeau and Annette Becker, *1914–1918: Understanding the Great War*, trans. Catherine Temerson (London: Profile, 2002), pp. 16–17. More generally, see also: Derek Penslar, *Jews and the Military* (Princeton: Princeton University Press, 2013), p. 8.

13. Alan Kramer, *Dynamic of Destruction: Culture and Mass Killing in the First World War* (Oxford: Oxford University Press, 2007), p. 68.

14. Fritz Fischer, *Griff nach der Weltmacht: Die Kriegszielpolitik des kaiserlichen Deutschland 1914/18* (Düsseldorf: Droste, 1961).

15. Werner Mosse, 'Einleitung: Deutsches Judentum und Liberalismus', in Beate-Carola Padtberg (ed.), *Das deutsche Judentum und der Liberalismus = German Jewry and Liberalism* (Sankt Augustin: COMDOK, 1986), pp. 15–21.

16. George Mosse, *German Jews beyond Judaism* (Bloomington: Indiana University Press, 1985), pp. 56–7; Edgar Feuchtwanger, 'The Jewishness of Conservative Politicians: Disraeli and Stahl', in Michael Brenner, Rainer Liedtke and David Rechter (eds), *Two Nations: British and German Jews in Comparative Perspective* (Tübingen: Mohr Siebeck, 1999), pp. 222–39.

17. Konrad Jarausch, *The Enigmatic Chancellor: Bethmann Hollweg and the Hubris of Imperial Germany* (New Haven: Yale University Press, 1973), p. 187; Fischer, *Griff*, pp. 186–7; Alastair Thompson, *Left Liberals, the State, and Popular Politics in Wilhelmine Germany* (Oxford: Oxford University Press, 2000), pp. 375–9.

18. Adam Seipp, *The Ordeal of Peace: Demobilization and the Urban Experience in Britain and Germany, 1917–1921* (Farnham: Ashgate, 2009), pp. 1–9.

19. Hans-Ulrich Wehler, *The German Empire, 1871–1918* (Leamington Spa: Berg, 1985); Hannah Arendt, *The Origins of Totalitarianism* (London: Allen & Unwin, 1958); Jürgen Zimmerer (ed.), *Von Windhuk nach Auschwitz? Beiträge zum Verhältnis von Kolonialismus und Holocaust* (Berlin: LIT, 2011).

20. Peter Fritzsche, *Germans into Nazis* (Cambridge, Mass.: Harvard University Press, 1998), p. 7.

21. Robert Gerwarth and John Horne, 'Paramilitarism in Europe after the Great War: An Introduction', in Robert Gerwarth and John Horne (eds), *War in Peace: Paramilitary Violence in Europe after the Great War* (Oxford: Oxford University Press, 2012), pp. 1–18, p. 3.

22. Richard Bessel, *Germany after the First World War* (Oxford: Oxford University Press, 1993), p. 260; Ulrich Herbert, *Best: Biographische Studien über Radikalismus, Weltanschauung und Vernunft, 1903–1989* (Bonn: Dietz, 1996).

23. Richard Bessel, *Nazism and War* (London: Phoenix, 2004), pp. 23–33.

24. Alexandra Kaiser, *Von Helden und Opfern: Eine Geschichte des Volkstrauertages* (Frankfurt: Campus, 2010), pp. 176–85; Martina Steber and Bernhard Gotto, 'Volksgemeinschaft: Writing the Social History of the Nazi Regime', in Martina Steber and Bernhard Gotto (eds), *Visions of a Community in Nazi Germany: Social Engineering and Private Lives* (Oxford: Oxford University Press, 2014), pp. 1–28, p. 8.

25. Ulrich Herbert, 'Was haben die Nationalsozialisten aus dem Ersten Weltkrieg gelernt?', in Gerd Krumeich (ed.), *Nationalsozialismus und Erster Weltkrieg* (Essen: Klartext, 2010), pp. 21–32; Vejas Gabriel Liulevicius, *War Land on the Eastern Front: Culture, National Identity, and German Occupation in World War I* (Cambridge: Cambridge University Press, 2000), p. 272.

26. For a similar point but in respect of colonialism, see: Davis, *Colonialism*, pp. 255–6.

Chapter 1 Precedents

1. 'Fiat justitia et pereat res publica', *Preußische Zeitung – Kreuz-Zeitung*, 14 July 1914, p. 1.

2. Werner Angress, 'Der jüdische Offizier in der neueren deutschen Geschichte, 1813–1918', in Ursula Breymayer, Bernd Ulrich and Karin Wieland (eds), *Willensmenschen: Über*

deutsche Offiziere (Frankfurt: Fischer, 1999), pp. 67–78, p. 73. In the Habsburg army in contrast there were approximately 25,000 Jewish officers: István Deák, 'Jewish Soldiers in Austro-Hungarian Society', *Leo Baeck Memorial Lecture*, 34 (1990), pp. 3–29, p. 22.

3. Ute Frevert, *A Nation in Barracks: Modern Germany, Military Conscription and Civil Society* (Oxford: Berg, 2004), p. 161.

4. Martin Kitchen, *The German Officer Corps 1890–1914* (Oxford: Clarendon, 1968), pp. 22–48.

5. Werner Angress, 'Prussia's Army and the Jewish Reserve Officer Controversy before World War I', *Leo Baeck Institute Yearbook*, 17 (1972), pp. 19–42.

6. 'Beförderungen', *K.C.-Blätter*, November–December 1914, p. 281.

7. Christopher Clark, *The Sleepwalkers: How Europe went to War in 1914* (London: Penguin, 2013), pp. 367–403.

8. 'Erzherzog Franz Ferdinand', *Wiener Zeitung*, 30 June 1914, p. 1.

9. 'Erzherzog Franz Ferdinand', *Die Wahrheit*, 3 July 1914, pp. 3–4.

10. Arthur Stern, *In bewegter Zeit: Erinnerungen und Gedanken eine jüdischen Nervenarztes* (Jerusalem: Rubin Mass, 1968), p. 68.

11. Theodor Kirchberger, 'Lebenserinnerungen', LBINY, ME1057, p. 50; Charlotte Stein-Pick, 'Die verlorene Heimat', LBINY, ME619.

12. 'Die Einweihung des neuen Krankenhauses', *Gemeindeblatt der jüdischen Gemeinde zu Berlin*, 10 July 1914, pp. 85–9.

13. 'Korrespondenzen und Nachrichten', *Allgemeine Zeitung des Judentums*, 17 July 1914, pp. 13–14.

14. Peter Pulzer, 'The Return of Old Hatreds', in Michael Meyer (ed.), *German-Jewish History in Modern Times – Volume 3: Integration in Dispute, 1871–1918* (New York: Columbia University Press, 1997), pp. 196–251.

15. Rainer Liedtke and David Rechter, 'Introduction: German Jewry and the Search for Normality', in Rainer Liedtke and David Rechter (eds), *Towards Normality? Acculturation and Modern German Jewry* (Tübingen: Mohr Siebeck, 2003), pp. 1–12, p. 2.

16. Avraham Barkai, *'Wehr Dich!' Der Centralverein deutscher Staatsbürger jüdischen Glaubens 1893–1938* (Munich: Beck, 2002).

17. Hagit Lavsky, *Before Catastrophe: The Distinctive Path of German Zionism* (Detroit: Wayne State University Press, 1996), pp. 22–3.

18. 'Jüdischer Verlag', *Jüdische Rundschau*, 3 July 1914, p. 290.

19. Samuel Chotzinoff, *A Lost Paradise: Early Reminiscences* (New York: Arno, 1975), pp. 39–45.

20. Alexander Granach, *Da geht ein Mensch: Lebensroman eines Schauspielers* (Munich: Herbig, 1973), pp. 200–3.

21. Jack Wertheimer, *Unwelcome Strangers: East European Jews in Imperial Germany* (Oxford: Oxford University Press, 1987), pp. 56, 184.

22. C.C. Aronsfeld, 'German Jews in Victorian England', *Leo Baeck Institute Yearbook*, 7 (1962), pp. 312–29.

23. M.J. Bonn, *Wandering Scholar* (London: Cohen & West, 1949), pp. 170–2; Patricia Clavin, '"A Wandering Scholar" in Britain and the USA, 1933–45: The Life and Work of Moritz Bonn', in Anthony Grenville (ed.), *Refugees from the Third Reich in Britain* (Amsterdam: Rodopi, 2002), pp. 27–42.

24. Clark, *Sleepwalkers*, pp. 412–16.

25. Werner Mosse, 'Wilhelm II and the Kaiserjuden: A Problematical Encounter', in Jehuda Reinharz and Walter Schatzberg (eds), *The Jewish Response to German Culture: From the Enlightenment to the Second World War* (Hanover: University Press of New England, 1985), pp. 164–94, p. 170.

26. Max Warburg, *Aus meinen Aufzeichnungen* (New York: E.M. Warburg, 1952), pp. 29–31; 'Der Kaiser in Hamburg-Altona', *Hamburger Fremdenblatt*, 23 June 1914, p. 18; Niall Ferguson, *Paper and Iron: Hamburg Business and German Politics in the Era of Inflation, 1897–1927* (Cambridge: Cambridge University Press, 1995), pp. 43–4, 93–4.

27. Isabel Hull, *The Entourage of Kaiser Wilhelm II, 1888–1918* (Cambridge: Cambridge University Press, 1982), p. 172.

28. Gottlieb von Jagow to Albert Ballin, 15 July 1914; Gottlieb von Jagow, 20 July 1914, in Karl Kautsky (ed.), *Die deutschen Dokumente zum Kriegsausbruch 1914* (Berlin: Deutsche Verlagsgesellschaft für Politik und Geschichte, 1922), pp. 82–4, 116.

29. Jonathan Steinberg, 'Diplomatie als Wille und Vorstellung: Die Berliner Mission Lord Haldanes im Februar 1912', in Herbert Schottelius and Wilhelm Deist (eds), *Marine und Marinepolitik im kaiserlichen Deutschland 1871–1914* (Düsseldorf: Droste, 1972), pp. 263–82, p. 274.

30. Winston Churchill, *The World Crisis – Volume I: 1911–1914* (London: Bloomsbury, [1950] 2015), p. 137.

31. Bernhard Huldermann, *Albert Ballin* (Oldenburg: Gerhard Stalling, 1922), pp. 301–2.

32. 'Zur Verwirklichung des Zionismus', *Jüdische Rundschau*, 31 July 1914, p. 333; 'Zum 9. Av', *Allgemeine Zeitung des Judentums*, p. 361.

33. Alon Confino, *The Nation as a Local Metaphor: Württemberg, Imperial Germany and National Memory, 1871–1918* (Chapel Hill: University of North Carolina Press, 1997).

34. 'Der Ernst der Lage', *Vossische Zeitung*, 27 July 1914, p. 1.

35. Jeffrey Verhey, *The Spirit of 1914: Militarism, Myth and Mobilization in Germany* (Cambridge: Cambridge University Press, 2000), p. 54.

36. 'Kundgebungen der Sozialdemokratie', *Die Post*, 29 July 1914, LAB, A Pr. Br. Rep. 030, Nr. 15805.

37. Kenneth Calkins, *Hugo Haase: Demokrat und Revolutionär* (Berlin: Colloquium, 1976), pp. 53–5; Georges Haupt, *Socialism and the Great War: The Collapse of the Second International* (Oxford: Clarendon, 1972), p. 253.

38. Eduard David, 31 July 1914, in Susanne Miller (ed.), *Das Kriegstagebuch des Reichstagsabgeordneten Eduard David 1914 bis 1918* (Düsseldorf: Droste, 1966), pp. 28–9.

39. Peter Pulzer, *Jews and the German State: The Political History of a Minority, 1848–1933* (Detroit: Wayne State University Press, 2003), p. 163.

40. 'Die eisernen Würfel rollen!', *Vorwärts*, 3 August 1914, p. 1.

41. Wolfdieter Bihl (ed.), *Deutsche Quellen zur Geschichte des Ersten Weltkrieges*, vol. 29 (Darmstadt: Wissenschaftliche Buchgesellschaft, 1991), p. 49.

42. 'Die Kriegssitzung des Reichstages', *Berliner Tageblatt*, 5 August 1914, pp. 5–6.

43. Pulzer, *Jews and the German State*, p. 46.

44. Benjamin Carter Hett, *Crossing Hitler: The Man Who Put the Nazis on the Witness Stand* (Oxford: Oxford University Press, 2008), p. 14.

45. Monika Richarz, 'Demographic Developments', in Michael Meyer (ed.), *German-Jewish History in Modern Times – Volume 3: Integration in Dispute, 1871–1918* (New York: Columbia University Press, 1997), pp. 7–34, p. 15.

46. Deborah Hertz, *How Jews Became Germans: The History of Conversion and Assimilation in Berlin* (New Haven: Yale University Press, 2007), pp. 13, 199.

47. 'Unter den Waffen', *Im deutschen Reich*, September 1914, pp. 341–3; 'Krieg', *Im deutschen Reich*, September 1914, pp. 337–8.

48. 'Krieg', *Im deutschen Reich*, September 1914, pp. 337–8.

49. Ludwig Strauss to Martin Buber, 30 September 1914, in Grete Schaeder (ed.), *Martin Buber: Briefwechsel aus sieben Jahrzehnten – Band I: 1897–1918* (Heidelberg: Schneider, 1972), pp. 371–3.

50. Jarausch, *Enigmatic*.

51. 'Die Kriegssitzung des Reichstags', *Vossische Zeitung*, 5 August 1914, p. 3.

52. 'Der vierte August', *Berliner Tageblatt*, 5 August 1914, p. 2.

53. *The Truth about Germany: Facts about the War* (Berlin, 1914), pp. 8, 26.

54. 'In schicksalsschwerer Zeit', *Liberales Judentum*, August 1914, pp. 157–9, p. 158.

55. 'Der Krieg', *Im deutschen Reich*, January 1915, pp. 2–24, p. 13.

56. 'Russische Spitzel und ihre Opfer', *Jüdische Rundschau*, 21 August 1914, p. 349.

57. *Der Krieg und wir Juden: Gesammelte Aufsätze von einem deutschen Juden* (Berlin: Louis Lamm, 1915), p. 12.

58. Some 14,000 Jews had taken part in the clashes against the French: Christine Krüger, *'Sind wir denn nicht Brüdern?' Deutsche Juden im nationalen Krieg 1870/71* (Paderborn:

Schöningh, 2006), p. 63; Frank Kühlich, *Die deutschen Soldaten im Krieg von 1870/71* (Frankfurt: Peter Lang, 1995), p. 55.

59. 'Ein Wort zur Lage', *Berliner Tageblatt*, 31 July 1914, p. 4.
60. Friedrich Meinecke, *Die deutsche Erhebung von 1914* (Stuttgart: Cotta'sche, 1915), pp. 39–46.
61. Walther Rathenau to Fanny Künstler, late July 1914, in Alexander Jaser, Clemens Picht and Ernst Schulin (ed.), *Briefe, 1914–1922* (Düsseldorf: Droste, 2006), p. 1346.

Chapter 2 War Enthusiasm

1. 'Mobilmachung', p. 1, 'Deutschlands Mobilmachung', *Vossische Zeitung*, 2 August 1914, p. 2; 'Berlin am Abend der Mobilmachung', *Vossische Zeitung*, 2 August 1914, p. 3.
2. 'Der Bettag am 5. August', *Allgemeine Zeitung des Judentums*, 14 August 1914, pp. 385–8.
3. 'Der allgemeine Bettag', *Im deutschen Reich*, September 1914, pp. 344–9.
4. Verhey, *Spirit*, p. 91.
5. 'An die deutschen Juden', *Im deutschen Reich*, September 1914, p. 339.
6. 'Deutsche Juden!', *Jüdische Rundschau*, 7 August 1914, p. 343.
7. Alexander Watson, ' "For Kaiser and Reich": The Identity and Fate of the German Volunteers, 1914–1918', *War in History*, 12 (1) (2008), pp. 44–74, pp. 48, 56.
8. Protokoll der ersten Sitzung des Ausschusses für Kriegsstatistik, 19 September 1914, CJA, 1.75C, Ve1, Nr. 224 #12847.
9. Dorothee Wierling, *Eine Familie im Krieg: Leben, Sterben und Schreiben 1914–1918* (Göttingen: Wallstein, 2013), p. 43–55.
10. H.C. Plaut, 'Memories of a German Jew', Leeds University Special Collections, GE28, p. 98.
11. Isaac Hurwitz to Kriegsministerium, 5 August 1914, CJA, 1.75C, Ve1, Nr. 417, #13040.
12. 'Meine letzten Tage in Paris', *Aschaffenburger Zeitung*, 10 August 1914, p. 1.
13. 'Die jüngsten deutschen Soldaten', *Im deutschen Reich*, October 1914, p. 394; 'Bejahrte jüdische Kriegsfreiwillige', *Im deutschen Reich*, October 1914, p. 403.
14. *Er kommt wieder*, LAB, A Pr. Br. Rep. 030–05–02, Nr. 6015, pp. 11–12.
15. Otte, *Jewish Identities*, pp. 145–59, 187–8.
16. Friedrich Stampfer, *Erfahrungen und Erkenntnisse* (Cologne: Verlag für Politik und Wissenschaft, 1958), p. 168.
17. 'Kriegsantisemitismus', *Jüdische Rundschau*, 11 September 1914, p. 362.
18. 'Burgfrieden', *Israelitisches Gemeindeblatt*, 4 September 1914, pp. 362–3.
19. CV to Bethmann Hollweg, 20 October 1914, BArch Berlin, R43/908.
20. Gerda Luft, *Chronik eines Lebens für Israel* (Stuttgart: Erdmann, 1983), p. 271.
21. 'Bericht des Pflegeamtes des Almosenkastens der israelitischen Gemeinde über dessen Wirksamkeit im Jahre 1914', IfS, V/390.
22. Stefan Goebel, 'Schools', in Jay Winter and Jean-Louis Robert (ed.), *Capital Cities at War: Paris, London, Berlin 1914–1919 – Volume 2: A Cultural History* (Cambridge: Cambridge University Press, 2007), pp. 188–234, pp. 192–7.
23. Kriegsministerium, 16 August 1914, BArch MA, PH2/217.
24. 'Aus der Bewegung', *Blau-Weiss-Blätter*, October 1914, p. 14.
25. 'Die Pflichten unserer Frauen und Jungfrauen gegen das Vaterland', *Allgemeine Zeitung des Judentums*, 21 August 1914, p. 400.
26. Käthe Frankenthal, *Der dreifache Fluch: Jüdin, Intellektuelle, Sozialistin – Lebenserinnerungen einer Ärtztin in Deutschland und im Exil* (Frankfurt: Campus, 1981), pp. 57–9.
27. Astrid Stölzle, 'Einführung', in Susanne Rueß and Astrid Stölzle, *Das Tagebuch der jüdischen Kriegskrankenschwester Rosa Bendit, 1914 bis 1917* (Stuttgart: Franz Steiner, 2012), pp. 7–8, p. 7.
28. Gustav Feldmann, 'Das Jüdische Schwesternheim Stuttgart im Weltkrieg', [undated], CAHJP, P32, Nr. 19.
29. Martina Steer, 'Nation, Religion, Gender: The Triple Challenge of Middle-Class Jewish Women in World War I', *Central European History*, 48 (2) (2015), pp. 176–98, p. 183.

30. Helene Meyer-Stargard, 'Monatsbericht September', [1914], CJA, 1.75C, Ge1, Nr. 956, #10846.
31. Deutsch-Israelitische Gemeindebund, 9 August 1914, CJA, 1.75C, Ge1, Nr. 959, #10849.
32. Auguste Victoria-Krankenhaus vom Roten Kreuz to Jüdische Arbeiterkolonie, 15 August 1914, and Kalischer to Oscar Cassel, 30 August 1914, both in: CJA, 1.75C, Ge1, Nr. 959, #10849.
33. 'Das Rote Kreuz gegen den Antisemitismus', *Im deutschen Reich*, January–February 1915, pp. 31–2.
34. Arnold Zweig to Helene Weyl, 27 August 1914, in Georg Wenzel (ed.), *Arnold Zweig 1887–1968: Werk und Leben in Dokumentation und Bildern* (Berlin: Aufbau, 1978), pp. 61–3.
35. Ludwig Geiger, *Die deutschen Juden und der Krieg* (Berlin: Schwetschke, 1915), p. 68. See also: Penslar, *Military*, p. 159.
36. Bernhardt Albert Mayer, 19 November 1914, CJA, 1.75C, Ve1, Nr. 417, #13040.
37. Ludwig Geiger, *Krieg und Kultur* (Berlin: Rudolf Mosse, 1915), pp. 7–11.
38. Berger, *Eisernes Kreuz*, p. 131.
39. Arthur Hantke, 12 November 1914, in Jehuda Reinharz (ed.), *Dokumente zur Geschichte des deutschen Zionismus, 1882–1933* (Tübingen: Mohr, 1981), pp. 158–60.
40. 'Der Krieg und das liberale Judentum', *Liberales Judentum*, September 1914, p. 188.
41. Martin Buber to Hans Kohn, 30 September 1914, in Schaeder, *Martin Buber: Briefwechsel*, p. 370.
42. Micheline Prüter-Müller and Peter Wilhelm Schmidt (eds), *Hugo Rosenthal: Lebenserinnerungen* (Bielefeld: Verlag für Regionalgeschichte, 2000), p. 271.
43. Holger Herwig, 'War in the West, 1914–1916', in John Horne (ed.), *A Companion to World War I* (Oxford: Wiley-Blackwell, 2012), pp. 49–63, p. 51.
44. The precise origins of the 'Schlieffen Plan' have been fiercely contested; see: Terrence Zuber, *Inventing the Schlieffen Plan: German War Planning, 1871–1914* (Oxford: Oxford University Press, 2002); Robert Foley, 'The Real Schlieffen Plan', *War in History*, 13 (1) (2006), pp. 91–115.
45. Gottfried Sender to Dr Spanier, 9 August 1914, in M. Spanier (ed.), *Leutnant Sender: Blätter der Erinnerung für seine Freunde* (Hamburg: Blogau, 1915), p. 12.
46. Harry Marcuse to Hedwig Hirschmann, 9 August 1914, in Barbara Reisner (ed.), *Kriegsbriefe 1914–1918: Dr. Harry & Mimi Marcuse* (London: Lulu, 2013), pp. 9–10.
47. Gottfried Sender to Dr Gutmann, 28 August 1914, in Spanier, *Sender*, pp. 14–15.
48. 'Zwei Feldpostbriefe', *Jüdische Rundschau*, 2 October 1914, p. 383.
49. Rolf Gustav Haebler, *In Memoriam Ludwig Frank* (Mannheim: Allgemeine Zeitung, 1954), pp. 47–9; 'Ludwig Frank', *Liberales Judentum*, October 1914, p. 214; 'Ludwig Frank: Ein deutscher Jude', *Im deutschen Reich*, October 1914, pp. 374–6.
50. Karl Baedeker, *Belgium and Holland: A Handbook for Travellers* (Leipzig: Baedeker, 1885), p. 182.
51. John Horne and Alan Kramer, *German Atrocities, 1914: A History of Denial* (New Haven: Yale University Press, 2001), p. 39.
52. Felix Theilhaber, *Schlichte Kriegserlebnisse* (Berlin: Louis Lamm, 1916), p. 10.
53. Oskar Brieger, [September 1914], in Eugen Tannenbaum (ed.), *Kriegsbriefe deutscher und österreichischer Juden* (Berlin: Neuer Verlag, 1915), pp. 96–8.
54. Horne and Kramer, *German Atrocities*, pp. 94–8.
55. 'Aus unserer Feldpost-Briefmappe', *K.C.-Blätter*, November–December 1914, p. 304.
56. 'Juden als Kolonialkrieger', *Der Schild*, 15 May 1925, p. 186; 'Jüdische Kolonialsoldaten', *Frankfurter Israelitisches Gemeindeblatt*, June 1930, p. 409.
57. Harry Marcuse to Mimi Marcuse, 3 September 1914, in Reisner, *Kriegsbriefe*, p. 27; Harry Marcuse to Mimi Marcuse, 7 September 1914, in Reisner, *Kriegsbriefe*, pp. 29–32.
58. Alexander Watson, ' "Unheard-of Brutality": Russian Atrocities against Civilians in East Prussia, 1914–1915', *Journal of Modern History*, 86 (4) (2014), pp. 780–825, p. 823.
59. Ausschuss des Vebandes der Synagogengemeinden Ostpreußens to Vorstand der Synagogengemeinde Lötzen, 24 August 1916, CJA, 1.75A, LO1, Nr. 11, #4708.

60. Victor Klemperer, *Curriculum Vitae: Erinnerungen 2, 1881–1918* (Berlin: Aufbau, 1996), p. 201.

61. Anna von der Goltz, *Hindenburg: Power, Myth, and the Rise of the Nazis* (Oxford: Oxford University Press, 2009), p. 19.

62. 'Die Woche', *Allgemeine Zeitung des Judentums*, 18 September 1914, pp. 447–51, p. 449.

63. Paul Goldmann, *Beim Generalfeldmarschall von Hindenburg: Ein Abend im Hauptquartier* (Berlin: Concordia, 1914), p. 25.

64. Jay Winter, 'Demography', in Horne (ed.), *Companion*, pp. 248–62, p. 250.

65. Herbert Sulzbach, *With the German Guns: Four Years on the Western Front* (Barnsley: Pen & Sword, 1998), p. 27.

66. Richard Friedmann, 4 September 1914, in *Kriegsbriefe gefallener deutscher Juden mit einem Geleitwort von Franz Josef Strauß* (Stuttgart: Seewald, 1961), pp. 46–7.

67. *Kriegs-Bericht der Salia*, 1 October 1915, p. 3.

68. Harry Marcuse to Mimi Marcuse, 17 October 1915, in Reisner, *Kriegsbriefe*, p. 173.

69. Roger Chickering, *The Great War and Urban Life in Germany: Freiburg, 1914–1918* (Cambridge: Cambridge University Press, 2007), p. 72.

70. 'Ehrentafel', *K.C.-Blätter*, September 1914, p. 275; 'Nachruf', *Herzl-Bund-Blätter*, February–March 1915, p. 191.

71. Theodor Wolff, 21 August 1914, in Bernd Sösemann (ed.), *Tagebücher, 1914–1919: Der Erste Weltkrieg und die Entstehung der Weimarer Republik in Tagebüchern, Leitartikeln und Briefen des Chefredakteurs am 'Berliner Tageblatt' und Mitbegründers der 'Deutschen Demokratischen Partei'* (Boppard am Rhein: Boldt, 1984), p. 89.

72. Hans Peter Hanssen, 31 August 1914, in Hans Peter Hanssen, *Diary of a Dying Empire* (Port Washington: Kennikat Press, 1973), p. 60.

73. Ludwig Rosenthal, *Die große Zeit im Spiegel ernster Tage* (Cologne, 1914), p. 3.

74. 'Aus den Kriegserinnerungen eines Militärarztes im Jahre 1870', *Allgemeine Zeitung des Judentums*, 25 September 1914, pp. 461–2; 'Feldpost-Briefe', *Im deutschen Reich*, October–December 1914, pp. 388–92.

75. Chickering, *Great War and Urban Life*, pp. 73–4.

76. 'Alte und neue Makkabäer', *Jüdische Rundschau*, 28 August 1914, pp. 353–5.

77. 'Der heilige Krieg', *Allgemeine Zeitung des Judentums*, 4 September 1914, pp. 421–2.

78. Ernst Lissauer, 1915, cited in Elisabeth Albanis, 'Ostracised for Loyalty: Ernst Lissauer's Propaganda Writing and its Reception', *Leo Baeck Institute Yearbook*, 43 (1998), pp. 195–224, p. 214.

79. Elisabeth Albanis, *German-Jewish Cultural Identity from 1900 to the Aftermath of the First World War: A Comparative Study of Moritz Goldstein, Julius Bab and Ernst Lissauer* (Tübingen: Niemeyer, 2002), p. 231.

80. Ernst Lissauer, 'Haßgesang gegen England', in Ernst Lissauer (ed.), *Worte in die Zeit-Flugblätter 1914*, Blatt I (1914), pp. 1–2.

81. See: Albanis, *German-Jewish Cultural Identity*, p. 180.

82. Egmont Zechlin, *Die deutsche Politik und die Juden im Ersten Weltkrieg* (Göttingen: Vandenhoeck & Ruprecht, 1969), p. 97.

83. Albanis, *German-Jewish Cultural Identity*, pp. 235–6.

84. Bernhard Goldschmidt to Verband der deutschen Juden, 27 January 1915, CJA, 1.75C Ve1, Nr. 417, #13040.

85. 'Die Kriegssitzung des Reichstages', *Berliner Tageblatt*, 5 August 1914, pp. 5–6.

86. Gotthart Schwarz, *Theodor Wolff und das 'Berliner Tageblatt': Eine liberale Stimme in der deutschen Politik, 1906–1933* (Tübingen: J.C.B. Mohr, 1968), pp. 44–5.

87. 'Der Krieg', *Im deutschen Reich*, January 1915, p. 11.

88. Eduard David, 29 August 1914, in Miller, *Kriegstagebuch*, pp. 28–9.

89. Christian Schölzel, *Walther Rathenau: Eine Biographie* (Paderborn: Ferdinand Schöningh, 2006), pp. 182–3.

90. Jarausch, *Enigmatic Chancellor*, p. 191.

91. Rainer Hering, *Konstruierte Nation: Der Alldeutsche Verband, 1890 bis 1939* (Hamburg: Christians, 2003), p. 135.

92. Fischer, *Griff*, p. 181.

93. Walther Rathenau to Bethmann Hollweg, 7 September 1914, in Walther Rathenau, *Politische Briefe* (Dresden: Reissner, 1929), pp. 9–16, p. 9; Albert Ballin to Admiral von Tirpitz, 1 October 1914, in Alfred von Tirpitz (ed.), *Politische Dokumente* (Stuttgart: Cotta, 1924), pp. 130–5, p. 134.

94. Fischer, *Griff*, pp. 114, 127.

95. Frank Wende, *Die belgische Frage in der deutschen Politik des Ersten Welktriegs* (Hamburg: Eckart Böhme, 1969), pp. 70–5.

96. Rathenau to Mollendorf, 8 August 1914, in Rathenau, *Politische*, pp. 6–7.

97. Georg Solmssen to Direktion der Disconto-Gesellschaft, 2 December 1914, in Harold James and Martin Müller (eds), *Georg Solmssen: Ein deutscher Bankier – Briefe aus einem halben Jahrhundert 1900–1956* (Munich: Beck, 2012), pp. 88–93.

98. 'Zangwill Urges Jews to Support Allies', *New York Times*, 10 September 1914, p. 1.

99. Sophie de Schaepdrijver, 'Occupation, Propaganda and the Idea of Belgium', in Aviel Roshwald and Richard Stites (eds), *European Culture in the Great War: The Arts, Entertainment and Propaganda, 1914–1918* (Cambridge: Cambridge University Press, 1999), pp. 267–94, p. 269.

100. 'Der Krieg', *Im deutschen Reich*, January 1915, p. 14.

101. Martin Buber to Frederik van Eeden, October 1914, in Schaeder, *Martin Buber: Briefwechsel*, pp. 374–80, p. 379.

102. Robert Cohen, 'Arnold Zweig's War Novellas of 1914', in Bernd Hüppauf (ed.), *War, Violence and the Modern Condition* (Berlin: De Gruyter, 1997), pp. 277–90, p. 287.

103. Julius Bab, 'Deutschland', in Julius Bab (ed.), *Menschenstimme: Gedichte aus der Kriegszeit 1914–1918* (Stettin: Norddeutscher Verlag für Literatur und Kunst, 1920), p. 13.

104. Julius Bab, 'Die Belgier', in Julius Bab, *Am Rande der Zeit: Betrachtungen 1914/15* (Berlin: Oesterheld, 1915), pp. 30–4, p. 30.

105. Jutta Höfel, *Der belgische Lyriker Emile Verhaeren* (Frankfurt: Peter Lang, 1994), p. 47.

106. Jürgen von Ungern-Sternberg and Wolfgang von Ungern-Sternberg, *Der Aufruf 'An die Kulturwelt': Das Manifest der 93 und die Anfänge der Kriegspropaganda im Ersten Weltkrieg* (Stuttgart: F. Steiner, 1996).

Chapter 3 Total War

1. 31 December 1914, in Sösemann, *Tagebücher*, p. 145.

2. 'Die Silvesternacht', *Berliner Tageblatt*, 1 January 1915, p. 4.

3. Robert Asprey, *The German High Command at War: Hindenburg and Ludendorff and the First World War* (London: Little Brown, 1993), p. 109. For positive press reports, see: 'Günstiger Stand der Schlacht bei Paris', *Vossische Zeitung*, 14 September 1914, p. 1.

4. On Germany's gradual path to total war, see: Roger Chickering, 'World War I and the Theory of Total War: Reflections on the British and German Cases, 1914–1915', in Roger Chickering and Stig Förster (eds), *Great War, Total War: Combat and Mobilization on the Western Front, 1914–1918* (Cambridge: Cambridge University Press, 2000), pp. 35–53.

5. Sulzbach, *With the German Guns*, p. 25.

6. Eric Osborne, *Britain's Economic Blockade of Germany, 1914–1919* (London: Frank Cass, 2004), p. 108.

7. Gerhard A. Ritter, 'The Kaiser and his Ship Owner: Albert Ballin, the HAPAG Shipping Company and the Relationship between Industry and Politics in Imperial Germany and the Early Weimar Republic', in Hartmut Berghoff, Jürgen Kocka and Dieter Ziegler (eds), *Business in the Age of Extremes: Essays in Modern German and Austrian Economic History* (Cambridge: Cambridge University Press, 2013), pp. 15–39, pp. 31–2; Albert Ballin and Philipp Heineken to Bethmann Hollweg, 22 December 1914, in Werner Basler (ed.), *Deutschlands Annexionspolitik in Polen und im Baltikum* (Berlin: Rütten & Loening, 1962), p. 363.

8. Belinda Davis, *Home Fires Burning: Food, Politics, and Everyday Life in World War I Berlin* (Chapel Hill: University of North Carolina Press, 2000), p. 22; Avner Offer, *The First World War: An Agrarian Interpretation* (Oxford: Clarendon, 1989), pp. 300–1.

9. Lamar Cecil, *Albert Ballin: Business and Politics in Imperial Germany, 1888–1918* (Princeton: Princeton University Press, 1967), p. 217.

10. Dr Lübbert, *Die Zentraleinkaufsgesellschaft* (Berlin: Kriegspresseamt, 1917), p. 7.
11. Warburg, *Aufzeichnungen*, p. 38.
12. Gerald Feldman, *Army, Industry and Labor in Germany, 1914–1918* (Princeton: Princeton University Press, 1966), p. 102.
13. Alice Salomon, 'Kriegsdienst im deutschen Haushalt', *Die Frauenfrage, Zentralblatt des Bundes deutscher Frauenvereine*, 1 February 1915, pp. 161–4, p. 162.
14. Theodor Wolff, 3 December 1915, in Sösemann, *Tagebücher*, p. 317.
15. Henriette Fürth, *Kleines Kriegskochbuch: Ein Ratgeber für sparsames Kochen* (Frankfurt: Jobst, 1916), p. 33.
16. 'Speisegebote in Kriegszeit', *Gemeindblatt der jüdischen Gemeinde zu Berlin*, 12 February 1915, p. 15.
17. Theodor Wolff, 5 November 1915, in Sösemann, *Tagebücher*, p. 307.
18. Minna Schwarz and Lilli Manes, 'Protokol', 29 December 1914, CJA, 1.75C, Ge1, Nr. 956, #10846.
19. Steven Schouten, 'Fighting a Kosher War: German Jews and Kashrut in the First World War', in Ina Zweiniger-Bargielowska, Rachel Duffett and Alain Drouard (eds), *Food and War in Twentieth Century Europe* (Farnham: Ashgate, 2011), pp. 41–58, p. 43.
20. 'Speisegebote', p. 15.
21. Vorstand der israelitischen Gemeinde Frankfurt to Deutsch-Israelitischer Gemeindebund, 17 February 1915, CJA, 1.75C, Ge1, Nr. 964, #10854.
22. *Frankfurter Israelitisches Familienblatt*, 6 November 1914, pp. 7–8.
23. Hanns Falk, *Die Juden in den Kriegsgesellschaften* (Berlin: Philo, 1920), p. 11.
24. Walther Rathenau, *Die Organisation der Rohstoffversorgung: Vortrag gehalten in der Deutschen Gesellschaft 1914 am 20. Dezember 1915* (1915), pp. 6–8.
25. Schölzel, *Rathenau*, pp. 175–6.
26. Rathenau to Fanny Künstler, 1 September 1914, in Margarete von Eynern (ed.), *Briefe: Walther Rathenau, ein preussischer Europäer* (Berlin: Vogt, 1955), pp. 117–18.
27. Rathenau, *Rohstoffversorgung*, p. 9.
28. Rathenau to Gerhard von Mutius, 10 October 1914, in von Eynern, *Briefe*, pp. 125–7.
29. Kurt Wiedenfeld, *Rohstoffversorgung* (Berlin: Kriegspresseamt, 1917), p. 4.
30. Schölzel, *Rathenau*, p. 164.
31. Gerhard Hecker, *Walther Rathenau und sein Verhältnis zu Militär und Krieg* (Boppard: Harald Boldt, 1983), pp. 244–5.
32. Ernst Lange to Feldzeugmeisterei, 13 November 1915, IfS, W2–5/1.096.
33. Vermittlungs-Stelle für Heereslieferung to Handelskammer, 22 November 1915, IfS, W2–5/1.096.
34. Moritz Goldstein, *Berliner Jahre: Erinnerungen 1880–1933* (Munich: Verlag Dokumentation, 1977), p. 80.
35. See the discussion of this anti-Semitic discourse in 'Eine Konfessionsstatistik der Kriegsgesellschaften', *Berliner Tageblatt*, 15 November 1919, p. 5.
36. Rathenau to Fanny Künstler, 21 February 1915, in von Eynern, *Briefe*, pp. 135–6.
37. Wiedenfeld, *Rohstoffversorgung*, p. 19.
38. 'Bericht der Direktion an die ordentliche Generalversammlung der Aktionäre der Metallgesellschaft vom 29. Dezember 1914 über das Geschäftsjahr vom 1. Oktober 1913 bis 30. September 1914', Hessisches Wirtschaftsarchiv, Abt. 119, Nr. 152.
39. Hecker, *Rathenau*, p. 229.
40. Michael Dorrmann, *Eduard Arnhold (1848–1925): Eine biographische Studie zu Unternehmer- und Mäzenatentum im Deutschen Kaiserreich* (Berlin: Akademie, 2002), pp. 220–2.
41. Von Kries, 'Vierteljahrsbericht des Verwaltungschefs bei dem General-Gouvernement Warschau', 31 December 1915, p. 14, in BArch MA, PH30/II/10.
42. Theo Balderston, 'War Finance and Inflation in Britain and Germany, 1914–1918', *The Economic History Review*, 42 (2) (1989), pp. 222–42, p. 237.
43. Cyrus Adler, *Jacob Schiff: His Life and Letters* (New York: Doubleday, 1928), p. 259.

44. Konrad Roesler, *Die Finanzpolitik des Deutschen Reiches im Ersten Weltkrieg* (Berlin: Duncker & Humboldt, 1967), p. 206.
45. Dorrmann, *Arnhold*, p. 220.
46. 'Vereinsnachrichten', *Im deutschen Reich*, October 1915, p. 223.
47. Hilfs-Ausschuss für deutsche u. österreichische Flüchtlinge aus Belgien, 16 October 1914, IfS, S/363.
48. 'Aufruf für die aus Feindesland vetriebenen Deutschen', *Frankfurter Zeitung*, 18 October 1914, p. 6.
49. 'Jüdische Lesehalle', *Israelitisches Gemeindeblatt*, 4 September 1914, p. 365.
50. Till van Rahden, 'Die Grenze vor Ort: Einbürgerung und Ausweisung ausländischer Juden in Breslau 1860–1918', *Tel Aviver Jahrbuch für deutsche Geschichte*, 27 (1998), pp. 47–69, p. 62.
51. 21 October 1914, CJA, 1.75C, Ve1, Nr. 169, #12792.
52. 'Die "Russen" in Berlin', *Jüdische Rundschau*, 11 September 1914, p. 362.
53. Der Bade-Inspektor, 12 September 1914, IfS, Sport und Badeamt, Nr. 382.
54. Wertheimer, *Unwelcome Strangers*, pp. 157–61.
55. Vorstand der Israelitischen Religionsgemeinde zu Chemnitz to Verband der Deutschen Juden, 15 December 1914, CJA, 1.75C, Ve1, Nr. 417, #13040.
56. Bernhard Kahn, 'Memoirs', LBINY, ME344a, pp. 4–8.
57. Klibansky to Königliche Polizei-Präsidium, 16 November 1914, Institut für Stadtgeschichte Frankfurt, S/147.
58. Ulrich Herbert, *Geschichte der Ausländerpolitik in Deutschland* (Munich: Beck, 2001), p. 86.
59. Kahn, 'Memoirs', p. 10.
60. Matthew Stibbe, *British Civilian Internees in Germany: The Ruhleben Camp, 1914–18* (Manchester: Manchester University Press, 2008), pp. 28–41.
61. Israel Cohen, *The Ruhleben Prison Camp: A Record of Nineteen Months' Internment* (London: Methuen, 1917), pp. 40–50.
62. Albert Einstein to Paul Ehrenfest, December 1914, in Robert Schuman, A.J. Kox, Michel Janssen and József Illy (eds), *The Collected Papers of Albert Einstein – Volume 8: The Berlin Years – Correspondence, 1914–1918* (Princeton: Princeton University Press, 1998), pp. 46–7.
63. Carl von Clausewitz, *On War*, cited in Hew Strachan, *Clausewitz's* On War (New York: Atlantic Monthly Press, 2007), p. 129.
64. Annika Mombauer, *Helmuth von Moltke and the Origins of the First World War* (Cambridge: Cambridge University Press, 2001), pp. 174–5.
65. Michael Geyer, 'German Strategy in the Age of Machine Warfare, 1914–1945', in Peter Paret (ed.), *Makers of Modern Strategy from Machiavelli to the Nuclear Age* (Oxford: Clarendon, 1998), pp. 527–97, p. 535.
66. Eugen Mittwoch, *Deutschland, die Türkei und der heilige Krieg* (Berlin: Kameradschaft, 1914).
67. 'Eine Entscheidung', *Jüdische Rundschau*, 6 November 1914, p. 1.
68. Stefan Vogt, 'Zionismus und Weltpolitik: Die Auseinandersetzung der deutschen Zionisten mit dem deutschen Imperialismus und Kolonialismus 1890–1918', *Zeitschrift für Geschichtswissenschaft*, 60 (7/8) (2012), pp. 596–697, p. 609.
69. 'Die politische Bedeutung des Zionismus', *Das größere Deutschland: Wochenschrift für Deutsche Welt- und Kolonial-Politik*, 27 February 1915, pp. 290–8, p. 298.
70. 2 January 1915, PA–AA, R20944.
71. Walther Rathenau to Major G. von Diezelsky, 3 May 1915, in Rathenau, *Politische*, pp. 38–9.
72. Zechlin, *Die deutsche Politik*, p. 98.
73. Hermann Cohen, ' "Du sollst nicht einhergehen als ein Verleumder": Ein Appell an die Juden Amerikas', in Bruno Strauß (ed.), *Hermann Cohens Jüdische Schriften* (Berlin: Schwetschke, 1924), pp. 229–36, p. 234.
74. 'Germany Refuses to Halt Submarine Warfare', *Washington Herald*, 31 May 1915, p. 1.

75. 'Lusitania Death Toll 1346', *Public Ledger*, 8 May 1915, p. 1.

76. 'Italiens Hetzer', *Vossische Zeitung*, 10 May 1915, p. 1.

77. Cecil, *Ballin*, pp. 266–75.

78. 'Das nasse Dreieck', *Frankfurter Zeitung*, 5 January 1915, p. 1.

79. Wolff, 9 February 1915, in Sösemann, *Tagebücher*, p. 159.

80. Albert Ballin to Admiral von Capelle, 21 January 1915, BArch MA, N253/101.

81. Joachim Schröder, *Die U-Boote des Kaisers: Die Geschichte des deutschen U-Boot-Krieges gegen Großbritannien im Ersten Weltkrieg* (Bonn: Bernhard & Graefe, 2003), pp. 28–9.

82. Fritz Stern, *Dreams and Delusions: The Drama of German History* (London: Weidenfeld & Nicolson, 1987), p. 54.

83. Margit Szöllösi-Janze, *Fritz Haber, 1868–1934: Eine Biographie* (Munich: Beck, 1998), p. 58.

84. Ibid., pp. 268–70.

85. Ibid., pp. 322–35.

86. Carl Lichnock, 'Der 1. Deutsche Gas-Angriff am 22.4.1915', BArch MA, PH14/37.

87. 'Geschosse mit giftigen Gasen', *Vossische Zeitung*, 23 April 1915, p. 1.

88. Fritz Haber, 'Die Chemie im Kriege', in Fritz Haber (ed.), *Fünf Vorträge aus den Jahren 1920–1923* (Berlin: Julius Springer, 1924), pp. 25–41, p. 35.

89. Richard Willstätter, *Aus meinem Leben: Von Arbeit, Muße und Freunden* (Weinheim: Verlag Chemie, 1958), p. 252.

90. Sulzbach, *With the German Guns*, p. 68.

91. Otto Lummitsch, 'Meine Erinnerungen an Geheimrat Prof. Haber', July–August 1955, Archiv der Max-Planck-Gesellschaft, Dept. Va, Rep. 5, 1480; Willstätter, *Leben*, p. 230.

92. Klemperer, *Curriculum*, p. 316.

93. Kriegsministerium, 6 March 1915, BArch MA, PH7/27.

94. Kriegsministerium to das K. stellv. Gen. Kdo. I.II.III. A.K, 5 December 1915, Kriegsarchiv, Stv. Gen. Kdo. I.b.A.K., Nr. 755; Kriegsministerium, 10 May 1915, BArch MA, PH7/27.

95. Thomas Weber, *Hitler's First War: Adolf Hitler, the Men of the List Regiment, and the First World War* (Oxford: Oxford University Press, 2010), p. 215. By late 1916, 941 German Jews had served as officers: 'Nachweisung der beim Heere befindlichen wehrpflichtigen Juden', 26 January 1917, HstAS, M1/4, Bü1271.

96. Fritz Herz, 20 September 1914, in Tannenbaum, *Kriegsbriefe*, pp. 28–9.

97. 'Das Eiserne Kreuz erhielten', *K.C.-Blätter*, January–February 1915, p. 314.

98. Eugen Beer to Verband der deutschen Juden, 7 May 1915, CJA, 1.75C, Ve1, Nr. 213, #12854.

99. 'Jüdische Feldgeistliche', *Im deutschen Reich*, October 1914, p. 397; Kriegsministerium to Armee-Ober-Kommando VI, 13 September 1914, Kriegsarchiv, Stv. Gen. Kdo. I.b.A.K., Nr. 381. On the army rabbis, see: Sarah Panter, *Jüdische Erfahrungen und Loyalitätskonflikte im Ersten Weltkrieg* (Göttingen: Vandenhoeck & Ruprecht, 2014), pp. 190–6.

100. Leo Baeck, 'Berichte des Feldgeistlichen Rabbiner Dr. Leo Baeck an den Vorstand der jüdischen Gemeinde', *Gemeindeblatt der jüdischen Gemeinde zu Berlin*, 13 November 1914, pp. 140–1.

101. See Baerwald's publication list in Sabine Hank, Hermann Simon and Uwe Hank (eds), *Feldrabbiner in den deutschen Streitkräften des Ersten Weltkrieges* (Berlin: Hentrich & Hentrich, 2013), p. 37.

102. Ibid., pp. 31, 99, 160, 194, 457.

103. Report, 16 September 1915, CJA, 1.75c, Ve1, Nr. 368, #12991.

104. Bruno Italiener to Verband der deutschen Juden, 24 September 1914, in Hank, Simon and Hank, *Feldrabbiner*, pp. 265–7.

105. Wilde to Ausschuss des Verbandes der Deutschen Juden, 4 November 1914, CJA, 1.75C, Ve1, Nr. 376, #12999.

106. Hank, Simon and Hank, *Feldrabbiner*, p. 9; Patrick Houlihan, *Catholicism and the Great War: Religion and Everyday Life in Germany and Austria-Hungary, 1914–1922* (Cambridge: Cambridge University Press, 2015), p. 79.

107. Klemperer, *Curriculum*, p. 362.
108. Centralverein to Verband der deutschen Juden, 23 November 1914, CJA, 1.75C, Ve1, Nr. 417, #13040; Centralverein to Eisenbahn-Regiment Nr. 1 Ersatzbataillon, 10 April 1915, Zentralarchiv, B.3/52, Nr. 3.
109. David Fine, *Jewish Integration in the German Army in the First World War* (Berlin: De Gruyter, 2012), p. 18.

Chapter 4 Annexations

1. Max Warburg cited in Ferguson, *Paper*, p. 137.
2. Kristin Kopp, 'Gray Zones: On the Inclusion of "Poland" in the Study of German Colonialism', in Michael Perrudin, Jürgen Zimmerer and Katy Heady (eds), *German Colonialism and National Identity* (New York: Routledge, 2011), pp. 33–42, p. 36.
3. Walter Wolff, 'Memoirs of a German Jew, 1887–1966', LBINY, ME957, p. 22.
4. 'Petition der sechs Wirtschaftsverbände an der Reichskanzler', 20 May 1915, in Salomon Grumbach, *Das annexionistische Deutschland* (Lausanne: Payot, 1917), pp. 123–31, p. 126.
5. Robert Nelson (ed.), *Germans, Poland, and Colonial Expansion to the East: 1850 through the Present* (Basingstoke: Palgrave Macmillan, 2009).
6. 'Petition der Professoren an den Reichskanzler', in Grumbach, *Annexionistische*, pp. 132–40, p. 135.
7. Seeberg petition signatories, Zentral- und Landesbibliothek Berlin, Nachlass Deißmann, Nr. 553.
8. Hans Thierbach, 'Lebenslauf', in Hans Thierbach (ed.), *Adolf Grabowsky Leben und Werk: Dem Altmeister der politischen wissenschaften als Fest- und Dankesgabe gewidmet* (Cologne: Carl Heymanns, 1963), pp. 135–52.
9. Adolf Grabowsky, 'Die Weltmacht', *Das neue Deutschland*, 28 October 1914, in Grumbach, *Annexionistische*, p. 213.
10. Adolf Grabowsky, 'Der innere Imperialismus', *Das neue Deutschland*, 27 February 1915, in ibid., pp. 117–22.
11. *Stenographisches Protokoll der Verhandlungen des VI. Zionisten Kongresses in Basel* (1903), pp. 42–53.
12. Davis Trietsch, *Die Welt nach dem Kriege* (Berlin: Puttkammer & Mühlbrecht, 1915); Davis Trietsch, *Kriegsziele gegen England* (Berlin: Puttkammer & Mühlbrecht, 1915), p. 6; Davis Trietsch, *Russland* (Berlin: Basch, 1915), p. 3.
13. Elzbieta Ettinger, *Rosa Luxemburg: A Life* (London: Harrap, 1987), pp. 197–205.
14. Eduard Bernstein, Hugo Haase and Karl Kautsky, 'Das Gebot der Stunde', 19 June 1915, in Ernst Haase (ed.), *Hugo Haase: Sein Leben und Wirken* (Berlin: Ottens, 1929), pp. 225–7.
15. John Röhl, 'Germany', in Keith Wilson (ed.), *Decisions for War, 1914* (London: UCL Press, 1995), pp. 27–54, p. 32.
16. 'Die Delbrück-Dernberg Petition', in Grumbach, *Annexionistische*, pp. 409–11.
17. Albert Ballin to Theodor Wolff, 13 July 1915 in Sösemann, *Tagebücher*, pp. 890–1.
18. Ismar Becker to Sigmund Feist, 7 March 1915, in Sabine Hank and Hermann Simon (eds), *Feldpostbriefe jüdischer Soldaten 1914–1918* (Teetz: Heinrich & Heinrich, 2002), pp. 82–3.
19. Asprey, *German High Command*, pp. 185–91.
20. Almut Linder-Wirsching, 'Patrioten im Pool: Deutsche und französische Kriegsberichterstatter im Ersten Weltkrieg', in Ute Daniel (ed.), *Augenzeugen: Kriegsberichterstattung vom 18. zum 21. Jahrhundert* (Göttingen: Vandenhoeck & Ruprecht, 2006), pp. 113–40, p. 122.
21. Fritz Wertheimer, *Von der Weichsel bis zum Dnjestr* (Stuttgart: Deutsche Verlags-Anstalt, 1915), pp. 56, 87, 102.
22. 'Der Sinn der Befreiung', *Jüdische Rundschau*, 23 September 1915, p. 317.
23. Wertheimer, *Weichsel*, p. 110.

24. Rebecca Kobrin, *Jewish Bialystok and its Diaspora* (Bloomington: Indiana University Press, 2010), pp. 96–7.

25. Steven Aschheim, *Brothers and Strangers: The East European Jew in German and German-Jewish Consciousness, 1800–1923* (Madison: University of Wisconsin Press, 1982), pp. 157–63.

26. 'Generalbericht für die Mitglieder des "Komitees fuer den Osten" ', December 1914, PA–AA, R10503.

27. 'An die Juden in Polen', *Berliner Tageblatt*, 1 September 1914, p. 2.

28. Zosa Szajkowski, 'The German Appeal to the Jews of Poland, August 1914', *Jewish Quarterly Review*, 59 (4) (1969), pp. 311–20, p. 315.

29. Henriette Hannah Bodenheimer (ed.), *Prelude to Israel: The Memoirs of M. I. Bodenheimer* (New York: Yoseloff, 1963), pp. 242–8.

30. Bodenheimer, *Prelude*, pp. 249–50.

31. Komitee für den Osten to Hindenburg, 29 November 1914, LBINY, MF13.

32. Fritz Wertheimer, *Im polnischen Winterfeldzug mit der Armee Mackensen* (Stuttgart: Deutsche Verlags-Anstalt, 1915), p. 179.

33. Franz Oppenheimer and Max Bodenheimer, 'Generalbericht für die Mitglieder des Komitees für den Osten', December 1914, PA–AA, R10503.

34. Deutsche Vereinigung für die Interessen der osteuropäischen Juden, October 1915, BArch Berlin, R1501/119802.

35. Davis Trietsch, *Juden und Deutsche: Eine Sprach- und Interessengemeinschaft* (Vienna: R. Löwit, 1915), p. 58.

36. Max Bodenheimer, 'Bericht über die im Auftrage "Komitees für den Osten" im Mai–Juni 1915 unternommene Reise nach Russisch-Polen', June 1915, LBINY, AR7185.

37. 'Protokoll der Sitzung des geschäftsführenden Ausschusses', 23 March 1915, cited in Aschheim, *Brothers*, p. 158.

38. Unterarzt Köhler to Sigmund Feist, 15 March 1915, in Hank and Simon, *Feldpostbriefe*, pp. 356–60.

39. Max Hoffmann, 29 October 1914, in Major-General Max Hoffmann, *War Diaries and Other Papers* (London: Martin Secker, 1929), p. 48.

40. Leopold Rosenak to Verband der deutschen Juden, 26 April 1915, in Hank, Simon and Hank, *Feldrabbiner*, pp. 364–6.

41. '1. (3.) Vierteljahrsbericht des Verwaltungschefs bei dem General-Gouvernement Warschau', 21 July 1915–1 October 1915, BArch MA, PH30/II/9.

42. Eugene Kent, 12 February 1915, Imperial War Museum London, 12/22/1.

43. Emanuel Carlebach, 24 February 1916, in Alexander Carlebach, 'A German Rabbi goes East', *Leo Baeck Institute Yearbook*, 6 (1961), pp. 60–121, pp. 85–7.

44. Paul Weindling, *Epidemics and Genocide in Eastern Europe, 1890–1945* (Oxford: Oxford University Press, 2000), p. 79.

45. Friedemann to Bodenheimer, 30 April 1915, LBINY, MF13.

46. 'Strassenhandel', *Zeitung der X. Armee*, 13 January 1916, p. 3.

47. Aschheim, *Brothers*, p. 147.

48. 'Im Abenddämmern', *Zeitung der X. Armee*, 9 December 1915, pp. 4–5; Robert Nelson, *German Soldier Newspapers of the First World War* (Cambridge: Cambridge University Press, 2011), pp. 224–36.

49. Vierteljahrsbericht des Verwaltungschefs bei dem General-Gouvernement Warschau, 1 January 1916–30 March 1916, in BArch MA, PH30/II/11.

50. Kurt Levy, 25 September 1914, in Tannenbaum, *Kriegsbriefe*, pp. 40–2.

51. Klemperer, *Curriculum*, p. 487.

52. Arnold Tänzer, 'Kriegserinnerungen', LBINY, ME640, pp. 24–5.

53. Carlebach, 27 January 1916, in Carlebach, 'German Rabbi', pp. 70–5.

54. Arnold Tänzer, 'Von einer Reise zur Front bei Pinsk', *Feldzeitung der Bugarmee*, 8 January 1916, p. 2.

55. 'Reise der Herrn Justizrat Dr. Bodenheimer und Friedemann', 6 May 1915, LBINY, MF13.

56. Nathan Birnbaum, *Den Ostjuden ihr Recht!* (Vienna: R. Löwit, 1915), p. 16.
57. Adolf Grabowsky, *Die polnische Frage* (Berlin: Carl Heymanns, 1916), p. 28.
58. Walther Rathenau to Bethmann Hollweg, 30 August 1915, in Rathenau, *Politische*, pp. 45–9.
59. Liulevicius, *War Land*, p. 54.
60. S. Ansky, *The Enemy at his Pleasure: A Journey Through the Jewish Pale of Settlement during World War I* (New York: Henry Holt, 2002), p. 212.
61. Hilfsverein der deutschen Juden, 'Aufruf für die notleidenden Juden', LBINY, MF13.
62. Kahn, 'Memoirs', p. 25; Sammy Gronemann, *Hawdoloh und Zapfenstreich: Erinnerungen an die ostjüdische Etappe 1916–18* (Berlin: Jüdischer Verlag, 1924), p. 144.
63. Erich Ludendorff, *My War Memories, 1914–1918* (London: Hutchinson, 1919), pp. 178–9.
64. Liulevicius, *War Land*, p. 57.
65. Minister des Innern to Reichskanzler, 3 September 1915, BArch Berlin, R1501/119802.
66. Hermann Strack to Arthur Zimmermann, 3 February 1917, BArch Berlin, R1501/119803.
67. Judith Schrag-Haas, 'Erinnerungen an meinen Vater, Ludwig Haas', LBINY, ME581.
68. Gouverneur von Puttkamer, 'Noch einiges zum Ostjudenproblem', Sonderabdruck aus der Nummer 11 des Tags, 14 January 1916, LBINY, MF13.
69. Gronemann, *Hawdoloh*, p. 24.
70. Klemperer, *Curriculum*, p. 477.
71. Letter to Vize-Feldwebel Salinger, 5 June 1915, LBINY, MF13.
72. Gronemann, *Hawdoloh*, pp. 33, 87.
73. Ismar Freund, 'Die Ostjuden im Spiegel der Geschichte', *Zeitung der X. Armee*, 1 February 1916, p. 127.
74. Zosa Szajkowski, 'The Struggle for Yiddish during World War I: The Attitude of German Jewry', *Leo Baeck Institute Yearbook*, 9 (1964), pp. 131–58, p. 140; Jesse Kauffman, 'Schools, State-Building and National Conflict in German Occupied Poland, 1915–1918', in Jennifer Keene and Michael Neiberg (eds), *Finding Common Ground: New Directions in First World War Studies* (Leiden: Brill, 2011), pp. 113–38.
75. David Biale, *Gershom Scholem: Kabbalah and Counter-History* (Cambridge, Mass.: Harvard University Press, 1982), p. 26.
76. Franz Rosenzweig to his parents, 6 April 1917, pp. 182–3; Franz Rosenzweig to his mother, 28 May 1918, pp. 320–2, both in Edith Rosenzweig (ed.), *Franz Rosenzweig Briefe* (Berlin: Schocken, 1935).
77. Theodor Rosenthal, 'Tagebuch', LBINY, ME908, pp. 31, 41.
78. Nelson, *German Soldier Newspapers*, p. 231.
79. Aviel Roshwald, 'Jewish Cultural Identity in Eastern and Central Europe during the Great War', in Roshwald and Stites, *European Culture*, pp. 89–126, pp. 120–1.
80. Hermann Struck and Herbert Eulenberg, *Skizzen aus Litauen, Weissrussland und Kurland* (Berlin: Stilke, 1916), pp. 1, 41, 51.
81. Klemperer, *Curriculum*, p. 474.
82. Ludwig Bernhard and Leo Wegener, 'Die Ostgrenze', 18 August 1914, BArch MA, N30/34.
83. Georg Fritz, *Die Ostjudenfrage: Zionismus und Grenzschluß* (Munich: Lehmanns, 1915), p. 43.
84. Ibid.
85. 'Besprechung zwischen Dr. Oppenheimer, Rechtsanwalt Rosenbaum und Dr. Jacobson', 14 October 1915, LBINY, MF13.
86. Willy Cohn, 'Zukunftsfragen des deutschen Judentums', *Allgemeine Zeitung des Judentums*, 26 November 1915, p. 1.
87. Kurt Alexander, 'Deutschland und die Ostjudenfrage', *Im deutschen Reich*, January 1916, p. 25.
88. [Wirtschaftliche Vereinigung] to Bethmann Hollweg, 24 August 1915, PA–AA, R10504.
89. Edgar Jaffe, 'Deutschlands Ostgrenzen jetzt und in Zukunft', PA–AA, R21574. See also: Imanuel Geiss, *Der polnische Grenzstreifen 1914–1918: Ein Beitrag zur deutschen Kriegszielpolitik im Ersten Weltkrieg* (Hamburg: Matthiesen, 1960), p. 52.

90. Wolfgang Heinze, 'Ostjüdische Einwanderung', *Preußische Jahrbücher*, October 1915, pp. 98–117.

91. 'Deutschland und die Ostjudenfrage', *Im deutschen Reich*, October 1915, pp. 195–213; 'Die chinesische Mauer', *Jüdische Rundschau*, 15 October 1915, pp. 335–6.

92. 'Unterredung der Herren Dr. Oppenheimer und Dr. Friedemann mit Graf Wastarp', 28 June 1915, LBINY, MF13.

93. Max Bodenheimer, 'Einwanderungsbeschränkung der Ostjuden', *Süddeutsche Monatshefte*, February 1916, pp. 731–5, p. 735.

94. 'Protokoll der Unterredung zwischen den Herren Professor Dr. Sobernheim und Dr. Oppenheimer mit Herrn Ministerialdirektor Dr. Lewald vom Ministerium des Innern', 18 March 1916, LBINY, MF13.

95. Deutsche Vereinigung für die Interessen der osteuropäischen Juden, October 1915, BArch Berlin, R1501/119802.

96. Alfred Friedemann, 'Streng vertraulich', [undated], LBINY, MF13.

97. Levy to Bodenheimer, 3 August 1915, LBINY, MF13.

98. Bertha Pappenheim to Sophie Mamelok, 18 August 1917, in Dora Edinger (ed.), *Bertha Pappenheim: Leben und Schriften* (Frankfurt: Ner-Tamid, 1963), p. 43.

Chapter 5 Celebrating Destruction

1. 'Vaterländische Feier in Bochum', *Märkischer Sprecher*, 5 June 1916, p. 5; 'Aus Anlaß der Seeschlacht am Skagerrak', *Im deutschen Reich*, May–June 1916, p. 127.

2. Isaac Goldstein is listed as a casualty in Michael Adler (ed.), *British Jewry Book of Honour* (London: Caxton, 1922), p. 92.

3. Karl Weißkopf, 4 April 1916, in *Kriegsbriefe gefallener deutscher Juden*, pp. 126–7.

4. Max Hirschberg, *Jude und Demokrat: Erinnerungen eines Muenchener Rechtsanwalts 1883 bis 1939* (Munich: Oldenbourg, 1998), p. 93.

5. Kramer, *Dynamic*, pp. 183, 232–3; Isabel Hull, *Absolute Destruction: Military Culture and the Practices of War in Imperial Germany* (Ithaca: Cornell University Press, 2004).

6. Max Liebermann, 'Englands schwerer Traum', *Kriegszeit: Künstlerflugblätter*, 30 September 1914, p. 23; Max Liebermann, 'Krieg auf Erden', *Kriegszeit: Künstlerflugblätter*, 24 December 1914, p. 74.

7. Magnus Hirschfeld, *Warum hassen uns die Völker? Eine kriegspsychologische Betrachtung* (Bonn: Weber, 1915), p. 10.

8. Biale, *Gershom Scholem*, pp. 60–4.

9. Raffael Scheck, *Alfred von Tirpitz and German Right-Wing Politics, 1914–1930* (Boston: Humanities Press, 1998).

10. Arthur Schlossmann, 'Neue Grundlagen der Bevölkerungspolilik', 19 February 1916, in Grumbach, *Annexionistische*, p. 221.

11. Robert Friedberg, address to the Prussian parliament, 17 January 1916, in ibid., p. 70.

12. Otto Landsberg, 6 January 1916 in ibid., p. 113.

13. Rathenau to Ludendorff, 8 January 1916, in Rathenau, *Politische*, p. 54.

14. Georg Bernhard, *Die Kriegspolitik der Vossischen Zeitung* (Berlin: Ullstein, 1919), p. 5.

15. Roger Chickering, *Imperial Germany and the Great War, 1914–1918* (Cambridge: Cambridge University Press, 2004), p. 66.

16. See: Joanna Bourke, *An Intimate History of Killing: Face-to-Face Killing in Twentieth-Century Warfare* (London: Granta, 1999), p. 2.

17. K. Wachsner, 'Sturmangriff auf Bethincourt', *Der Schild*, 13 March 1936, p. 5.

18. Julius Marx, 18 August 1914, in Julius Marx, *Kriegs-Tagebuch eines Juden* (Frankfurt: Ner-Tamid-Verlag, 1964), p. 15.

19. Stephen Westman, *Surgeon with the Kaiser's Army* (London: Kimber, 1968), p. 58.

20. Ibid., p. 59.

21. Walter C., 30 August 1914, in Tannenbaum, *Kriegsbriefe*, p. 7.

22. Martin Feist, 18 October 1914, LBINY, AR6300.

23. Joanna Bourke, *Dismembering the Male: Men's Bodies, Britain and the Great War* (London: Reaktion, 1996), pp. 214–15.
24. Peter Fritzsche, *A Nation of Fliers: German Aviation and the National Imagination* (Cambridge, Mass.: Harvard University Press, 1992), pp. 62–3.
25. Felix Theilhaber, *Jüdische Flieger im Weltkrieg* (Berlin: Verlag der Schild, 1924), p. 87.
26. Julius Marx, 18 August 1914, in Marx, *Kriegs-Tagebuch*, p. 171.
27. Hans Senft to Sigmund Feist, 17 July 1916, in Hank and Simon, *Feldpostbriefe*, p. 576.
28. Georg Luft to Sigmund Feist, 25 October 1916, in ibid., p. 469.
29. Sönke Neitzel and Harald Welzer, *Soldaten: On Fighting, Killing, and Dying – The Secret World War II Tapes of German POWs* (London: Simon & Schuster, 2011), p. 54.
30. Rabbiner Dr N.A. Nobel, 'Kriegspredigten', 1914, CAHJP, P75, Nr. 51.
31. Abraham Glaßberg, *Im Kriegsjahr 1914/15* (Berlin, 1915), p. 2.
32. Todd Presner, *Muscular Judaism: The Jewish Body and the Politics of Regeneration* (New York: Routledge, 2007), pp. 196–7.
33. Nahum Goldmann, *Der Geist des Militarismus* (Berlin: Deutsche Verlagsanstalt, 1915), p. 40.
34. Nahum Goldmann, *Memories: The Autobiography of Nahum Goldmann – The Story of a Lifelong Battle by World Jewry's Ambassador at Large*, trans. Helen Sebba (London: Weidenfeld & Nicolson, 1970), p. 51.
35. George Mosse, *Fallen Soldiers: Reshaping the Memory of the World Wars* (Oxford: Oxford University Press, 1990), p. 127.
36. Ulrike Heikaus, 'Krieg! Juden zwischen den Fronten 1914–1918: Eine Wechselausstellung im Jüdischen Museum München', in Ulrike Heikaus and Julia Köhne (eds), *Krieg! 1914–1918: Juden zwischen den Fronten* (Berlin: Hentrich & Hentrich, 2014), pp. 8–44, p. 21.
37. Wolff, 24 December 1914, in Sösemann, *Tagebücher*, p. 143.
38. Eiserner Hindenburg von Berlin, 'Abbildungen und Preise der Nägel und Schilder', Archiv der Max-Planck-Gesellschaft, I, Abt. KWG, Rep. 1A, Nr. 641.
39. Dietlinder Munzel-Everling, *Kriegsnagelungen, Wehrmann in Eisen, Nagel-Roland, Eisernes Kreuz* (Wiesbaden: Archimedicx, 2008), pp. 18–24.
40. 'Der Bamberger eiserne Ritter', *Im deutschen Reich*, July–August 1916, p. 182.
41. Hilfskommission 1915 für Palästina, 1915, CJA, 1.75A, Lo1, Nr. 11, #4708.
42. Fritz Mayer to Frau Hirsch, 10 February 1917, LBINY, AR25042.
43. Mosse, *Fallen Soldiers*, pp. 70–106.
44. Bourke, *Dismembering*, p. 214.
45. Emil Levy to Verband der deutschen Juden, 8 November 1914, in Hank, Simon and Hank, *Feldrabbiner*, pp. 332–5.
46. Rosa Bendit, 9 November 1916, in Susanne Rueß and Astrid Stölzle, *Das Tagebuch der jüdischen Kriegskrankenschwester Rosa Bendit, 1914 bis 1917* (Stuttgart: Franz Steiner, 2012), pp. 138–9.
47. Emil Kronheim to Verband der deutschen Juden, 1 October 1918, in Hank, Simon and Hank, *Feldrabbiner*, p. 289.
48. Leo van Bergen, *Before My Helpless Sight: Suffering, Dying and Military Medicine on the Western Front, 1914–1918* (Farnham: Ashgate, 2009), pp. 479–92.
49. Hank, Simon and Hank, *Feldrabbiner*, p. 592.
50. 'Soldatengräber', *Der Israelit*, 16 November 1916, p. 2.
51. 'Feldrabbiner-Konferenz am 11. September 1916 in Brüssel im Hotel des Boulevards', in Hank, Simon and Hank, *Feldrabbiner*, pp. 504–6.
52. George Mosse, 'Jews and the German War Experience, 1914–1918', *Leo Baeck Memorial Lecture*, 21 (1977), pp. 3–28, p. 7.
53. Gronemann, *Hawdoloh*, p. 102.
54. 'Siegfried Dembinski', *Hamburger Familienblatt*, 17 May 1915, p. 7; 'Dr Arthur Süßmann', *Gemeindeblatt der jüdischen Gemeinde zu Berlin*, 10 November 1916, p. 127.
55. 'Hamburg', *Allgemeine Zeitung des Judentums*, 27 November 1914, p. 15.
56. Vorstand der Deutsch-Israelitischen Gemeinde to Friedhofsbüro, 13 November 1914, StAHH, 325–1, Nr. 272.

57. Judith Prokasky, 'Treue zu Deutschland und Treue zum Judentum: Das Gedenken an die deutschen jüdischen Gefallenen des Ersten Weltkrieges', *Aschkenas: Zeitschrift für Geschichte und Kultur der Juden*, 9 (2) (1999), pp. 503–16, p. 515.

58. Joseph Roth, 'Lebende Kriegsdenkmäler', in Klaus Westerman (ed.), *Berliner Saisonbericht: Unbekannte Reportage und journalistische Arbeiten, 1920–39* (Cologne: Kiepenheuer und Witsch, 1984), pp. 85–90.

59. 'Dr. Salzberger: Aus meinem Kriegstagebuch', *Liberales Judentum*, January 1915, pp. 2–10.

60. Bendit, 9 May 1916 and 12 May 1916, in Rueß and Stölzle, *Tagebuch*, p. 115.

61. Susan Grayzel, *Women's Identities at War: Gender, Motherhood and Politics in Britain and France during the First World War* (Chapel Hill: University of North Carolina Press, 1999), p. 11.

62. Sabine Hank, Hermann Simon and Uwe Hank, 'Einleitung', in Hank, Simon and Hank, *Feldrabbiner*, pp. 7–15, p. 13.

63. Artur Michaelson to Sigmund Feist, 26 June 1916, in Hank and Simon, *Feldpostbriefe*, pp. 497–8.

64. 'Aus dem Krankenhause der jüdischen Gemeinde', *Gemeindeblatt der jüdischen Gemeinde zu Berlin*, 11 February 1916, p. 25.

65. Paul Silex and Betty Hirsch, *Bericht über unsere dreijährige Tätigkeit an der Blinden-Lazarettschule des Vereinslazaretts St. Maria Viktoria-Heilanstalt zu Berlin* (Berlin: Lazarettschule, 1918), pp. 33, 66.

66. Hilfsbund für Kriegsbeschädigte jüdische Soldaten, [1916]; Reichsausschuss für Kriegsbeschädigtenfürsorge to Staatskommissar für die Regelung der Kriegswohlfahrts-pflege in Preussen, 8 March 1917, GStA PK, I. HA, Rep. 191, Nr. 3285.

67. Susanne Thesing, ' "Krieg": Ein graphischer Zyklus von Ludwig Meidner', in Gerda Breuer and Ines Wagemann (eds), *Ludwig Meidner: Zeichner, Maler, Literat 1884–1966* (Stuttgart: Gerd Hatje, 1991), pp. 96–105, p. 101.

68. Käthe Mendels, 'Geschichte meiner Familie im Ersten Weltkrieg', in Andreas Lixl-Purcell (ed.), *Erinnerungen deutsch-jüdischer Frauen, 1900–1990* (Leipzig: Reclam, 1992), pp. 74–93.

69. Anna Lindemann, 'Probleme der Fürsorge für weibliche Kriegerhinterbliebene', *Das neue Deutschland*, 10 November 1915, pp. 441–5, p. 442.

70. Dorothea Bernhard and Siddy Wronsky, 'Hinterbliebenenfürsorge', August 1915, BArch Berlin, R43/2415.

71. 'Kriegerwitwe', *Israelitisches Gemeindeblatt*, 12 April 1918, p. 6.

72. Nationalstiftung für die Hinterbliebenen der im Kriege Gefallenen, 'Aufruf', [undated], BArch Berlin, R43/2415.

73. 'Konzert zu Gunsten der Hinterbliebenen im Felde gefallener Elberfelder Krieger', 31 January 1915, CAHJP, D/Be4, Nr. 202.

74. Niall Ferguson, *The Pity of War, 1914–1918* (London: Penguin, 1999), p. 369.

75. Rosenthal, 'Tagebuch', pp. 45–9.

76. Uta Hinz, *Gefangen im Großen Krieg: Kriegsgefangenschaft in Deutschland 1914–1921* (Essen: Klartext, 2006), pp. 246–7.

77. Georg Wurzer, *Die Kriegsgefangenen der Mittelmächte in Russland im Ersten Weltkrieg* (Göttingen: V&R Unipress, 2005), p. 61.

78. Rosenthal, 'Tagebuch', pp. 45–9.

79. Max Pinkus to Simon, 1 October 1914, LBINY, AR7030.

80. H. Podey to Max Pinkus, 9 October 1914, LBINY, AR7030.

81. Max Pinkus to Dänische Rote Kreuz, 31 October 1914, Max Pinkus to Centralnachweisbureau des Reichsmarineamtes, 24 November 1914, LBINY, AR7030.

82. Uta Hinz, 'Humanität im Krieg? Internationales Rotes Kreuz und Kriegsgefangenenhilfe im Ersten Weltkrieg', in Jochen Oltmer (ed.), *Kriegsgefangene im Europa des Ersten Weltkrieges* (Paderborn: Schöningh, 2006), pp. 216–36, pp. 223–4.

83. Adolf Vischer, *Die Stacheldraht-Krankheit: Beiträge zur Psychologie des Kriegsgefangenen* (Zurich: Rascher, 1918); Rosenthal, 'Tagebuch', pp. 47–8.

84. Manchester Shechita Board, General Minutes, 12 September 1915, Greater Manchester County Record Office, GB127.M448.
85. Reichsverband für jüdische Kriegsgefangenenfürsorge to Kommissar für Wohlfahrtspflege, Köngl. Polizei-Präsidium, 19 December 1916, GStA PK, I. HA, Rep. 191, Nr. 3289.
86. 'Verzeichnis der mit der Seelsorge an den Gefangenen jüdischer Konfession betrauten', 15 April 1915, BArch MA, PH2/231.
87. 'Jüdische Gefangenenseelsorge im Lager Grafenwöhr', *Das Jüdische Echo*, 11 June 1915, pp. 182–4.
88. Rabbinate München and Ansbach to Rabbinate im Königreich Bayern, 16 April 1916, CJA, 1.75B, Su1, Nr. 1, #9733.
89. Dr M. Weinberg, 'Aufruf', CJA, 1.75B, Su1, Nr. 1, #9733.
90. 'Bei den juedischen Kriegsgefangenen in Heilsberg', *Ost und West*, December 1916, pp. 473–8.
91. Max Simonsohn, 'Bericht über meine Tätigkeit und Erfahrungen in der Gefangenen-Seelsorge', 5 January 1915, CJA, 1.75C, Ge1, Nr. 965, #10855.
92. Gefangenendepot Stuttgart, 22 January 1915, HstAS, M1/4, Bü980.
93. 'Gefangenenseelsorge', p. 184.
94. Landrabbiner to Deutsch Israelitischer Gemeindebund, 12 January 1915, CJA, 1.75C, Ge1, Nr. 965, #10855.
95. Israel Nussbaum, *'Gut Schabbes!' Jüdisches Leben auf dem Lande: Aufzeichnungen eines Lehrers (1869–1942)* (Berlin: Jüdische Verlagsanstalt, 2002), p. 189.
96. Dr Weingarten to Deutsch-Israelitischer Gemeindebund, 2 January 1915, CJA, 1.75C, Ge1, Nr. 965, #10855.

Chapter 6 The 'Other'

1. Omer Bartov, 'Defining Enemies, Making Victims: Germans, Jews, and the Holocaust', *American Historical Review*, 103 (3) (1998), pp. 771–816, p. 774.
2. Von Loebell, 15 December 1915, GStA PK, I. HA Rep. 77, Tit. 863a, Nr. 6; Ludendorff, 17 July 1915, HStAS, M33/2, Bü681.
3. Hull, *Absolute Destruction*, p. 331.
4. 'Der Kaiser an das Volk und an das Heer', *Berliner Tageblatt*, 1 August 1916, p. 1.
5. Der Vorstand der israelitischen Gemeinde, 'Bekanntmachung', 16 March 1916, Universitätsbibliothek Frankfurt am Main, Fm/Kg 1/638a, Nr. 34.
6. Volker Standt, *Köln im Ersten Weltkrieg* (Göttingen: Optimus, 2014), pp. 250–64.
7. Marie Munk, 'Memoirs', 1961, LBINY, ME332, pp. VIII, 13.
8. Luft, *Chronik*, pp. 43–4.
9. Charlotte Landau-Mühsam, 'Meine Erinnerungen', LBINY, ME381, p. 44.
10. Emanuel Wurm, 27 March 1916, in Ralph Haswell Lutz (ed.), *The Fall of the German Empire 1914–1918*, vol. II (New York: Octagon, 1969), pp. 166–8, p. 167.
11. Bauer, Feldpolizeidirektor, 'Stimmung in Bayern', 3 August 1916, BArch MA, PH2/476. On conditions in Bavaria, see: Benjamin Ziemann, *Front und Heimat: Ländliche Kriegserfahrungen im südlichen Bayern 1914–1923* (Essen: Klartext, 1997), pp. 308–13.
12. *Berliner Tageblatt*, 16 May 1916, pp. 8 and 12.
13. Davis, *Home Fires Burning*, pp. 133–4.
14. Dietrich Woywod, 'Deutscher Nationalausschuss für einen ehrenvollen Frieden (DNA) Gegründet 1916', in Dieter Fricke (ed.), *Die bürgerlichen Parteien in Deutschland*, vol. I (Leipzig: Bibliographisches Institut, 1968), pp. 487–8.
15. Matthew Stibbe, *German Anglophobia and the Great War, 1914–1918* (Cambridge: Cambridge University Press, 2001), p. 125.
16. Georg Bernhard, 'Land oder Geld', in Ernst Jäckh (ed.), *Der Deutsche Krieg* (Stuttgart: DVA, 1916), pp. 1–25, p. 13; 'An der Schwelle des 3. Kriegsjahres', *Märkischer Sprecher*, 2 August 1916, p. 3.
17. Stibbe, *German Anglophobia*, pp. 137, 148–51.

18. Volksausschuss für rasche Niederkämpfung Englands, 'Mitgliederliste für Bayern', September 1917, GStA PK, VI. HA, Nl. Kapp, W., Nr. 665.

19. Josef Hofmiller, 'Erinnerung', in *Paul Nikolaus Cossmann zum sechzigsten Geburtstag am 6. April 1929* (Munich: R. Oldenbourg, 1929), pp. viii–xxviii, p. xxiv.

20. 'Der Staat, sein Wesen und seine Organisation', *Süddeutsche Monatshefte*, March 1916, pp. 999–1016; 'England als Feind', April 1915, *Süddeutsche Monatshefte*, pp. 97–100; 'Tirpitz', April 1916, *Süddeutsche Monatshefte*, pp. 1–2; 'Schöpferische und unschöpferische Politik', July 1916, *Süddeutsche Monatshefte*, pp. 409–10.

21. Martin Kitchen, *The Silent Dictatorship: The Politics of the German High Command under Hindenburg and Ludendorff, 1916–1918* (London: Croom Helm, 1976), p. 28.

22. Ezechiel Hasgall to Moritz Hasgall, 30 August 1916, in Hank, Simon and Hank, *Feldrabbiner*, p. 262.

23. 'Eine Erklärung Ballins', *Hamburger Nachrichten*, 30 September 1916, p. 5.

24. Herbert Sulzbach, 31 August 1916, in Sulzbach, *With the German Guns*, pp. 87–8.

25. Kitchen, *Silent Dictatorship*.

26. Gerhard Hecker, ' "Metallum-Aktiengesellschaft": Industrielle und staatliche Interessenidentität im Rahmen des Hindenburg-Programmes', *Militärgeschichtliche Zeitschrift*, 35 (1) (1984), pp. 113–40, p. 115.

27. Wolff, 3 November 1916, in Sösemann, *Tagebücher*, p. 453.

28. Hebert Czapski to Sigmund Feist, 26 December 1916, in Hank and Simon, *Feldpostbriefe*, p. 161.

29. See Presner, *Muscular Judaism*.

30. Die Vorstandschaft der isr. Lehrerbildungsanstalt Würzburg to K. Regierung von Unterfranken, 14 August 1916, CAHJP, D/Wu3, Nr. 3.

31. Dr Horwitz to Lehrer Mannheim, 12 January 1916, CJA, 1.75C, Ve1, Nr. 364, #12987.

32. Ludger Heid, *Ostjuden: Bürger, Kleinbürger, Proletarier – Geschichte einer jüdischen Minderheit im Ruhrgebiet* (Essen: Klartext, 2011), pp. 138–9.

33. Hugo Haase to Ernst Haase, 21 November 1916, in Haase, *Hugo Haase: Sein Leben*, p. 134.

34. Gertrud Bäumer and Alice Bensheimer, 26 November 1916, LAB, B. Rep. 235–01, MF 2737.

35. Bund Deutscher Frauenvereine, to Verbände und Zweigvereine des Bundes Deutscher Frauenvereine, 10 February 1917, LAB, B. Rep. 235–01, MF 2745.

36. Hansjörg Vollmann, *Eigenständigkeit und Konzernintegration: Die Cassella, ihre Eigentümer und ihr Führungspersonal* (Darmstadt: Hessisches Wirtschaftsarchiv, 2011), p. 182.

37. Brigitte Hatke, *Hugo Stinnes und die drei deutsch-belgischen Gesellschaften von 1916* (Stuttgart: Franz Steiner, 1990), p. 83.

38. Harold James, 'Georg Solmssen: Eine biographische Annäherung', in James and Müller, *Solmssen*, pp. 11–52, p. 16.

39. Wende, *Die belgische frage*, pp. 71–2.

40. Rathenau to Ludendorff, 16 September 1916, in Nationalversammlung (ed.), *Das Werk des Untersuchungsausschusses der Verfassungsgebenden Deutschen Nationalversammlung und des deutschen Reichstages 1919–1928*, vol. 3:1 (Berlin: Deutsche Verlagsgesellschaft für Politik und Gesellschaft, 1925–30).

41. 'Schwierigkeiten in der Versorgung der Gaswerke mit Kohlen', 2 June 1916, GStA PK, I. HA, Rep. 121, Nr. 8590.

42. Caesar Wollheim, *Der Kohlenmarkt im zweiten Kriegsjahr* (Berlin: H.S. Hermann, 1916), p. 17.

43. Franz Oppenheimer, *Weltwirtschaft und Nationalwirtschaft* (Berlin: Fischer, 1915), p. 70.

44. Otto Braun to Arnold Wahnschaffe, 15 June 1917, BArch Berlin, R1501/119389. See also: Jens Thiel, '*Menschenbassin Belgien': Anwerbung, Deportation und Zwangsarbeit im Ersten Weltkrieg* (Essen: Klartext, 2007), pp. 148–55.

45. Rathenau to Ludendorff, 23 October 1916, in Rathenau, *Politische*, p. 66.

46. Ludwig Haas, 7 May 1917, cited in Christian Westerhoff, *Zwangsarbeit im Ersten Weltkrieg: Deutsche Arbeitskräftepolitik im besetzten Polen und Litauen 1914–1918* (Paderborn: Schöningh, 2012), p. 236.

47. Westerhoff, *Zwangsarbeit*, p. 112.

48. Ibid., p. 257; Ludger Heid, *Maloche – nicht Mildtätigkeit: ostjüdische Arbeiter in Deutschland 1914–1923* (Hildesheim: Olms, 1995), p. 101.

49. Heid, *Maloche*, pp. 132–4.

50. Westerhoff, *Zwangsarbeit*, pp. 127, 215–16; Liulevicius, *War Land*, p. 73. See also: Andrew Noble Koss, 'World War I and the Remaking of Jewish Vilna' (PhD, Stanford University, 2010).

51. Rathenau to Ludendorff, 6 November 1916, in Rathenau, *Politische*, pp. 70–3.

52. Jochen Oltmer, 'Einführung: Funktionen und Erfahrungen von Kriegsgefangenschaft im Europa des Ersten Weltkrieges', in Oltmer, *Kriegsgefangene*, pp. 11–23, p. 16; Gerhard Höpp, *Muslime in der Mark: Als Kriegsgefangene und Internierte in Wünsdorf und Zossen* (Berlin: Das Arabische Buch, 1999).

53. Felix von Luschan, *Kriegsgefangene: 100 Steinzeichnungen von Hermann Struck* (Berlin: Dietrich Reimer, 1916), p. 3.

54. Margaret Olin, 'Jews among the People: Visual Archives in German Prison Camps during the Great War', in Reinhard Johler, Christian Marchetti and Monique Scheer (eds), *Doing Anthropology in Wartime and War Zones: World War I and the Cultural Sciences in Europe* (Bielefeld: Transcript, 2010), pp. 255–79, p. 258.

55. Heather Jones, 'A Missing Paradigm? Military Captivity and the Prisoner of War, 1914–18', in Matthew Stibbe (ed.), *Captivity, Forced Labour and Forced Migration in Europe during the First World War* (London: Routledge, 2013), pp. 19–48, p. 37.

56. Marie Roosen-Runge-Mollwo (ed.), *Adolph Goldschmidt 1863–1944: Lebenserinnerungen* (Berlin: Deutsche Verlag für Kunstwissenschaft, 1989), pp. 190–1.

57. Janos Riesz, 'Afrikanische Kriegsgefangene in deutschen Lagern während des Ersten Weltkriegs', in Michael Hofmann and Rita Morrien (eds), *Deutsch-afrikanische Diskurse in Geschichte und Gegenwart: Literatur- und kulturwissenschaftliche Perspektiven* (Amsterdam: Rodophi, 2012), pp. 71–106, p. 82.

58. Andrew Evans, *Anthropology at War: World War I and the Science of Race in Germany* (Chicago: University of Chicago Press, 2010), p. 164.

59. Rudolf Marcuse, 'Völkertypen' (Leipzig, 1919).

60. Rudolf Marcuse, 'Voelkertypen aus dem Weltkrieg', *Ost und West*, 1919 (11–12), pp. 281–6, p. 282.

61. Luschan, *Kriegsgefangene*.

62. To Generalkommando des 1. Armeekorps, 5 May 1916, Kriegsarchiv, Stv. Gen. Kdo. I.b.A.K., Nr. 1660.

63. K. Polizeidirektion Munich to Stellv. Generalkommando K.B. 1. Armeekorps, 5 August 1916, Kriegsarchiv, Stv. Gen. Kdo. I.b.A.K., Nr. 1660.

64. Der Präsident des Kriegsernähungsamts to ausserpreusssische Bundesregierungen, 8 August 1916, HstAS, E40/72, Bü30.

65. K. Bezirksamt Eggenfelden to Stellv. Generalkommando I. b. A. K München, 18 December 1916, Kriegsarchiv, Stv. Gen. Kdo. I.b.A.K., Nr. 980.

66. Kriegsministerium to Minister des Innern, 4 March 1916, HStAS, M77/1 Bü413.

67. Benjamin Ziemann, *Gewalt in Ersten Weltkrieg: Töten – Überleben – Verweigern* (Essen: Klartext, 2013), p. 95.

68. Klemperer, *Curriculum*, pp. 538–9.

69. K. Bolz to Generalkommando München, 27 July 1916 and I. Erz.-Batl. 3. Inf-Rgt. 7. Komp., to Generalkommando München, both in Kriegsarchiv, Stv. Gen. Kdo. I.b.A.K., Nr. 549. More generally, see: Christoph Jahr, *Gewöhnliche Soldaten: Desertion und Deserteure im deutschen und britischen Heer 1914–1918* (Göttingen: Vandenhoeck & Ruprecht, 1998), p. 263.

70. Dietz Behring, *The Stigma of Names: Antisemitism in German Daily Life, 1812–1933* (Cambridge: Polity, 1992), p. 5.

71. Johannes Leicht, *Heinrich Claß 1868–1953: Die politische Biographie eines Alldeutschen* (Paderborn: Schöningh, 2012), p. 224; Alfred Roth cited in Zechlin, *Die deutsche Politik*, p. 522.

72. Der Chef des Stabes, Oberkommando in den Marken to Ministerium des Innern, 3 September 1916, BArch Berlin, R1501/113714.

73. Max Below to Generalkommando des 1. Armeekorps, 6 June 1916, Kriegsarchiv, Abt. IV, Stv. Gen. Kdo. I.b.A.K., Nr. 1660.
74. Holger Herwig, *The German Naval Officer Corps: A Social and Political History 1890–1918* (Oxford: Clarendon, 1973), p. 96; Angress, 'Das deutsche Militär', p. 79.
75. Rosenthal, 'Die Ehre', pp. 51–2.
76. Julius Marx, 2 November 1916, in Marx, *Kriegstagebuch*, p. 138.
77. Adam Tooze, *Statistics and the German State, 1900–1945* (Cambridge: Cambridge University Press, 2001), p. 65.
78. Geschäftsordnung des Ausschusses für die statistischen Erhebungen über die Beteiligung der Juden am Kriege, 1915, CJA, 1.75C, Ve1, Nr. 222 #12845.
79. Ferdinand Werner, 17 June 1916, cited in Rosenthal, 'Die Ehre', p. 52.
80. Rosenthal, 'Die Ehre', p. 54.
81. Christopher Dowe, *Matthias Erzberger: Ein Leben für die Demokratie* (Stuttgart: W. Kohlhammer, 2011), p. 64.
82. Stibbe, *British Civilian Internees*, p. 59.
83. Angress, 'Das deutsche Militär', pp. 80–1.
84. Helmut Reichold, *Adolf Wild von Hohenborn: Briefe und Tagebuchaufzeichnungen des preußischen Generals als Kriegsminister und Truppenführer im Ersten Weltkrieg* (Boppard am Rhein: Harald Boldt, 1986), p. 6.
85. 'Nochmals – Judenzählung!', *Der Schild*, 17 May 1926, p. 154.
86. 'Judenzählung 1916', *Der Schild*, 3 May 1926, p. 134.
87. Appelbaum, *Loyal Sons*, p. 250; Zechlin, *Die deutsche Politik*, p. 538.
88. Paula Glück, 12 January 1917, in Hank, Simon and Hank, *Feldrabbiner*, p. 285.
89. Leopold Rosenak to Verband der deutschen Juden, 24 December 1916, in ibid., p. 373.
90. Jakob Sonderling to Ausschuss des Verbandes der Deutschen Juden, 29 December 1916, in ibid., p. 417.
91. 73. Sitzung, 3 November 1916, in 'Verhandlungen des Deutschen Reichstags': online at http://www.reichstagsprotokolle.de/rtbiiauf.html (accessed 30 January 2017).
92. 'Die Glaubens-Statistik im Heere', *Im deutschen Reich*, November–December 1916, p. 243; 'Judenzählung', *Jüdische Rundschau*, 27 October 1916, p. 351.
93. 'Die Rede des Reichtagsabgeordneten Dr. Haas', *Im deutschen Reich*, November–December 1916, p. 258–64.
94. Hermann von Stein to Oskar Cassel, 3 January 1917, BArch Berlin, R43/908; Angress, 'Das deutsche Militär', pp. 83–7.
95. Armee-Oberkommando 4, 9 October 1916, HStAS, M33/2, Bü681.

Chapter 7 Breakdown

1. Leo Baeck Institut Jerusalem (ed.), *Sechzig Jahre gegen den Strom: Ernst A. Simon – Briefe von 1917–1984* (Tübingen: Mohr Siebeck, 1998), p. 1.
2. Ernst Simon, 'Unser Kriegserlebnis', in Ernst Simon (ed.), *Brücken: Gesammelte Aufsätze* (Heidelberg: Lambert Schneider, 1965), pp. 17–23, p. 22.
3. Christhard Hoffmann, 'Between Integration and Rejection: The Jewish Community in Germany 1914–1918', in John Horne (ed.), *State, Society and Mobilization in Europe during the First World War* (Cambridge: Cambridge University Press, 1997), pp. 89–104; Clemens Picht, 'Zwischen Vaterland und Volk: Das deutsche Judentum im Ersten Weltkrieg', in Wolfgang Michalka (ed.), *Der Erste Weltkrieg: Wirkung, Wahrnehmung, Analyse* (Munich: Piper, 1994), pp. 736–55; Paul Mendes-Flohr, 'The "Kriegserlebnis" and Jewish Consciousness', in Wolfgang Benz (ed.), *Jüdisches Leben in der Weimarer Republik = Jews in the Weimar Republic* (Tübingen: Mohr Siebeck, 1998), pp. 225–37.
4. 'Ehrentafel', *K.C.-Blätter*, May–June–July 1917, p. 869.
5. Martin Salomonski, *Jüdische Seelsorge an der Westfront* (Berlin: Lamm, 1918), p. 9; Martin Salomonski, *Ein Jahr an der Somme* (Frankfurt an der Oder: Trowitsch & Sohn, 1917), pp. 76, 81.
6. Klemperer, *Curriculum*, p. 366.

7. Arnold Zweig, 'Judenzählung vor Verdun', *Jüdische Rundschau*, 22 December 1916, pp. 4–5.

8. Marx, *Kriegs-Tagebuch*, p. 138.

9. Ibid., p. 144.

10. Georg Salzberger, *Aus meinem Kriegstagebuch* (Frankfurt: Voigt & Gleiber, 1916), p. 131.

11. Bernd Ulrich, 'Die Desillusionierung der Kriegsfreiwilligen von 1914', in Wolfram Wette (ed.), *Der Krieg des kleinen Mannes: Eine Militärgeschichte von unten* (Munich: Piper, 1992), pp. 110–26, p. 121.

12. Arnold Zweig to Willi Handl, 3 February 1915, in Wenzel, *Zweig*, p. 71.

13. Marx, *Kriegs-Tagebuch*, p. 112.

14. 'Dr. Salzberger: Aus meinem Kriegstagebuch', *Liberales Judentum*, July–August 1916, pp. 89–95.

15. Arnold Zweig to Martin Buber, 15 February 1917, in Wenzel, *Zweig*, p. 74.

16. 'Die innere Wandlung unserer jüdischen Feldgrauen', *Frankfurter Israelitisches Familienblatt*, 29 November 1918, in Hank, Simon and Hank, *Feldrabbiner*, p. 400.

17. Edward Madigan, *Faith under Fire: Anglican Chaplains and the Great War* (Basingstoke: Palgrave Macmillan, 2011), p. 249. See for example: Isaac Rosenberg, 27 September 1918, in Fred Gottlieb (ed.), *My Opa: The Diary of a German Rabbi* (Jerusalem: Chaim Mazo, 2005), p. 185.

18. Salzberger, *Kriegstagebuch*, p. 129.

19. Julius Goldstein, 19 July 1917, in Uwe Zuber (ed.), *Julius Goldstein. Der jüdische Philosoph in seinen Tagebüchern: 1873–1929, Hamburg – Jena – Darmstadt* (Wiesbaden: Kommission für die Geschichte der Juden in Hessen, 2008), pp. 142–3.

20. Martin Buber, 'Die Losung', *Der Jude*, April 1916, pp. 1–3; Eleonore Lappin, *Der Jude, 1916–1928: Jüdische Moderne zwischen Universalismus und Partikularismus* (Tübingen: Mohr Siebeck, 2000), pp. 68–70.

21. Lappin, *Jude*, pp. 60–1.

22. B., 'Judenzählung', *Der Jude*, November 1916, p. 564.

23. Aberbach, *European Jews*, p. 164.

24. Willy Cohn, *Verwehte Spuren: Erinnerungen an das Breslauer Judentum vor seinem Untergang* (Cologne: Böhlau, 1995), p. 225.

25. 'Aus den Bundesverbänden und -Vereinen', *Die Frauenfrage: Zentralblatt des Bundes Deutscher Frauenvereine*, 1 March 1917, p. 35.

26. Max Hermann Maier, *'In uns verwoben tief und wunderbar': Erinnerungen an Deutschland* (Frankfurt: Josef Knecht, 1972), p. 100.

27. 'Vereinsnachrichten', *Im deutschen Reich*, September 1917, p. 372; 'Maximillian Horwitz', *Im deutschen Reich*, November 1917, pp. 434–44, p. 441.

28. Davis, *Home Fires Burning*, p. 180.

29. 'Kohlrüben, Wruken, Bodenkohlrabi, Steckrüben anstatt Kartofeln', LAB, B. Rep. 235–01, MF2752.

30. Davis, *Home Fires Burning*, p. 184.

31. Margarete Sallis-Freudenthal, *Ich habe mein Land gefunden: Autobiographischer Rückblick* (Frankfurt: Josef Knecht, 1977), pp. 52–3.

32. Sulzbach, *With the German Guns*, p. 93.

33. See also: Karin Huser, *'Haltet gut Jontef und seid herzlichst geküsst': Feldpostbriefe des Elsässer Juden Henri Levy von der Ostfront (1916–1918)* (Zurich: Chronos, 2014), pp. 113–15.

34. Abschrift aus dem Schreiben des Armeerabbiners S. Levi, 10 February 1917, CJA, 1.75C, Ve1, Nr. 227 #12850.

35. Bendit, 25 October 1916, in Rueß and Stölzle, *Tagebuch*, pp. 137–8.

36. K.u.K. Majestät to Aron Tänzer, 5 November 1916, LBINY, AR485; Kaiserlich Osmanisches Ernährungsamt to Dr Oppenheimer, 21 March 1917, LBINY, AR4105.

37. Julius Goldstein, 21 December 1916, in Zuber, *Philosoph*, p. 135.

38. 'Protokoll der Sitzung des Gesamtsusschusses', 20 April 1917, CJA, 1.75C, Ve1, Nr. 227, #12850; Sulzbach, *With the German Guns*, p. 93.

39. Maier, *Erinnerungen*, p. 101.

40. Riess von Scheurnschloss to Wahnschaffe, 16 January 1917, BArch MA, FB1898N.
41. 'Städtische Nachrichten', *Bonner Zeitung*, 2 October 1917, p. 2; *Coburger Zeitung*, 2 October 1917, p. 1.
42. Ernst Lissauer, 'Hindenburg', *Front*, 30 September 1917, pp. 2–4.
43. Schul- und Talmud-Torah-Vorstand der jüdischen Gemeinde, 24 October 1917, CJA, 1.75C, Ge1, Nr. 956, #10846.
44. Andrew Donson, *Youth in the Fatherless Land: War Pedagogy, Nationalism and Authority in Germany, 1914–1918* (Cambridge, Mass.: Harvard University Press, 2010), pp. 173–4, 197.
45. Alice Salomon, 'Vom Leben deutscher Helferinnen in einer östlichen Etappe', *Die Frauenfrage, Zentralblatt des Bundes deutscher Frauenvereine*, 1 November 1917, pp. 153–5.
46. Lion Wolff, *Durch Nacht zum Licht, durch Kampf zum Sieg* (Tempelburg: Manig, 1917), p. 44.
47. Pferde-Depot der Truppen to Kriegsamstelle Magdeburg, 26 January 1918; Kaiserl. Deutsches Militär-Gouvernement Siedlce to Kriegsamtstelle Warschau, 27 December 1917, BArch MA, PH2/776.
48. Ute Daniel, *Arbeiterfrauen in der Kriegsgesellschaft: Beruf, Familie und Politik im Ersten Weltkrieg* (Göttingen: Vandenhoeck & Ruprecht, 1989), p. 93.
49. 'Lebenslauf von Sophie Hellmann', LBINY, AR6436.
50. Gefangenenlager I Stuttgart, 3 April 1917, HstAS, M1/4, Bü958.
51. Fritz Haber to Farbwerke Lucius und Brüning, 12 June 1917, Archiv der Max-Planck-Gesellschaft, Dept. Va, Rep. 5, 516.
52. Szöllösi-Janze, *Haber*, pp. 365–8.
53. Fritz Haber, 18 September 1917, Archiv der Max-Planck-Gesellschaft, Dept. Va, Rep. 5, 1616.
54. Davis Trietsch, *Afrikanische Kriegsziele* (Berlin: Süsserott, 1917), pp. 1, 30.
55. Karl Emil Schabinger Freiherr von Schowingen, 'Weltgeschichtliche Mosaiksplitter: Erlebnisse und Erinnerungen eines kaiserlichen Dragomans' (Baden-Baden, 1967), pp. 128–31.
56. Alexander Watson, *Ring of Steel: Germany and Austria-Hungary at War, 1914–1918* (London: Allen Lane, 2014), p. 421.
57. Holger Herwig, 'Total Rhetoric, Limited War: Germany's U-Boat Campaign, 1917–1918', in Roger Chickering and Stig Förster (eds), *Great War, Total War: Combat and Mobilization on the Western Front, 1914–1918* (Cambridge: Cambridge University Press, 2000), pp. 189–206, p. 194.
58. Wolff, 20 March 1916, in Sösemann, *Tagebücher*, p. 362. For example, 'U-Boot Krieg und Parlament', *Vossische Zeitung*, 18 March 1916, p. 3.
59. W. Loewenfeld to Zimmermann, 25 April 1916, PA–AA, R21529.
60. Bernhard, *Kriegspolitik*, p. 21.
61. Wolff, 26 January 1917, in Sösemann, *Tagebücher*, p. 475; Warburg, *Aufzeichnungen*, p. 55.
62. Baldur Kaulisch, 'Die Auseinandersetzungen über den uneingeschränkten U-Boot-Krieg innerhalb der herrschenden Klassen im zweiten Halbjahr 1916 und seine Eröffnung im Februar 1917', in Fritz Klein (ed.), *Politik im Krieg 1914–1918* (Berlin: Akademie, 1964), pp. 90–118, pp. 97–8.
63. 'U-Bootspende', 26 Februar 1917, BArch Berlin, R43/2415a; 'U-Boot-Spende', *Märkischer Sprecher*, 30 May 1917, BArch Berlin, R43/2415a.
64. Watson, *Ring of Steel*, p. 433.
65. Schröder, *U-Boote*, p. 437.
66. Zentralnachweiseamt für Kriegerverluste u. Kriegergräber, 'Militär-Dienstzeitbescheinigung', 31 August 1933, JMB, 2004/61/60.
67. Max Haller, 30 June, JMB, 2004/61/53.
68. Harald Bendert, *Die UC-Boote der Kaiserlichen Marine 1914–1918* (Hamburg: E.S. Mittler, 2001), pp. 98–9.
69. Max Haller, 22–23 August, JMB, 2004/61/53.

70. Rathenau to General von Seeckt, 1 March 1917, in Rathenau, *Politische*, pp. 100–3.
71. 'The President Calls for War Without Hate', *New York Tribune*, 3 April 1917, p. 1.
72. 'Kriegszustand', *Vossische Zeitung*, 3 April 1917, pp. 1–2.
73. Gebr. Arnhold, 'Das Wirtschaftsleben während der Kriegszeit', 28 April 1917, BArch MA, N30/9.
74. Hans-Ulrich Wehler, *Deutsche Gesellschaftsgeschichte 1914–1949* (Munich: Beck, 2003), p. 135.
75. Gustav Mayer, 26 April 1917, in Gottfried Niedhart (ed.), *Gustav Mayer, als deutsch-jüdischer Historiker in Krieg und Revolution 1914–1920* (Munich: Oldenbourg, 2009), p. 115.
76. Oberkommando in den Marken to Kriegsministerium, 17 April 1917, BArch MA, PH2/414.
77. Kriegsministerium, 'Nachrichten über Arbeiterbewegung', 18 May 1917, BArch MA, PH2/414; Calkins, *Haase*, p. 142.
78. Leicht, *Claß*, p. 243.
79. 'Proclamation of the Independent Social-Democratic Party', 20 April 1917, in Lutz, *Fall*, p. 45.
80. 'Hindenburgbrief und Munitionsstreik', *Alldeutsche Blätter*, 28 April 1917, p. 195; 'Modell Cohn', *Mitteilungen aus dem Verein zur Abwehr des Antisemitismus*, 16 May 1917, pp. 15–16.
81. 101. Sitzung, 5 May 1917, in 'Verhandlungen des Deutschen Reichstags': online at http://www.reichstagsprotokolle.de/rtbiiauf.html (accessed 30 January 2017).
82. 'Zur Reichstagsrede des Herrn Abg. Dr. Cohn', *Im deutschen Reich*, July–August 1917, pp. 314–15.
83. *Kölnische Volkszeitung*, 8 July 1917, in Lutz, *Fall*, p. 275.
84. Chickering, *Imperial Germany*, p. 161.
85. 'Annahme der Friedensresolution im Reichstage', *Berliner Tageblatt*, 20 July 1917, p. 1.
86. 116. Sitzung, 19 July 1917, in 'Verhandlungen des Deutschen Reichstags': online at http://www.reichstagsprotokolle.de/rtbiiauf.html (accessed 30 January 2017); Eduard David, 19 July 1917, in Miller, *Kriegstagebuch*, pp. 248–9.
87. Zechlin, *Die deutsche Politik*, p. 548.
88. Eugen Zimmermann, 'Albert Ballins Fahrt ins grosse Hauptquartier', GStA PK, BPH, Rep. 192, Nl Zimmermann, E., Nr. 17.
89. 'Bethmann', *Süddeutsche Monatshefte*, August 1917, pp. 621–7; Hugo Haase to Ernst Haase, 27 July 1917, in Haase, *Hugo Haase: Sein Leben*, pp. 148–9.
90. Werner Jochmann, 'Die Ausbreitung des Antisemitismus', in Werner Mosse (ed.), *Deutsches Judentum in Krieg und Revolution, 1916–1923* (Tübingen: Mohr, 1971), pp. 409–510, p. 432.
91. For this view, see: Anthony Kauders, 'Legally Citizens: Jewish Exclusion from the Weimar Polity', in Wolfgang Benz, Anthony Paucker and Peter Pulzer (eds), *Jüdisches Leben in der Weimarer Republik = Jews in the Weimar Republic* (Tübingen: Mohr Siebeck, 1998), pp. 159–172, p. 160.
92. 'Die Verantwortlichen', *Vossische Zeitung*, 19 July 1917, pp. 1–2.
93. Adolf Grabowsky, 'Wahre und falsche Weltpolitik', *Das neue Deutschland*, 1 October 1917, pp. 1–6; 'Zu den Friedenserklärung des Reichstags', *Süddeutsche Monatshefte*, September 1917, p. 735. On Cossmann, see: Karl Alexander von Müller, *Aus Gärten der Vergangenheit* (Stuttgart: Gustav Klipper, 1951), p. 485.
94. Wehler, *Gesellschaftsgeschichte*, p. 125; Richard Stegmann, *Die Erben Bismarcks: Parteien und Verbände in der Spätphase der Wilhelmischen Deutschlands – Sammlungspolitik 1897–1918* (Cologne: Kiepenheuer & Witsch, 1970), p. 508.
95. Daniel Hope, *Familienstücke: Eine Spurensuche* (Hamburg: Rowohlt, 2008), p. 92; Auswärtiges Amt, 18 May 1918, BArch Berlin, R43/1422b.
96. Heinz Hagenlücke, *Deutsche Vaterlandspartei: Die nationale Rechte am Ende des Kaiserreiches* (Düsseldorf: Droste, 1997), p. 174.
97. 'Die Deutsche Vaterlandspartei und der Antisemitismus', *Im deutschen Reich*, March 1918, pp. 104–6.

98. Martin Ulmer, *Antisemitismus in Stuttgart 1871–1933: Studien zum öffentlichen Diskurs und Alltag* (Berlin: Metropol, 2011), pp. 196–7.
99. David Nirenberg, *Anti-Judaism: The Western Tradition* (London: Norton, 2013), pp. 428–39.
100. Erich Schlesinger to Mainzer, 12 May 1917, in *K.C.-Blätter*, May 1917, pp. 875–6; Bendit, 27 March 1917, in Rueß and Stölzle (eds), *Tagebuch*, p. 148.
101. Heinemann Stern, *Warum hassen sie uns eigentlich? Jüdisches Leben zwischen den Kriegen* (Düsseldorf: Droste, 1970), p. 101; William Katz, *Ein jüdisch-deutsches Leben, 1904–1939–1978* (Tübingen: Katzmann, 1980), p. 59.
102. Ziemann, *Gewalt*, p. 86.
103. Weber, *Hitler's First War*, pp. 176–7.
104. Ulrich Sieg, *Jüdische Intellektuelle im Ersten Weltkrieg: Kreigserfahrungen, weltanschauliche Debatten und kulturelle Neuentwürfe* (Berlin: Akademie, 2001), pp. 242–3.
105. Martin Buber to Werner Kraft, 15 March 1917, in Schaeder, *Martin Buber: Briefwechsel*, pp. 477–8.
106. Ulrich Sieg, 'Bekenntnis zu nationalen und universalen Werten: jüdische Philosophen im Deutschen Kaiserreich', *Historische Zeitschrift*, 263 (1996), pp. 609–39, pp. 622–6.
107. Arthur Hantke, 22 November 1917, in Reinharz, *Dokumente*, pp. 200–2.
108. 'Was will das liberale Judentum?', *Liberales Judentum*, January 1918, pp. 1–3, p. 2.
109. Hans Jonas, *Erinnerungen* (Frankfurt: Insel, 2003), p. 57; Gershom Scholem, *Von Berlin nach Jerusalem: Jugenderinnerungen* (Frankfurt: Suhrkamp, 1977), p. 110.

Chapter 8 Myths of Defeat

1. Arnold Tänzer, *Geschichte der Juden in Brest-Litowsk* (Berlin: Louis Lamm, 1918), p. 6.
2. Representative of Kaiser Wilhelm II to Arnold Tänzer, 23 March 1918; Ludendorff to Arnold Tänzer, 6 February 1918; representative of Hindenburg to Arnold Tänzer, 4 February 1918. All in LBINY, AR485.
3. 'Der Kaiser an Heer und Flotte', *Coburger Zeitung*, 3 January 1918, p. 1.
4. Rahel Straus, *Wir lebten in Deutschland: Erinnerungen einer deutschen Jüdin, 1880–1933* (Stuttgart: DVA, 1961), p. 215.
5. Davis, *Home Fires Burning*, p. 222; K. Polizeidirektion, 11 March 1918, Kriegsarchiv, Stv. Gen. Kdo. I.b.A.K., Nr. 552.
6. Stephen Bailey, 'The Berlin Strike of January 1918', *Central European History*, 13 (2) (1980), pp. 158–74, pp. 159–60; Hugo Haase, *Reichstagsreden gegen die Kriegspolitik* (Berlin: Neues Vaterland, 1919), p. 150; Bernhard Grau, *Kurt Eisner, 1867–1919: Eine Biographie* (Munich: Beck, 2001), pp. 335–6.
7. Uwe Lohalm, *Völkischer Radikalismus: Die Geschichte des Deutschvölkischen Schutz- und Trutz-Bundes 1919–1923* (Hamburg: Leibnitz, 1970), p. 74.
8. 'Die Streikbewegung in Groß-Berlin', *Berliner Tageblatt*, 29 January 1918, p. 2.
9. Rathenau to Fedor von Perbandt, 7 February 1918, in Rathenau, *Politische*, pp. 170–1.
10. 'Die Woche', *Allgemeine Zeitung des Judentums*, 8 February 1918, p. 63.
11. 'Wirkungen', *Vossische Zeitung*, 1 February 1918, p. 1.
12. Rainer Sammet, *'Dolchstoss': Deutschland und die Auseinandersetzung mit der Niederlage im Ersten Weltkrieg (1918–1933)* (Berlin: Trafo, 2003), p. 207.
13. 'Überwachungsbericht der 5. Armee', 24 February 1918, in Bernd Ulrich and Benjamin Ziemann (eds), *Frontalltag im Ersten Weltkrieg: Quellen und Dokumente* (Frankfurt: Fischer, 1994), pp. 136–7; Victor Ehrenberg to Eduard Meyer, 2 February 1918, in Gert Audring, Christhard Hoffmann and Jürgen von Ungern-Sternberg (eds), *Eduard Meyer – Victor Ehrenberg: Ein Briefwechsel, 1914–1930* (Berlin: Akademie, 1990), p. 99.
14. Ziemann, *Gewalt*, pp. 122–3.
15. Sulzbach, *With the German Guns*, p. 144.
16. Wehler, *Deutsche Gesellschaftsgeschichte*, p. 152.
17. Ludendorff, *My War Memories*, p. 562; 'A People's Peace', *The Times*, 8 March 1918, p. 3.
18. Ludger Heid, *Oskar Cohn: Ein Sozialist und Zionist im Kaiserreich und in der Weimarer Republik* (Frankfurt: Campus, 2002), p. 157.

19. Susanne Miller, *Burgfrieden und Klassenkampf: Die deutsche Sozialdemokratie im Ersten Weltkrieg* (Düsseldorf: Droste, 1974), p. 367.
20. 'Die Laus im Pelz', *Auf Vorposten*, March–April 1918, pp. 522–6. More generally: Saul Friedländer, 'Die politischen Veränderung der Kriegszeit', in Mosse (ed.), *Deutsches Judentum*, pp. 27–65, p. 46.
21. 142. Sitzung, 18 March 1918, in 'Verhandlungen des Deutschen Reichstags': online at http://www.reichstagsprotokolle.de/rtbiiauf.html (accessed 30 January 2017).
22. Rathenau to Major Steinbömer, 1 March 1918, in Rathenau, *Politische*, p. 173.
23. Klemperer, *Curriculum*, p. 608.
24. Davis Trietsch, *Georgien und der Kaukasus* (Berlin: Deutsch-Georgische Gesellschaft, 1918), pp. 10–15, 24–7.
25. Fischer, *Griff*, pp. 724, 756; Manfred Nebelin, *Ludendorff: Diktatur im Ersten Weltkrieg* (Munich: Siedler, 2010), pp. 380–1.
26. 'Die Woche', *Allgemeine Zeitung des Judentums*, 8 March 1918, p. 111.
27. Amitai, 'Chronik', *Der Jude*, 1918–19, Heft 2, pp. 55–61, p. 56.
28. 'Die Woche', p. 111; Heid, *Cohn*, p. 159.
29. 'VIOD', *Neue jüdische Monatshefte*, 10 March 1918, pp. 263–4; Panter, *Jüdische Erfahrungen*, p. 283.
30. 'Städtische Nachrichten', *Bonner Zeitung*, 4 March 1918, p. 2.
31. Henri Levy to his parents, 3 March 1918, in Huser, *Feldpostbriefe*, pp. 135–6.
32. Watson, *Ring of Steel*, p. 517.
33. Gronemann, *Hawdoloh*, pp. 223–6.
34. Ibid., p. 227.
35. Kaiserlich Deutsche Gesandschaft, 14 March 1918, PA–AA, R14134.
36. Chickering, *Great War and German Life*, p. 551.
37. Vaterländischer Frauen-Verein to Staatskommissar für die Regelung der Kriegswohlfahrtspflege in Preussen, 28 February 1918, GStA PK, I. HA, Rep. 191, Nr. 3733.
38. Reichsbank-Direktorium, 17 February 1918, LBINY, AR6455.
39. Israelitische Oberkirchenbehörde to Rabbiner u. Vorsänger, 18 March 1918, HstAS, E130a, Bü1203.
40. Anton Kaes, *Shell Shock Cinema: Weimar Culture and the Wounds of War* (Princeton: Princeton University Press, 2009), p. 144.
41. 'Der Sieg des Schwertes', *Vossische Zeitung*, 25 March 1918, p. 1.
42. 'Umschau', *Im deutschen Reich*, April 1917, pp. 155–7.
43. 'Flucht aus Sibirien', *Vossische Zeitung*, 16 April 1918, p. 2; 'Die Flucht eines Berliner Juden aus Sibirien', *Im deutschen Reich*, April 1918, p. 174.
44. Walter Foerster to Goldmann, 18 April 1918, *K.C.-Blätter*, May–June 1918, pp. 1061–2; Alfred Baruch to Sigmund Feist, 12 April 1918, in Hank and Simon, *Feldpostbriefe*, p. 55.
45. Chickering, *Imperial Germany*, pp. 179–80.
46. Asprey, *German High Command*, p. 398.
47. Fuchs to Goldmann, 5 April 1918, *K.C.-Blätter*, March–April 1918, pp. 1025–6; Ludwig Hirsch, 17 July 1918, in Max Freundenthal (ed.), *Kriegsgedenkbuch der israelitischen Kultusgemeinde Nürnberg* (Nuremberg: Rosenfeld's, 1920), p. 122.
48. Victor Ehrenberg to Eduard Meyer, 24 July 1918, in Audring, Hoffmann and Ungern-Sternberg, *Meyer*, pp. 102–3.
49. Georg Alexander von Müller, 12 June 1918, in Walter Görlitz (ed.), *The Kaiser and his Court: The Diaries, Note Books and Letters of Admiral Georg Alexander von Müller, Chief of the Naval Cabinet, 1914–1918* (London: Macdonald, 1961), p. 361.
50. To: Stellv. Generalkommando I.A.K. München, 11 July 1918, Kriegsarchiv, Stv. Gen. Kdo. I.b.A.K., Nr. 553.
51. 'Die Juden im Weltkriege', July 1918, Kriegsarchiv, Stv. Gen. Kdo. I.b.A.K., Nr. 1895.
52. Central-Verein to Stellv. Generalkommando München, 5 August 1918, Kriegsarchiv, Stv. Gen. Kdo. I.b.A.K., Nr. 1878.
53. Holländer to Fuchs, 4 February 1918, Zentralarchiv, B.3/52, Nr. 3.
54. Heid, *Maloche*, p. 12.

55. Stadtdirektion Stuttgart to Stellv. Generalkommando Stuttgart, 7 May 1918, HstAS, M77/1, Bü875.
56. 'Zeitungsstimmen', *Im deutschen Reich*, March 1918, p. 135.
57. Wolfgang Heinze, 'Internationale jüdische Beziehungen', *Preußische Jahrbücher*, September 1917, pp. 340–66, p. 358.
58. Trude Maurer, *Ostjuden in Deutschland 1918–1933* (Hamburg: Hans Christians Verlag, 1986), p. 39.
59. Der Verwaltungschef beim Generalgouvernement Warschau to Kreischefs und Polizeipräsidenten, 24 May 1918, BArch Berlin, R1501/11320.
60. Moses Zitron, 17 June 1918, BArch Berlin, R1501/113720; Trude Maurer, 'Medizinalpolitik und Antisemitismus: Die deutsche Politik der Grenzsperre gegen Ostjuden im Ersten Weltkrieg', *Jahrbücher für Geschichte Osteuropas*, 33 (1985), pp. 205–30, p. 211.
61. 'Deutsche Grenzsperre gegen Ostjuden', *Im deutschen Reich*, September 1918, p. 360.
62. Bernhard Chaskel to Centralverein, 23 May 1918, CJA, 1.75C, Ve1, Nr. 169, #12792.
63. 'Grenzschluß gegen Juden in Deutschland', *Jüdische Rundschau*, 26 July 1918, p. 1.
64. Heid, *Maloche*, p. 70.
65. 'Die ostjüdischen Arbeiter in Deutschland', 12 April 1918, BArch Berlin, R1501/113720.
66. Vereinigung Jüdischer Organisationen Deutschlands to Graf von Hertling, 26 June 1918, BArch Berlin, R1501/113720.
67. Franz Oppenheimer to Hermann Struck, 3 May 1918, LBINY, MF13.
68. 'Aufzeichnung über die Besprechung am 15. April 1918 im Reichsamt des Innern, betreffend die Regelung der Beschäftigung und Abschiebung der im Inland befindlichen polnischen Juden', R1501/113719.
69. Aba Strazhas, 'Die Tätigkeit des Dezernats für jüdische Angelegenheiten in der "Deutschen Militärverwaltung Ober Ost" ', in Andrew Ezergailis and Gert von Pistohlkors (eds), *Die Baltischen Provinzen Russlands zwischen den Revolutionen von 1905 und 1917* (Cologne: Böhlau, 1982), pp. 315–29, p. 325.
70. Paul von Hintze cited in Nebelin, *Ludendorff*, p. 462.
71. Nebelin, *Ludendorff*, p. 490.
72. Ludwig Hirsch, 27 September 1918, in *Kriegsbriefe gefallener deutscher Juden*, p. 58.
73. Helmut Freund, 'Skizzen und Bilder aus dem Kriegstagebuch eines angehenden Arztes', LBINY, ME264, p. 295.
74. Watson, *Ring of Steel*, p. 528.
75. 29. Inf. Div to Gruppe Endres, 16 October 1918, BArch MA, PH8-I/549.
76. Herbert Czapski to Sigmund Feist, 29 October 1918, in Hank and Simon, *Feldpostbriefe*, p. 190.
77. Alexander Watson, *Enduring the Great War: Combat, Morale and Collapse in the German and British Armies, 1914–1918* (Cambridge: Cambridge University Press, 2008), p. 215. There has been considerable debate over the causes and extent of German indiscipline; see: Wilhelm Deist, 'The Military Collapse of the German Empire', *War in History*, 3 (2) (1996), pp. 186–207; Ziemann, *Gewalt*, pp. 134–53; Jahr, *Soldaten*.
78. Watson, *Enduring*, p. 204.
79. 'Ehrentafel', *K.C.-Blätter*, September–October 1918, p. 1137.
80. 'Armee-Tagesbefehl', 24 August 1918, HstAS, M33/2, Bü634.
81. Siegfried Klein to Jakob Guttmann, 10 September 1918, in Hank, Simon and Hank, *Feldrabbiner*, p. 287.
82. Alice Bensheimer to Verband deutscher Hausfrauenvereine, 4 October 1918, LAB, B. Rep 235-01, MF2752.
83. 'Politische Umgruppierung', *Vossische Zeitung*, 9 October 1918, pp. 1–2.
84. Walther Rathenau to Heinrich Scheüch, 9 October 1918, in Rathenau, *Politische*, pp. 188–91.
85. 'Vorbedingungen des Friedens', *Vossische Zeitung*, 25 October 1918, p. 1.
86. Max Warburg cited in Saul Friedländer, 'Political Transformations during the War and their Effect on the Jewish Question', in Herbert Strauss (ed.), *Hostages of Modernization:*

Studies on Modern Antisemitism 1870–1933/39, vol. 3/1 (Berlin: Walter de Gruyter, 1933), pp. 150–64, p. 156.

87. Max von Baden, *Erinnerungen und Dokumente* (Hamburg: Severus, [1927] 2011), p. 382.
88. 'Ein dunkler Tag', *Vossische Zeitung*, 7 October 1918; Michael Geyer, 'Insurrectionary Warfare: The German Debate about a *Levée en Masse* in October 1918', *Journal of Modern History*, 73 (3) (2001), pp. 459–527.
89. 'Frieden oder Endkampf', *Vossische Zeitung*, 23 October 1918, p. 1; 'Wilsons Antwort auf die deutsche Antwort', *Vossische Zeitung*, 16 October 1918, pp. 1–2.
90. 'Der Rücktritt Ludendorffs', *Berliner Tageblatt*, 27 October 1918, p. 1.

Chapter 9 The End

1. 'Cheering Crowds', *The Times*, 12 November 1918, p. 10.
2. Joseph Levy, 'Mein Leben in Deutschland vor und nach 1933', LBINY, ME383, pp. 23–4.
3. 'Noch keine Antwort des Kaisers', *Berliner Tageblatt*, 8 November 1918, p. 1.
4. Verhey, *Spirit*, pp. 206–14.
5. Lorenz Beckhardt, *Der Jude mit dem Hakenkreuz: Meine deutsche Familie* (Berlin: Aufbau, 2014), p. 87.
6. Otto Meyer, 13 November 1918, 21 November 1918, 6 December 1918 and 9 December 1918, in Andreas Meyer (ed.), *Als deutscher Jude im Ersten Weltkrieg: Der Fabrikant und Offizier Otto Meyer* (Berlin: be.bra, 2014), pp. 127–30.
7. Friedrich Rülf to Verband der deutschen Juden, 12 December 1918, in Hank, Simon and Hank, *Feldrabbiner*, p. 380.
8. Straus, *Wir lebten in Deutschland*, p. 226.
9. Note, 11 November 1918, LAB, B. Rep 235–01, MF2742.
10. Josephine Levy-Rathenau, 'Frauengedanken zur sozialen. Übergangsfürsorge', *Zeitschrift für das Armenwesen*, January–March 1918, p. 21.
11. Birthe Kundrus, *Kriegerfrauen: Familienpolitik und Geschlechterverhältnisse im Ersten und Zweiten Weltkrieg* (Hamburg: Christians, 1995), p. 208.
12. Max Sichel, 'Nervöse Folgezustände von Alkohol und Syphilis bei den Juden', *Zeitschrift für Demographie und Statistik der Juden*, August–December 1919, pp. 137–41, p. 139.
13. Ebert to Fanny Joseph, 9 November 1918, LBINY, AR6179.
14. Tim Grady, *The German-Jewish Soldiers of the First World War in History and Memory* (Liverpool: Liverpool University Press, 2011), pp. 65–76.
15. 'Ein Mahnwort in letzter Stunde!', *Israelitisches Familienblatt*, 29 November 1918, p. 2.
16. 'Albert Ballin †', *Hamburger Nachrichten*, 10 November 1918, p. 9.
17. Jörn Leonhard, *Die Büchse der Pandora: Geschichte des Ersten Weltkrieges* (Munich: Beck, 2014), p. 895.
18. Erwin Hoeft, *Fahnen wehen in aller Welt* (Bonn: Bonner Fahnenfabrik, 1956), pp. 22–3; Schölzel, *Rathenau*, p. 227.
19. 'Ist das wahr?', *Bonner Zeitung*, 10 November 1918, p. 3; 'Zur Aufklärung', *Bonner Zeitung*, 12 November 1918, p. 3.
20. 'Was wollte Gott?', *Der Reichsbote*, 15 May 1919, p. 1.
21. 111. Sitzung, 28 October 1919, in 'Verhandlungen des Deutschen Reichstags': online at http://www.reichstagsprotokolle.de/rtbiiauf.html (accessed 30 January 2017).
22. Falk, *Kriegsgesellschaften*, p. 16; Walther Rathenau to Reinhard Mumm, 20 May 1919, BArch Berlin, N2203/272.
23. Otto Armin, *Die Juden in den Kriegs-Gesellschaften und in der Kriegs-Wirtschaft* (Munich: Deutscher Volksverlag, 1921).
24. Wolff, 10 November 1918, in Sösemann, *Tagebücher*, p. 649.
25. 'Der Erfolg der Revolution', *Berliner Tageblatt*, 10 November 1918, p. 1.
26. Max Liebermann to Max Lehrs, 19 November 1918, in Ernst Braun (ed.), *Max Liebermann: Briefe – Band 6: 1916–1921* (Baden-Baden: Deutscher Wissenschafts-Verlag, 2016), pp. 265–6.

27. 'Die Woche', *Allgemeine Zeitung des Judentums*, 15 November 1918, p. 545.
28. 'Revolution', *Jüdische Rundschau*, 15 November 1918, p. 1.
29. Werner Angress, 'Juden im politischen Leben der Revolutionszeit', in Mosse (ed.), *Deutsches Judentum*, pp. 137–315, pp. 159–63; Charlotte Landau-Mühsam, 'Meine Erinnerungen', LBINY, ME381, pp. 44–5.
30. Judith Schrag-Haas, 'Erinnerungen an meinen Vater', LBINY, ME581, p. 14.
31. Ettinger, *Luxemburg*, p. 228; 'Was will der Spartakusbund?', *Die Rote Fahne*, 14 December 1918, pp. 1–2.
32. Philipp Loewenfeld, 'Memoiren', LBINY, ME404, p. 208.
33. Sebastian Haffner, *Failure of a Revolution: Germany 1918–19* (London: Andre Deutsch, 1973), pp. 165–6.
34. Bonn, *Wandering Scholar*, p. 198.
35. 'Sind wir frei?', *Vossische Zeitung*, 13 January 1919, p. 1.
36. Walter Liek, 'Der Anteil des Judentums an dem Zusammenbruch Deutschlands', *Deutschlands Erneuerung*, January 1919, pp. 29–43, p. 30.
37. 'Die arische Abstammung Liebknechts', *Im deutschen Reich*, February 1919, p. 75.
38. 'Die Woche', *Allgemeine Zeitung des Judentums*, 20 December 1918, p. 603.
39. Arthur Brenner, *Emil J. Gumbel: Weimar German Pacifist and Professor* (Leiden: Brill, 2001), p. 7.
40. Emil Julius Gumbel, *Zwei Jahre Mord* (Berlin: Verlag neues Vaterland, 1921), p. 63.
41. Emil Julius Gumbel, *Vier Jahre politischer Mord* (Berlin: Verlag der neuen Gesellschaft, 1922), pp. 78–80.
42. George Mosse, *Germans and Jews: The Right, the Left, and the Search for a 'Third Force' in Pre-Nazi Germany* (London: Orbach & Chambers, 1971), p. 48.
43. 'Richter Lynch', *Vossische Zeitung*, 16 January 1919, p. 4.
44. Siegfried Weinberg to Rat der Volksbeauftragten, 24 January 1919, BArch Berlin, R43/2494o.
45. 'Der dritte Mordplan im Edenhotel', *Die Rote Fahne*, 21 April 1929, pp. 5–6.
46. Klaus Gietinger, *Eine Leiche im Landwehrkanal: Die Ermordung der Rosa L.* (Berlin: Verlag 1900, 1995), pp. 5–6.
47. 'Die Ermordung Liebknechts und Rosa Luxemburgs', *Berliner Tageblatt*, 9 May 1919, p. 5.
48. H.C. Plaut, 'Memories of a German Jew', Leeds University Special Collections, GE28, p. 165.
49. Bernhard Kahn, 'Memoirs, 1914–1921', LBINY, ME344a, pp. 61–6.
50. Fritz Dispeker, 'Ausweis', 9 May 1919, JMB, 2002/24/53; Dr Koppel to Dellevie, 15 March 1933, Wiener Library, London, MF Doc55/82, CV2582.
51. Originally historians saw most veterans as brutalised: Mosse, *Fallen Soldiers*. This theory has come in for considerable revision: Bessel, *Germany*; Benjamin Ziemann, *Contested Commemorations: Republican War Veterans and Weimar Political Culture* (Cambridge: Cambridge University Press, 2013).
52. Alfred Neumeyer, *Lichter und Schatten: Eine Jugend in Deutschland* (Munich: Prestel, 1967), pp. 103, 164–5.
53. Bonn, *Wandering Scholar*, p. 219.
54. 'Deutsche Juden in Nachkriegskämpfen', *Der Schild*, 31 May 1935, p. 6.
55. Hagen Schulze, *Freikorps und Republik 1918–1920* (Boppard am Rhein: Harald Boldt, 1969), pp. 96–9.
56. 'Ein neues Antisemitenblatt und sein Herausgeber', *Im deutschen Reich*, July 1919, pp. 320–3.
57. 'Die Woche', *Allgemeine Zeitung des Judentums*, 31 January 1919, p. 3.
58. 'Der Geiselmord in München', *Im deutschen Reich*, July 1919, p. 343.
59. 'Die unannehmbaren Friedensbedingungen', *Berliner Tageblatt*, 8 May 1919, p. 1.
60. Warburg, *Aufzeichnungen*, p. 79.
61. Hans Meyer, 'Melchior als Mensch und Diplomat', in *Carl Melchior: Ein Buch des Gedenkens und der Freundschaft* (Tübingen: J.C.B. Mohr, 1967), pp. 131–40, p. 136.

62. 'Aus dem Inhalt des Friedenvertrages', *Allgemeine Zeitung des Judentums*, 16 May 1919, p. 209; 'Die Friedensbedingungen', *Jüdische Rundschau*, 16 May 1919, p. 268.
63. 'Ja oder Nein?', *Vossische Zeitung*, 8 May 1919, p. 1.
64. Walther Rathenau, 'Das Ende', *Die Zukunft*, 31 May 1919, pp. 248–50.
65. Andreas Stuhlmann, 'Vom "Schlafwandler" zum Kriegsgegner: Die Wandlungen des Maximilian Harden', *Simon Dubnow Institut Yearbook*, 13 (2014), pp. 309–35.
66. Maximilian Harden, *Von Versailles nach Versailles* (Hellerau: Im Avalun, 1927), p. 636.
67. Friedrich Thimme, *Maximilian Harden am Pranger* (Berlin: Verlag der 'Neuen Woche', 1919), p. 16.
68. Heid, *Cohn*, p. 191.
69. 'Die Friedensbedingungen', *Jüdische Rundschau*, 16 May 1919, p. 268.
70. Kurt Joseph, 'No Homesickness', LBINY, ME338, pp. 28–30.
71. Dorrmann, *Arnhold*, p. 237.
72. Berthold Haase, 'Mein Leben, was in ihm geschah, und wie ich es erlebte', LBINY, ME249.
73. 'Aus unserer Gemeinde', *Mitteilungen der Jüdischen Reformgemeinde zu Berlin*, 15 September 1921, pp. 15–16.
74. T. Hunt Tooley, *National Identity and Weimar Germany: Upper Silesia and the Eastern Border 1918–1922* (Lincoln: University of Nebraska Press, 1997), p. 235; Heid, *Cohn*, p. 33.
75. Emanuel Kirschner, 'Erinnerungen aus meinem Leben, Streben und Wirken', LBINY, ME361, pp. 134–6.
76. 138. Sitzung, 26 October 1921, in 'Verhandlungen des Deutschen Reichstags': online at http://www.reichstagsprotokolle.de/rtbiiauf.html (accessed 30 January 2017).
77. 'Die Zustände in Rybnik', *Berliner Tageblatt*, 25 May 1921, p. 4; Philipp Nielsen, ' "Der Schlageter Oberschlesiens": jüdische Deutsche und die Verteidigung ihrer Heimat im Osten', in Uwe Neumärker (ed.), *'Das war mal unsere Heimat . . .': Jüdische Geschichte im preußischen Osten* (Berlin: Stiftung Flucht, Vertreibung, Versöhnung, 2013), pp. 85–91.
78. Crim, *Antisemitism*, p. 23.
79. Joseph, 'Homesickness', pp. 30–1.
80. 'Zeitschau', *Im deutschen Reich*, September 1921, pp. 248–53.
81. Matthias Hambrock, *Die Etablierung der Außenseiter: Der Verband nationaldeutscher Juden 1921–1935* (Cologne: Böhlau, 2003), pp. 398, 410.
82. Josef Lange, 'Mein Leben' (1935), LBINY, ME380.
83. Moritz Föllmer, 'The Problem of National Solidarity in Interwar Germany', *German History*, 23 (2) (2005), pp. 202–31, pp. 208–9.
84. Annemarie Sammartino, *The Impossible Border: Germany and the East, 1914–1922* (Ithaca: Cornell University Press, 2010), p. 96.
85. Wilhelm Lustig, 'Erinnerungen aus der Zeit der Volksabstimmung in Oberschlesien', LBINY, ME407a, p. 2.
86. Julia Roos, 'Women's Rights, Nationalist Anxiety, and the "Moral" Agenda in the Early Weimar Republic: Revisiting the Black "Horror" Campaign against France's African Occupation Troops', *Central European History*, 42 (3) (2009), pp. 473–508; Evans, *Anthropology*, p. 167.
87. Deutscher Volksbund, 'Rettet die Ehre', 1920, LAB, B. Rep. 235–01, MF 2753; Roos, 'Rights', pp. 479–80.
88. Der Magistrat Frankfurt, 21 February 1919, IfS Frankfurt, S/240.
89. 'Pogrome in Polen und Galizien', *Neue jüdische Monatshefte*, 10 November 1918, pp. 51–8.
90. Jochen Oltmer, *Migration und Politik in der Weimarer Republik* (Göttingen: Vandenhoeck & Ruprecht, 2005), pp. 240–1.
91. Joseph Roth, 'The Orient on Hirtenstrasse', 1921, in Joseph Roth, *What I Saw: Reports from Berlin 1920–33*, trans. Michael Hofmann (London: Granta, 2003), pp. 31–4.
92. 'Aus den Repräsentantensitzungen', *Gemeindeblatt der jüdischen Gemeinde zu Berlin*, 13 May 1921, p. 42.

93. 'Wandersturm', *Im deutschen Reich*, December 1920, pp. 365–72.

94. Max Naumann, *Vom nationaldeutschen Juden* (Berlin: Albert Goldschmidt, 1920), p. 21.

95. Maurer, *Ostjuden*, pp. 110–12, 130.

96. Sammet, '*Dolchstoss*', pp. 115–22.

97. Philipp Loewenfeld, 'Memoirs', LBINY, ME404, p. 564.

98. Gerd Krumeich, 'Die Dolchstoß-Legende', in Étienne François and Hagen Schulze (eds), *Deutsche Erinnerungsorte* (Munich: Beck, 2001), pp. 585–99, p. 588.

99. Gronemann, *Hawdoloh*, p. 244.

100. 'Ansprachen Eberts und Wermuths an die einziehenden Truppen', *Berliner Tageblatt*, 10 December 1918, p. 2; Wolfgang Schivelbusch, *The Culture of Defeat: On National Trauma, Mourning and Recovery* (London: Granta, 2003), p. 203.

101. Oberst Bauer, *Konnten wir den Krieg vermeiden, gewinnen, abbrechen? Drei Fragen* (Berlin: August Scherl, 1919), p. 62.

102. 'Die Stellung der Demokratie', *Berliner Tageblatt*, 24 June 1919, p. 1; Sammet, '*Dolchstoss*', p. 103.

103. Georg Solmssen, 'Zusammenbruch und Wiederaufbau der deutschen Volkswirtschaft', 14 January 1919, in Georg Solmssen (ed.), *Beiträge zur Deutschen Politik und Wirtschaft 1900–1933: Gesammelte Aufsätze und Vorträge* (Munich: Duncker & Humblot, 1934), pp. 31–56, pp. 34–5; 'Städtische Nachrichten', *Kölnische Zeitung*, 16 January 1919, p. 2.

104. Bonn, *Wandering Scholar*, pp. 245–6.

105. 'Die Vernehmung Ludendorffs vor dem Ausschuß', *Berliner Tageblatt*, 19 November 1919, p. 4.

106. Boris Barth, *Dolchstoßlegenden und politische Desintegration: Das Trauma der deutschen Niederlage im Ersten Weltkrieg, 1914–1933* (Düsseldorf: Droste, 2003), p. 330.

107. 'Bericht über die Verhandlungen des Geschäftsführenden Ausschusses in Bamberg am 16. und 17. Februar 1919', BArch Berlin, R8048/205; 'Erklärung des Alldeutschen Verbandes', *Alldeutsche Blätter*, 1 March 1919, pp. 65–9.

108. Otto Armin, *Die Juden im Heere: Eine statistische Untersuchung nach amtlichen Quellen* (Munich: Deutscher Volks-Verlag, 1919), pp. 7–8.

109. Rosenthal, '*Die Ehre*', p. 118.

Epilogue

1. Ernst Kantorowicz to Robert Sproul, 4 October 1949, LBINY, AR7216.

2. David Abulafia, 'Kantorowicz and Frederick II', *History*, 62 (2) (1977), pp. 193–210.

3. Bessel, *Germany*, p. 283; Matthew Stibbe, *Germany 1914–1933: Politics, Society and Culture* (Harlow: Longman, 2010), pp. 4–5.

4. Moritz Föllmer and Graf Rüdiger (eds), *Die 'Krise' der Weimarer Republik: Zur Kritik eines Deutungsmusters* (Frankfurt: Campus, 2005); Benjamin Ziemann, 'Weimar was Weimar: Politics, Culture and the Emplotment of the German Republic', *German History*, 28 (4) (2010), pp. 542–71, pp. 553–6.

5. Anthony McElligott, *Rethinking the Weimar Republic: Authority and Authoritarianism, 1916–1936* (London: Bloomsbury, 2014).

6. Young-Sun Hong, *Welfare, Modernity, and the Weimar State, 1919–1933* (Princeton: Princeton University Press, 1998); Dorothy Rowe, *Representing Berlin: Sexuality and the City in Imperial and Weimar Germany* (Aldershot: Ashgate, 2003); Peter Gay, *Weimar Culture: The Outsider as Insider* (New York: Norton, 1968).

7. Peter Fritzsche, 'Did Weimar Fail?', *Journal of Modern History*, 68 (3) (1996), pp. 629–56.

8. Matthias Eberle, *World War I and the Weimar Artists: Dix, Grosz, Beckmann, Schlemmer* (New Haven: Yale University Press, 1985); Arnold Zweig, *Der Streit um den Sergeanten Grischa* (Potsdam: Kiepenheuer, 1928); Erich Maria Remarque, *Im Westen nichts Neues* (Berlin: Propyläen, 1929).

9. Robert Whalen, *Bitter Wounds: German Victims of the Great War 1914–1939* (Ithaca: Cornell University Press, 1984).

10. Wolfgang Pyta, *Hindenburg: Herrschaft zwischen Hohenzollern und Hitler* (Munich: Siedler, 2007).
11. Bessel, *Germany*, p. 283.
12. Harry Marcuse to Mimi Marcuse, 7 April 1918, in Reisner, *Kriegsbriefe*, pp. 516–17.
13. Ernst-Heinrich Schmidt, 'Zürndorfer-Waldmann: Das Schicksal einer Familie deutscher Frontkämpfer jüdischer Abstammung und jüdischen Glaubens 1914 bis 1945', in Militärgeschichtliches Forschungsamt (ed.), *Deutsche jüdische Soldaten 1914–1945* (Herford: Mittler, 1987), pp. 197–212, p. 201.
14. Gebrüder Alsberg to Gemeindeblatt der Deutsch-Israelitischen Gemeinde zu Hamburg, 13 July 1925, StAHH, 522–1, Nr. 628a.
15. Ernst Warschauer, 'In Memoriam: Rechtsanwalt Kurt Wolff, Oppeln', LBINY, AR4005.
16. *Frankfurter Israelitisches Gemeindeblatt*, June 1930, p. 412; ibid., October 1931, p. 52. This contrasts with the suggestion that the Jewish wounded were not visible: Penslar, *Military*, p. 182.
17. Whalen, *Bitter Wounds*; Deborah Cohen, *The War Come Home: Disabled Veterans in Britain and Germany, 1914–1939* (Berkeley: University of California Press, 2001).
18. Charlotte Hamburger, 'Die Familie und das Leben des Hans Hamburger, 1854–1953', LBINY, ME1504.
19. Regina Schulte, 'The Sick Warrior's Sister: Nursing during the First World War' in Lynn Abrams and Elizabeth Harvey (eds), *Gender Relations in German History: Power, Agency and Experience from the Sixteenth to the Twentieth Century* (London: UCL Press, 1996), pp. 121–41, p. 134.
20. Helen Boak, *Women in the Weimar Republic* (Manchester: Manchester University Press, 2013).
21. Steer, 'Nation, Religion, Gender', p. 194.
22. Gerald Feldman, *The Great Disorder: Politics, Economy, and Society in the German Inflation, 1914–1924* (Oxford: Oxford University Press, 1997), pp. 516–17.
23. Levy, 'Leben', LBINY, ME383, p. 26.
24. Brenner, *Gumbel*, pp. 44–7.
25. Kramer, *Dynamic*, p. 320.
26. 'Pfingstkongreß der Deutschen Landmannschaft', *Coburger Zeitung*, 25 May 1926, p. 1.
27. Judith Prokasky, 'Gestorben wofür? Die doppelte Funktionalisierung der deutsch-jüdischen Kriegerdenkmäler am Beispiel Guben', in Dieter Hübener, Kristina Hübener and Julius Schoeps (eds), *Kriegerdenkmale in Brandenburg: Von den Befreiungskriegen 1813/15 bis in die Gegenwart* (Berlin: be.bra. 2003), pp. 203–14.
28. Ziemann, *Contested Commemorations*, pp. 147–54.
29. 'Von der Frühjahrsoffensive 1928', *Der Schild*, 16 May 1928, pp. 165–6; 'Kriegserinnerungen', *Der Schild*, 22 February 1926, p. 59; Tim Grady, 'Fighting a Lost Battle: The Reichsbund jüdischer Frontsoldaten and the Rise of National Socialism', *German History*, 28 (1) (2010), pp. 1–20.
30. Winson Chu, *The German Minority in Interwar Poland* (Cambridge: Cambridge University Press, 2012), pp. 21–6.
31. Liulevicius, *War Land*, pp. 247–51.
32. Gronemann, *Hawdoloh*.
33. Chu, *German Minority*, pp. 40–9. See in particular: Michael Burleigh, *Germany Turns Eastwards: A Study of Ostforschung in the Third Reich* (Cambridge: Cambridge University Press, 1988).
34. Ingo Haar, 'German *Ostforschung* and Anti-Semitism', in Ingo Haar and Michael Fahlbusch (eds), *German Scholars and Ethnic Cleansing, 1920–1945* (Oxford: Berghahn, 2005), pp. 1–27.
35. Verhey, *Spirit*, p. 208.
36. Ian Kershaw, ' "Volksgemeinschaft": Potenzial und Grenzen eines neuen Forschungskonzepts', *Vierteljahrshefte für Zeitgeschichte*, 59 (1) (2011), pp. 1–17, pp. 6–7; Michael Wildt, *Hitler's* Volksgemeinschaft *and the Dynamics of Racial Exclusion: Violence against Jews in Provincial Germany, 1919–1939*, trans. Bernard Heise (Oxford: Berghahn, 2012), p. 16.

37. Ziemann, *Front und Heimat*, pp. 340–70.
38. Michael Brenner, *The Renaissance of Jewish Culture in Weimar Germany* (New Haven: Yale University Press, 1996), pp. 36–65; Michael Brenner and Derek Penslar (eds), *In Search of Jewish Community: Jewish Identities in Germany and Austria, 1918–1933* (Bloomington: Indiana University Press, 1998).
39. Steer, 'Nation, Religion, Gender', p. 191.
40. Satzungen des Vaterländischen Bundes jüdischer Frontsoldaten, 1919, Wiener Library, London; Der Herzl-Bund (ed.), *Den gefallenen Brüdern* (Berlin: Siegfried Scholem, 1919[?]), p. 9.
41. Martin Sabrow, *Der Rathenaumord: Rekonstruktion einer Verschwörung gegen die Republik von Weimar* (Munich: Oldenbourg, 1994), pp. 86–103.
42. David Clay Large, ' "Out with the Ostjuden": The Scheunenviertel Riots in Berlin, November 1923', in Christhard Hoffmann, Werner Bergmann and Helmut Walser Smith (eds), *Exclusionary Violence: Antisemitic Riots in Modern German History* (Ann Arbor: University of Michigan Press, 2002), pp. 123–40, p. 131.
43. 'Das Abflauen der Unruhen', *Berliner Tageblatt*, 8 November 1923, p. 6.
44. Sammet, *'Dolchstoss'*, p. 245.
45. Ziemann, *Contested Commemorations*, pp. 29–30.
46. Reichsbund jüdischer Frontsoldaten, 1000 Mark Belohnung, Wiener Library, London.
47. Dirk Schumann, *Politische Gewalt in der Weimarer Republik 1918–1933: Kampf um die Straße und Furcht vor dem Bürgerkrieg* (Essen: Klartext, 2001); Sabine Behrenbeck, 'Heldenkult oder Friedensmahnung? Kriegerdenkmale nach beiden Weltkriegen', in Gottfried Niedhart und Dieter Riesenberger (eds), *Lernen aus dem Krieg? Deutsche Nachkriegszeiten, 1918 und 1945: Beiträge zur historischen Friedensforschung* (Munich: Beck, 1992), pp. 344–64, pp. 347–8.
48. Fritz Stern, *Five Germanys I Have Known* (New York: Farrar, Straus and Giroux, 2006), p. 77.
49. Holger Skor, ' "Weil wir den Krieg kennen . . .": Deutsche und französische Frontsoldaten in der NS-Friedenspropaganda', in Gerd Krumeich (ed.), *Nationalsozialismus und Erster Weltkrieg* (Essen: Klartext, 2010), pp. 175–90, p. 177. Martin Broszat, *Hitler and the Collapse of Weimar Germany* (Leamington Spa: Berg, 1987), p. 91.
50. Richard Bessel, 'The Nazi Capture of Power', *Journal of Contemporary History*, 39 (2) (2004), pp. 169–88.
51. 'Der Fackelzug der SA und des Stahlhelm', *Spandauer Zeitung*, 31 January 1933, pp. 2–3.
52. Verhey, *Spirit*, p. 223.
53. Richard Evans, *The Coming of the Third Reich* (London: Penguin, 2004), p. 310.
54. Bessel, *Germany*, p. 281; Ludolf Herbst, *Das nationalsozialistische Deutschland 1933–1945* (Frankfurt: Suhrkamp, 1996), p. 9.
55. Herbert, 'Was haben die Nationalsozialisten'.
56. Bessel, *Nazism*, p. 14.
57. Adolf Hitler, 1924, cited in Herbert, 'Was haben die Nationalsozialisten', p. 31.
58. Grady, *German-Jewish Soldiers*, pp. 130–2, 139.
59. Martin Kutz, 'Fantasy, Reality, and Modes of Perception in Ludendorff's and Goebbels's Concept of "Total War" ', in Roger Chickering, Stig Förster and Bernd Greiner (eds), *A World at Total War: Global Conflict and the Politics of Destruction, 1937–1945* (Cambridge: Cambridge University Press, 2005), pp. 189–206.
60. Herbst, *Das nationalsozialistische Deutschland*, pp. 59–60.
61. Ian Kershaw, *Hitler 1889–1936: Hubris* (London: Penguin, 1998), p. 184.
62. Wilhelm Deist, *The Wehrmacht and German Rearmament* (Basingstoke: Macmillan, 1981), pp. 36–53.
63. Harold James, 'The Weimar Economy', in Anthony McElligott (ed.), *Weimar Germany* (Oxford: Oxford University Press, 2009), pp. 102–26, p. 125.
64. Adolf Hitler, 31 May 1921, cited in Geoffrey Stoakes, *Hitler and the Quest for World Dominion* (Leamington Spa: Berg, 1986), p. 155.

65. Shelley Baranowski, *Nazi Empire: German Colonialism and Imperialism from Bismarck to Hitler* (Cambridge: Cambridge University Press, 2011), pp. 140–1; Geoff Eley, *Nazism as Fascism: Violence, Ideology, and the Ground of Consent in Germany 1930–1945* (New York: Routledge, 2013), pp. 137–9.

66. Michael Kater, *Hitler Youth* (Cambridge, Mass.: Harvard University Press, 2006), p. 29.

67. Whalen, *Bitter Wounds*, p. 175.

68. Karin Hausen, 'The "Day of National Mourning" in Germany', in Gerald Sider and Gavin Smith (eds), *Between History and Histories: The Making of Silences and Commemorations* (Toronto: University of Toronto Press, 1997), pp. 127–46, p. 138.

69. Tim Mason, 'The Legacy of 1918 for National Socialism', in Anthony Nicholls and Erich Matthias (eds), *German Democracy and the Triumph of Hitler* (London: George Allen, 1971), pp. 215–39, p. 226; Herbst, *Das nationalsozialistische Deutschland*, pp. 240–2.

70. Saul Friedländer, *Nazi Germany and the Jews: The Years of Persecution, 1933–1939* (London: Weidenfeld & Nicolson, 1997), p. 168.

71. Alain Boureau, *Kantorowicz: Stories of a Historian*, trans. Stephen Nichols and Gabrielle Spiegel (Baltimore: Johns Hopkins University Press, 2001), pp. 77–80.

72. Moshe Zimmermann, *Die Deutschen Juden 1914–1945* (Munich: Oldenbourg, 1997), pp. 80–4.

73. Adolf Hitler, speech to the Reichstag, 30 January 1939, in Jeremy Noakes and Geoffrey Pridham (eds), *Nazism 1919–1945: Foreign Policy, War and Racial Extermination* (Exeter: University of Exeter Press, 1997), p. 441.

74. Hans Mommsen, 'Hitler's Reichstag Speech of 20 January 1939', *History and Memory*, 9 (1/2) (1997), pp. 147–61, p. 153.

BIBLIOGRAPHY

Archival Sources

Archiv der Max-Planck-Gesellschaft, Berlin

I, Abt. KWG, Rep. 1A: Kaiser-Wilhelm-Gesellschaft
Dept. Va, Rep. 5: Haber Collection

Auswärtiges Amt–Politisches Archiv, Berlin (PA–AA)

R10503: Juden in Russland
R10504: Juden in Russland
R14134: Die Juden in der Türkei
R20944: Die Juden
R21529: U-Bootskrieg
R21574: Die Zukunft Polens

Bayerisches Hauptstaatsarchiv, Abteilung Kriegsarchiv, Munich (Kriegsarchiv)

Stv. Gen. Kdo. I.b.A.K: Stellvertretendes Generalkommado I. Armee-Korps

Bundesarchiv, Berlin (BArch Berlin)

N2203: Reinhard Mumm
R43: Reichskanzlei
R1501: Reichsministerium des Innern
R8048: Alldeutscher Verband

Bundesarchiv-Militärarchiv, Freiburg (BArch MA)

BW1: Bundesministerium der Verteidigung
FB1898N: Zählung und Musterung der wehrpflichtigen Juden
PH2: Preußisches Kriegsministerium
PH7: Stellvertretende Generalkommandos der Preußischen Armee
PH8-I: Infanterie-Divisionen der Preußischen Armee
PH14: Dienststellen und Einheiten des Ingenieurkorps und der Pioniertruppen der Preußischen
  Armee

PH30/II: Kaiserliches Generalgouvernement Warschau
N253: Alfred Tirpitz
N30: Hans von Beseler

Central Archive for the History of the Jewish People, Jerusalem (CAHJP)

D/Be4: Berlin, Juedische Gemeinde
D/Wu3: Wuerzburg, ILBA
P32: Sammlung Gustav Feldmann
P75: Sammlung Flora und Jacob Rothschild

Centrum Judaicum Archiv, Berlin (CJA)

1.75A: Jüdische Gemeinden
1.75B: Gemeindeverbände und Rabbinate
1.75C: Organisationen

Geheimes Staatsarchiv Preußischer Kulturbesitz, Berlin (GStA PK)

I. HA Rep. 77: Ministerium des Innern
I. HA, Rep. 191: Ministerium für Volkswohlfahrt
I. HA, Rep. 121: Ministerium für Handel und Gewerbe, Berg-, Hütten- und Salinenverwaltung
VI. HA, Nl. Kapp, W.: Kapp, Wolfgang
BPH, Rep. 192, Nl Zimmermann, E.: Zimmermann, Eugen

Greater Manchester County Record Office

GB127.M448.: Manchester Shechita Board

Hessisches Wirtschaftsarchiv, Darmstadt

Abt. 119: Metallgesellschaft

Hauptstaatsarchiv Stuttgart (HstAS)

E40: Ministerium der auswärtigen Angelegenheiten
E130a: Staatsministerium
M1/4: Kriegsministerium
M33/2: Generalkommando XIII. Armeekorps
M77/1: Stellvertretendes Generalkommando XIII. A.K.

Imperial War Museum Archive, London

12/22/1: Private Papers of Eugene Kent

Institut für Stadtgeschichte, Frankfurt am Main (IfS)

Sport und Badeamt
S/147: Ausweisung von Ausländern
S/240: Ausländischer Arbeiter
S/363: Flüchtlingsfürsorge
V/390: Israelitischer Almosenkasten
W2–5: Industrie- und Handelskammer

Jüdisches Museum Berlin – Archiv (JMB)

2002/24: Fritz Dispeker Collection
2004/61: Max Haller Collection

Landesarchiv Berlin (LAB)

A Pr. Br. Rep. 030: Polizeipräsidium Berlin
B. Rep. 235–01: Bund Deutscher Frauenvereine

Leeds University Special Collections, Leeds

GE28: H.C. Plaut Collection
MS1062: Robert Ehrmann Papers

Leo Baeck Institute Archive, New York (LBINY)

AR485: Arnold Taenzer Collection
AR4005: Kurt Wolff
AR4105: Arthur Oppenheimer Collection
AR4472: Schönmann Family Collection
AR6147: Halberstadt Family Collection
AR6179: Fanny Joseph and Eva Goertz Collection
AR6455: Emanuel Fraenkel Family Collection
AR6300: Martin Feist Collection
AR6436: Hellmann-Kromwell Family Collection
AR7030: Pinkus Family Collection
AR7185: Robert Weltsch Collection
AR7216: Ernst Kantorowicz Collection
AR25042: Sussmann-Hirsch Family Collection
ME249: Berthold Haase
ME264: Helmut Freund
ME332: Marie Munk
ME338: Kurt Joseph
ME344a: Bernhard Kahn
ME361: Emanuel Kirschner
ME380: Josef Lange
ME381: Charlotte Landau-Mühsam
ME383 : Joseph Levy
ME404: Philipp Loewenfeld
ME407a: Wilhelm Lustig
ME581: Judith Schrag-Haas
ME619: Charlotte Stein-Pick
ME640: Arnold Tänzer
ME908: Theodor Rosenthal
ME957: Walter Wolff
ME1057: Theodor Kirchberger
ME1504: Charlotte Hamburger
MF13: Komitee für den Osten

Staatsarchiv Hamburg (StAHH)

325–1: Friedhofsverwaltung
522–1: Jüdische Gemeinden

Universitätsbibliothek Frankfurt am Main

Fm/Kg 1/638a Judaica Frankfurt

Wiener Library, London

MF Doc55: Centralverein Records

*Zentralarchiv zur Erforschung der Geschichte der Juden in Deutschland, Heidelberg
(Zentralarchiv)*

B.3/52: Materialsammlung Hobohm

Zentral- und Landesbibliothek Berlin

Nachlass Deißmann

Newspapers

Alldeutsche Blätter, 1917, 1919.
Allgemeine Zeitung des Judentums, 1914–15, 1918–19.
Aschaffenburger Zeitung, 1914.
Auf Vorposten, 1918.
Berliner Tageblatt, 1914–19, 1921–23.
Blau-Weiss-Blätter, 1914.
Bonner Zeitung, 1917–18.
Coburger Zeitung, 1917–18, 1926.
Deutschlands Erneuerung, 1919.
Feldzeitung der Bugarmee, 1916.
Frankfurter Israelitisches Familienblatt, 1914.
Frankfurter Israelitisches Gemeindeblatt, 1930–31.
Frankfurter Zeitung, 1914–15.
Die Frauenfrage: Zentralblatt des Bundes Deutscher Frauenvereine, 1915, 1917.
Front, 1917.
Gemeindeblatt der jüdischen Gemeinde zu Berlin, 1914–16, 1921.
Das größere Deutschland: Wochenschrift für Deutsche Welt- und Kolonial-Politik, 1915.
Hamburger Fremdenblatt, 1914–15.
Hamburger Nachrichten, 1916, 1918.
Herzl-Bund-Blätter, 1915.
Im deutschen Reich, 1914–21.
Der Israelit, 1916.
Israelitisches Familienblatt, 1918.
Israelitisches Gemeindeblatt, 1914–15.
Der Jude, 1916, 1918–19.
Das Jüdische Echo, 1915.
Jüdische Rundschau, 1914–19.
K.C.-Blätter, 1914–15, 1917–18.
Kölnische Zeitung, 1919.
Kriegs-Bericht der Salia, 1915.
Kriegszeit: Künstlerflugblätter, 1914.
Liberales Judentum, 1914–15, 1918.
Lustige Blätter, 1914.
Märkischer Sprecher, 1916.
Mitteilungen der Jüdischen Reformgemeinde zu Berlin, 1919.
Mitteilungen aus dem Verein zur Abwehr des Antisemitismus, 1917.

Das neue Deutschland, 1915, 1917.
Neue jüdische Monatshefte, 1918.
New York Times, 1914.
New York Tribune, 1917.
Ost und West, 1916, 1919.
Preußische Jahrbücher, 1915, 1917.
Preußische Zeitung – Kreuz-Zeitung, 1914.
Public Ledger, 1915.
Der Reichsbote, 1919.
Die Rote Fahne, 1918–19, 1929.
Der Schild, 1925–28, 1935–36.
Spandauer Zeitung, 1933.
Süddeutsche Monatshefte, 1915–17, 1924.
The Times, 1918.
Vorwärts, 1914.
Vossische Zeitung, 1914–19.
Die Wahrheit, 1914.
Washington Herald, 1915.
Wiener Zeitung, 1914.
Zeitschrift für das Armenwesen, 1918.
Zeitschrift für Demographie und Statistik der Juden, 1918.
Zeitung der X. Armee, 1915–16.
Die Zukunft, 1919.

Published Primary Sources

Adler, Cyrus, *Jacob Schiff: His Life and Letters* (New York: Doubleday, 1928).
Adler, Michael (ed.), *British Jewry Book of Honour* (London: Caxton, 1922).
Ansky, S., *The Enemy at his Pleasure: A Journey Through the Jewish Pale of Settlement during World War I* (New York: Henry Holt, 2002).
Armin, Otto, *Die Juden im Heere: Eine statistische Untersuchung nach amtlichen Quellen* (Munich: Deutscher Volks-Verlag, 1919).
— *Die Juden in den Kriegs-Gesellschaften und in der Kriegs-Wirtschaft* (Munich: Deutscher Volksverlag, 1921).
Audring, Gert, Christhard Hoffmann and Jürgen von Ungern-Sternberg (eds), *Eduard Meyer – Victor Ehrenberg: Ein Briefwechsel, 1914–1930* (Berlin: Akademie, 1990).
Bab, Julius, *Am Rande der Zeit: Betrachtungen 1914/15* (Berlin: Oesterheld, 1915).
— (ed.), *Menschenstimme: Gedichte aus der Kriegszeit 1914–1918* (Stettin: Norddeutscher Verlag für Literatur und Kunst, 1920).
Baden, Max von, *Erinnerungen und Dokumente* (Hamburg: Severus, [1927] 2011).
Baedeker, Karl, *Belgium and Holland: A Handbook for Travellers* (Leipzig: Baedeker, 1885).
Basler, Werner (ed.), *Deutschlands Annexionspolitik in Polen und im Baltikum* (Berlin: Rütten & Loening, 1962).
Bauer, Oberst, *Konnten wir den Krieg vermeiden, gewinnen, abbrechen? Drei Fragen* (Berlin: August Scherl, 1919).
Beckhardt, Lorenz, *Der Jude mit dem Hakenkreuz: Meine deutsche Familie* (Berlin: Aufbau, 2014).
Bernhard, Georg, *Die Kriegspolitik der Vossischen Zeitung* (Berlin: Ullstein, 1919).
— 'Land oder Geld', in Ernst Jäckh (ed.), *Der Deutsche Krieg* (Stuttgart: DVA, 1916), pp. 1–25.
Bihl, Wolfdieter (ed.), *Deutsche Quellen zur Geschichte des Ersten Weltkrieges*, vol. 29 (Darmstadt: Wissenschaftliche Buchgesellschaft, 1991).
Birnbaum, Nathan, *Den Ostjuden ihr Recht!* (Vienna: R. Löwit, 1915).
Bodenheimer, Henriette Hannah (ed.), *Prelude to Israel: The Memoirs of M.I. Bodenheimer* (New York: Yoseloff, 1963).
Bonn, M.J., *Wandering Scholar* (London: Cohen & West, 1949).

Braun, Ernst (ed.), *Max Liebermann: Briefe – Band 6: 1916–1921* (Baden-Baden: Deutscher Wissenschafts-Verlag, 2016).

Carlebach, Alexander, 'A German Rabbi goes East', *Leo Baeck Institute Yearbook*, 6 (1961), pp. 60–121.

Chotzinoff, Samuel, *A Lost Paradise: Early Reminiscences* (New York: Arno, 1975).

Churchill, Winston, *The World Crisis – Volume I: 1911–1914* (London: Bloomsbury, [1950] 2015).

Cohen, Israel, *The Ruhleben Prison Camp: A Record of Nineteen Months' Internment* (London: Methuen, 1917).

Cohn, Willy, *Verwehte Spuren: Erinnerungen an das Breslauer Judentum vor seinem Untergang* (Cologne: Böhlau, 1995).

Edinger, Dora (ed.), *Bertha Pappenheim: Leben und Schriften* (Frankfurt: Ner-Tamid, 1963).

Eliel, Carol, *The Apocalyptic Landscapes of Ludwig Meidner* (Munich: Prestel, 1989).

Eynern, Margarete von (ed.), *Briefe: Walther Rathenau, ein preussischer Europäer* (Berlin: Vogt, 1955).

Falk, Hanns, *Die Juden in den Kriegsgesellschaften* (Berlin: Philo, 1920).

Frankenthal, Käthe, *Der dreifache Fluch: Jüdin, Intellektuelle, Sozialistin – Lebenserinnerungen einer Ärtztin in Deutschland und im Exil* (Frankfurt: Campus, 1981).

Freundenthal, Max (ed.), *Kriegsgedenkbuch der israelitischen Kultusgemeinde Nürnberg* (Nuremberg: Rosenfeld's, 1920).

Fritz, Georg, *Die Ostjudenfrage: Zionismus und Grenzschluß* (Munich: Lehmanns, 1915).

Fürth, Henriette, *Kleines Kriegskochbuch: Ein Ratgeber für sparsames Kochen* (Frankfurt: Jobst, 1916).

Geiger, Ludwig, *Die deutschen Juden und der Krieg* (Berlin: Schwetschke, 1915).

— *Krieg und Kultur* (Berlin: Rudolf Mosse, 1915).

Glaßberg, Abraham, *Im Kriegsjahr 1914/15* (Berlin, 1915).

Goldmann, Nahum, *Der Geist des Militarismus* (Berlin: Deutsche Verlagsanstalt, 1915).

— *Memories: The Autobiography of Nahum Goldmann – The Story of a Lifelong Battle by World Jewry's Ambassador at Large*, trans. Helen Sebba (London: Weidenfeld & Nicolson, 1970).

Goldmann, Paul, *Beim Generalfeldmarschall von Hindenburg: Ein Abend im Hauptquartier* (Berlin: Concordia, 1914).

Goldstein, Moritz, *Berliner Jahre: Erinnerungen 1880–1933* (Munich: Verlag Dokumentation, 1977).

Görlitz, Walter (ed.), *The Kaiser and his Court: The Diaries, Note Books and Letters of Admiral Georg Alexander von Müller, Chief of the Naval Cabinet, 1914–1918* (London: Macdonald, 1961).

Gottlieb, Fred (ed.), *My Opa: The Diary of a German Rabbi* (Jerusalem: Chaim Mazo, 2005).

Grabowsky, Adolf, *Die polnische Frage* (Berlin: Carl Heymanns, 1916).

Granach, Alexander, *Da geht ein Mensch: Lebensroman eines Schauspielers* (Munich: Herbig, 1973).

Gronemann, Sammy, *Hawdoloh und Zapfenstreich: Erinnerungen an die ostjüdische Etappe 1916–18* (Berlin: Jüdischer Verlag, 1924).

Grumbach, Salomon, *Das annexionistische Deutschland* (Lausanne: Payot, 1917).

Gumbel, Emil Julius, *Vier Jahre politischer Mord* (Berlin: Verlag der neuen Gesellschaft, 1922).

— *Zwei Jahre Mord* (Berlin: Verlag neues Vaterland, 1921).

Haase, Ernst (ed.), *Hugo Haase: Sein Leben und Wirken* (Berlin: Ottens, 1929).

Haase, Hugo, *Reichstagsreden gegen die Kriegspolitik* (Berlin: Neues Vaterland, 1919).

Haber, Fritz (ed.), *Fünf Vorträge aus den Jahren 1920–1923* (Berlin: Julius Springer, 1924).

Hank, Sabine and Hermann Simon (eds), *Feldpostbriefe jüdischer Soldaten 1914–1918* (Teetz: Heinrich & Heinrich, 2002).

Hank, Sabine, Hermann Simon and Uwe Hank (eds), *Feldrabbiner in den deutschen Streitkräften des Ersten Weltkrieges* (Berlin: Hentrich & Hentrich, 2013).

Hanssen, Hans Peter, *Diary of a Dying Empire* (Port Washington: Kennikat Press, 1973).

Harden, Maximilian, *Von Versailles nach Versailles* (Hellerau: Im Avalun, 1927).

Hirschberg, Max, *Jude und Demokrat: Erinnerungen eines Muenchener Rechtsanwalts 1883 bis 1939* (Munich: Oldenbourg, 1998).

Hirschfeld, Magnus, *Warum hassen uns die Völker? Eine kriegspsychologische Betrachtung* (Bonn: Weber, 1915).

Hoeft, Erwin, *Fahnen wehen in aller Welt* (Bonn: Bonner Fahnenfabrik, 1956).

Hoffmann, Major-General Max, *War Diaries and Other Papers* (London: Martin Secker, 1929).

Hofmiller, Josef, 'Erinnerung', in *Paul Nikolaus Cossmann zum sechzigsten Geburtstag am 6. April 1929* (Munich: R. Oldenbourg, 1929), pp. viii–xxviii.

Hope, Daniel, *Familienstücke: Eine Spurensuche* (Hamburg: Rowohlt, 2008).

Huldermann, Bernhard, *Albert Ballin* (Oldenburg: Gerhard Stalling, 1922).

Huser, Karin, *'Haltet gut Jontef und seid herzlichst geküsst': Feldpostbriefe des Elsässer Juden Henri Levy von der Ostfront (1916–1918)* (Zurich: Chronos, 2014).

James, Harold and Martin Müller (eds), *Georg Solmssen: Ein deutscher Bankier – Briefe aus einem halben Jahrhundert 1900–1956* (Munich: Beck, 2012).

Jaser, Alexander, Clemens Picht and Ernst Schulin (eds), *Briefe, 1914–1922* (Düsseldorf: Droste, 2006).

Jewish Theological Seminary of America (ed.), *Past Perfect: The Jewish Experience in Early 20th Century Postcards* (New York: Jewish Theological Seminary of America, 1997).

Jonas, Hans, *Erinnerungen* (Frankfurt: Insel, 2003).

Katz, William, *Ein jüdisch-deutsches Leben, 1904–1939–1978* (Tübingen: Katzmann, 1980).

Kautsky, Karl (ed.), *Die deutschen Dokumente zum Kriegsausbruch 1914* (Berlin: Deutsche Verlagsgesellschaft für Politik und Geschichte, 1922).

Klemperer, Victor, *Curriculum Vitae: Erinnerungen 2, 1881–1918* (Berlin: Aufbau, 1996).

Der Krieg und wir Juden: Gesammelte Aufsätze von einem deutschen Juden (Berlin: Louis Lamm, 1915).

Kriegsbriefe gefallener deutscher Juden mit einem Geleitwort von Franz Josef Strauß (Stuttgart: Seewald, 1961).

Leo Baeck Institut Jerusalem (ed.), *Sechzig Jahre gegen den Strom: Ernst A. Simon – Briefe von 1917–1984* (Tübingen: Mohr Siebeck, 1998).

Lissauer, Ernst (ed.), *Worte in die Zeit: Flugblätter 1914*, Blatt I (1914).

Lübbert, Dr, *Die Zentraleinkaufsgesellschaft* (Berlin: Kriegspresseamt, 1917).

Ludendorff, Erich, *My War Memories, 1914–1918* (London: Hutchinson, 1919).

Luft, Gerda, *Chronik eines Lebens für Israel* (Stuttgart: Erdmann, 1983).

Luschan, Felix von, *Kriegsgefangene: 100 Steinzeichnungen von Hermann Struck* (Berlin: Dietrich Reimer, 1916).

Lutz, Ralph Haswell (ed.), *The Fall of the German Empire 1914–1918*, vol. II (New York: Octagon, 1969).

Maier, Max Hermann, *'In uns verwoben tief und wunderbar': Erinnerungen an Deutschland* (Frankfurt: Josef Knecht, 1972).

Marcuse, Rudolf, 'Völkertypen' (Leipzig, 1919).

Marx, Julius, *Kriegs-Tagebuch eines Juden* (Frankfurt: Ner-Tamid-Verlag, 1964).

Meinecke, Friedrich, *Die deutsche Erhebung von 1914* (Stuttgart: Cotta'sche, 1915).

Mendels, Käthe, 'Geschichte meiner Familie im Ersten Weltkrieg', in Andreas Lixl-Purcell (ed.), *Erinnerungen deutsch-jüdischer Frauen, 1900–1990* (Leipzig: Reclam, 1992), pp. 74–93.

Meyer, Andreas (ed.), *Als deutscher Jude im Ersten Weltkrieg: Der Fabrikant und Offizier Otto Meyer* (Berlin: be.bra, 2014).

Meyer, Hans, 'Melchior als Mensch und Diplomat', in *Carl Melchior: Ein Buch des Gedenkens und der Freundschaft* (Tübingen: J.C.B. Mohr, 1967), pp. 131–40.

Miller, Susanne (ed.), *Das Kriegstagebuch des Reichstagsabgeordneten Eduard David 1914 bis 1918* (Düsseldorf: Droste, 1966).

Mittwoch, Eugen, *Deutschland, die Türkei und der heilige Krieg* (Berlin: Kameradschaft, 1914).

Müller, Karl Alexander von, *Aus Gärten der Vergangenheit* (Stuttgart: Gustav Klipper, 1951).

Nationalversammlung (ed.), *Das Werk des Untersuchungsausschusses der Verfassungsgebenden Deutschen Nationalversammlung und des deutschen Reichstages 1919–1928*, vol. 3:1 (Berlin: Deutsche Verlagsgesellschaft für Politik und Gesellschaft, 1925–30).

Naumann, Max, *Vom nationaldeutschen Juden* (Berlin: Albert Goldschmidt, 1920).

Neumeyer, Alfred, *Lichter und Schatten: Eine Jugend in Deutschland* (Munich: Prestel, 1967).

Niedhart, Gottfried (ed.), *Gustav Mayer, als deutsch-jüdischer Historiker in Krieg und Revolution 1914–1920* (Munich: Oldenbourg, 2009).

Noakes, Jeremy and Geoffrey Pridham (eds), *Nazism 1919–1945: Foreign Policy, War and Racial Extermination* (Exeter: University of Exeter Press, 1997).

Nussbaum, Israel, *'Gut Schabbes!' Jüdisches Leben auf dem Lande: Aufzeichnungen eines Lehrers (1869–1942)* (Berlin: Jüdische Verlagsanstalt, 2002).

Oppenheimer, Franz, *Weltwirtschaft und Nationalwirtschaft* (Berlin: Fischer, 1915).

Prüter-Müller, Micheline and Peter Wilhelm Schmidt (eds), *Hugo Rosenthal: Lebenserinnerungen* (Bielefeld: Verlag für Regionalgeschichte, 2000).

Rathenau, Walther, *Die Organisation der Rohstoffversorgung: Vortrag gehalten in der Deutschen Gesellschaft 1914 am 20. Dezember 1915* (1915).

— *Politische Briefe* (Dresden: Reissner, 1929).

Reinharz, Jehuda (ed.), *Dokumente zur Geschichte des deutschen Zionismus, 1882–1933* (Tübingen: Mohr, 1981).

Reisner, Barbara (ed.), *Kriegsbriefe 1914–1918: Dr. Harry & Mimi Marcuse* (London: Lulu, 2013).

Remarque, Erich Maria, *Im Westen nichts Neues* (Berlin: Propyläen, 1929).

Roosen-Runge-Mollwo, Marie (ed.), *Adolph Goldschmidt 1863–1944: Lebenserinnerungen* (Berlin: Deutsche Verlag für Kunstwissenschaft, 1989).

Rosenthal, Ludwig, *Die große Zeit im Spiegel ernster Tage* (Cologne, 1914).

Rosenzweig, Edith (ed.), *Franz Rosenzweig Briefe* (Berlin: Schocken, 1935).

Roth, Joseph, *What I Saw: Reports from Berlin 1920–33*, trans. Michael Hofmann (London: Granta, 2003).

Rueß, Susanne and Astrid Stölzle, *Das Tagebuch der jüdischen Kriegskrankenschwester Rosa Bendit, 1914 bis 1917* (Stuttgart: Franz Steiner, 2012).

Salomonski, Martin, *Ein Jahr an der Somme* (Frankfurt an der Oder: Trowitsch & Sohn, 1917).

— *Jüdische Seelsorge an der Westfront* (Berlin: Lamm, 1918).

Sallis-Freudenthal, Margarete, *Ich habe mein Land gefunden: Autobiographischer Rückblick* (Frankfurt: Josef Knecht, 1977).

Salzberger, Georg, *Aus meinem Kriegstagebuch* (Frankfurt: Voigt & Gleiber, 1916).

Schabinger, Karl Emil, Freiherr von Schowingen, 'Weltgeschichtliche Mosaiksplitter: Erlebnisse und Erinnerungen eines kaiserlichen Dragomans' (Baden-Baden, 1967).

Schaeder, Grete (ed.), *Martin Buber: Briefwechsel aus sieben Jahrzehnten – Band I: 1897–1918* (Heidelberg: Schneider, 1972).

Scholem, Gershom, *Von Berlin nach Jerusalem: Jugenderinnerungen* (Frankfurt: Suhrkamp, 1977).

Schuman, Robert, A.J. Kox, Michel Janssen and József Illy (eds), *The Collected Papers of Albert Einstein – Volume 8: The Berlin Years – Correspondence, 1914–1918* (Princeton: Princeton University Press, 1998).

Silex, Paul and Betty Hirsch, *Bericht über unsere dreijährige Tätigkeit an der Blinden-Lazarettschule des Vereinslazaretts St. Maria Viktoria-Heilanstalt zu Berlin* (Berlin: Lazarettschule, 1918).

Simon, Ernst (ed.), *Brücken: Gesammelte Aufsätze* (Heidelberg: Lambert Schneider, 1965).

Solmssen, Georg (ed.), *Beiträge zur Deutschen Politik und Wirtschaft 1900–1933: Gesammelte Aufsätze und Vorträge* (Munich: Duncker & Humblot, 1934).

Sösemann, Bernd (ed.), *Tagebücher, 1914–1919: Der Erste Weltkrieg und die Entstehung der Weimarer Republik in Tagebüchern, Leitartikeln und Briefen des Chefredakteurs am 'Berliner Tageblatt' und Mitbegründers der 'Deutschen Demokratischen Partei'* (Boppard am Rhein: Boldt, 1984).

Spanier, M. (ed.), *Leutnant Sender: Blätter der Erinnerung für seine Freunde* (Hamburg: Blogau, 1915).

Stampfer, Friedrich, *Erfahrungen und Erkenntnisse* (Cologne: Verlag für Politik und Wissenschaft, 1958).

Stenographisches Protokoll der Verhandlungen des VI. Zionisten Kongresses in Basel (1903).

Stern, Arthur, *In bewegter Zeit: Erinnerungen und Gedanken eine jüdischen Nervenarztes* (Jerusalem: Rubin Mass, 1968).

Stern, Fritz, *Dreams and Delusions: The Drama of German History* (London: Weidenfeld & Nicolson, 1987).

— *Five Germanys I Have Known* (New York: Farrar, Straus and Giroux, 2006).

Stern, Heinemann, *Warum hassen sie uns eigentlich? Jüdisches Leben zwischen den Kriegen* (Düsseldorf: Droste, 1970).

Straus, Rahel, *Wir lebten in Deutschland: Erinnerungen einer deutschen Jüdin, 1880–1933* (Stuttgart: DVA, 1961).

Strauß, Bruno (ed.), *Hermann Cohens Jüdische Schriften* (Berlin: Schwetschke, 1924).

Struck, Hermann and Herbert Eulenberg, *Skizzen aus Litauen, Weissrussland und Kurland* (Berlin: Stilke, 1916).

Sulzbach, Herbert, *With the German Guns: Four Years on the Western Front* (Barnsley: Pen & Sword, 1998).

Tannenbaum, Eugen (ed.), *Kriegsbriefe deutscher und österreichischer Juden* (Berlin: Neuer Verlag, 1915).

Tänzer, Arnold, *Geschichte der Juden in Brest-Litowsk* (Berlin: Louis Lamm, 1918).

Theilhaber, Felix, *Jüdische Flieger im Weltkrieg* (Berlin: Verlag der Schild, 1924).

— *Schlichte Kriegserlebnisse* (Berlin: Louis Lamm, 1916).

Thimme, Friedrich, *Maximilian Harden am Pranger* (Berlin: Verlag der 'Neuen Woche', 1919).

Tirpitz, Alfred von (ed.), *Politische Dokumente* (Stuttgart: Cotta, 1924).

Trietsch, Davis, *Afrikanische Kriegsziele* (Berlin: Süsserott, 1917).

— *Georgien und der Kaukasus* (Berlin: Deutsch-Georgische Gesellschaft, 1918).

— *Juden und Deutsche: Eine Sprach- und Interessengemeinschaft* (Vienna: R. Löwit, 1915).

— *Kriegsziele gegen England* (Berlin: Puttkammer & Mühlbrecht, 1915).

— *Russland* (Berlin: Basch, 1915).

— *Die Welt nach dem Kriege* (Berlin: Puttkammer & Mühlbrecht, 1915).

The Truth about Germany: Facts about the War (Berlin, 1914).

Ulrich, Bernd and Benjamin Ziemann (eds), *Frontalltag im Ersten Weltkrieg: Quellen und Dokumente* (Frankfurt: Fischer, 1994).

Vischer, Adolf, *Die Stacheldraht-Krankheit: Beiträge zur Pyschologie des Kriegsgefangenen* (Zurich: Rascher, 1918).

Warburg, Max, *Aus meinen Aufzeichnungen* (New York: E.M. Warburg, 1952).

Wenzel, Georg (ed.), *Arnold Zweig 1887–1968: Werk und Leben in Dokumentation und Bildern* (Berlin: Aufbau, 1978).

Wertheimer, Fritz, *Im polnischen Winterfeldzug mit der Armee Mackensen* (Stuttgart: Deutsche Verlags-Anstalt, 1915).

— *Von der Weichsel bis zum Dnjestr* (Stuttgart: Deutsche Verlags-Anstalt, 1915).

Westerman, Klaus (ed.), *Berliner Saisonbericht: Unbekannte Reportage und journalistische Arbeiten, 1920–39* (Cologne: Kiepenheuer und Witsch, 1984).

Westman, Stephen, *Surgeon with the Kaiser's Army* (London: Kimber, 1968).

Wiedenfeld, Kurt, *Rohstoffversorgung* (Berlin: Kriegspresseamt, 1917).

Wierling, Dorothee, *Eine Familie im Krieg: Leben, Sterben und Schreiben 1914–1918* (Göttingen: Wallstein, 2013).

Willstätter, Richard, *Aus meinem Leben: Von Arbeit, Müe und Freunden* (Weinheim: Verlag Chemie, 1958).

Wolff, Lion, *Durch Nacht zum Licht, durch Kampf zum Sieg* (Tempelburg: Manig, 1917).

Wollheim, Caesar, *Der Kohlenmarkt im zweiten Kriegsjahr* (Berlin: H.S. Hermann, 1916).

Zuber, Uwe (ed.), *Julius Goldstein: Der jüdische Philosoph in seinen Tagebüchern, 1873–1929* (Wiesbaden: Kommission für die Geschichte der Juden in Hessen, 2008).

Zweig, Arnold, *Der Streit um den Sergeanten Grischa* (Potsdam: Kiepenheuer, 1928).

Websites

Verhandlungen des Deutschen Reichstags: online at http://www.reichstagsprotokolle.de/rtbi-iauf.html (accessed 30 January 2017).

Secondary Sources

Aberbach, David, *The European Jews, Patriotism and the Liberal State 1789–1939: A Study of Literature and Social Psychology* (New York: Routledge, 2013).

Albanis, Elisabeth, *German-Jewish Cultural Identity from 1900 to the Aftermath of the First World War: A Comparative Study of Moritz Goldstein, Julius Bab and Ernst Lissauer* (Tübingen: Niemeyer, 2002).
— 'Ostracised for Loyalty: Ernst Lissauer's Propaganda Writing and its Reception', *Leo Baeck Institute Yearbook*, 43 (1998), pp. 195–224.
Angress, Werner, 'Das deutsche Militär und die Juden im Ersten Weltkrieg', *Militärgeschichtliche Mitteilungen*, 19 (1976), pp. 77–146.
— 'Juden im politischen Leben der Revolutionszeit', in Werner Mosse (ed.), *Deutsches Judentum in Krieg und Revolution, 1916–1923* (Tübingen: J.C.B. Mohr, 1971), pp. 137–315.
— 'Der jüdische Offizier in der neueren deutschen Geschichte, 1813–1918', in Ursula Breymayer, Bernd Ulrich and Karin Wieland (eds), *Willensmenschen: Über deutsche Offiziere* (Frankfurt: Fischer, 1999), pp. 67–78.
— 'Prussia's Army and the Jewish Reserve Officer Controversy before World War I', *Leo Baeck Institute Yearbook*, 17 (1972), pp. 19–42.
Appelbaum, Peter, *Loyal Sons: Jews in the German Army in the Great War* (London: Vallentine Mitchell, 2014).
Arendt, Hannah, *The Origins of Totalitarianism* (London: Allen & Unwin, 1958).
Aronsfeld, C.C., 'German Jews in Victorian England', *Leo Baeck Institute Yearbook*, 7 (1962), pp. 312–29.
Aschheim, Steven, *Brothers and Strangers: The East European Jew in German and German-Jewish Consciousness, 1800–1923* (Madison: University of Wisconsin Press, 1982).
— *In Times of Crisis: Essays on European Culture, Germans, and Jews* (Madison: University of Wisconsin Press, 2001).
Asprey, Robert, *The German High Command at War: Hindenburg and Ludendorff and the First World War* (London: Little Brown, 1993).
Audoin-Rouzeau, Stéphane and Annette Becker, *1914–1918: Understanding the Great War*, trans. Catherine Temerson (London: Profile, 2002).
Bailey, Stephen, 'The Berlin Strike of January 1918', *Central European History*, 13 (2) (1980), pp. 158–74.
Balderston, Theo, 'War Finance and Inflation in Britain and Germany, 1914–1918', *The Economic History Review*, 42 (2) (1989), pp. 222–42.
Baranowski, Shelley, *Nazi Empire: German Colonialism and Imperialism from Bismarck to Hitler* (Cambridge: Cambridge University Press, 2011).
Barkai, Avraham, *'Wehr Dich!' Der Centralverein deutscher Staatsbürger jüdischen Glaubens 1893–1938* (Munich: Beck, 2002).
Barth, Boris, *Dolchstoßlegenden und politische Desintegration: Das Trauma der deutschen Niederlage im Ersten Weltkrieg, 1914–1933* (Düsseldorf: Droste, 2003).
Bartov, Omer, 'Defining Enemies, Making Victims: Germans, Jews, and the Holocaust', *American Historical Review*, 103 (3) (1998), pp. 771–816.
Behrenbeck, Sabine, 'Heldenkult oder Friedensmahnung? Kriegerdenkmale nach beiden Weltkriegen', in Gottfried Niedhart und Dieter Riesenberger (eds), *Lernen aus dem Krieg? Deutsche Nachkriegszeiten, 1918 und 1945: Beiträge zur historischen Friedensforschung* (Munich: Beck, 1992), pp. 344–64.
Behring, Dietz, *The Stigma of Names: Antisemitism in German Daily Life, 1812–1933* (Cambridge: Polity, 1992).
Bendert, Harald, *Die UC-Boote der Kaiserlichen Marine 1914–1918* (Hamburg: E.S. Mittler, 2001).
Bergen, Leo van, *Before My Helpless Sight: Suffering, Dying and Military Medicine on the Western Front, 1914–1918* (Farnham: Ashgate, 2009).
Berger, Michael, *Eisernes Kreuz und Davidstern: Die Geschichte Jüdischer Soldaten in Deutschen Armeen* (Berlin: Trafo, 2006).
Bessel, Richard, *Germany after the First World War* (Oxford: Oxford University Press, 1993).
— 'The Nazi Capture of Power', *Journal of Contemporary History*, 39 (2) (2004), pp. 169–88.
— *Nazism and War* (London: Phoenix, 2004).
Biale, David, *Gershom Scholem: Kabbalah and Counter-History* (Cambridge, Mass.: Harvard University Press, 1982).

Boak, Helen, *Women in the Weimar Republic* (Manchester: Manchester University Press, 2013).

Boureau, Alain, *Kantorowicz: Stories of a Historian*, trans. Stephen Nichols and Gabrielle Spiegel (Baltimore: Johns Hopkins University Press, 2001).

Bourke, Joanna, *Dismembering the Male: Men's Bodies, Britain and the Great War* (London: Reaktion, 1996).

— *An Intimate History of Killing: Face-to-Face Killing in Twentieth-Century Warfare* (London: Granta, 1999).

Brenner, Arthur, *Emil J. Gumbel: Weimar German Pacifist and Professor* (Leiden: Brill, 2001).

Brenner, Michael, *The Renaissance of Jewish Culture in Weimar Germany* (New Haven: Yale University Press, 1996).

Brenner, Michael and Derek Penslar (eds), *In Search of Jewish Community: Jewish Identities in Germany and Austria, 1918–1933* (Bloomington: Indiana University Press, 1998).

Brodersen, Ingke and Rüdiger Dammann, *Geschichten einer Ausstellung: Zwei Jahrtausende deutsch-jüdische Geschichte* (Berlin: Jüdisches Museum Berlin, 2002).

Broszat, Martin, *Hitler and the Collapse of Weimar Germany* (Leamington Spa: Berg, 1987).

Burleigh, Michael, *Germany Turns Eastwards: A Study of Ostforschung in the Third Reich* (Cambridge: Cambridge University Press, 1988).

Calkins, Kenneth, *Hugo Haase: Demokrat und Revolutionär* (Berlin: Colloquium, 1976).

Cecil, Lamar, *Albert Ballin: Business and Politics in Imperial Germany, 1888–1918* (Princeton: Princeton University Press, 1967).

Charles, Daniel, *Between Genius and Genocide: The Tragedy of Fritz Haber, Father of Chemical Warfare* (London: Jonathan Cape, 2005).

Chickering, Roger, *The Great War and Urban Life in Germany: Freiburg, 1914–1918* (Cambridge: Cambridge University Press, 2007).

— *Imperial Germany and the Great War, 1914–1918* (Cambridge: Cambridge University Press, 2004).

— 'World War I and the Theory of Total War: Reflections on the British and German Cases, 1914–1915', in Roger Chickering and Stig Förster (eds), *Great War, Total War: Combat and Mobilization on the Western Front, 1914–1918* (Cambridge: Cambridge University Press, 2000), pp. 189–206.

Chu, Winson, *The German Minority in Interwar Poland* (Cambridge: Cambridge University Press, 2012).

Clark, Christopher, *The Sleepwalkers: How Europe Went to War in 1914* (London: Penguin, 2013).

Clavin, Patricia, ' "A Wandering Scholar" in Britain and the USA, 1933–45: The Life and Work of Moritz Bonn', in Anthony Grenville (ed.), *Refugees from the Third Reich in Britain* (Amsterdam: Rodopi, 2002), pp. 27–42.

Cohen, Deborah, *The War Come Home: Disabled Veterans in Britain and Germany, 1914–1939* (Berkeley: University of California Press, 2001).

Cohen, Robert, 'Arnold Zweig's War Novellas of 1914', in Bernd Hüppauf (ed.), *War, Violence and the Modern Condition* (Berlin: De Gruyter, 1997), pp. 277–90.

Confino, Alon, *The Nation as a Local Metaphor: Württemberg, Imperial Germany and National Memory, 1871–1918* (Chapel Hill: University of North Carolina Press, 1997).

Crim, Brian, *Antisemitism in the German Military Community and the Jewish Response* (Langham: Rowman & Littlefield, 2014).

Daniel, Ute, *Arbeiterfrauen in der Kriegsgesellschaft: Beruf, Familie und Politik im Ersten Weltkrieg* (Göttingen: Vandenhoeck & Ruprecht, 1989).

Davis, Belinda, *Home Fires Burning: Food, Politics, and Everyday Life in World War I Berlin* (Chapel Hill: University of North Carolina Press, 2000).

Davis, Christian, *Colonialism, Antisemitism, and Germans of Jewish Descent in Imperial Germany* (Ann Arbor: University of Michigan Press, 2012).

Deák, István, 'Jewish Soldiers in Austro-Hungarian Society', *Leo Baeck Memorial Lecture*, 34 (1990), pp. 3–29.

Deist, Wilhelm, 'The Military Collapse of the German Empire', *War in History*, 3 (2) (1996), pp. 186–207.

— *The Wehrmacht and German Rearmament* (Basingstoke: Macmillan, 1981).

Donson, Andrew, *Youth in the Fatherless Land: War Pedagogy, Nationalism and Authority in Germany, 1914–1918* (Cambridge, Mass.: Harvard University Press, 2010).

Dorrmann, Michael, *Eduard Arnhold (1848–1925): Eine biographische Studie zu Unternehmer- und Mäzenatentum im Deutschen Kaiserreich* (Berlin: Akademie, 2002).

Dowe, Christopher, *Matthias Erzberger: Ein Leben für die Demokratie* (Stuttgart: W. Kohlhammer, 2011).

Eberle, Matthias, *World War I and the Weimar Artists: Dix, Grosz, Beckmann, Schlemmer* (New Haven: Yale University Press, 1985).

Eley, Geoff, *Nazism as Fascism: Violence, Ideology, and the Ground of Consent in Germany 1930– 1945* (New York: Routledge, 2013).

Endelman, Todd, *Broadening Jewish History: Towards a Social History of Ordinary Jews* (Oxford: The Littman Library of Jewish Civilization, 2011).

Ettinger, Elzbieta, *Rosa Luxemburg: A Life* (London: Harrap, 1987).

Evans, Andrew, *Anthropology at War: World War I and the Science of Race in Germany* (Chicago: University of Chicago Press, 2010).

Evans, Richard, *The Coming of the Third Reich* (London: Penguin, 2004).

Feldman, Gerald, *Army, Industry and Labor in Germany, 1914–1918* (Princeton: Princeton University Press, 1966).

— *The Great Disorder: Politics, Economy, and Society in the German Inflation, 1914–1924* (Oxford: Oxford University Press, 1997).

Ferguson, Niall, *Paper and Iron: Hamburg Business and German Politics in the Era of Inflation, 1897–1927* (Cambridge: Cambridge University Press, 1995).

— *The Pity of War, 1914–1918* (London: Penguin, 1999).

Feuchtwanger, Edgar, 'The Jewishness of Conservative Politicians: Disraeli and Stahl', in Michael Brenner, Rainer Liedtke and David Rechter (eds), *Two Nations: British and German Jews in Comparative Perspective* (Tübingen: Mohr Siebeck, 1999), pp. 222–39.

Fine, David, *Jewish Integration in the German Army in the First World War* (Berlin: De Gruyter, 2012).

Fischer, Fritz, *Griff nach der Weltmacht: Die Kriegszielpolitik des kaiserlichen Deutschland 1914/18* (Düsseldorf: Droste, 1961).

Foley, Robert, 'The Real Schlieffen Plan', *War in History*, 13 (1) (2006), pp. 91–115.

Föllmer, Moritz, 'The Problem of National Solidarity in Interwar Germany', *German History*, 23 (2) (2005), pp. 202–31.

Föllmer, Moritz and Graf Rüdiger (eds), *Die 'Krise' der Weimarer Republik: Zur Kritik eines Deutungsmusters* (Frankfurt: Campus, 2005).

Frevert, Ute, *A Nation in Barracks: Modern Germany, Military Conscription and Civil Society* (Oxford: Berg, 2004).

Friedländer, Saul, *Nazi Germany and the Jews: The Years of Persecution, 1933–1939* (London: Weidenfeld & Nicolson, 1997).

— 'Political Transformations during the War and their Effect on the Jewish Question', in Herbert Strauss (ed.), *Hostages of Modernization: Studies on Modern Antisemitism 1870– 1933/39*, vol. 3:1 (Berlin: Walter de Gruyter, 1933), pp. 150–64.

— 'Die politischen Veränderung der Kriegszeit', in Werner Mosse (ed.), *Deutsches Judentum in Krieg und Revolution, 1916–1923* (Tübingen: J.C.B. Mohr, 1971), pp. 27–65.

Fritzsche, Peter, 'Did Weimar Fail?', *Journal of Modern History*, 68 (3) (1996), pp. 629–56.

— *Germans into Nazis* (Cambridge, Mass.: Harvard University Press, 1998).

— *A Nation of Fliers: German Aviation and the National Imagination* (Cambridge, Mass.: Harvard University Press, 1992).

Gay, Peter, *Weimar Culture: The Outsider as Insider* (New York: Norton, 1968).

Geiss, Imanuel, *Der polnische Grenzstreifen 1914–1918: Ein Beitrag zur deutschen Kriegszielpolitik im Ersten Weltkrieg* (Hamburg: Matthiesen, 1960).

Gerwarth, Robert and John Horne, 'Paramilitarism in Europe after the Great War: An Introduction', in Robert Gerwarth and John Horne (eds), *War in Peace: Paramilitary Violence in Europe after the Great War* (Oxford: Oxford University Press, 2012), pp. 1–18.

Geyer, Michael, 'German Strategy in the Age of Machine Warfare, 1914–1945', in Peter Paret (ed.), *Makers of Modern Strategy from Machiavelli to the Nuclear Age* (Oxford: Clarendon, 1998), pp. 527–97.

— 'Insurrectionary Warfare: The German Debate about a *Levée en Masse* in October 1918', *Journal of Modern History*, 73 (3) (2001), pp. 459–527.

Gietinger, Klaus, *Eine Leiche im Landwehrkanal: Die Ermordung der Rosa L.* (Berlin: Verlag 1900, 1995).

Goebel, Stefan, 'Schools', in Jay Winter and Jean-Louis Robert (ed.), *Capital Cities at War: Paris, London, Berlin 1914–1919 – Volume 2: A Cultural History* (Cambridge: Cambridge University Press, 2007), pp. 188–234.

Goltz, Anna von der, *Hindenburg: Power, Myth, and the Rise of the Nazis* (Oxford: Oxford University Press, 2009).

Grady, Tim, 'Fighting a Lost Battle: The Reichsbund Jüdischer Frontsoldaten and the Rise of National Socialism', *German History*, 28 (1) (2010), pp. 1–20.

— *The German-Jewish Soldiers of the First World War in History and Memory* (Liverpool: Liverpool University Press, 2011).

Grau, Bernhard, *Kurt Eisner, 1867–1919: Eine Biographie* (Munich: Beck, 2001).

Grayzel, Susan, *Women's Identities at War: Gender, Motherhood and Politics in Britain and France during the First World War* (Chapel Hill: University of North Carolina Press, 1999).

Haar, Ingo, 'German *Ostforschung* and Anti-Semitism', in Ingo Haar and Michael Fahlbusch (eds), *German Scholars and Ethnic Cleansing, 1920–1945* (Oxford: Berghahn, 2005), pp. 1–27.

Haebler, Rolf Gustav, *In Memoriam Ludwig Frank* (Mannheim: Allgemeine Zeitung, 1954).

Haffner, Sebastian, *Failure of a Revolution: Germany 1918–19* (London: Andre Deutsch, 1973).

Hagenlücke, Heinz, *Deutsche Vaterlandspartei: Die nationale Rechte am Ende des Kaiserreiches* (Düsseldorf: Droste, 1997).

Hambrock, Matthias, *Die Etablierung der Außenseiter: Der Verband nationaldeutscher Juden 1921–1935* (Cologne: Böhlau, 2003).

Hank, Sabine, Hermann Simon and Uwe Hank, 'Einleitung', in Sabine Hank, Hermann Simon and Uwe Hank (eds), *Feldrabbiner in den deutschen Streitkräften des Ersten Weltkrieges* (Berlin: Hentrich & Hentrich, 2013), pp. 7–15.

Hatke, Brigitte, *Hugo Stinnes und die drei deutsch-belgischen Gesellschaften von 1916* (Stuttgart: Franz Steiner, 1990).

Haupt, Georges, *Socialism and the Great War: The Collapse of the Second International* (Oxford: Clarendon, 1972).

Hausen, Karin, 'The "Day of National Mourning" in Germany', in Gerald Sider and Gavin Smith (eds), *Between History and Histories: The Making of Silences and Commemorations* (Toronto: University of Toronto Press, 1997), pp. 127–46, p. 138.

Hecker, Gerhard, ' "Metallum-Aktiengesellschaft": Industrielle und staatliche Interessenidentität im Rahmen des Hindenburg-Programmes', *Militärgeschichtliche Zeitschrift*, 35 (1) (1984), pp. 113–40.

— *Walther Rathenau und sein Verhältnis zu Militär und Krieg* (Boppard: Harald Boldt, 1983).

Heid, Ludger, *Maloche – nicht Mildtätigkeit: ostjüdische Arbeiter in Deutschland 1914–1923* (Hildesheim: Olms, 1995).

— *Oskar Cohn: Ein Sozialist und Zionist im Kaiserreich und in der Weimarer Republik* (Frankfurt: Campus, 2002).

— *Ostjuden: Bürger, Kleinbürger, Proletarier – Geschichte einer jüdischen Minderheit im Ruhrgebiet* (Essen: Klartext, 2011).

Heikaus, Ulrike, 'Krieg! Juden zwischen den Fronten 1914–1918: Eine Wechselausstellung im Jüdischen Museum München', in Ulrike Heikaus and Julia Köhne (eds), *Krieg! 1914–1918: Juden zwischen den Fronten* (Berlin: Hentrich & Hentrich, 2014), pp. 8–44.

Herbert, Ulrich, *Best: Biographische Studien über Radikalismus, Weltanschauung und Vernunft, 1903–1989* (Bonn: Dietz, 1996).

— *Geschichte der Ausländerpolitik in Deutschland* (Munich: Beck, 2001).

— 'Was haben die Nationalsozialisten aus dem Ersten Weltkrieg gelernt?', in Gerd Krumeich (ed.), *Nationalsozialismus und Erster Weltkrieg* (Essen: Klartext, 2010), pp. 21–32.

Herbst, Ludolf, *Das nationalsozialistische Deutschland 1933–1945* (Frankfurt: Suhrkamp, 1996).

Hering, Rainer, *Konstruierte Nation: Der Alldeutsche Verband, 1890 bis 1939* (Hamburg: Christians, 2003).

Hertz, Deborah, *How Jews Became Germans: The History of Conversion and Assimilation in Berlin* (New Haven: Yale University Press, 2007).

Herwig, Holger, *The German Naval Officer Corps: A Social and Political History 1890–1918* (Oxford: Clarendon, 1973).

— 'Total Rhetoric, Limited War: Germany's U-Boat Campaign, 1917–1918', in Roger Chickering and Stig Förster (eds), *Great War, Total War: Combat and Mobilization on the Western Front, 1914–1918* (Cambridge: Cambridge University Press, 2000), pp. 189–206.

— 'War in the West, 1914–1916', in John Horne (ed.), *A Companion to World War I* (Oxford: Wiley-Blackwell, 2012), pp. 49–63.

Hett, Benjamin Carter, *Crossing Hitler: The Man Who Put the Nazis on the Witness Stand* (Oxford: Oxford University Press, 2008).

Hinz, Uta, *Gefangen im Großen Krieg: Kriegsgefangenschaft in Deutschland 1914–1921* (Essen: Klartext, 2006).

— 'Humanität im Krieg? Internationales Rotes Kreuz und Kriegsgefangenenhilfe im Ersten Weltkrieg', in Jochen Oltmer (ed.), *Kriegsgefangene im Europa des Ersten Weltkrieges* (Paderborn: Schöningh, 2006), pp. 216–36.

Höfel, Jutta, *Der belgische Lyriker Emile Verhaeren* (Frankfurt: Peter Lang, 1994).

Hoffmann, Christhard, 'Between Integration and Rejection: The Jewish Community in Germany 1914–1918', in John Horne (ed.), *State, Society and Mobilization in Europe during the First World War* (Cambridge: Cambridge University Press, 1997), pp. 89–104.

Hong, Young-Sun, *Welfare, Modernity, and the Weimar State, 1919–1933* (Princeton: Princeton University Press, 1998).

Horne, John and Alan Kramer, *German Atrocities, 1914: A History of Denial* (New Haven: Yale University Press, 2001).

Houlihan, Patrick, *Catholicism and the Great War: Religion and Everyday Life in Germany and Austria-Hungary, 1914–1922* (Cambridge: Cambridge University Press, 2015).

Hull, Isabel, *Absolute Destruction: Military Culture and the Practices of War in Imperial Germany* (Ithaca: Cornell University Press, 2004).

— *The Entourage of Kaiser Wilhelm II, 1888–1918* (Cambridge: Cambridge University Press, 1982).

Jahr, Christoph, *Gewöhnliche Soldaten: Desertion und Deserteure im deutschen und britischen Heer 1914–1918* (Göttingen: Vandenhoeck & Ruprecht, 1998).

James, Harold, 'Georg Solmssen: Eine biographische Annäherung', in Harold James and Martin Müller (eds), *Georg Solmssen: Ein deutscher Bankier – Briefe aus einem halben Jahrhundert 1900–1956* (Munich: Beck, 2012), pp. 11–52.

— 'The Weimar Economy', in Anthony McElligott (ed.), *Weimar Germany* (Oxford: Oxford University Press, 2009), pp. 102–26.

Jarausch, Konrad, *The Enigmatic Chancellor: Bethmann Hollweg and the Hubris of Imperial Germany* (New Haven: Yale University Press, 1973).

Jochmann, Werner, 'Die Ausbreitung des Antisemitismus', in Werner Mosse (ed.), *Deutsches Judentum in Krieg und Revolution, 1916–1923* (Tübingen: Mohr, 1971), pp. 409–510.

Jones, Heather, 'A Missing Paradigm? Military Captivity and the Prisoner of War, 1914–18', in Matthew Stibbe (ed.), *Captivity, Forced Labour and Forced Migration in Europe during the First World War* (London: Routledge, 2013), pp. 19–48.

Kaes, Anton, *Shell Shock Cinema: Weimar Culture and the Wounds of War* (Princeton: Princeton University Press, 2009).

Kaiser, Alexandra, *Von Helden und Opfern: Eine Geschichte des Volkstrauertages* (Frankfurt: Campus, 2010).

Kauders, Anthony, 'Legally Citizens: Jewish Exclusion from the Weimar Polity', in Wolfgang Benz, Anthony Paucker and Peter Pulzer (eds), *Jüdisches Leben in der Weimarer Republik = Jews in the Weimar Republic* (Tübingen: Mohr Siebeck, 1998), pp. 159–72.

Kauffman, Jesse, 'Schools, State-Building and National Conflict in German Occupied Poland, 1915–1918', in Jennifer Keene and Michael Neiberg (eds), *Finding Common Ground: New Directions in First World War Studies* (Leiden: Brill, 2011), pp. 113–38.

Kaulisch, Baldur, 'Die Auseinandersetzungen über den uneingeschränkten U-Boot-Krieg innerhalb der herrschenden Klassen im zweiten Halbjahr 1916 und seine Eröffnung im Februar 1917', in Fritz Klein (ed.), *Politik im Krieg 1914–1918* (Berlin: Akademie, 1964), pp. 90–118.

Kershaw, Ian, *Hitler 1889–1936: Hubris* (London: Penguin, 1998).

— ' "Volksgemeinschaft": Potenzial und Grenzen eines neuen Forschungskonzepts', *Vierteljahrshefte für Zeitgeschichte*, 59 (1) (2011), pp. 1–17.

Kitchen, Martin, *The German Officer Corps 1890–1914* (Oxford: Clarendon, 1968).

— *The Silent Dictatorship: The Politics of the German High Command under Hindenburg and Ludendorff, 1916–1918* (London: Croom Helm, 1976).

Kobrin, Rebecca, *Jewish Bialystok and its Diaspora* (Bloomington: Indiana University Press, 2010).

Kopp, Kristin, 'Gray Zones: On the Inclusion of "Poland" in the Study of German Colonialism', in Michael Perrudin, Jürgen Zimmerer and Katy Heady (eds), *German Colonialism and National Identity* (New York: Routledge, 2011), pp. 33–42.

Koss, Andrew Noble, 'World War I and the Remaking of Jewish Vilna' (PhD, Stanford University, 2010).

Kramer, Alan, *Dynamic of Destruction: Culture and Mass Killing in the First World War* (Oxford: Oxford University Press, 2007).

Krüger, Christine, *'Sind wir denn nicht Brüdern?' Deutsche Juden im nationalen Krieg 1870/71* (Paderborn: Schöningh, 2006).

Krumeich, Gerd, 'Die Dolchstoß-Legende', in Étienne François and Hagen Schulze (eds), *Deutsche Erinnerungsorte* (Munich: Beck, 2001), pp. 585–99.

Kundrus, Birthe, *Kriegerfrauen: Familienpolitik und Geschlechterverhältnisse im Ersten und Zweiten Weltkrieg* (Hamburg: Christians, 1995).

Kutz, Martin, 'Fantasy, Reality, and Modes of Perception in Ludendorff's and Goebbels's Concept of "Total War" ', in Roger Chickering, Stig Förster and Bernd Greiner (eds), *A World at Total War: Global Conflict and the Politics of Destruction, 1937–1945* (Cambridge: Cambridge University Press, 2005), pp. 189–206.

Lappin, Eleonore, *Der Jude, 1916–1928: Jüdische Moderne zwischen Universalismus und Partikularismus* (Tübingen: Mohr Siebeck, 2000).

Large, David Clay, '"Out with the Ostjuden": The Scheunenviertel Riots in Berlin, November 1923', in Christhard Hoffmann, Werner Bergmann and Helmut Walser Smith (eds), *Exclusionary Violence: Antisemitic Riots in Modern German History* (Ann Arbor: University of Michigan Press, 2002), pp. 123–40.

Lavsky, Hagit, *Before Catastrophe: The Distinctive Path of German Zionism* (Detroit: Wayne State University Press, 1996).

Leicht, Johannes, *Heinrich Claß 1868–1953: Die politische Biographie eines Alldeutschen* (Paderborn: Schöningh, 2012).

Leonhard, Jörn, *Die Büchse der Pandora: Geschichte des Ersten Weltkrieges* (Munich: Beck, 2014).

Liedtke, Rainer and David Rechter, 'Introduction: German Jewry and the Search for Normality', in Rainer Liedtke and David Rechter (eds), *Towards Normality? Acculturation and Modern German Jewry* (Tübingen: Mohr Siebeck, 2003), pp. 1–12.

Linder-Wirsching, Almut, 'Patrioten im Pool: Deutsche und französische Kriegsberichterstatter im Ersten Weltkrieg', in Ute Daniel (ed.), *Augenzeugen: Kriegsberichterstattung vom 18. zum 21. Jahrhundert* (Göttingen: Vandenhoeck & Ruprecht, 2006), pp. 113–40.

Lipp, Anne, *Meinungslenkung im Krieg: Kriegserfahrungen deutscher Soldaten und ihre Deutung 1914–1918* (Göttingen: Vandenhoeck & Ruprecht, 2002).

Liulevicius, Vejas Gabriel, *War Land on the Eastern Front: Culture, National Identity, and German Occupation in World War I* (Cambridge: Cambridge University Press, 2000).

Lohalm, Uwe, *Völkischer Radikalismus: Die Geschichte des Deutschvölkischen Schutz- und Trutz-Bundes 1919–1923* (Hamburg: Leibnitz, 1970).

Madigan, Edward, *Faith under Fire: Anglican Chaplains and the Great War* (Basingstoke: Palgrave Macmillan, 2011).

Mason, Tim, 'The Legacy of 1918 for National Socialism', in Anthony Nicholls and Erich Matthias (eds), *German Democracy and the Triumph of Hitler* (London: George Allen, 1971), pp. 215–39.

Maurer, Trude, *Ostjuden in Deutschland 1918–1933* (Hamburg: Hans Christians Verlag, 1986).

McElligott, Anthony, *Rethinking the Weimar Republic: Authority and Authoritarianism, 1916–1936* (London: Bloomsbury, 2014).

Mendes-Flohr, Paul, 'The "Kriegserlebnis" and Jewish Consciousness', in Wolfgang Benz (ed.), *Jüdisches Leben in der Weimarer Republik = Jews in the Weimar Republic* (Tübingen: Mohr Siebeck, 1998), pp. 225–37.

Miller, Susanne, *Burgfrieden und Klassenkampf: Die deutsche Sozialdemokratie im Ersten Weltkrieg* (Düsseldorf: Droste, 1974).

Mombauer, Annika, *Helmuth von Moltke and the Origins of the First World War* (Cambridge: Cambridge University Press, 2001).

Mommsen, Hans, 'Hitler's Reichstag Speech of 20 January 1939', *History and Memory*, 9 (1/2) (1997), pp. 147–61.

Mosse, George, *Fallen Soldiers: Reshaping the Memory of the World Wars* (Oxford: Oxford University Press, 1990).

— *Freud, Jews and Other Germans: Masters and Victims in Modernist Culture* (Oxford: Oxford University Press, 1979).

— *German Jews beyond Judaism* (Bloomington: Indiana University Press, 1985).

— *Germans and Jews: The Right, the Left, and the Search for a 'Third Force' in Pre-Nazi Germany* (London: Orbach & Chambers, 1971).

— 'Jews and the German War Experience, 1914–1918', *Leo Baeck Memorial Lecture*, 21 (1977), pp. 3–28.

Mosse, Werner, 'Einleitung: Deutsches Judentum und Liberalismus', in Beate-Carola Padtberg (ed.), *Das deutsche Judentum und der Liberalismus = German Jewry and Liberalism* (Sankt Augustin: COMDOK, 1986), pp. 15–21.

— 'Wilhelm II and the Kaiserjuden: A Problematical Encounter', in Jehuda Reinharz and Walter Schatzberg (eds), *The Jewish Response to German Culture: From the Enlightenment to the Second World War* (Hanover: University Press of New England, 1985), pp. 164–94.

Munzel-Everling, Dietlinder, *Kriegsnagelungen, Wehrmann in Eisen, Nagel-Roland, Eisernes Kreuz* (Wiesbaden: Archimedicx, 2008).

Nebelin, Manfred, *Ludendorff: Diktatur im Ersten Weltkrieg* (Munich: Siedler, 2010).

Neitzel, Sönke and Harald Welzer, *Soldaten: On Fighting, Killing, and Dying – The Secret World War II Tapes of German POWs* (London: Simon & Schuster, 2011).

Nelson, Robert, *German Soldier Newspapers of the First World War* (Cambridge: Cambridge University Press, 2011).

— (ed.), *Germans, Poland, and Colonial Expansion to the East: 1850 through the Present* (Basingstoke: Palgrave Macmillan, 2009).

Nielsen, Philipp, ' "Der Schlageter Oberschlesiens": Jüdische Deutsche und die Verteidigung ihrer Heimat im Osten', in Uwe Neumärker (ed.), *'Das war mal unsere Heimat . . .': Jüdische Geschichte im preußischen Osten* (Berlin: Stiftung Flucht, Vertreibung, Versöhnung, 2013), pp. 85–91.

Nirenberg, David, *Anti-Judaism: The Western Tradition* (London: Norton, 2013).

Offer, Avner, *The First World War: An Agrarian Interpretation* (Oxford: Clarendon, 1989).

Olin, Margaret, 'Jews among the People: Visual Archives in German Prison Camps during the Great War', in Reinhard Johler, Christian Marchetti and Monique Scheer (eds), *Doing Anthropology in Wartime and War Zones: World War I and the Cultural Sciences in Europe* (Bielefeld: Transcript, 2010), pp. 255–79.

Oltmer, Jochen, 'Einführung: Funktionen und Erfahrungen von Kriegsgefangenschaft im Europa des Ersten Weltkrieges', in Jochen Oltmer (ed.), *Kriegsgefangene im Europa des Ersten Weltkrieges* (Paderborn: Ferdinand Schöningh, 2006), pp. 11–23.

— *Migration und Politik in der Weimarer Republik* (Göttingen: Vandenhoeck & Ruprecht, 2005).

Osborne, Eric, *Britain's Economic Blockade of Germany, 1914–1919* (London: Frank Cass, 2004).

Otte, Marline, *Jewish Identities in German Popular Entertainment, 1890–1933* (Cambridge: Cambridge University Press, 2006).

Panter, Sarah, *Jüdische Erfahrungen und Loyalitätskonflikte im Ersten Weltkrieg* (Göttingen: Vandenhoeck & Ruprecht, 2014).

Penslar, Derek, *Jews and the Military* (Princeton: Princeton University Press, 2013).

Picht, Clemens, 'Zwischen Vaterland und Volk: Das deutsche Judentum im Ersten Weltkrieg', in Wolfgang Michalka (ed.), *Der Erste Weltkrieg: Wirkung, Wahrnehmung, Analyse* (Munich: Piper, 1994), pp. 736–55.

Presner, Todd, *Muscular Judaism: The Jewish Body and the Politics of Regeneration* (New York: Routledge, 2007).

Prokasky, Judith, 'Gestorben wofür? Die doppelte Funktionalisierung der deutsch-jüdischen Kriegerdenkmäler am Beispiel Guben', in Dieter Hübener, Kristina Hübener and Julius Schoeps (eds), *Kriegerdenkmale in Brandenburg: Von den Befreiungskriegen 1813/15 bis in die Gegenwart* (Berlin: be.bra. 2003), pp. 203–14.

— 'Treue zu Deutschland und Treue zum Judentum: Das Gedenken an die deutschen jüdischen Gefallenen des Ersten Weltkrieges', *Aschkenas: Zeitschrift für Geschichte und Kultur der Juden*, 9 (2) (1999), pp. 503–16.

Pulzer, Peter, *Jews and the German State: The Political History of a Minority, 1848–1933* (Detroit: Wayne State University Press, 2003).

Pyta, Wolfgang, *Hindenburg: Herrschaft zwischen Hohenzollern und Hitler* (Munich: Siedler, 2007).

Rahden, Till van, 'Die Grenze vor Ort: Einbürgerung und Ausweisung ausländischer Juden in Breslau 1860–1918', *Tel Aviver Jahrbuch für deutsche Geschichte*, 27 (1998), pp. 47–69.

— *Juden und andere Breslauer: Die Beziehungen zwischen Juden, Protestanten und Katholiken in einer deutschen Grossstadt von 1860 bis 1925* (Göttingen: Vandenhoeck & Ruprecht, 2000).

Reichold, Helmut, *Adolf Wild von Hohenborn: Briefe und Tagebuchaufzeichnungen des preußischen Generals als Kriegsminister und Truppenführer im Ersten Weltkrieg* (Boppard am Rhein: Harald Boldt, 1986).

Richarz, Monika, 'Demographic Developments', in Michael Meyer (ed.), *German-Jewish History in Modern Times – Volume 3: Integration in Dispute, 1871–1918* (New York: Columbia University Press, 1997).

Riesz, Janos, 'Afrikanische Kriegsgefangene in deutschen Lagern während des Ersten Weltkriegs', in Michael Hofmann and Rita Morrien (eds), *Deutsch-afrikanische Diskurse in Geschichte und Gegenwart: Literatur- und kulturwissenschaftliche Perspektiven* (Amsterdam: Rodophi, 2012), pp. 71–106.

Ritter, Gerhard A., 'The Kaiser and his Ship Owner: Albert Ballin, the HAPAG Shipping Company and the Relationship between Industry and Politics in Imperial Germany and the Early Weimar Republic', in Hartmut Berghoff, Jürgen Kocka and Dieter Ziegler (eds), *Business in the Age of Extremes: Essays in Modern German and Austrian Economic History* (Cambridge: Cambridge University Press, 2013), pp. 15–39.

Roesler, Konrad, *Die Finanzpolitik des Deutschen Reiches im Ersten Weltkrieg* (Berlin: Duncker & Humboldt, 1967).

Röhl, John, 'Germany', in Keith Wilson (ed.), *Decisions for War, 1914* (London: UCL Press, 1995), pp. 27–54.

Roos, Julia, 'Women's Rights, Nationalist Anxiety, and the "Moral" Agenda in the Early Weimar Republic: Revisiting the Black "Horror" Campaign against France's African Occupation Troops', *Central European History*, 42 (3) (2009), pp. 473–508.

Rosenthal, Jacob, *'Die Ehre des jüdischen Soldaten': Die Judenzählung im Ersten Weltkrieg und ihre Folgen* (Frankfurt: Campus, 2007).

Roshwald, Aviel, 'Jewish Cultural Identity in Eastern and Central Europe during the Great War', in Aviel Roshwald and Richard Stites (eds), *European Culture in the Great War: The Arts, Entertainment, and Propaganda, 1914–1918* (Cambridge: Cambridge University Press, 1999), pp. 89–126.

Rosman, Moshe, *How Jewish is Jewish History?* (Oxford: The Littman Library of Jewish Civilization, 2007).

Rowe, Dorothy, *Representing Berlin: Sexuality and the City in Imperial and Weimar Germany* (Aldershot: Ashgate, 2003).

Sabrow, Martin, *Der Rathenaumord: Rekonstruktion einer Verschwörung gegen die Republik von Weimar* (Munich: Oldenbourg, 1994).

Sammartino, Annemarie, *The Impossible Border: Germany and the East, 1914–1922* (Ithaca: Cornell University Press, 2010).

Sammet, Rainer, *'Dolchstoss': Deutschland und die Auseinandersetzung mit der Niederlage im Ersten Weltkrieg (1918–1933)* (Berlin: Trafo, 2003).

Schaepdrijver, Sophie de, 'Occupation, Propaganda and the Idea of Belgium', in Aviel Roshwald and Richard Stites (eds), *European Culture in the Great War: The Arts, Entertainment and Propaganda, 1914–1918* (Cambridge: Cambridge University Press, 1999), pp. 267–94.

Scheck, Raffael, *Alfred von Tirpitz and German Right-Wing Politics, 1914–1930* (Boston: Humanities Press, 1998).

Schivelbusch, Wolfgang, *The Culture of Defeat: On National Trauma, Mourning and Recovery* (London: Granta, 2003).

Schmidt, Ernst-Heinrich, 'Zürndorfer-Waldmann: Das Schicksal deutscher Frontkämpfer jüdischer Abstammung und jüdischen Glaubens und ihrer Familien 1914 bis 1945', in Frank Nägler (ed.), *Deutsche jüdische Soldaten: Von der Epoche der Emanzipation bis zum Zeitalter der Weltkriege* (Hamburg: E.S. Mittler, 1996), pp. 177–89.

Schölzel, Christian, *Walther Rathenau: Eine Biographie* (Paderborn: Ferdinand Schöningh, 2006).

Schouten, Steven, 'Fighting a Kosher War: German Jews and Kashrut in the First World War', in Ina Zweiniger-Bargielowska, Rachel Duffett and Alain Drouard (eds), *Food and War in Twentieth Century Europe* (Farnham: Ashgate, 2011), pp. 41–58.

Schröder, Joachim, *Die U-Boote des Kaisers: Die Geschichte des deutschen U-Boot-Krieges gegen Großbritannien im Ersten Weltkrieg* (Bonn: Bernhard & Graefe, 2003).

Schulze, Hagen, *Freikorps und Republik 1918–1920* (Boppard am Rhein: Harald Boldt, 1969).

Schumann, Dirk, *Politische Gewalt in der Weimarer Republik 1918–1933: Kampf um die Straße und Furcht vor dem Bürgerkrieg* (Essen: Klartext, 2001).

Schwarz, Gotthart, *Theodor Wolff und das 'Berliner Tageblatt': Eine liberale Stimme in der deutschen Politik, 1906–1933* (Tübingen: J.C.B. Mohr, 1968).

Seipp, Adam, *The Ordeal of Peace: Demobilization and the Urban Experience in Britain and Germany, 1917–1921* (Farnham: Ashgate, 2009).

Sieg, Ulrich, 'Bekenntnis zu nationalen und universalen Werten: Jüdische Philosophen im Deutschen Kaiserreich', *Historische Zeitschrift*, 263 (1996), pp. 609–39.

— *Jüdische Intellektuelle im Ersten Weltkrieg: Kreigserfahrungen, weltanschauliche Debatten und kulturelle Neuentwürfe* (Berlin: Akademie, 2001).

Skor, Holger, ' "Weil wir den Krieg kennen . . .": Deutsche und französische Frontsoldaten in der NS-Friedenspropaganda', in Gerd Krumeich (ed.), *Nationalsozialismus und Erster Weltkrieg* (Essen: Klartext, 2010), pp. 175–90.

Smith, Helmut Walser, 'The Vanishing Point of German History: An Essay on Perspective', *History & Memory*, 17 (2005), pp. 269–95.

Standt, Volker, *Köln im Ersten Weltkrieg* (Göttingen: Optimus, 2014).

Steber, Martina and Bernhard Gotto, 'Volksgemeinschaft: Writing the Social History of the Nazi Regime', in Martina Steber and Bernhard Gotto (eds), *Visions of a Community in Nazi Germany: Social Engineering and Private Lives* (Oxford: Oxford University Press, 2014), pp. 1–28.

Steer, Martina, 'Nation, Religion, Gender: The Triple Challenge of Middle-Class Jewish Women in World War I', *Central European History*, 48 (2) (2015), pp. 176–98.

Stegmann, Dirk, *Die Erben Bismarcks: Parteien und Verbände in der Spätphase der Wilhelmischen Deutschlands – Sammlungspolitik 1897–1918* (Cologne: Kiepenheuer & Witsch, 1970).

Steinberg, Jonathan, 'Diplomatie als Wille und Vorstellung: Die Berliner Mission Lord Haldanes im Februar 1912', in Herbert Schottelius and Wilhelm Deist (eds), *Marine und Marinepolitik im kaiserlichen Deutschland 1871–1914* (Düsseldorf: Droste, 1972), pp. 263–82.

Stibbe, Matthew, *British Civilian Internees in Germany: The Ruhleben Camp, 1914–18* (Manchester: Manchester University Press, 2008).

— *German Anglophobia and the Great War, 1914–1918* (Cambridge: Cambridge University Press, 2001).

— *Germany 1914–1933: Politics, Society and Culture* (Harlow: Longman, 2010).

Stoakes, Geoffrey, *Hitler and the Quest for World Dominion* (Leamington Spa: Berg, 1986).

Stölzle, Astrid, 'Einführung', in Susanne Rueß and Astrid Stölzle, *Das Tagebuch der jüdischen Kriegskrankenschwester Rosa Bendit, 1914 bis 1917* (Stuttgart: Franz Steiner, 2012), pp. 7–8.

Strachan, Hew, *Clausewitz's On War* (New York: Atlantic Monthly Press, 2007).

Strazhas, Aba, 'Die Tätigkeit des Dezernats für jüdische Angelegenheiten in der "Deutschen Militärverwaltung Ober Ost"', in Andrew Ezergailis and Gert von Pistohlkors (eds), *Die Baltischen Provinzen Russlands zwischen den Revolutionen von 1905 und 1917* (Cologne: Böhlau, 1982), pp. 315–29.

Stuhlmann, Andreas, 'Vom "Schlafwandler" zum Kriegsgegner: Die Wandlungen des Maximilian Harden', *Simon Dubnow Institute Yearbook*, 13 (2014), pp. 309–35.

Szajkowski, Zosa, 'The German Appeal to the Jews of Poland, August 1914', *Jewish Quarterly Review*, 59 (4) (1969), pp. 311–20.

— 'The Struggle for Yiddish during World War I: The Attitude of German Jewry', *Leo Baeck Institute Yearbook*, 9 (1964), pp. 131–58.

Szöllösi-Janze, Margit, *Fritz Haber, 1868–1934: Eine Biographie* (Munich: Beck, 1998).

Thesing, Susanne, ' "Krieg": Ein graphischer Zyklus von Ludwig Meidner', in Gerda Breuer and Ines Wagemann (eds), *Ludwig Meidner: Zeichner, Maler, Literat 1884–1966* (Stuttgart: Gerd Hatje, 1991), pp. 96–105.

Thiel, Jens, *'Menschenbassin Belgien': Anwerbung, Deportation und Zwangsarbeit im Ersten Weltkrieg* (Essen: Klartext, 2007).

Thierbach, Hans (ed.), *Adolf Grabowsky Leben und Werk: Dem Altmeister der politischen Wissenschaften als Fest- und Dankesgabe gewidmet* (Cologne: Carl Heymanns, 1963).

Thompson, Alastair, *Left Liberals, the State, and Popular Politics in Wilhelmine Germany* (Oxford: Oxford University Press, 2000).

Tooley, T. Hunt, *National Identity and Weimar Germany: Upper Silesia and the Eastern Border 1918–1922* (Lincoln: University of Nebraska Press, 1997).

Tooze, Adam, *Statistics and the German State, 1900–1945* (Cambridge: Cambridge University Press, 2001).

Ulmer, Martin, *Antisemitismus in Stuttgart 1871–1933: Studien zum öffentlichen Diskurs und Alltag* (Berlin: Metropol, 2011).

Ulrich, Bernd, 'Die Desillusionierung der Kriegsfreiwilligen von 1914', in Wolfram Wette (ed.), *Der Krieg des kleinen Mannes: Eine Militärgeschichte von unten* (Munich: Piper, 1992), pp. 110–26.

Ungern-Sternberg, Jürgen von and Wolfgang von Ungern-Sternberg, *Der Aufruf 'An die Kulturwelt': Das Manifest der 93 und die Anfänge der Kriegspropaganda im Ersten Weltkrieg* (Stuttgart: F. Steiner, 1996).

Verhey, Jeffrey, *The Spirit of 1914: Militarism, Myth and Mobilization in Germany* (Cambridge: Cambridge University Press, 2000).

Vogt, Stefan, 'Zionismus und Weltpolitik: Die Auseinandersetzung der deutschen Zionisten mit dem deutschen Imperialismus und Kolonialismus 1890–1918', *Zeitschrift für Geschichtswissenschaft*, 60 (7/8) (2012), pp. 596–697.

Vollmann, Hansjörg, *Eigenständigkeit und Konzernintegration: Die Cassella, ihre Eigentümer und ihr Führungspersonal* (Darmstadt: Hessisches Wirtschaftsarchiv, 2011).

Watson, Alexander, *Enduring the Great War: Combat, Morale and Collapse in the German and British Armies, 1914–1918* (Cambridge: Cambridge University Press, 2008).

— '"For Kaiser and Reich": The Identity and Fate of the German Volunteers, 1914–1918', *War in History*, 12 (1) (2008), pp. 44–74.

— *Ring of Steel: Germany and Austria-Hungary at War, 1914–1918* (London: Allen Lane, 2014).

— ' "Unheard-of Brutality": Russian Atrocities against Civilians in East Prussia, 1914–1915', *Journal of Modern History*, 86 (4) (2014), pp. 780–825.

Watson, Janet, *Fighting Different Wars: Experience, Memory and the First World War in Britain* (Cambridge: Cambridge University Press, 2006).

Weber, Thomas, *Hitler's First War: Adolf Hitler, the Men of the List Regiment, and the First World War* (Oxford: Oxford University Press, 2010).

Wehler, Hans-Ulrich, *Deutsche Gesellschaftsgeschichte 1914–1949* (Munich: Beck, 2003).

— *The German Empire, 1871–1918* (Leamington Spa: Berg, 1985).

Weindling, Paul, *Epidemics and Genocide in Eastern Europe, 1890–1945* (Oxford: Oxford University Press, 2000).

Wende, Frank, *Die belgische Frage in der deutschen Politik des Ersten Weltkriegs* (Hamburg: Eckart Böhme, 1969).

Wertheimer, Jack, *Unwelcome Strangers: East European Jews in Imperial Germany* (Oxford: Oxford University Press, 1987).

Westerhoff, Christian, *Zwangsarbeit im Ersten Weltkrieg: Deutsche Arbeitskräftepolitik im besetzten Polen und Litauen 1914–1918* (Paderborn: Schöningh, 2012).

Whalen, Robert, *Bitter Wounds: German Victims of the Great War 1914–1939* (Ithaca: Cornell University Press, 1984).

Wildt, Michael, *Hitler's* Volksgemeinschaft *and the Dynamics of Racial Exclusion: Violence against Jews in Provincial Germany, 1919–1939*, trans. Bernard Heise (Oxford: Berghahn, 2012).

Winter, Jay, 'Demography', in Johne Horne (ed.), *A Companion to World War I* (Oxford: Wiley-Blackwell, 2012), pp. 248–62.

Woywod, Dietrich, 'Deutscher Nationalausschuß für einen ehrenvollen Frieden (DNA) Gegründet 1916', in Dieter Fricke (ed.), *Die bürgerlichen Parteien in Deutschland*, vol. I (Leipzig: Bibliographisches Institut, 1968), pp. 487–8.

Wurzer, Georg, *Die Kriegsgefangenen der Mittelmächte in Russland im Ersten Weltkrieg* (Göttingen: V&R Unipress, 2005).

Zechlin, Egmont, *Die deutsche Politik und die Juden im Ersten Weltkrieg* (Göttingen: Vandenhoeck & Ruprecht, 1969).

Ziemann, Benjamin, *Contested Commemorations: Republican War Veterans and Weimar Political Culture* (Cambridge: Cambridge University Press, 2013).

— *Front und Heimat: Ländliche Kriegserfahrungen im südlichen Bayern 1914–1923* (Essen: Klartext, 1997).

— *Gewalt in Ersten Weltkrieg: Töten – Überleben – Verweigern* (Essen: Klartext, 2013).

— 'Weimar was Weimar: Politics, Culture and the Emplotment of the German Republic', *German History*, 28 (4) (2010), pp. 542–71.

Zimmerer, Jürgen (ed.), *Von Windhuk nach Auschwitz? Beiträge zum Verhältnis von Kolonialismus und Holocaust* (Berlin: LIT, 2011).

Zimmermann, Moshe, *Die Deutschen Juden 1914–1945* (Munich: Oldenbourg, 1997).

Zuber, Terrence, *Inventing the Schlieffen Plan: German War Planning, 1871–1914* (Oxford: Oxford University Press, 2002).

INDEX